FUNCTIONAL ADMINISTRATION IN PHYSICAL AND HEALTH EDUCATION

FUNCTIONAL ADMINISTRATION IN PHYSICAL AND HEALTH EDUCATION

M. L. Johnson
Southeastern Louisiana University

Houghton Mifflin Company • Boston
Atlanta • Dallas • Geneva, Ill. • Hopewell, N.J. •
Palo Alto • London

To those theorists, researchers, and
teachers who have raised our level of
knowledge, and on whose shoulders we
stand today.

Printed in the U.S.A

Library of Congress Catalog Card Number: 76–13089

ISBN: 0–395–20635–9

CONTENTS

PART TWO—BASIC PROGRAMS

PREFACE

The quality of a physical and health education program reflects the quality of its managerial leadership. Although adequate equipment and facilities are important, a professional staff at each level—classroom, department, and system-wide—is the most important element in a successful program. Because personnel is so critical a factor, the main thrust of *Functional Administration in Physical and Health Education* is toward developing the staff's management competencies.

Administration of physical and health education involves a diverse set of topics that must be effectively integrated into a single ongoing program. In the past, textbooks have been primarily directed toward the management of functions in the day-to-day routine. These functions, however, are important only in the light of the desired student outcomes. Therefore, an attempt has been made here to integrate these diverse functions of the day-to-day routine by using the systems approach to management. Management theory and research from both inside and outside the physical and health education disciplines are discussed because creative theory and data from empirical research are essential to programs of the future.

Physical and health educators have often tried short cuts to management. Indexed handbooks that supply answers to common problems are widely used. Some of them categorically state the exact percentage of time that must be given to each activity in the curriculum as if all students' needs were identical. Reliance on such handbooks is called a *tool* orientation. A *concept* orientation, which this textbook advocates, means operating with adaptable management principles. A concept orientation requires a more profound understanding of the discipline than the handbook approach. The advantage of the concept orientation is that students, staff personnel, and the entire school situation can be accurately assessed in order to formulate the best strategy for achieving the desired student outcomes.

Functional Administration in Physical and Health Education covers physical and health education administration from elementary through secondary school, though many of the management concepts could be applied to public recreation, college, and university programs.

Part I describes the administrative context. Systems management and administrative philosophy are introduced and applied to physical and health education. Part II describes the actual school programs that are to be managed. Both traditional and innovative ideas are included to take account of personal preferences. Part III, "Supportive Operations," explores in independent chapters certain general topics applicable to more than one of the basic programs. The case examples are intended to stimulate reflective analysis of typical problems, and original materials are included to allow convenient review of ideas and issues. The correlated *Study Guide* requires several types of responses to reinforce concepts. The complete instructional package is designed to foster the development of critical management competencies.

I would like gratefully to acknowledge the many people who have helped to put this book into print. First, recognition should be given to my wife Anne who served as typist, editor, and encourager throughout these trying years of writing. The several manuscript reviewers include Attorney Tom Matheny; William Douglas, West Virginia University; James Belisle, Indiana University; Robert Antonacci, Temple University; Carl Erickson, Kent State University; William Helms, University of Cincinnati; and especially Ed Coates, West Virginia University. My own colleagues who helped with comments and ideas were Dr. Betty Baker, Dr. Joan Paul, Mr. Larry Hymel, and Mr. Hubert Smith. A special thanks goes to Dr. Clea E. Parker who permitted the publication of materials from Southeastern Louisiana University. The team of typists includes Joy Miles, Becki Baker, Becki Boyd, Rhonda Jones, Denise Hebert, and Ardis Tucker.

M. L. JOHNSON

I.
ADMINISTRATIVE OPERATIONS

1.

SYSTEMS MANAGEMENT IN PHYSICAL AND HEALTH EDUCATION

After reading this chapter, each student should be able to:

Identify the elements of systems management.

Relate physical and health education objectives to the general objectives of education.

Describe the major outcomes the program should foster in the life of each student.

Plan a systems management strategy for improving the transformation process in physical and health education programming.

3

Let us assume that society needs to be improved through education of its youth, and that a teaching technology exists that can effect a positive transformation in student behavior. Assume further that the desired outcomes of physical and health education programs are known and agreed upon. Even with all these conditions met, education will not take place! A final unifying process is needed to cause components of the system to function smoothly. This unifying process is called management.

Management is generally defined as the process of setting and achieving organizational goals. The school is an open system, and the physical and health education department is a subsystem of the school. Each school has a set of overall organizational goals, within which each department pursues specific goals related to its subject area. Management is responsible for integrating departmental goals into the overall objectives of the school as a whole.

School Accountability

When investors allocate resources, they expect a fair return on their original investment. Since schools represent an investment by society, teachers and administrators must offer a good return on that investment. How long would a business survive if the productivity of one of its major departments was never called to account? Physical and health education, as a subsystem of the school, must be able to demonstrate what progress students have made. Educational accountability is basic to effective learning, efficient administration, and good community relations.

Accountability is simply the responsibility to answer for resources that have been used. As a process it is the systematic comparison of resource input with organizational output. Teachers and administrators fulfill this responsibility by reporting the type and degree of student achievement.

A recent legal controversy reported by Saretsky (1973) aptly illustrates the duty of schools to report the type and degree of student learning. Educational experiences must be professionally structured, student progress must be monitored, and accurate information must be furnished to parents. In the Peter Doe case, the parents of a high school student were continually told that their son was doing "fine." Nevertheless the young man graduated from high school with fifth-grade level reading proficiency. The irate parents have charged that the schools were negligent in their duty. Regardless of the outcome of this litigation, the Peter Doe case will stimulate educators to formulate and execute instructional programs precisely—to develop program accountability. What is the implication of "The Strangely Significant Case of Peter Doe" for physical and health education specifically?

THE STRANGELY SIGNIFICANT CASE OF PETER DOE

According to the attorney for the plaintiff, the Peter Doe case is a first step on the part of parents to use the judicial system to force schools to provide quality education to society's youth. The plaintiff filed suit against the local and state school systems for one million dollars because of the failure of the school systems to provide him with an adequate education. "Peter Doe" apparently possessed normal intelligence, he had no record of serious disciplinary problems, and he was regularly promoted each year until he had been graduated from high school. Throughout his school career his parents were assured that his reading level was normal. Shortly after graduation from high school, the young man was examined by two reading specialists. Both specialists diagnosed his reading ability at approximately the fifth grade level.

The plaintiff alleged that the schools were liable on nine distinct legal grounds. The charges include general negligence, misrepresentation, and breach of statutory duty. The complaint contends that as a result of the acts and omissions of the schools, the plaintiff lost potential earning power and has suffered mental distress and suffering.

The Peter Doe suit is apparently a test case intended to probe the limits of educational malpractice. Advocates of educational reform could use such a case to provoke court actions as a means of improving educational practices. Implications of the case are both threatening and encouraging. On one hand, school systems are threatened by the thought of laying the weight of judgment of complex educational programs in the hands of a few judges who are untrained in the scope and sequence of education. On the other hand, such class action suits may serve as a catalyst for bringing needs of the schools to public attention.

G. Saretsky, "The Strangely Significant Case of Peter Doe," *Phi Delta Kappan,* 54 (1973), 589–592.

Society and the Educative Process

Every society that has endured long enough to establish a historical identity has had some form of educative process. In the process of education, information and skills that the adult generation considered important were taught in an informal or formal manner. Youth of primitive cultures underwent a training period prior to being accepted as adults. To be eligible for the transition from childhood to adult status, youths were often required to complete certain difficult tasks. While present-day American culture is far removed from the primitive state, the transitional process of education is continued. Seldom do physically painful rites figure in the transformation from child to adult, but there are social and psychological rites that can be extremely traumatic.

Classical Greek culture developed a rudimentary educational system. Both literary and athletic competence were fundamental to the educated Greek. Youth of Athens and Sparta were given literary training and physical education. Athenian physical education stressed esthetic goals, while Spartan physical education emphasized combative skills and physical fitness. As you read the excerpt from *Life and Education in Early Societies,* try to identify similarities and differences between Athenian and American education. What was the Athenian concept of general education? What kind of relationship did physical education have to Athenian general education? To whom was the schoolmaster accountable?

LIFE AND EDUCATION IN EARLY SOCIETIES

Greeks commonly regarded Homer as the "educator of all Hellas." When literary institutions for youth first arose at Athens is unknown. Whenever they may have been established, the increase of literary activity and publication of laws in the seventh and sixth centuries imply the existence of some sort of formal instruction. Herodotus refers to a school of 120 boys at Chios about 494 B.C. Pausanias mentions one at Astypalaea, a little earlier, with about sixty boys.

A balance of mental and physical education was sought at Athens. The palaestra (wrestling place) and the music school were to give that training in music and literature for the soul and exercise for the body which was thought essential for freeborn youth. At his seventh year a boy was permitted to enter school; he might continue there a long or a short period, depending on the wealth and wishes of his parents, up to the age of fifteen or sixteen. Both palaestra and music school were private institutions, though Troezen is said to have provided Athenian refugees with free education. They were not compulsory in the present sense of the term, though Plato says that the laws required the father to have his sons taught music and gymnastics; and a law, credited to Solon, required all boys to learn to swim and to know their letters. Enforcement of the laws regarding safeguards of morals was under the jurisdiction of the Areopagus until its powers were curtailed, and the laws themselves fell into neglect.

The training of the gymnasium (for those fifteen to eighteen years of age) continued the exercises of the palaestra in a more strenuous fashion and perfected them. But in addition to these, youth now attended to riding, driving, the torch race, the race armor, and hunting—though the latter was less encouraged in Athens than at Sparta, especially after wild game had become scarce. For riding there were special academies, and of course, special fees, which made it a sport for those who could afford to pay. Rowing, swimming, and dancing in the public chorus were also a part of the education of many youths of this age. A knowledge of the laws was required, Plato says, but we hear nothing of systematic instruction.

T. Woody, *Life and Education in Early Societies,* The Macmillan Company, New York, 1949, pp. 298 ff.

Figure 1.1 Ask not what Steve can do for track, but rather what track can do for Steve's development.

Ellis Herwig, Stock Boston

Prescription and Control

Schools function primarily to train the younger generations to operate effectively in the social order. Paradoxically, in order to participate in the complex inter-relationships of modern society, individuals must develop skills that will make them independent. Society demands that each person acquire a fund of basic information, salable skills to apply in employment, and creative problem-solving abilities. School curricular experiences should therefore result in development of skills, acquisition of a fund of information, and adoption of social attitudes. Society prescribes that students leave school equipped to become contributing members of the social order. Edwards and Richey (1947) maintain that educated youth must also be capable of bringing about changes in schools and the social order.

Every school program, including recreation, interschool athletics, health education, and the instructional physical education program, is legally justified on the basis of what that program can do to change patterns of student behavior. Consider the development of the modern educational establishment. Originally society said, "Let us designate someone to teach our children." In the first schools individuals or small groups of children were taught by a wise and skilled adult. As educational structures grew more complex, their reason for being remained the same. Modern education has evolved from the one-teacher school to complex

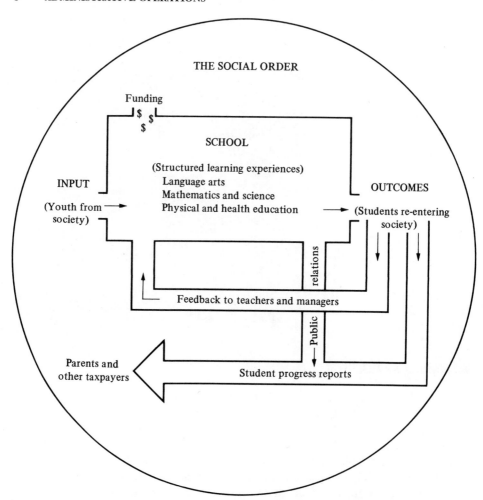

Figure 1.2 The cycle of school accountability within the social order.

local school systems. Bond issues are passed for building construction. Taxes levied for teachers' salaries and general operations are justified in terms of training the community's youth. Accordingly, every school program from athletics to school buses to cafeterias derives its legal basis from educative benefits to the student. The relationship between school and society is shown in Figure 1.2.

Several educational commissions have examined the concept of the overall school program and attempted to relate it to the needs of youth and of society. In order for physical education teachers to properly interpret their programs to students and parents, they must understand the relationship between school and society. The American Association of School Administrators functions as a mediating force between the society and the school. Which of the imperatives listed by this commission help to provide a basis for physical and health education programs?

IMPERATIVES IN EDUCATION

For half of a century professional educators have attempted to frame concise statements defining the educational needs of youth in the American social order. For example, a partial list of imperative outcomes for secondary school youth is as follows:

All youth need to develop and maintain good health and physical fitness and mental health.

All youth need to understand the rights and duties of the citizen of a democratic society, and to be diligent and competent in the performance of their obligations as members of the community and citizens of the state and nation, and to have an understanding of the nations and peoples of the world.

All youth need to understand the significance of the family for the individual and society and the conditions conducive to successful family life.

All youth need to know how to purchase and use goods and services intelligently, understanding both the values received by the consumer and the economic consequences of their acts.

All youth need opportunities to develop their capacities to appreciate beauty in literature, art, music, and nature.

All youth need to be able to use their leisure time well and to budget it wisely, balancing activities that yield satisfaction to the individual with those that are socially useful.

All youth need to develop respect for other persons, to grow in their insight into ethical values and principles, to be able to live and work cooperatively with others, and to grow in the moral and spiritual values of life.

AASA, "Foreword" to *Imperatives in Education,* American Association of School Administrators, Washington, D.C., 1966, p. 1.

The relationship of school programs to society has been defined by law and interpreted by the courts. Physical and health education areas are justifiable only insofar as they educate youth to become more effective members of society. Hence the main thrust of school experiences must be geared to the development of individuals rather than the development of winning teams.

Systems Management

A *system* is a complex, organized whole in which parts function to constitute a unit. Each school is a management system, because the subsystems of departments and teachers cooperate to accomplish organizational goals. *Systems management* is the application of a part–whole behavior model to organizational production. Let us see what this means.

The traditional view of management was a static, one-directional model whereby students and teachers performed prescribed functions, with little chance to express their own ideas or frustrations. Conversely, the "open" system approach to management utilizes all of the leadership potential existing within students and teachers. The systems approach to management is a highly accountable process.

Characteristics of Systems

Before the systems concept is applied further to physical and health education management, its basic components must be clarified. Figure 1.3 shows the components necessary for a system. Every system is a cycle or a combination of cycles. The solar system has great cyclical complexity, and the earth's biosphere is a macrocycle with several microcycles. Systems management in the school was also

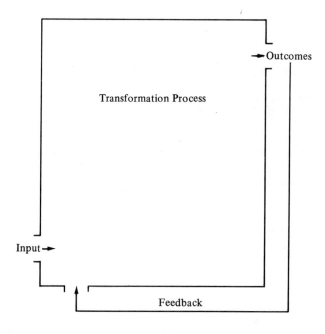

Outcomes

Transformation Process

Input

Feedback

Figure 1.3 The basic components of a system.

shown as a cycle in Figure 1.1; input received from society was transformed within the school and subsequently emerged as output returned to society.

Litterer (1969) describes several characteristic properties of a general system. Among them are the following: (1) interrelatedness of objects, attributes, and events; (2) wholeism; (3) goal seeking; (4) regulation; (5) inputs and outputs; (6) transformation; (7) hierarchy of subsystems; (8) entropy; (9) differentiation of subsystem function; and (10) equifinality. Four properties are apparent within the simple model shown in Figure 1.3. These components are described as follows:

1. Input.   Resources are fed into the system from outside.
2. Transformation process.   Organizational goals are accomplished by application of technology to the input.
3. Outcomes.   Organizational output may consist of final products returned to the environment or secondary input fed into other systems.
4. Feedback.   Control of input and the transformation process is derived from monitoring the outcomes.

Open Systems and Outcomes

Systems that continuously receive new input are called *open systems*. Systems management emphasizes how the relationships between organizational parts function to achieve outcomes. Emphasis is on management to achieve outcomes. Popham (1969) presents an outcomes-oriented approach to teaching, including a comparison between the process orientation and the outcomes orientation.

THE PROCESS OR THE OUTCOME

The single most important deficiency in American education is its preoccupation with instructional process. This overriding concern with procedures rather than the results produced by those procedures manifests itself in many ways. We see teachers judged according to the methods they use ("She has excellent chalkboard techniques and fine bulletin boards"). Innovation is lauded for its own sake ("Now there's a *really* new instructional approach!"). Teachers design classroom instructional sequences by asking themselves "What shall I do?" rather than the appropriate question, which is "What do I wish my learners to become?"

A Means Orientation

There is an essential distinction between educators who possess a means orientation and those who possess an outcomes orientation. Those who are captivated by questions of instructional process may well be descendants of the educational methods enthusiasts so prevalent during the early half of this century. More likely they bear no such lineage—it's just a great deal easier to be concerned with instructional methods rather than with whether those methods are effective.

Anyone who has seriously tried to develop criterion measures with which to assess a major instructional program will readily attest to the difficulty of such an enterprise. Simple, low-level objectives, of course, are easily assessed. All educators, or so it seems, are skilled in testing a student's ability to memorize. But assessing high-level cognitive outcomes or attitudinal attainments—this is a taxing task. The really worthwhile goals of education are invariably the most difficult to measure.

An Outcome Orientation

An educator who focuses on outcomes, not process, is usually committed to the belief that teachers exist primarily to modify learners. More generally, formal education is viewed as an enterprise which is designed to *change* human beings so that they are better, wiser, more efficient, etc. If this basic assumption is correct (alternative assumptions appearing eminently untenable), then the educator's principal tasks are to (1) identify the kinds of modifications he wishes to promote, (2) design instructional procedures which he hopes will promote them, and (3) find out whether the procedures were successful. Only if the hoped-for changes in learner behavior have been attained is the instructional process considered effective. Because the criterion by which the success of an instructional process will be judged must be measurable learner behavior, the outcomes-oriented educator cleaves exclusively to objectives amenable to measurement. Whether they are called "performance objectives," "behavioral goals," "operational objectives," or some equivalent phrase, they must be capable of post-instructional assessment.

W. J. Popham, "Focus on Outcomes: A Guiding Theme of ES '70 Schools," *Phi Delta Kappan,* 51 (1969), 208–210.

School administrators are concerned with producing outcomes, though more sophisticated criteria are needed to assess output. Mager (1962) stresses the need to state educational goals in behavioral terms. Teachers are encouraged to specify what student behaviors should accrue from the learning experiences in their classrooms. Behavioral objectives define outcomes in an observable and measurable way. School managers are similarly accountable for their contribution to student outcomes, and the behavioral concept is easily applied to school management. Writing statements of management objectives involves the same basic assumptions as classroom instruction statements. The expected behavior must be explicitly defined, and it must be stated in a manner that will allow measurements to be made. For example, a behavioral objective in professional productivity might be: "Each teacher in the department of physical and health education will

*Figure 1.4 They are neatly dressed in uniforms,
but how much have they learned?*

score above the fiftieth percentile on the teacher performance profile" or "The
department chairman will rank above the fiftieth percentile on a work climate
and effectiveness scale." Both statements are explicit and measurable management criteria.

Systems Analysis of Physical and Health Education

Physical and health education programs benefit from systems management because of its inherent efficiency and relevance. Emphasizing the outcomes of a
program makes it more likely that educational experiences will promote student
achievement. *Systems analysis* is a method of examining the parts of a cycle and
the relationships between them in order to increase organizational effectiveness.
Since systems are cycles or sets of cycles, a system can be analyzed by starting at
either the beginning or the end. Actually, an outcomes orientation implies that
the educators begin with the projected outcome and subsequently structure the
experiences that will precipitate those outcomes. For purpose of analysis, we will
describe a logical flow from input to output here.

Input

Input into a system is called *resources*. Closed systems contain a finite amount of
resources, and when those resources are exhausted the systems cease functioning.
The tendency for systems to become disorganized or decrease in energy potential
is called *entropy*. By contrast, open systems can continue functioning indefinitely
because of constant renewal of resources. Three categories of input into schools
are (1) students, (2) funding, and (3) community ideas.

Students

Student populations reflect the recent stabilization of birth rates. If the goal of zero population growth is achieved, the school population should reach long-term stability. Though from the standpoint of the school system children attending schools are "input," they could also be described as "partially trained output" of the various family systems. Students are not totally naive, and they have individual needs and interests.

Funding

Funds for school operation are supplied mainly by state and local governments. Buildings, materials, and teacher services are the major categories of school expenditures. The systemic relationship between the community and its schools is dramatized by the success or failure of local school-tax elections. School revenue is an input factor that is partially predicated on student outcomes. Resources are related to outcomes by using the planning-programming-budgeting system described in Chapter 7.

Community Ideas

Citizens and political leaders have definite ideas about the function of their schools. For example, the schools in Nazi Germany were blatantly used for propaganda purposes because of input from political leaders. Youth fitness was a major component of school life because of state requirements.

School administrators should solicit the views of all citizens. Idea input is good public relations, and it helps to insure that student outcomes will approximate community expectations. Preliminary input from citizens is essential for the success of such controversial programs as family life education.

Transformation Processes

Transformation processes include the school context, educational experiences prestructured for the students, and the professional staff. The systems concept of school management dictates that we perceive student, teacher, and administrator behavior as subsystems of an integrated whole. If all groups are participating in the transformation process, the school is like a clock mechanism whose many subcycles are coordinated to yield the desired outcome. Kast and Rosenzweig (1970) identified five subsystems in a sociotechnical system, all of which interrelated to produce output. The five primary subsystems are: (1) goals and values; (2) technology; (3) structure; (4) psychosocial factors; and (5) management. Applied to schools, the transformation process can be illustrated as in Figure 1.5.

TRANSFORMATION PROCESS (School)

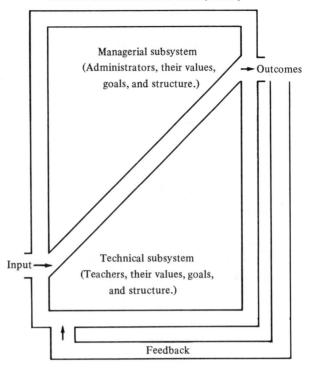

Figure 1.5 Subsystems of the school transformation process.

The Managerial Subsystem

How is management related to input and outcomes? Managers cause instruction to take place in the class context. Systems-oriented managers identify critical functions within the schools and assign major emphasis accordingly. Procedure-oriented managers attend to details of staffing, securing resources, and reporting, whereas outcomes-oriented managers emphasize activities critical to student achievement, such as functional goal-setting, motivation, and outcomes assessment. One such management objective would be: "To have all nonhandicapped students enrolled in physical education achieve at least the fiftieth percentile on a standardized youth fitness test." Physical and health education administrators perform management functions in the three major areas: (1) quality of instruction; (2) dynamics within the faculty; and (3) school learning climate.

Quality of Instruction. The school manager is legally responsible for the quality of instruction presented by teachers. In-service training is a useful method for improving instruction; however, in-service programs themselves can become a process orientation for managers. The middle-level manager should be instrumental in determining conceptual objectives; the teacher develops operational objectives. Some secondary school student outcomes to be affected indirectly by physical education managers are as follows:

> to develop sufficient endurance for each normal student to run a mile in seven minutes
> to develop skill in basketball to enable each student to execute ten out of twenty free throws
> to develop the social behavior in basketball whereby every player voluntarily calls his or her own fouls

Faculty Dynamics. Effective teacher production is largely a function of management. The manager has the primary responsibility for setting the production tone of the work group. Work attitudes and conflicts among faculty members signal management problems. Though faculty group dynamics is a secondary factor, it has much effect on teacher productivity. Some examples of faculty dynamics objectives for managers are as follows:

> to develop cohesion and positive interaction within the faculty group
> to develop the decision-making skills necessary for participatory management
> to cause each staff member personally to set and achieve professional goals

School Learning Climate. The school context also has significant effect on student achievement and teacher performance. Urban and rural schools present different problems. Some management objectives for the school context follow. Though writing reports and such tasks are important, this category is cited last because it does not deal directly with the student.

> to schedule students in physical and health education classes of from twenty-five to thirty-five students
> to develop and use a cumulative physical and health record card for each student
> to develop and use a special physical and health education report card that specifically describes each student's status or achievement

The Technical Subsystem

Teachers are assumed to possess certain competencies that can be applied in the transformation process to achieve student outcomes. Subject-matter training and mastery of teaching techniques are important technical competencies that affect student behavior modification.

Singer and Dick (1974) describe a systems approach to the teaching of physical education. Their systems approach is built on a detailed analysis of teacher behavior, including evaluation and feedback for subsequent modification of the program. The Singer and Dick model, shown in Figure 1.6, is a diagram of the technical subsystem shown in Figure 1.5. Note that the criterion of being a complete cycle is a characteristic of the model.

Outcomes

Outcomes of a physical and health education program are cited herein to stimulate clear thinking about end products of school experience. Instructional effects in physical and health education can be identified and measured as readily as any other of the structured school experiences. Administration should facilitate student progress in a socially desirable direction. The school principal, the department head, and each teacher must be conversant with the potential outcomes of a physical and health education program.

A general discussion of desired outcomes is included in this chapter because of the obvious overlap of outcomes for the various programs. The physical educa-

Figure 1.6 Systems approach model for instruction. (From Teaching Physical Education: A Systems Approach *by R. N. Singer and W. Dick. Copyright © 1974 by Houghton Mifflin Company. Reprinted by permission.)*

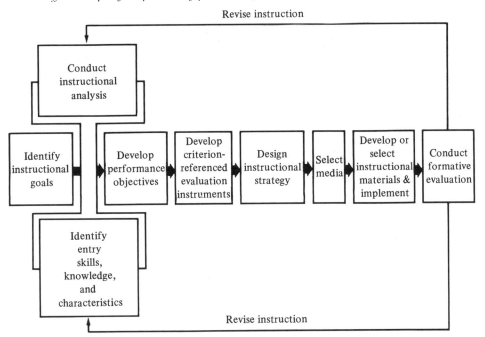

tion instruction, school recreation program, and interschool athletic programs have individual differences, but they also have much in common. Health education and physical education share concern with weight control and exercise physiology and sociological and psychological outcomes. Within the mainstream of physical education, general objectives include development of (1) physiological efficiency; (2) psychomotor fluency; (3) social efficiency; and (4) knowledge and appreciation of sports and related activities. Contemporary health instruction objectives tend to cluster around the areas of personal and environmental health. Figure 1.7 shows the projected outcomes in summary form. Outcomes in physical and health education can be quantified through verbal tests, motor achievement tests, and performance ratings.

Programs Related to Physical Education

Researchers (Dotson and Stanley 1972; Rosentswieg 1969; and Wilson 1969) have identified the major categories of outcomes that are projected from programs related to physical education. No single, ultimate outcome accrues from all physical education. Instead, four major clusters of outcomes are projected from school experiences in physical education.

Physical Efficiency. Physical efficiency refers to the ability of the body to perform sustained motor tasks. Cardiorespiratory endurance, flexibility, and skeletal muscle strength and endurance are the main factors in physical efficiency. No single activity will develop physical efficiency for all motor tasks, however. Fitness for motor performance is specific to the individual person's lifestyle and to its potential hazards. For example, a person cannot be physically fit to excel in all motor tasks, including long-distance swimming, running, and climbing. Running exercise makes a better runner but not necessarily a better swimmer. However, all normal people can develop motor performance capability that will enable them

Figure 1.7 *Projected outcomes of programs related to physical and health education.*

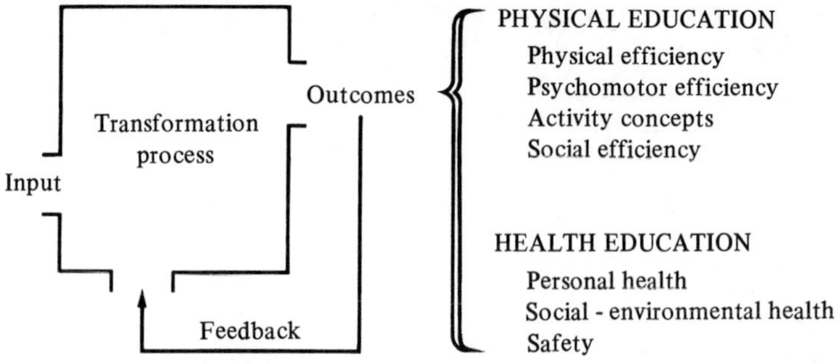

to survive most psychophysical hazards in their environment (see Cooper 1969).

Physical efficiency develops in direct proportion to the frequency, intensity, and type of exercise performed. Motor performance capability fluctuates: physical efficiency may be gained, lost, and later regained. It is the duty of the school to encourage students to develop and maintain physical efficiency. Some specific physical efficiency outcomes derived from engaging in vigorous motor tasks are cited here. Many of the physical efficiency outcomes are readily measured—and thus easily reportable to both students and parents.

Psychomotor Efficiency. Psychomotor movement fluency is the ability to perform a wide variety of motor tasks in an accurate, graceful, and efficient manner. *Movement patterning* is the medium through which all products and by-products of physical education are derived. The development of physical efficiency, social efficiency, and cognitive skills are all predicated on the use of movement patterns. Movement patterns can be either highly structured as in sports or relatively unstructured as in some movement education.

Fluency in self-expression is a highly desirable attribute. Graphic language and art forms are commonly used media for self-expression. Psychomotor skills vital to physical education programs are also effective media for self-expression. The development of fluency in motor skills includes basic motor patterns, movement as self-expression, and lifetime sports skills. Layman (1960) presents a classic description of the contributions of exercise and sports to mental health and social adjustment.

The acquisition of basic locomotor and manipulative skills is an important developmental outcome. As is true of other developmental tasks, there is an optimal time for developing fluency in motor skills. If proficiency is not achieved at the optimal time in the individual's development, patterns will not be as efficient or fluent as they could have been. The movement patterns of individuals who learn to play a sport after reaching adulthood are often characterized by jerky, abrupt movements. Adults with low motor skills can learn to perform motor tasks. However, they have a very limited "motor vocabulary" for use in learning the new motor tasks (Gallagher 1970). Obviously, physical education programs in the elementary schools should stress timely development of fundamental skills.

Activity Concepts. The development of motor-related concepts includes the primary factors of knowledge and appreciation. In order to play even the simplest of games, the participant must possess an understanding of rules and playing procedures. Elementary school students often ask their teachers, "What is the object of the game?" Furthermore, patterns of activity begun in the formal school years should be continued beyond graduation. The student should develop an understanding of sports and a positive attitude toward vigorous activity. Not only

Terry McKoy, I. O. E.

Figure 1.8 Acquisition of re-creational motor skills is a major outcome of physical education programs.

Southeastern Louisiana University

Southeastern Louisiana University

Figure 1.9 Players must know the rules and strategy in order to use their skills effectively.

should students know how to exercise, but they should know why exercise benefits the human body and how much personal satisfaction they can experience from exercising. Cognitive outcomes are easily measured components of the physical education program. Materials on concept development have been published by AAHPER (1970) and Corbin *et al.* (1970).

Social Efficiency. Social efficiency has been defined as sensitivity to, and respect for, the needs and rights of self and others. Physical education programs have been described as laboratories for social learning. Social aspects of the physical education program include personal–social development and group acculturation. Great potential for socialization is present in games and sports. However, the degree and type of social learning is a function of the quality of adult leadership. Nelson and Johnson (1968) studied sociometric status in physical education classes. They found that positive shifts in social acceptance could be effected by conscious effort on the part of the teacher. The study showed that changes in sociometric ratings did not occur automatically either with or without physical activity. Social learning is demonstrated in game participation only when the teacher has intentionally structured experiences to foster socialization.

Southeastern Louisiana University

Figure 1.10 Games and sports can help to create positive social interactions.

School Health

School health is an omnibus concept including health instruction, health services, and school environment. Each of these three components is included in school management—though health services and school environment are frequently handled by nonteaching staff. Chapter 6 includes a discussion of health services and school environment. Description of health instruction is included here to further identify the outcomes of a comprehensive physical and health education program.

Individuals must understand health concepts in order to know themselves and their environment. Health is related to physical education in that both areas pertain to the efficient physical and social functioning of the individual. Health education is unique because of the special topics that are usually addressed in the program. The major areas of health education are personal health and social–environmental health and safety.

Personal Health. What health problems are relevant to the individual student? Emphasis should be placed on those topics that the students are particularly interested in. Participation in a comprehensive health education program should foster good health habits, good health attitudes, and a fund of sound knowledge about health problems. Personal health education may include such topics as sex education, nutrition, grooming, dental hygiene, mental health, drug abuse, and safety.

Instructional outcomes of health experiences are both cognitive and affective. *Cognitive outcomes* are fact acquisition and problem-solving skills. *Affective outcomes* are the student's feelings about health problems and the student's personal value structures. Many traditional health programs emphasized only exposure to health facts. This traditional orientation is seriously questioned by Zazzaro (1973). For example, reliable research data indicate that some well-intended visual aids on drug abuse actually teach students how to inject high-risk drugs. Scare tactics used by law-enforcement officers and ex-addicts may also have a reverse effect. A good health instruction program furnishes students with information *and* value clarification relative to action alternatives.

Social–Environmental Health. What health problems effect individuals in society and in their interaction with the environment? People have always tended to be spoilers and polluters. The accelerated rate of pollution and the world population explosion have forced society to reflect seriously on this problem. Health education can serve as a tool for developing attitudes and disseminating basic information regarding pollution, communicable diseases, and social problems. The health teacher should select the most critical issues for instruction. Outcomes

Figure 1.11 By monitoring the heart rate every week during a school term the effects of exercise can be experienced firsthand.

within the area of social health problems would include attitudes about and knowledge of venereal disease, population control, and social conflicts. Outcomes related to environmental health would include resources management, waste disposal, and recycling.

Safety. What safety practices are essential for students at each grade level? General safety education is intended to reduce the number and severity of accidents. Since elementary and secondary students sometimes have limited capability to foresee hazards, they tend to exhibit high-risk behavior. Student safety outcomes should include identification of hazards, accident prevention, and first aid for injury.

Feedback

Continuous feedback is the fourth requisite of any management system. Feedback is information an individual or group derives about the effects of some behavior. The behavior may be an individual teacher's instructional attempts. Or the behavioral effects may be a cooperative attempt by an entire faculty to implement a program. Feedback has been merely an incidental component of traditional management, but systems management mounts an aggressive campaign to obtain and use feedback.

Examples of management feedback include: (1) performance results of students—grades and standardized tests; (2) performance of staff members—teacher evaluation and student achievement in each teacher's classes; (3) program effectiveness—relevance of school experiences and effectiveness of program components; and (4) manager effectiveness—assessment of administrative behavior. Feedback in school management is based directly on student outcomes. Outcomes feedback is channeled back to the transformation process for use in subsequent decision making. For further information review the works of Haberstroh (1969), Roberts (1969), and Tannenbaum (1968). Materials for evaluating management, instruction, coaching, and the various physical and health education programs are included in the Student Guide for the respective chapters.

References

AAHPER. *Knowledge and Understanding in Physical Education.* American Association for Health, Physical Education and Recreation, Washington, D.C., 1970.

AASA. "Foreword" to *Imperatives in Education.* American Association of School Administrators, Washington, D.C., 1966.

COOPER, K. H. "The Role of Exercise in Our Contemporary Society." *JOHPER*, 40 (1969), 22–25.

CORBIN, C., L. J. DOWELL, R. LINDSEY, and H. TOLSON. *Concepts in Physical Education.* Wm. C. Brown Company, Dubuque, Iowa, 1970.

DOTSON, C. O., and W. J. STANLEY. "Values of Physical Activity Perceived by Male University Students." *Research Quarterly,* 43 (1972), 148–156.

EDWARDS, N., and H. G. RICHEY. *The School in the American Social Order.* Houghton Mifflin Company, Boston, 1947.

GALLAGHER, J. D. "Motor Learning Characteristics of Low-skilled College Men." *Research Quarterly,* 41 (1970), 59–67.

HABERSTROH, C. J. "Control as an Organizational Process." In *Organizations: Vol. II,* edited by J. A. Litterer. John Wiley & Sons, New York, 1969.

KAST, F. E., and J. D. ROSENZWEIG. *Organization and Management: A Systems Approach.* McGraw-Hill Book Company, New York, 1970.

LAYMAN, EMMA A. "Contributions of Exercise and Sports to Mental Health and Social Adjustment." In *Science and Medicine of Exercise and Sports,* edited by Warren B. Johnson. Harper & Brothers, New York, 1960.

LITTERER, J. A. *Organizations: Vol. II.* John Wiley & Sons, New York, 1969.

MAGER, R. F. *Preparing Instructional Objectives.* Fearon Publishers, Belmont, Calif., 1962.

NELSON, J. K., and B. L. JOHNSON. "Effects of Varied Techniques in Organizing Class Competition upon Changes in Socio-metric Status." *Research Quarterly,* 39 (1968), 643–649.

POPHAM, W. J. "Focus on Outcomes: A Guiding Theme of ES '70 Schools." *Phi Delta Kappan,* 51 (1969), 208–210.

ROBERTS, E. B. "Industrial Dynamics and the Design of Management Controls Systems." In *Organizations: Vol. II,* edited by J. A. Litterer. John Wiley & Sons, New York, 1969.

ROSENTSWIEG, J. "A Ranking of the Objectives of Physical Education." *Research Quarterly,* 40 (1969), 783–787.

SARETSKY, G. "The Strangely Significant Case of Peter Doe." *Phi Delta Kappan,* 54 (1973), 589–592.

SINGER, R. N., and W. DICK. *Teaching Physical Education: A Systems Approach.* Houghton Mifflin Company, Boston, 1974.

TANNENBAUM, A. S. *Control in Organizations.* McGraw-Hill Book Company, New York, 1968.

WILSON, C. "Diversities of Meanings of Physical Education." *Research Quarterly,* 40 (1969), 211–214.

WOODY, T. *Life and Education in Early Societies.* The Macmillan Company, New York, 1949.

ZAZZARO, J. "Drug Education: Is Ignorance Bliss?" *Nation's Schools,* 92 (1973), 29–33.

2.
THE
FUNCTIONAL
MANAGER

After reading this chapter, each student should be able to:

Define and give examples for each of the four components of the management process.

Identify the competencies related to success in the various physical and health education management positions.

Describe the three classical management philosophies.

Write a self-analysis of management philosophy.

Analyze school situations and recommend the most effective management strategy.

27

Educational managers use various tactics in trying to resolve school problems. The object is to resolve the issue in a way that will prevent related problems from cropping up in the future. A problem is not resolved if it recurs in a slightly different form. Almost every issue confronting the school manager has ramifications for students, teachers, administrators, and the community. The effective administrator resolves the issue in a way that will maximize the positive effects on all parties concerned.

Most technical problems can be rather easily resolved, such as the question, "What type of exercise program will produce the greatest gains in muscular strength?" But problems involving people and their interrelationships are more complicated. Students learn largely in response to the teacher, and teacher performance is affected by staff relationships. The school manager is most instrumental in setting the staff production level. (The terms *manager* and *administrator* are used here interchangeably.) School personnel respond favorably or unfavorably to the behavior of the person in charge. Administrators can *affect* teachers so that they work, or they can *disaffect* teachers. It is improbable that a disaffected teacher will be able to motivate a class to full learning production.

What is effective management? Obviously, there is no formula applicable to all situations. In exploring the functional manager concept, the following questions will be probed: (1) What is the procedure used in managing? (2) What do managers do? (3) What management style best promotes good morale and

Figure 2.1 The four steps of the management process integrated into the systems approach.

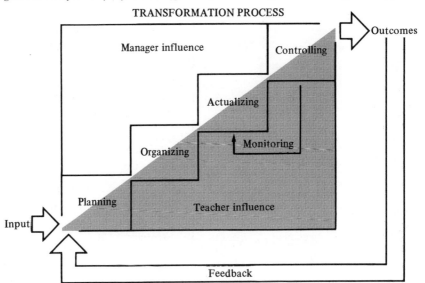

productivity in physical and health education? Within the transformation process of systems management, both teachers and administrators cooperatively fill their respective roles. Figure 2.1 shows how the four steps of the management process are integrated into a systemic approach.

School Management

The average administrator in physical and health education spends too much time handling details. The field needs leaders who can envision the whole spectrum of educational possibilities. Creating innovative programs requires the ability to dream of what might be *and* the drive to realize that dream. An organization seldom rises higher than its leadership. The quality of their ideas enables an organization to become outstanding.

The Management Process

Certain management steps are always followed (though they can be structured less or more formally) in accomplishing a goal. The steps of planning, organizing, actualizing, and controlling advance a concept from idea to completed project. Individual staff members within the school can usually be appointed to perform some of the major tasks. For example, a school system may have a consultant for

Figure 2.2 Management by objectives helps identify the tasks that are essential to operating a program.

planning school facilities, a visual aids coordinator for *organizing* materials, a specialist to *perform* model teaching, and game officials for *controlling* athletic contests. Both teachers and department heads are usually multirole managers. The multirole manager sequentially performs all the steps in the school management process.

Planning. The type and extent of planning depend upon the nature of the task. Some tasks are done "on impulse" with very little attention to planning details. Simple problems require little conscious planning, while complex problems in curriculum construction require planning by teachers and specialists. Educational planning is simply the act of preselecting events that will take place in a school term. Systematic programming dictates the sequence in which organizing, actualizing, and controlling will be used. For example, disciplinary action in an individual case may take only a few minutes, but the mature teacher will have a basic plan for handling common categories of behavior problems.

Planning in systems management is done in reverse order when an outcomes orientation is used. First the desired outcomes are stated, then a system is devised that will achieve the outcomes. By moving backward through the system, planners can analyze each subsystem for its probable contribution to outcomes. For amplification of organizational planning theory and applications see Branch (1966).

Organizing. The specific organizational pattern depends upon the task and the context. As the group becomes larger, for example, the organizational structure must be modified to include additional personnel. If more than one person works in the same task, organization is needed to prevent overlap and confusion. Each person's role must be defined in a job description that specifies relationships with other employees and expected responsibilities. Although organizing also includes securing materials and grouping students for instruction, most organizational theory addresses staff–line relationships. Classical theorists Gulick and Urwick (1937) advocate certain regimented principles of organization, whereas open-systems management continuously evaluates the success and merit of the organizational patterns in effect.

The line-and-staff organizational chart shown in Figure 2.4 can be modified in several ways to suit the specific situation and group. *Line positions* are the main boxes in the vertical *power* hierarchy. *Staff positions* are service positions, but either horizontal branched positions or lower-level line positions may be called staff. Which way do communications go? Routing communications through a strict chain of command can be ridiculous. For example, a teacher needs a box of chalk immediately. Routing a formal requisition through the principal to the business office and back to the janitor for release of the chalk would be a complete

Figure 2.3 *Teachers, coaches, and the department chairperson may play important roles in all four steps of the management process.*

Organizational charts show relationships within a system. Although there are several types of organizational charts, the basic principles of denoting relationships are somewhat standardized. An organizational chart is a static picture of a dynamic organism. Generally speaking, power increases in ascending order up the levels in the chart. The standard notations are as follows:

1. A box indicates a job position.

2. A vertical line indicates responsibility.

3. A vertical line with branches indicates that lower positions are responsible to a higher position.

4. A vertical or horizontal broken line indicates a special interest communication relationship.

5. A box beside the executive represents an advisory board.

6. A box directly above the executive represents a board of directors.

7. A box connected to the executive but not extending to the lower levels indicates an auxillary relationship (secretary, services, etc.)

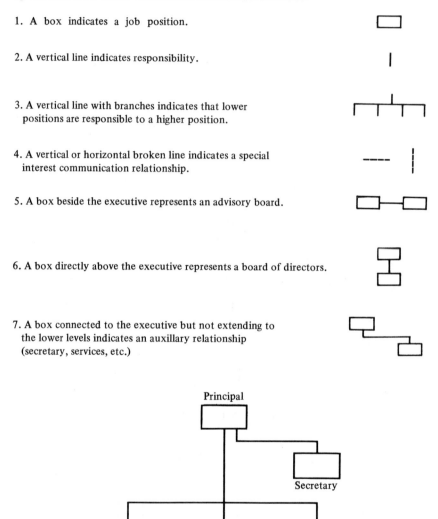

Figure 2.4 The traditional system of staff organization.

waste of time. A more flexible approach is to encourage communication flow directly to and from work areas. Carzo and Yanouzas (1967) describe the systems approach to formal organization.

Actualizing. Actualizing is defined as causing events to happen in accordance with the predetermined sequence. Students do not learn from curriculum planning or from staff organization. Students learn when the planned educational activities evoke behavioral responses. Managers and teachers function as the transformation between the plan and the student. In the school actualizing process, teachers set up the conditions to encourage student learning, and administrators try to structure conditions under which instructors will teach effectively. The basic problem of actualizing is how to cause that desired action—effective learning or effective teaching—to occur.

But what makes people learn? What motivates a professional educator to perform at a higher rate than minimally required? Many answers to the motivation problem have been proposed by psychologists. The problem of actualizing involves both the *type* of task that is performed and the *rate* of attaining the goal of the task. Psychologists such as Leavitt (1964) and Schein and Bennis (1967) identify principles of stimulating productivity.

Controlling. Controlling is the fourth major component in the administrative process. Controlling is the procedure that insures that plans are followed and that a reasonable pace is maintained. To apply standards borrowed from industry, control insures at least minimum quality and quantity in production—in this case production of educational outcomes. Both quality of production and the physical property itself must be controlled, of course. On the one hand, student learning must be monitored, and on the other hand, school supplies must be accounted for regularly.

Within industry, a specialized team of agents examines the items produced to determine quality. If an item does not meet the company's quality-control standards, it is either recycled or sold as a "second" without the manufacturer's name. However, most schools have virtually no systemwide physical and health education quality/quantity control. The teacher applies most of the control procedures exercised in education. Control of student behavior problems occupies a significant part of the classroom teacher's time. But disciplinary control should be of secondary importance compared to quality/quantity learning control. Administration of standardized achievement tests in reading, health knowledge, motor skill, and physical fitness are attempts at quality control of the educational "product." General theory of organization control is further described by Cleland and King (1968) and Tannenbaum (1968).

Controlling is best accomplished by obtaining feedback from students and putting better procedures into practice wherever deficiencies come to light. For example, if testing data reveal that students in a school scored relatively low compared to national norms on a youth fitness test, the physical education manager should review the time allocated to vigorous activity. The following four steps trace the controlling process:

1. Set the standards that will be used for comparison.
2. Get complete information about teacher procedures and student learning.
3. Compare the production item with the appropriate standard.
4. Change the critical production factor if the production item is deficient. (See the Peter Doe case reported in Chapter 1.)

Property control is secondary in importance to classroom production control. Equipment and facilities used by the physical education program are some of the most expensive in the school, and they must be accounted for regularly. Every teacher's property-control program should include a regular inventory of equipment and supplies. Though some equipment will wear out and small items will get lost, control of damage and loss is essential to all programs.

Case Example: MANAGEMENT BY A MIDDLE-LEVEL EXECUTIVE

The state supervisor for physical and health education has informed the Washington County school superintendent that the school district will be dropped from accreditation unless improvements are made in curriculum. Among other inadequacies, there is no progressional program in physical education, whereby students move to increasingly complex skills from grade to grade. The health instruction program is also deficient. The county curriculum supervisor is given the job of developing an acceptable program.

Washington County contains forty-three elementary schools, fifteen junior high schools, and six senior high schools. Some of the schools have gymnasiums and some do not. Most of the elementary schools have physical and health education specialists, and all the secondary schools have a combination of coaches and teachers. Approximately one-third of the seventy physical and health education teachers lack minimum certification.

What planning procedures should the supervisor follow in developing an acceptable physical and health education curriculum?
1. Who should be brought in to help with the planning?
2. What should the planning group be trying to produce?
3. What procedures should be followed in making sure the planned product meets or exceeds state minimum standards?

4. What would an organization chart look like if the physical and health education teachers were directly responsible to the school principal and indirectly
responsible to the supervisor of instruction?
5. What kinds of motivation would be helpful in putting the curriculum plan
into effect?
6. What control procedures should be built into the plan to insure evaluation of
student achievement?

Management Competencies

Management entails the four general steps of planning, organizing, actualizing,
and controlling. But what management behavior is typical of physical and health
education department heads, teachers, and athletic directors? The specific management competencies of these educators can be determined by objective job
analysis or interview.

Program innovation is only one responsibility of the school manager. More
than half of the routine, day-to-day school operations are repetitive tasks. Good
administrators are able to keep details and concepts in proper perspective. School
administrators who concentrate *only* on handling routine details overlook major
educational reform. Conversely, concentrating *only* on theoretical concepts
leaves routine school operation floundering. Competency in both expediting details and conceiving major educational innovation coexist in effective administration. The dilemma of detail versus innovation applies to the classroom teacher
and to such middle-level managers as the principal or department chairperson.

Teacher Competencies

The classroom teacher is an administrator who takes part in all of the four steps
of the management process. The teacher applies the management functions directly to students, whereas the department chairperson works with the entire
staff. An analysis of the typical tasks of the manager in a physical education
classroom follows. Roundy (1967) identifies the competencies reported from a
sample of secondary school teachers. Which of the competency problems apply
to health instruction?

The general areas in which teachers were most often lacking competence were:
(1) dealing with classes that have large enrollments; (2) grading and reporting
pupil progress; (3) working in the area of adaptive physical education; and (4)
evaluating the effectiveness of the physical education program. Teaching the
specific activities of gymnastics and rhythms were the two areas where competency was most frequently lacking.

PROBLEMS IN TEACHING BOYS' PHYSICAL EDUCATION

Problem

The objectives of this study were (a) to identify and to rank in order of importance the problems teachers of boys' physical education at the secondary level were faced with in performing their roles as directors of learning, and (b) to identify and to rank the competencies needed by these teachers to deal more effectively with the problems.

Procedure

Thirty teachers and 19 administrators were interviewed in the states of California and Utah. Data from these interviews provided the basic material for the development of an inquiry form that was mailed to 526 physical education teachers and 176 administrators in California and Utah. Twenty-one problems and 144 competencies were identified and rated.

Results

Problem and related competencies	Percent indicating problem of		
	Major Concern	Minor Concern	Mean Ratio
Dealing with classes which have large enrollment	54.29	35.28	1.4471
Working with limited facilities and equipment	48.24	37.89	1.3436
Grading and reporting pupil progress	47.14	34.14	1.2841
Working in the area of adaptive physical education	44.71	38.11	1.2753
Evaluating the program	41.63	41.41	1.2467
Dealing with the small percentage of students who do not cooperate	41.41	39.87	1.2269
Providing effective and continuous motivation	38.11	40.31	1.1652
Developing a broad enough curriculum to meet the needs and interests of the students	35.68	38.55	1.0991

E. S. Roundy, "Problems of and Competencies Needed by Men Physical Education Teachers at the Secondary Level," *Research Quarterly*, 38 (1967), 274–282.

Middle-Level Manager Competencies

The superintendent of schools is the upper-level manager in the American education system. Middle-level managers in physical and health education include department chairpersons, head coaches, athletic directors, and supervisors of instruction. Although the duties of various middle-level managers are quite different, all middle-level management positions carry responsibility for coordinating programs and executing details of procedure. However, *the most important task for all management positions is motivating people to perform their own assigned tasks as well as they can* (see Chapter 8 for a general discussion of motivation).

The Department Chairperson. In departmentalized elementary and secondary schools, one person may be given middle-level management responsibility. Often the department chairperson is responsible for both physical and health instruction programs. Generally the department chairperson performs the four functions associated with the management process. Planning at the departmental level would include curriculum and facilities. Organizing functions include securing faculty, grouping students, and obtaining instructional materials. Actualizing would include attending to routine details and studying methodology of teaching. Controlling includes supervising teachers and accounting for money and materials. Obviously the department chairperson of a large elementary or secondary school needs released time from teaching duties or additional payment for the additional work.

The Athletic Director. Large school systems need a person designated to coordinate the athletic program. Many secondary schools designate a coach to serve as the director of athletics. An athletic director may serve as administrator for both boys' and girls' sports, or there may be separate directors. It is common practice to give a period of released time for the athletic director to perform routine functions. Athletic planning is improved when the athletic director has time to determine priorities among the sports and to develop long-range programs. Coordinating boys' and girls' sports and scheduling contests are organizing functions. Arranging ticket sales and transportation are important actualizing functions. Financial management is the major controlling function of the athletic director.

The athletic director is responsible for coordinating the entire athletic program. The director may be responsible to the school athletic committee and is directly responsible to the school principal. As a middle-echelon manager, the athletic director performs all four of the administrative functions. In large systems, other people may perform the actual coaching duties. Some of the athletic director's tasks are specified in more detail as follows.

Planning functions include:

1. Arrange long-range facilities improvements with the coaches.
2. Work out program for the year with individual coaches.
3. Establish program priorities with faculty athletic committee.
4. Review budget with individual coaches and school financial committee.
5. Organize Booster Club support program.

Organizing functions include:

1. Participate in athletic conference and national athletic association.
2. Cooperate with school principal in selection of coaches.
3. Coordinate the playing schedules of the various sports.
4. Certify athletic eligibility rosters.
5. Process coaches' requests for equipment.

Actualizing functions include:

1. Secure all team insurance and travel arrangements.
2. Print, advertise, and sell game tickets.
3. Promote programs through personal appearance and disseminating sports information.
4. Provide courtesy services for visiting teams.
5. Secure game officials through the athletic association.

Controlling functions include:

1. Observe practice sessions and games.
2. Develop crowd-control procedures.
3. Evaluate game officials.
4. Prepare annual financial report on income and expenses for each sport.
5. Prepare yearly athletic program report.

Management Philosophy

A wide variety of administrative styles exist in the field of physical and health education. Athletic directors, supervisors, department heads, and teachers develop individual behavior patterns that provide them with job satisfaction and protect them from their psychological vulnerabilities. When administrators exhibit consistency in their management style, they have developed a working *administrative philosophy.* Consistency in behavioral style simply means that once administrative philosophy has been established, decision making tends to follow a predictable pattern. Classically, administrative style has been described in terms of three orientations or philosophies: authoritarian management, laissez-faire management, and participatory management. Although the three philosophies have been generally well defined, relationships among them are poorly understood.

Relationships among the three administrative viewpoints can be illustrated as shown in Figure 2.5. Since the three philosophies are independent of one another and in mutual opposition, they are represented as extremes equidistant from a common origin—and from one another. Each line from origin to extreme is divided into five equal units, with a value of five assigned to each extreme position and a value of zero to the common origin. Thus each of the three lines is a six-point scale with value gradations from zero to five.

A tripolar rating scale provides a useful means of classifying administrators according to recurring behavior patterns. The three philosophies may be arranged arbitrarily in alphabetical order as authoritarian, laissez-faire, participatory, and each of the three philosophies may be ascribed a point value of from zero to five points. Three point values separated by colons and summing to a maximum of five would numerically represent a particular administrator's philosophy. Thus the classic authoritarian administrator would be suggested by the ratio 5:0:0, the classic participatory manager by 0:5:0, and the extreme laissez-faire type by 0:0:5.

Administrators committed to the extreme orientations are seldom found in real school situations. Instead of absolute styles, there are various gradations and

Figure 2.5 A tri-polar model of administrative philosophy.

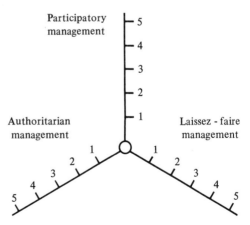

Table 1   *Scale value expressions of selected combinations of administrative philosophies*

TYPE OF EXECUTIVE BEHAVIOR	SCALE VALUE FOR EACH DIMENSION		
	Authoritarian	Laissez-faire	Participatory
Predominantly authoritarian plus some group participation	4 :	0 :	1
Predominantly group management plus some authoritarian practice	1 :	0 :	4
Predominantly laissez-faire plus some participatory management	0 :	4 :	1
Oscillates among the three philosophies	1.66 :	1.66 :	1.66

combinations that can be quantified via the numerical notation of the tripolar scale. For example, an executive who shows strong authoritarian behavior patterns seasoned with occasional group participation would be denoted by 4:0:1, as shown in Table 1.

Inexperienced students may question the need for an administrative philosophy. Does administrative style really have an effect on staff morale and productivity? And what administrative style is best suited to the field of physical and health education? Seidel (1970), invoking social–governmental theories fundamental to the Constitution of the United States, argues that administrators are largely responsible for faculty work attitudes.

ARE ADMINISTRATORS RESPONSIBLE FOR TEACHER UNREST?

Teacher unrest is a significant force in American education today. Often overlooked in rhetorical discussion of whether or not teachers should participate in strikes, "professional study days," or negotiations of any kind is the salient factor that the prototype teacher of yesteryear is obsolete.

Massive societal changes have caused a shift in the attitudes of many groups, but none has been so striking or so fundamental as that in the teaching profession. Teachers are seeking new, functional relationships with administrators. Today teachers have a high degree of creativity and special competence. Teachers are qualified to determine the best ways and means of teaching.

Although there is much room for improvement, salaries are increasing. Therefore, contrary to popular opinion, the unrest that is evident must be based also upon such factors as large classes, inadequate equipment, insufficient supplies, and an inordinate amount of record keeping and clerical work which seem to make teaching of secondary importance. Not the least among those factors is a demand for a voice in the management of the schools—a need to be heard in all decision making which affects the teacher.

Since many of these grievances are administrative in nature, those in administrative positions including department heads would be well advised to take a realistic look at themselves to ascertain if they are, indeed, contributing to lowered effectiveness. The formula seems clear: poor administrative practices = dissatisfied, inefficient teachers = ineffective education for students.

The group process, an important aspect of democracy, places a premium on cooperative social action. This process can be used by educational administrators to insure that teachers have a voice in establishing policies and procedures. Since in a democracy final authority and responsibility rest with the members of the group, it is desirable that the group utilize as much of these features as possible. Members of a group need to delegate to designated leaders only that degree of authority and responsibility which they themselves are incapable of handling.

B. Seidel, "Are Administrators Responsible for Teacher Unrest?" *The Physical Educator*, 27 (1970), 22–24.

Authoritarian Management

Authoritarian administrative philosophy is in effect when there is complete management of the work group by an upper-level power group. Employees work toward a goal they did not set using methods prescribed by someone in the upper levels of management. A strict line-and-staff organizational system is nearly always used. Channels of communication are rigidly followed in order for the system to work properly. The respective roles of subordinates and superiors are restrictive and explicity defined. A typical line-and-staff organizational chart appears in Figure 2.7. Upper-level managers may send directives down and require performance from any lower-level employee. Lower-level employees may send requests up to higher-level officials, but the request may be stopped or usurped by any higher-level official.

Assumptions of Authoritarian Management

Planning. The most qualified person occupies the highest position; hence, the chief administrator should do the planning for the organization. Obviously, the highest leadership role is filled by the most qualified person in the organization. Since the person with the most knowledge and skill is the leader, the leader should always make the plans. The official leader's plans will always be superior to those of lower-echelon workers.

Authoritarian (dominant power figure): "If you have a plan or problem come directly to me for clearance on the issue."

laissez-faire (personal independence): "If you are confronted with a problem, solve it as best you can---its your problem."

Participatory (group decision): "what are the issues, and what would be our best method for resolving the problem."

Figure 2.6 Interpersonal relationships in the three administrative philosophies.

Organizing. Individual workers find maximum security in a climate where they are protected by their superiors and where channels of communication are rigidly defined. If the leader protects the interests of the worker, then the worker reciprocally owes allegiance to the leader. The defined channels of communication in the chain of command must be followed to prevent disruption and inefficiency.

Actualizing. Responsibility for the organization's welfare rests with the administrator; therefore, the administrator must initiate each plan by issuing directives. Directives involve delegation of tasks and define the prerogatives and powers necessary for executing tasks. Responsibility for the welfare of the organization rests with the chief administrator; responsibility cannot be shared.

Controlling. Maximum production derives from a highly competitive context in which the administrator has the prerogative of punishment or reward. The use of

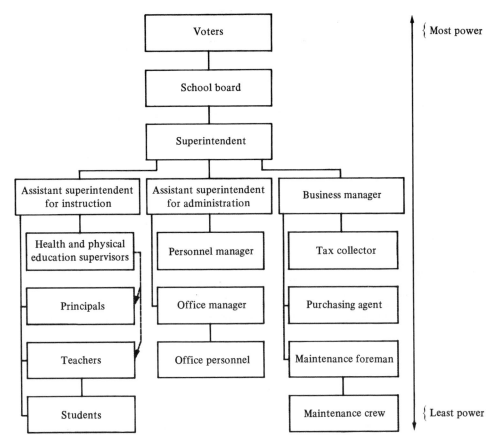

Figure 2.7 A typical organization chart used by authoritarian managers. Note the power-level labels on the right.

external rewards and implied punishments to create a dynamic, stressful climate is a legitimate controlling tool. A moderate level of anxiety produced by the presence of a higher-level officer is necessary before professional educators will produce near their maximum level.

Criticism of Authoritarian Management

Authoritarianism has been a popular form of government throughout the ages. Based on the doctrine of "divine right of kings," the authoritarian philosophy has been invoked by monarchs, dictators, and other heavy-handed administrators. Paternalistic ideas of protection and unquestioned loyalty characteristic of the Middle Ages persist today in the form of authoritarian administrative philosophy.

Case Example: THE MIDDLE-LEVEL AUTHORITARIAN ADMINISTRATOR

Mr. Pershing, the athletic director, received leadership training as a military officer. He believes that school affairs should be run like the affairs of a military unit. A primary purpose of the school experience is to develop an orderly, disciplined student attitude. Students and teachers who deviate from the behavior code defined in the school's operating manual are quickly caught and punished.

To Mr. Pershing, participation in athletics is a way for students to learn discipline. He believes mass drills and prolonged calisthenic exercises are especially useful for developing character. Mr. Pershing is loudly praised by some of the parents who feel that disciplined programs help to control their children at home.

Staff meetings in athletic departments are characterized by a brisk lecture by Mr. Pershing on the dangers of a "soft society." Schedules and duties are handed out at the staff meetings. The entire junior high school and high school athletic program is based on physical fitness. The lower-level schools serve as a farm system for middle- and upper-level school athletics. There is a high level of agreement in staff meetings because Mr. Pershing does not tolerate opposing points of view. Staff members who have disagreed with Mr. Pershing have been transferred to other schools or dismissed at the end of the probationary contract.

Ascendency to management positions is largely based on loyalty to upper-level managers. For a brilliant exposé of traditional management, see Peter (1969).

Some claim that less educated and unskilled people tend to prefer authoritarian rule because of the relative security that it offers. Whatever the merits of that argument, the present-day teacher hardly fits the description! Today's educators are fully able to think and act on their own initiative without slavish dependence on the edicts of an external taskmaster. Authoritarian management does have the theoretical advantage of producing quick short-term results and may be mandated for emergency situations that preclude group involvement.

Figure 2.8 Authoritarian management is highly domineering.

THE BORN LOSER   by Art Sansom

Use of merit raises or implied threat to raise the anxiety level of educators is a classic example of inappropriate use of power. Since the teacher–student relationship in the classroom is a complex variable, heightened anxiety on the part of teacher or student serves only to impede educational progress. What is the relationship between administrative behavior and work-group morale and production? The motivations applied by authoritarian leaders are often harsh. As pointed out by Ulrich and Ayrin (1962), harsh extrinsic stimuli can produce disruptive, noncreative behavior. Harmful stimuli cause rats to fight each other or to attack a nearby object. Similarly, when a faculty experiences strong noxious stimuli, the result may be a direct verbal attack on the authoritarian figure responsible. Alternatively, if the leadership figure is perceived as too strong to attack, the hostile response will be directed toward another, convenient object. (All too often, the scapegoat is the student.) While staff members are attacking each other, their students, or an outside figure, very little progress can be made toward the real goal of education. School managers can cause a general state of arousal among faculty members by verbal abuse, antagonism, and/or personal rejection of teachers.

AGGRESSION

Response of lower animals to stressors has been studied by several researchers. While no single kind of response can be categorically predicted in response to a stressor like electric shock, aggressive behavior is frequently elicited. It has been observed that if two apparently friendly rats are subjected to painful electric shock, they begin to fight defensively. The stereotyped fighting or boxing position is assumed by the rats. Rats continue to attack each other as long as they are subjected to the painful electric shock.

Reflexive fighting in shocked animals may be due to generalized arousal rather than antisocial aggressive tendency. A formerly shocked animal tends not to fight a second rat introduced shortly after the shock is terminated. If only one rat is shocked, the animal tends to try escape or avoidance maneuvers—climbing upon the other rat to get off the electrified grid. The reflexive fighting stance and boxing procedures elicited by electric shock have few of the kicking, biting, and wrestling components of normal rat fighting.

The stress induced by electric shock may be directed toward anything nearby. If another animal is not present, the shocked rat may attack inanimate objects during his period of extreme arousal. However, rats are capable of discrimination even during periods of shock pain. Wild rats will seldom attack familiar inanimate objects. Young rats will attack each other, but not their mother, during shock.

R. N. Johnson, *Aggression in Man and Animals*, W. B. Saunders Company, Philadelphia, 1972.

Laissez-faire Management

In actual practice, very few administrators fit the classic type of the laissez-faire administrator. However, the laissez-faire approach is frequently used in combination with one or more of the other administrative forms of behavior. *Laissez-faire administration* is in effect when individuals in the group are allowed to operate independently as they desire. Personnel in a laissez-faire atmosphere function as a loosely knit confederacy of individuals.

Assumptions of Laissez-faire Management

Planning. All persons in the organization must be allowed to develop their own plan for resolving the problems that directly affect them. Professional educators are highly trained to accomplish their assigned tasks. Teachers perform best when the central office sends the fewest managerial directives.

Organizing. A school system needs an organizational superstructure only for supportive functions. Since professional personnel perform their tasks best in an atmosphere of independence, the only purpose of a "skeleton organizational structure" is to perform such functions as pupil accounting and financial management.

Actualizing. Each individual teacher must be responsible for initiating the program that he or she plans. The entire school program is dependent upon the collective behavior of individual teachers. Where specific problems arise, the teacher should try to let the problem work itself out. Individual instructors should follow a deliberate pace in implementing programs in their areas of responsibility.

Controlling. Maximum production takes place in a climate free from competition and normative pressure. Individual teachers need freedom to interact creatively with their students. External pressures to perform tend to inhibit teacher performance in the instructional process. Teachers must evaluate student progress in terms of the behavioral objectives they have designed for the learning process.

Criticism of Laissez-faire Management

The laissez-faire idea gained prominence in the field of economics and government. The slogan, "The government that rules least rules best" is a succinct laissez-faire statement. As an administrative philosophy, the laissez-faire doctrine is probably more pertinent to state and national government than to school management. The assumption that professional educators will produce near their maximum level of their own volition is an interesting, but not necessarily a valid, idea.

Some of the basic ideas of the laissez-faire approach have merit. Each teacher needs some freedom of expression in program development and academic freedom in the classroom. Self-expression is an intrinsic motivator, it allows the individual teacher to be much more than another cog in the educational factory. Nevertheless laissez-faire dominance can be troublesome. Centralized quality-control procedures, for example, are contrary to the basic premises of the laissez-faire idea.

This highly informal administrative style may be appropriate for some management situations. The laissez-faire philosophy is common among the medical staffs of small hospitals, for example, (though a bureaucratic organization is used in most large hospitals). Physicians are considered competent professionals who do not need someone standing over them "cracking a whip" to make them produce. Neither teachers themselves nor the general public, however, conceive of teaching as a profession quite on a par with law or medicine. The key question is, "Are physical and health educators intrinsically motivated enough to perform best as independent professionals?"

Case Example: THE MIDDLE-LEVEL LAISSEZ-FAIRE ADMINISTRATOR

Ms. Graham, physical and health education coordinator for a city school district, believes that each teacher should handle all his or her school affairs. Discipline problems must be handled by each teacher in a manner that will encourage the students to maintain self-control. In a preventive discipline program, teachers and special speakers try to show each class the relationship between orderly behavior and school accomplishment. The students are made aware that learning is very difficult in a chaotic atmosphere.

Each teacher is responsible for developing her or his own course outline. Textbooks are furnished out of the school depository, but school supplies are purchased individually by the instructors from a small fund allocated at the beginning of the semester. Departments in some schools have banded together to develop a common syllabus; other departments have not done so. Elective physical and health education programs are being studied for possible adoption.

Ms. Graham does not visit the classes while instruction is under way. She occasionally holds in-service training sessions to refresh the instructors on teaching methods and to introduce new educational materials. Since research studies have shown that students learn at individual rates, she is encouraging teachers to develop individual learning programs. Competency-based physical and health education activities would allow individual students to pace themselves in their learning.

Participatory Management

The participatory management philosophy assumes an affirmative answer to the question, "Can people be trusted to guide their own steps wisely in a group project?" Egalitarianism, democracy, or *participatory management*, is in effect when primary responsibility for organizational operation rests with the individuals working directly on the task. If laissez-faire power resides in the individuals and authoritarian power in a taskmaster over the group, then participatory power resides in the work group itself.

Assumptions of Participatory Management

Planning. The people directly affected by a significant problem are in the best position to devise a solution. Whether the problem involves defining the teaching stations in a proposed building or ordering equipment for the following year, the teachers intimately familiar with what is needed in the local school should make the decisions. A plan developed cooperatively should be superior to the plans of separate individuals.

Organizing. An organizational framework should be used only to divide labor among the staff specialists. Individuals within the group possess different kinds of expertise. An organizational structure is necessary in large school systems to coordinate the various assigned roles. Communications within the system must flow multidirectionally, rather than down a strict chain of command.

Actualizing. Responsibility can be shared. The school executive should function primarily to coordinate efforts of the staff. The teaching staff is strongly motivated to execute the approved operational plan because they made the plan—it is the creation of all involved staff members.

Controlling. Maximum production derives from a climate where motivation is intrinsic and where there is little threat or intrastaff competition. Evaluation is the prerogative of the group. Individuals are pressured by the group members to meet the production goals set by the group.

Criticism of Participatory Management

The basic idea of democracy is intriguing, but even the Greeks restricted its prerogatives to educated people. All people are not capable of self-government. All educators, even with their academic degrees and experience, are not ready for full participation in the school operation. Educators are accustomed to a

Case Example: THE MIDDLE-LEVEL USE OF PARTICIPATORY MANAGEMENT

Ms. Lock is a physical and health education supervisor for a large, independent school district. She believes that all teachers should have a voice in the affairs that affect them. In-service meetings provide an open forum for debate and planning. Several teachers have strong feelings about what activities should be emphasized in the program. Disagreement is openly discussed on a professional level. Derogatory remarks about people are not accepted in staff meetings. Recently the physical and health education teachers in the school district were called together and assigned the task of constructing a syllabus to be used from kindergarten through high school. Committees were formed to work on its various parts. After all the committee reports had been compiled, the committee-of-the-whole reviewed the syllabus to make sure it was consistent, accurate, and workable. After one year of operation the group will be brought back together to evaluate the syllabus.

Ms. Lock often visits the schools while the classroom teacher is conducting lessons. When it is obvious that the production level of an individual teacher is low, Ms. Lock talks to the instructor privately. Her idea of supervision is to observe and retrain. Where several teachers need the same retraining, a small workshop is held for their benefit. Teachers are seldom fired or transferred to other schools. Frequent supervisory reports and sessions with assisting master teachers have proved effective in raising the production level of most probationary teachers.

modified form of authoritarian management, and drastic change is usually met with resistance and indifference at first. It is paradoxical that people in the American political democracy find the theories behind our form of government so difficult to apply in the educational context.

Participation in management offers a unique opportunity to tap the creative potential of the professional staff. Genuine participatory management helps to sustain interest in achieving the long-term goals of education. Personal identification with problems and solutions helps to insure enthusiastic execution of the management plan.

The group itself is charged with regulating production. If production is low, the members responsible are "brought into line" by other members of the group. Group pressure is a very potent force. Physical and health education teachers who show little planning and teaching effort can be ostracized, rebuffed, or encouraged by group members. However, the entire group's concept of an acceptable teaching job can be much lower than what they could do, what other groups are doing, or what higher-level administrators expect them to do. Conversely, the group can also be quite vicious to those who exceed the minimal teaching performance. High producers may tend to "show up" a substandard group, resulting in ostracism or threats directed against the high producer.

Which Management Approach?

Under the oppressive yoke of an authoritarian form of government, those who designed American democracy mutually affirmed that they would do away with every form of tyranny over the human mind. Two hundred years later, the revolution has yet to be seriously initiated in educational administration; the ideal of replacing authoritarianism with egalitarianism is far from realized. Participatory management does not deny the need for a functional administrative bureaucracy. Government of all complex organizations demands some sort of bureaucratic system. The critical issue in all three management philosophies is not whether a bureaucracy exists, but to what degree professional teachers are involved in the management decisions that affect them.

How can we establish that one administrative philosophy is superior to another? Validity and validation procedures are highly specific, and a particular administrative philosophy can be considered superior or inferior only with respect to the conditions in effect when its worth was assessed. Some of the important conditions that must be specified in the validation process are the nature of the task, whether complex or simple; type of personnel, whether trained or untrained; and the time factor, whether the operation involves a short-range or a long-range problem. In the context of education, educational administrators are operating within a realm where the task of the classroom teacher is complex, where classroom teachers are highly educated professional personnel, and where the time factor is very long.

The American public school system is an excellent proving ground for participatory administrative practices. American school teachers are well educated and can accept a share of the responsibility for the group enterprise. Education of the nation's youth is a complex task requiring both creativity and flexibility of the instructional staff. Calling upon skilled personnel to carry out complex tasks over a long period of time, the educational enterprise is an excellent medium for group deliberation, group action, and group evaluation.

References

BRANCH, M. C. *Planning: Aspects and Applications.* John Wiley & Sons, New York, 1966.

CARZO, R., JR., and J. N. YANOUZAS. *Formal Organization: A Systems Approach.* Richard D. Irwin and The Dorsey Press, Homewood, Ill., 1967.

CLELAND, D. I., and W. R. KING. *Systems Analysis and Project Management.* McGraw-Hill Book Company, New York, 1968.

GULICK, L., and L. URWICK, eds. *Papers on Science of Administration.* Institute of Public Administration, Columbia University, New York, 1937.

JOHNSON, R. N. *Aggression in Man and Animals.* W. B. Saunders Company, Philadelphia, 1972.

LEAVITT, H. J. *Managerial Psychology.* 2d ed. The University of Chicago Press, Chicago, 1964.

PETER, L. *The Peter Principle.* Bantam Books, New York, 1969.

ROUNDY, E. S. "Problems and Competencies Needed by Men Physical Education Teachers at the Secondary Level." *Research Quarterly,* 38 (1967), 274–282.

SCHEIN, E. H., and W. G. BENNIS. *Personal and Organizational Change through Group Methods.* John Wiley & Sons, New York, 1967.

SEIDEL, B. "Are Administrators Responsible for Teacher Unrest?" *Physical Educator,* 22 (1970), 22–24.

TANNENBAUM, A. *Control in Organizations.* McGraw-Hill Book Company, New York, 1968.

ULRICH, R., and N. H. AYRIN. "Reflexive Fighting in Response to Aversive Stimulation." *Journal of Experimental Analysis of Behavior,* 5 (1962), 511–520.

II.
BASIC
PROGRAMS

CHAPTER CONTENTS

Program Overview

Planning Procedures

Organizing

Actualizing

Controlling

3.

PHYSICAL EDUCATION INSTRUCTION

After reading this chapter, each student should be able to:

Describe the various types of instructional programs applicable to normal and to exceptional students.

Apply the four philosophies of physical education to selecting activities in a program.

Describe the management procedures of planning, organizing, actualizing, and controlling as applied to physical education instruction.

Analyze the strengths and weaknesses of traditional and alternative programs.

What is physical education? What are physical educators trying to accomplish? What is the best procedure for bringing about the desired results? *Physical education is the process of changing student behavior through the medium of physical activities.* Since body, emotions, and mind are so closely linked, behavior change in the physical, affective, or cognitive domain affects the other domains as well. If education is the process of changing student behavior, physical education is the school activity which causes behavior modification by means of such physical activities as rhythms, games, and gymnastics.

Program Overview

Several different types of programs have been developed because divergent opinions exist about what kinds of programs should be offered to which students. All professional physical educators do not agree in philosophy or program. Historically, there have been many systems of physical education. The advocates of German and Swedish gymnastics and European sports have strongly influenced physical education in America.

The Scope of the Normal Student Program

The program of activities must always be structured to fit student needs. Since student needs reflect the student's developmental stage at a particular time, programs will vary remarkably from entrance to graduation. The vertical curriculum from kindergarten through post-secondary school is described in the following paragraphs.

Preschool Programs

Preschool programs are generally designed to foster the acquisition of physical, mental, and social developmental skills. Some children have learned the basics of movement, perception, and social interaction from parents or siblings in the home. Too, there are homes in which movement and perceptual experiences may be limited. Accordingly, preschool physical education programs may be geared for normal or remedial development.

The physical education teacher, other teachers, and parents should all realize that preschool programs are designed to contribute to the general development of the child. In haste to please the teachers of language arts, some preschool programs have been perverted into massive reading-readiness programs. Certainly, basic concepts of directionality, handedness, and serial order could be included in a comprehensive preschool program. Physical education has its own objectives. If in achieving these objectives the child improves in reading level, such gains are "fringe benefits," not mainstream effects for this part of the program. McCormick *et al.* (1968) reported that significant gains in reading level are sometimes made by perceptual–motor-trained experimental groups. It is difficult to determine, however, whether reading gains result from specific motor–cognitive experiences or are caused by such accompanying variables as increased attention and improved self-image.

Elementary School Programs

Elementary school programs are usually designed to develop basic movement patterns and activity-related concepts. In elementary schools containing grades 1–6, there is a natural cleavage between the upper and lower levels. Adjustments must be made from an individualized perspective to an individual-in-a-group perspective. Physical education programs can play a key role in the success of the individual in adjusting to and benefiting from this change of emphasis.

Mastery of developmental tasks is especially critical in elementary school physical education. As in the preschool program, it is essential that each child achieve certain developmental skills at the proper time. As the human embryo grows, the biological code dictates that parts of the anatomy must develop at a *time of ascendency.* If the fingers do not emerge at their programmed time of ascendency in the first two months, the child will be born without fingers. If it does not take place at the time of ascendency, normal development will never occur. Similarly, the developmental tasks of children must be accomplished during the time of ascendency for *normal* maturation to occur. Havighurst (1953) emphasizes the importance of following the proper sequence in childhood instruction. Certainly the physical, mental, and social tasks of childhood are not as irremediable as formation of organs in the fetus. Nevertheless, the adult who learns to play tennis usually makes stiff, clumsy movements that lack the fluidity of one who learned to play in childhood. Research (Gallagher 1970) shows poor results in remedial programs designed to teach adults basic motor tasks. Muller (1969) has enumerated several developmental tasks of childhood such as (1) learning social communication; (2) learning the appropriate sexual role; and (3) learning the physical skills of games. Socialization and acquisition of locomotor and axial skills are essential developmental tasks of the elementary school level.

Junior High School Programs

Junior high schools were originally designed to offer an educational setting in which the child could freely explore areas of potential interest. Exploration is especially critical in this period because the child is in transition from parent-direction to mature self-direction. The physical education program should foster physical and social exploration, while emphasizing development in the critical maturation areas that are in their time of ascendency. Another organizational variation is called the middle school. *Middle schools* contain the true preadolescents of grades five, six, and seven.

Junior high schools are looked upon by some as preparatory schools for high school. The hard-line academic approach of beginning to develop high school competencies at the junior high level overlooks the fact that preadolescent students have distinct needs and interests of their own. The junior high school student is no longer interested in games of low organization—yet lacks the precise muscle control necessary for immediate success in individual sports in which implements are used. Though some individual sports can be learned, the group affiliation drive makes team activities attractive.

Senior High School Programs

The high school is the last formal educational experience for most students. Therefore, the high school teacher must complete the task of developing the projected student outcomes. By high school graduation, all normal students should have acquired at least the minimum competencies. The high school has the two-fold task of completing development in areas critical to the maturing adolescent and developing competence and attitudes conducive to a lifetime of satisfying physical activity.

The team sport and compulsory exercise programs typical of most high schools are disappearing. Vigorous team sports and compulsory exercises may be useful in raising the physical fitness levels of students. But calisthenics and such team sports as football have low carry-over potential to recreation in adult life. If the high school graduate does not have the skills necessary to compete in individual sports with satisfaction, and does not know *why* exercise is essential to life, the high school physical education program has failed. Mature adults learn new sports gingerly, and the positive effects of a compulsory exercise program will be dissipated in about the same amount of time it took to acquire fitness.

Post-Secondary School Programs

Physical education programs in colleges and universities should be designed to prepare the student for a lifetime of vigorous activity. Maturational development is virtually complete by late high school for girls and for most boys. Subsequent physical education activities should be designed to serve the recreational needs of adults, with less emphasis on such concepts as strength and endurance. There is little justification for including team sports, calisthenics, and gymnastics in a college physical education program. It is unfortunate but true that few opportunities for participation in team sports are available to adults who have not already become highly proficient during adolescence. Calisthenics inherently have a low motivation factor and would probably not be continued after college requirements were satisfied. Very few opportunities are available for adult gymnastic participation, and gymnastic stunts are difficult for adults to master or retain. Post-secondary physical education should consist of activities that encourage and allow lifetime participation. While there is no guarantee that an activity will be continued into adulthood, lifetime recreational sports activities are likeliest to last because facilities are available and motivation is high.

Special Programs for the Atypical Student

Students with serious psychomotor, cognition, and emotional problems need physical education as much as—or more than—the normal student. Most other students are surrounded by recreational opportunities in which they can spontaneously participate. The atypical child is often forced to sit passively because parents and teachers do not have time to offer the required individual attention. With some modification, many activities can be adapted to the atypical child's ability or the child can be "mainstreamed" into regular classes. We will consider three major categories of special physical education programs.

The Physically Handicapped

The *physically handicapped* child is one who is debilitated because of anatomical or physiological problems. Cerebral palsy, polio, spinal paralysis, muscular distrophy, blindness, stroke, and arthritis are medical problems that prevent students from participating in the regular physical education program. However, the presence of a physical disability does not always necessitate segregation of students into a special program. Remarkable athletic feats have been performed by persons with a severe disability. Seaman (1970) reported that physically handicapped children who participated in the regular program of activities had a more favorable attitude toward physical education than students enrolled in special programs. The orthopedically and neurologically handicapped secondary school students in the study apparently were not disabled so severely as to prevent them from engaging in most class activities.

There are many activities in which severely physically disabled students can participate. Certain modifications useful in special physical education programs should be adopted where appropriate.

Blindness. With little modification blind students can participate in swimming, wrestling, weight training, calisthenics, bowling, and track and field events. A wire line can be constructed to guide the blind student when he or she runs. Field events such as javelin, discus, and shot putting require little special assistance after the initial learning phase. Blind students can learn to shoot free throws in basketball, to play a complete game of golf, and to hit a softball.

Anatomical Handicaps. Anatomically handicapped students include those students with nonexistent or disabled arms or legs and those who are partially paralyzed. Such students may be able to participate in selected activities from the regular program. For example, one-armed and one-legged students can learn to play such games as basketball, tennis, badminton, and bowling. The lack of arms does not seriously impede performance in individual running events, and swimming is possible with flotation devices. Loss of one leg only slightly interferes with performance in gymnastics and swimming. Physiological dysfunction also includes students who grossly lack ability in hand-to-eye coordination and those who are paralyzed. Track and field events do not require high-level perceptual–motor functioning. Weight training and calisthenics are possible for the student with coordinative motor dysfunction. Partially paralyzed students may participate in such games as wheelchair basketball, archery, wheelchair bowling, modified calisthenics, weight training and swimming with flotation devices.

The Mentally Handicapped

Mental handicaps are customarily defined according to performance on standardized intelligence tests. Immediately below the normal range of intelligence are the educable mentally retarded (EMR), followed by the trainable mentally retarded (TMR), and the total-care patients. Many educable mentally retarded students and some trainable students may be enrolled in schools. Special education classes may be grouped together for their own physical education, or they may be included in some of the regular physical education classes. Physically the EMR and TMR students could compete with the normal student, but to include them in all the regular activities would prevent the instructor from teaching the cognitive aspects of physical education.

Programs for the EMR and TMR student can be quite similar to those of the regular program. Track and field events are especially desirable, along with a culminating activity such as the Special Olympics. Games of low organization are effective because they do not require high-level comprehension of complex rules and subtle strategy. Rhythms and combatives such as wrestling are recommended. In addition, special activities should be included for developing an awareness of body parts, directionality, and position in space relative to objects. Beter (1973) reported significant gains in cognitive and motor performance from concentrated work in perceptual–motor activities with a large group of EMR students.

The Emotionally Disturbed

The abnormal condition described by the term *emotional disorder* is an inability to function in normal daily activities. Mild cases are called *neuroses;* and severe conditions of inappropriate behavior are called *psychoses.* Though physical symptoms of abnormality characteristically appear in other forms of mental dysfunction (schizophrenia and paranoia, for example) the interdependence of mental and physical domains is especially apparent in depression. Mental depression has a corollary in physical depression. If a person no longer wants to live, the body will mirror the fact. Severe mental depression is almost always accompanied by sagging muscles and glazed eyes. In fact, severe mental depression is classically portrayed as a condition of physiological shock, the characteristics of which are lowered metabolism, low blood pressure, low heart rate, clammy skin, and vacant expression.

Since mental disorders are mirrored by the body, improvement in mental outlook should be demonstrated in physical characteristics. And it may conversely be true that improvement in body function can improve the student's mental outlook. Based on the assumption of mind–body functional unity, Lowen (1972) has proposed a series of exercises designed to draw patients out of severe depression. Some of the recommended activities are as follows: (1) backbend over stool, to deepen breathing; (2) shallow knee bend, sustained to fatigue; (3) touch toes, letting arms and head relax; (4) one-leg balance, sustained to fatigue; and (5) knee–chest position, allowing abdomen and chest to relax fully.

Vigorous exercises and games may have the cathartic effect of releasing emotions through movement. Games provide a social context in which withdrawn persons can experience interpersonal interaction, though the games should not be so complex as to introduce new frustrations. On the other hand, many emotionally disturbed people are in a constant state of tension, and they need to learn how to systematically reduce muscular contraction. Lyons and Lufkin (1967) reported that tension levels can be decreased by conscious effort in a training program. Instruction in tension control can help to reduce the physical expression of mild emotional disorders.

Philosophies of Physical Education Instruction

There are sharp differences in philosophy among physical educators. For example, a physiologically oriented teacher may emphasize running and calisthenics, while a sports-skill advocate would spend all the class time on team and individual games. Existing physical education programs of widely varied composition reflect different sides in a continuing philosophical debate. In order to understand the differences in programs, it is necessary to examine the various thought and action systems. Four currents of thought emerge from the literature of physical education. They correspond closely to physical efficiency, social efficiency, psychomotor efficiency, and activity concepts—the four major categories of outcomes identified in Chapter 1. Similarly, Eisner and Vallance (1974) have identified several conflicting conceptions of curriculum. Most difficulty in resolving curriculum conflicts springs from failure to recognize that the subject can be approached in several different ways. We will consider four logical categories of physical education curricula.

Somatic Realism

Somatic realism is an adaptation of the realist position to physical education—literally it means "body" plus "reality." Realism stresses dependence on observable objects, events, and constructions (see also Part II of Eisner and Vallance 1974). Therefore, a *somatic realist* is a person who places great emphasis on the human body and obvious changes produced by exercise. The Spartans in ancient Greece were somatic realists because they advocated and constantly trained for physical fitness and militancy. Subtypes within somatic realism include the body builders, the contact sport athletes, and some exercise physiologists. Though these three are quite different, they tend to view body development and exercise as an end in itself. They emphasize the physiological development objective.

Many physical educators apparently operate as somatic realists. Writers such as Cureton (1965), Berger and Mathus (1969), Morehouse and Miller (1971) and Karpovich and Sinning (1971) emphasize body development. Such activities as martial arts, calisthenics, weight training, track and field, and vigorous contact sports are favored by somatic realists.

Somatic Humanism

Somatic humanism is the integration of humanistic philosophy with physical education—literally it means "body" plus "human." Somatic humanism parallels the Eisner and Vallance (1974) category of self-actualization. Humanism is a system of thought focused upon natural human interests and activities. Therefore, a *somatic humanist* is a person who places greatest value on activities that flow naturally out of interaction with the physical and social environment. Performers who use physical activities as a creative art form are examples of somatic humanism. Subtypes within somatic humanism include many sport-skill enthusiasts, specialists in movement education, dancers, and athletes in the areas of creative movement. Originally, the German gymnastic system was developed around natural movements as a reaction to the scientific Swedish gymnastic system. Somatic humanists tend to emphasize the objective of psychomotor skill as an outcome of physical education.

Somatic humanists have produced a large volume of literature, and they are very influential in local physical education programs. Writers such as Brightbill (1961), Schurr (1967) and Gerhardt (1973) are typical. The movement-education advocates have made a very strong humanistic stand for varying the use of equipment. For example, while parallel bars could be restricted to classical gymnastic events, the same apparatus could be used by students to explore elevated walking, swinging, and crawling-through problems. Such activities as dance education and lifetime recreational sports are emphasized by somatic humanists.

Somatic Idealism

Somatic idealism is a paradox, for idealists have traditionally devoted little attention to the human body. Idealists may tend to be dualists, dividing mind from body. Idealism is the philosophy that maximizes use of the mind in defining reality. Therefore, a *somatic idealist* is a person who values ideas about the body and the conscious individuality of the person. This broad category may be construed to include both rationalism and existentialism. The Eisner and Vallance (1974) concept of academic rationalism parallels many ideas of the somatic idealists. Subtypes within somatic idealism include the reflective scholars and concept advocates. Somatic idealists emphasize activity concepts as objectives in their programs.

Somatic idealists are not the dominant group in physical education, but they tend to be articulate and persistent. Important works in this category have been published by Metheny (1965), Johnson *et al.* (1966), Corbin *et al.* (1970), AAHPER (1970), and Ulrich (1972). Somatic idealists use games, creative individual activities, and concept learning. For example, traditional (somatic realist) conditioning classes are taught *how* to execute exercises. Somatic idealists would stress an appreciation of *why* movement is necessary. The cognitive curriculum plan developed by Johnson *et al.* (1966) is designed to develop students' competency in assessing the residual effects of their own exercise. The basic idea of the "Toledo Plan" was to directly involve the learner in experiencing and recording the effects of an exercise program. Emphasis is on knowing about the results of exercise.

Social Pragmatism

Social pragmatism presents the case for considering games as only a means to development of important social concepts—literally it means "society" plus "functional." "Social" pertains to interpersonal interaction; "pragmatism" is the functional method of evaluating effectiveness. Therefore, a *social pragmatist* is a person who values development of the social order by functional reconstructional methods. Social pragmatists include physical educators who advocate ethical character development and many of the sport sociologists. Physical education is defined as education *through* the physical rather than education *of* the physical. Of course social pragmatists emphasize the socialization objective of physical education instruction. Data of Wilson (1969) and Rosentswieg (1969) indicate that pragmatists are a minority in the field, and yet they have a significant impact on physical education programs. The development of ethical character through game participation has been advocated by moralists such as Alley (1974) and Wooden (1972). Social pragmatism (Dewey 1916) was ably adapted to physical education by Williams (1930) and publicized by Oberteuffer (1945). Apparently a general rebirth of moral education is occurring. Purpel and Ryan (1975) describe the problems. Other writers, such as Voltmer and Esslinger (1975) and Johnson (1968), support the idea of socialization through physical activities. Team and individual sports are preferred because more ethically critical incidents occur therein than in calisthenics or gymnastics.

Planning

Anything worth doing is worth doing well. To do anything well requires fore-thought and planning. Planning involves specifying goals and defining the process to be used in reaching them. The subsequent steps of organizing, actualizing, and controlling are all dependent upon prior statements, projected outcomes, and the program blueprint.

Teachers are expected to state their objectives prior to beginning the program. Administrators too are expected to state their own objectives. The concept of management-by-objectives introduced in Chapter 1 is essential to good adminis-tration. Some exemplary management objectives for administrative planning of physical education instruction are as follows:

to identify major student needs in the school population
to state the minimal competencies expected of a student for each year's work
to develop a comprehensive strategy to achieve outcomes, a strategy that
   integrates the program with available facilities and the school calendar
to develop departmental policies that will simplify administration of routine
   problems
to evolve long-range departmental program goals

Program Planning

Planning is critical in physical education instruction programs. Many teachers find it too easy to "roll out the ball" and let the students have a free recreation period. Physical education can be plagued by problems concerning use of facili-ties and equipment. Planning should take place well before the school year begins, and all those affected by the program should be included in the planning group. According to the assumptions of the participatory management concept, teachers and administrators *involved* in program execution are in the best posi-tion to know what the students need. Student input into curriculum is highly desirable to the end that education become something done "with the student" rather than something done "to the student."

Assuming that several schools are represented, there are three phases of pro-gram planning. The first phase involves general recommendations by the teacher and administrator planning group—syllabus, administrative guide, etc. The second phase entails program planning at the local school level involving all the physical education teachers—departmental goals, sequence of activities, and facilities coordination. The third phase of physical education program planning is done by each individual teacher—unit and daily lesson plans. The products of the first planning phase are described as follows. The specific planning products of the department and individual teacher are discussed later in this chapter and in Chapters 4, 5, and 6.

Syllabus

A syllabus is a guide to program planning in which the goals of the program are defined and alternative activities for reaching the goals are identified. Theoretically, professional teachers should be able to structure the best learning experiences for the students. But in practice, many teachers lack the foresight, interest, or ability to develop a comprehensive curriculum. The syllabus also uniquely provides a basis for overall multischool program continuity from grade to grade. Elementary schools develop the basic competencies which are subsequently built upon by the junior and senior high schools. However, multigrade continuity is possible only if teachers at each level coordinate and plan the progression. Additionally, adoption of an official syllabus for the school district protects the teacher from a major category of lawsuits, as long as the recommended activities are utilized. See Chapter 10 for discussion and cases relative to program planning.

The planning group of teachers and administrators must study the overall situation before narrowing down to specific activities. State and local regulations on time and content of classes are a basic program framework. Official policy statements are available from the state department of education and the local school district office. Grieve (1971) has reviewed and summarized the various state legal requirements for physical education. For example, some states require physical and health education every year in the secondary school. Other states have a lesser requirement or an elective option.

Administrative Guide

Specific recommendations to school administrators are frequently omitted by planning groups. But the principal is the key manager of the local physical education program. For example, the principal who schedules students at three different grade levels in a single class virtually kills any teacher-paced progressional program. The principal who schedules all the athletes for last-period physical education in order to give varsity practice an early start has effectively eliminated the possibility of a broad spectrum of physical education experiences for the athletes.

Administrative guides produced by the planning group are usually a compromise between what the physical educators want and what the administrators think they can accept and enforce. If the administrator leaves the planning session convinced that the recommended program is impossible to enforce, he or she will not genuinely attempt to put the syllabus into effect. The minimum components of a physical education administrative guide include policy recommendations on (1) student classification; (2) student scheduling; (3) class size; (4) class time allotment; and (5) criteria for program evaluation.

Student Characteristics

All students do not fit the normal model for a particular grade level. Students mature at different rates, and those in a particular grade are also of different chronological ages. There may be as much as an eleven-month range in a grade level, and older students who have failed grades further complicate program planning. However, useful generalizations are possible about a specified age/grade level. A numerical average of student performance implies that scores fall above and below the mean. As a group of students matures, the mean performance should improve. Actually, students on both ends of the developmental range of the class may be performing at the rate of a lower- or higher-aged class.

Though some error always results from characterizing a group by its mean, curriculum developers need some firm estimate of developmental level. Much

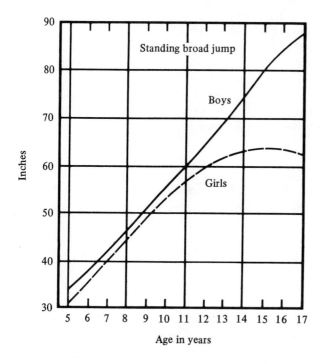

Figure 3.1 Longitudinal development in the standing broad jump. (From "Motor Development," by Anna Espenschade and Helen Eckert in Science and Medicine of Exercise and Sport, 2nd Ed., by Warren R. Johnson and E. R. Buskirk, Harper & Row, 1974.)

research has been conducted in child development. Figure 3.1 illustrates the mean rates of longitudinal student development in a selected motor skill. Curriculum planners can infer student needs from the characteristics graphed in Figure 3.1. It should be noted that many of the entry skills identified by Singer and Dick (1974) are predicated upon a student's maturational development. *Entry skills* are prerequisite competencies needed for learning successively more complex tasks.

Lower Elementary (grades 1-2-3/ages 6-7-8)

Social
1. Boys and girls tend to play in separate groups.
2. Spontaneous play groups of two to four individuals form.
3. Low-level cooperation and competition appear—as in jump rope activities.
4. Individuals perceive some basic principles of fair play in groups.

Mental/emotional
1. Attention span is shorter than for adolescents.
2. Individual is capable of following a sequential order of directions to complete a simple task.
3. Activities are largely self-centered.
4. Parents and teachers are primary models for value judgments.

Physical
1. Individual has difficulty in mastering fine motor skills.
2. There is much spontaneous movement.
3. Individual lacks endurance for sustained locomotor movements.
4. Limb–eye coordination is sufficiently developed for catching and kicking.

Upper Elementary (grades 4-5-6/ages 9-10-11)

Social
1. Considerable cleavage develops between boys' and girls' interests.
2. This is a period of strong gender-concept formation.
3. Boys respond to competition more than girls. (Strong 1968)
4. Boys' games tend to be rigorous, while girls' activities are more skilled and social.

Mental/emotional
1. Interest grows in community sports events, usually team sports.
2. The rudiments of highly organized games are understood.
3. Logic changes; individuals begin to reason deductively from their own experiences.
4. Teachers and ideal adults are the primary behavior models.

Physical
1. Mastery (patterns that will persist through adolescence) of basic locomotor and axial motor skills develops.

2. The individual is capable of sustaining maximal-heart-rate exercise of moderate duration.
3. The individual fatigues and recovers quickly.
4. There is an increase in muscle mass and a decrease in flexibility.

Junior High School (grades 7-8-9/ages 12-13-14)

Social
1. Heterosexual interest begins covertly with some pairing in later stages.
2. Much interest in the peer group and considerable peer group pressure to conform are evident.
3. Athletic prowess is associated with high social standing in the peer group.
4. Social and ethical value responses temporarily become inconsistent.

Mental/emotional
1. Moods tend to swing unexpectedly from euphoric to depressive.
2. Some reflective thinking in quiet times about the meanings of living.
3. Detailed verbal concepts are remembered, and responsibility is assumed.
4. The peer group is the primary basis for value judgments; there is some personal insecurity.

Physical
1. Individual experiences awkwardness in locomotor and axial movements.
2. Even so, locomotor and axial movement capabilities are developed more than fine manipulative motor movements.
3. There is a period of rapid growth in height; speed and endurance peak for girls.
4. Secondary sex characteristics develop.

Senior High School (grades 10-11-12/ages 15-16-17)

Social
1. Much overt and covert heterosexual interest is evidenced by much pairing and dating.
2. Peer groups and cliques are potent determiners of behavior.
3. Idealism and concern with unfairness and inequities emerge.
4. Social and ethical responses again increase in consistency and reliability.

Mental/emotional
1. The individual is capable of creative thought and can carry plans through to completion.
2. Complex problems, as in the sophisticated strategy of team sports, are understood.
3. Adult level of intelligence is reached in later grades.
4. Peer-group and adult values are being compared, as individual judgment develops.

Physical
1. Sprinting speed nears final adult level for boys.
2. Manipulative fine motor capability is near adult level.
3. Growth in height stabilizes, with development in strength and endurance continuing for boys.
4. Complete sexual maturity is reached in later grades.

Activity Selection

Games, sports, and rhythmic movements are the media by which student behavior is modified in physical education. Activities themselves are not end products. They are merely the means of achieving the end product of behavior modification. Not all activities will produce the same effect, however. For example, track and field activities may foster self-reliance and fitness, but very few ethically critical events normally occur in track and field to offer a "teachable moment" for improving social conduct. Conversely, team sports are excellent sources of incidents for development of group cooperation and social efficiency, but at the expense of individualization. The desired end product must be detailed in competency objectives before any teaching begins.

Objectives

Objectives are statements of intention that define the intermediate steps on the way to achieving full competency. As shown in Table 2, there are two levels of objectives. The general behavior goal is called a *terminal competency*. The categories of terminal competencies (physiological efficiency, psychomotor efficiency, etc.) were described in Chapter 1. Specific behavior goals are called *behavioral competencies*. Behavioral competencies define specifically what student performance is expected.

Prespecified intentions are important because they give direction and continuity to programs. However, the teacher's rhetoric about objectives is only valuable if attention is focused on instructional consequences. As Wilson (1969) pointed out, it is not uncommon to discover that what the teacher presented to the student produced an entirely unexpected result. His research showed considerable difference between the physical education objectives perceived by professional respondents and by high school students enrolled in physical education programs. There is some question whether students must perceive what is to be learned before they can learn it. In any case, the high school students in the study did not recognize many of the objectives or categories in which they were supposedly changing their behavior.

Once the end product has been defined, the program and its managers can be evaluated for effectiveness. Every staff should decide what competencies are to be expected of students—what constitutes a physically educated person. As

Table 2   *Prespecified instructional intentions with examples of terminal and behavioral competencies*

Terminal Competency	Behavioral Competency
Activity concepts	1. The student will be able to describe the mechanics of executing a set shot, two-hand pass, and dribble. 2. The student will be able to define the rules relating to double dribble, personal foul, and free throw. 3. The student will be able to describe zone defense and freelance offense.
Social efficiency	1. The student will be able to show self-control when a foul is called on him or her. 2. The student will be able to show self-control when flagrantly fouled. 3. The student will be able to encourage teammates to play fairly when opponents resort to unsportsman-like tactics.
Psychomotor skills	1. The student will be able to dribble a basketball the length of a standard court and back in sixty seconds. 2. The student will be able to execute the two-hand pass-and-catch against a wall ten feet away twenty times in sixty seconds. 3. The student will be able to make six baskets out of ten free throw attempts.
Physiological efficiency	1. The student will be able to sustain continuous play for fifteen minutes. 2. The student will be able to throw an overhand pass half the length of a standard court. 3. The student will be able to execute a maximum-jump-reach rebound simulation twenty times in sixty seconds.

pointed out by Shockley (1973), end-product behavior must be explicitly defined. In programs where end products are not specifically defined, student and teacher pace tends to be slow. Prespecifying competencies sets the scene for action. Students must be made aware of the expected competencies early in the instructional unit in order for them to work toward the goals. Defining behavioral objectives requires logical analysis of the activity to be used for student behavior change. Mager (1962) contributed much to the movement toward behavioral objectives, and Davis (1973) presents a good application to the field of physical

Figure 3.2 Objective: the student will successfully make six out of ten free throws on a standard basketball court.

education instruction. Davis also identifies correct and incorrect statements of behavioral objectives. The basic procedure for writing behavioral competencies involves the following steps:

1. Define observable behavior (shooting a free throw in basketball).
2. Specify the type of behavior desired (dribbling, shooting, and passing a basketball).
3. Set the competency criteria (make 4 out of 10 basketball free throws).

Criteria for Activity Selection

Physical educators have a wide spectrum of motor skills from which to choose curricular activities. Calisthenics, gymnastics, and team sports may be included in the curriculum for a particular grade level. However, activity selection must not be a random process nor should choices be based on the teacher's interests and proficiencies. Selection must be based on the twin criteria of what the student needs and what the activity has to offer.

Student Needs. Schools exist to help the student toward skill development, self-actualization, and socialization, goals which suggest that meeting student needs is of prime importance. For example, in elementary grades the student needs to acquire proficiency in the basic locomotor and axial movements. In junior and senior high school, students need to develop proficiency in motor skills that will be of use as they function as group or team members. Student needs are based on developmental characteristics at a particular age level.

Nature of the Activity. Activities vary widely in contributory potential and geographical interest. For example, in team sports the game of newcomb is relatively simple, while the similar game of volleyball requires a high degree of skill for all players on the team. In choosing curricular activities, the following questions should be asked about each alternative:

1. What will be the probable effect? For example, the probable effects of team sports include socialization, teamwork, and motor skill development. The probable effect must be consistent with the stated objectives of the course.
2. What is the difficulty level? Activities have been analyzed in terms of complexity level (amount of information) and organization (number of component parts) by Naylor and Briggs (1963), and Johnson (1972). Amount of necessary strength and endurance are also factors to consider in designating activities for the various age groups.
3. Are students interested in the activity? Geographic and socioeconomic factors are potent determiners of student interest. For example, there is much interest in wrestling in the mid-western states but very little interest in the southern states. Basketball is a popular activity in the inner-city areas, whereas golf would be less attractive to inner-city youth whose socioeconomic status has not made possible the purchase of special equipment or access to specialized playing areas.
4. Is a progressional sequence implied? For example, a definite progressional sequence is assumed in gymnastics: basic tumbling is a prerequisite to more advanced work in aerial gymnastics and related trampoline stunts. Also, when an activity is repeated, such as basketball, the second and subsequent offerings must introduce more advanced concepts.

Grade Placement of Activity. Where can a particular activity be used to maximum advantage? Such fundamental skills as perceptual–motor activities are best placed at the lower elementary school level. Active team games should be stressed in the junior high school, because of the physical and social needs of the student. Exploration in lifetime sports should be provided during the high school years because the high school is often the last formal educational experience. The task of curriculum developers is to make a fine discrimination between alternative activities and to recommend the optimal range of applicable grade levels.

For example, basic mat tumbling could be assigned to the upper elementary school, aerial gymnastics and elementary apparatus at the junior high level, and gymnastic apparatus and advanced tumbling in senior high school.

Activity Alternatives

A host of alternative activities are available. If the curriculum guide specifies team sports for grade eight, choices could be made among volleyball, football, rugby, speedball, soccer, basketball, and team handball. Where several sections of a grade are scheduled, the teachers must plan facilities use cooperatively. However, assigning all students of a particular grade to any activity, in lieu of alternates, on the sole basis of administrative convenience is not defensible. The teacher's function is analogous to that of a physician: she or he *prescribes* the activities that will produce the desired behavioral competencies. Activities offered in an elective program must also be rigorously screened. In the following lists, alternative activities are grouped according to probable grade-level designation. Categories of activities are listed on the left, and typical activities appear on the right for each category. Many activities could be subsumed under more than one category. For description of the activities cited, see Anderson, Elliot, and La Berge (1966), Gerhardt (1973), Schurr (1975), and Fait (1971).

Lower Elementary. Lower elementary programs should emphasize acquisition of fundamental movement skills. Programs should include movement to rhythm, exploration of movement in space, body–eye coordination, simple tumbling stunts, and simple games. Individual play and cooperative group activities are desirable, but competitive activities should be minimized for lower elementary children.

Activity category	*Activity examples*
Movement Exploration	Up, down, smallness, bigness, spin, upside-down, round, square
Axial skills	Catch, throw, climb, strike, hang, sling, kick
Locomotor movements	Walk, run, leap, hop, skip, jump, crawl, dodge, slide, step, gallop
Rhythms	Dance steps, step and clap in time, singing games
Mimetics	"Look like a tree, elephant, turtle, rabbit, camel, frog, building, scarecrow," follow the leader, Simon says
Story plays	Trip to the zoo, ride on the roller coaster, trip on a ship, the circus comes to town
Stunts	Side roll, forward roll, tip-up, heel slap, one-foot balance, line walk, heel click, rocket

Courtesy Lind Climber Co., Evanston, Illinois

Figure 3.3 There are several ways to solve the motor problem of going over a bar.

Self-testing	Sit-up, push-up, pull-up, jumping-jack, touch-toe
Relays (game race)	Duck walk, wheelbarrow, gym scooter, skip and run, tag the line
Low-organization games	Circle dodgeball, skip tag, fire on the mountain, four square, fox and chickens, wood tag

Upper Elementary. The upper elementary school child is capable of sustained attention to tasks of moderate strenuousness and complexity. Considerable attention needs to be given to enjoyable activities that foster the development of fundamental locomotor and axial skills. Movement exploration is desirable in the form of rhythms or gymnastics, and some competition can be introduced.

Activity category	*Activity examples*
Movement exploration	complex problems: dribble ball as low as possible, find the center of gravity in movement, swing around bar
Axial skills	Football (punt, pass, kick), baseball (hit, pitch, throw), rope climb, cargo net, soccer dribble, basketball (shoot, pass, and dribble)
Locomotor movements	Chinese jump rope, jump rope, high jump, long jump, standing broad jump, hopscotch, dodge ball, team dodge, obstacle course, hop, step, and jump

Rhythms	Tinklen sticks, singing games, simple folk dances, musical pantomimes
Gymnastics	Forward roll, backward roll, cartwheel, round-off, low balance beam, head stand, head spring, dual balancing
Self-testing	Push-up, pull-up, squat–thrust, sit-up, jump and full turn, jump and straddle, toe touch
Relays	Shuttle run, three-legged run, wheelbarrow, inchworm, crab walk, gym scooter, dribble
Lead-up games	Kickball, modified goal basketball, touch or flag football, speedball, softball

Junior High. Junior high and middle school physical education instruction programs should feature developmental activities that actively involve the large muscle groups. Combatives such as wrestling, rhythms, track and field events, gymnastics, and team sports such as speedball, soccer, football, volleyball and basketball are especially recommended. Rhythms such as folk and modern dance are also appropriate. Lifetime sports may be introduced, depending upon high school requirements and other vertical curriculum factors in the school system.

Figure 3.4 A vigorous activity like push ball is good for developing large muscle groups.

Courtesy GSC Athletic Equipment, San Pedro, California

Activity category	Activity examples
Combatives	Wrestling, judo, arm wrestling, tug-o-war, self-defense
Rhythms	Elementary modern dance, foreign folk dance, American folk dance
Aquatics	Floating, front crawl, back crawl, sidestroke, water sports
Gymnastics	Hand spring, one-hand cartwheel, hand stand, forward roll with half twist, elementary free exercise routine, pyramid building
Track and field	Sprinting, shot put, softball throw, 600-meter run, long jump, high jump, hop–step–jump, standing broad jump
Team games	Push ball, dodge ball, basketball, touch football, rugby, soccer, speedball, volleyball, team handball, field hockey, ice hockey
Self-testing	Push-up, pull-up, sit-up, touch toe, squat–thrust

Senior High. Senior high school programs should focus on vigorous activities that foster development in the maturing adolescent's critical areas and on activities in which lifetime participation is possible. Jogging, golf, tennis, swimming, archery, and cycling are recommended lifetime activities. Some provision should be made for concentrated work in preferred elective activities.

Activity category	Activity examples
Gymnastics	Basic trampoline, vaulting, parallel bars, balance beam, dual balancing, free exercise
Aquatics	Breast stroke, butterfly, diving, life saving, water games
Rhythms	Modern dance, foreign folk dance, American folk dance, social dance
Track and field	Sprinting, distance run, shot put, high jump, relays, hop–step–jump, long jump
Team sports	Advanced levels of basketball, volleyball, soccer, rugby, touch football
Conditioning	Calisthenics, weight training, power lifting, isometric training
Lifetime sports	Archery, badminton, bowling, golf, handball, tennis, cycling, fencing, self-defense

After activities have been designated for the various grade levels, a yearly plan should be constructed. Seasonal considerations, such as weather and number of daylight hours, should be taken into account. However, in dovetailing boys' and girls' programs, it may be necessary to teach some activities out of the traditional seasons. Activities should also be balanced for variety. If the AAHPER Youth Fitness test battery is to be administered twice yearly, the fall semester test could culminate a conditioning exercise unit and the second test could be used to cap a

Courtesy Wing Archery Co.

Figure 3.5 The later high school program should stress lifetime sports activities like archery.

spring track and field unit. Team sports could be alternated with individual sports, gymnastics, and combatives in order to provide variation. It is at least as true in physical education as in other pursuits that a change is as good as a rest!

Factors that Modify Programs

The ideal physical education program developed by curriculum planners often undergoes drastic changes when integrated into the overall class program of the local school. Model programs encounter uncooperative principals, unmotivated instructors, and less than ideal facilities. Complications involving professional personnel and the school–community context can arise and make modification of your original plans necessary.

Professional Personnel

Administrators have biases. They may believe in some parts of the program and reject other parts. Since the principal is the chief administrative officer in the local school, it is difficult to circumvent his or her disapproval. For example, the principal may want all the boys to participate in team sports and track and field in order to discover students who could be used in the varsity sports program. This principal would reject individual sports in the physical education program because individual sports have very little varsity interest. Furthermore, coaches of team sports are commonly assigned to teach physical education. The natural bias of such a coach often prevents aggressive and diversified physical education programming.

The greatest threat to a progressive program of physical education is indifference. Many school principals believe that physical education and athletics are synonomous—the main difference being that people pay to see the more highly skilled students perform. Indifferent administrators may herd large groups of students from several grades into a single class for convenience in scheduling. Indifferent teachers may also sit idly by and watch students play the same game day after day. Or the teacher may use the class period to work with the highly skilled, leaving the less skilled to fend for themselves. Those dedicated teachers who want to improve local programs in spite of other lethargic personnel should work with interested parents to effect improvements.

Case Example: PLANNING FOR PHYSICAL EDUCATION INSTRUCTION

The Washington County school system has funded a curriculum workshop to develop scope-and-sequence classroom guides for physical education. Competent male and female representatives from the elementary and secondary schools have been named workshop participants. Money is also available for bringing in outside consultants.

The secondary school principals have been lax in physical and health education program enforcement. None of the secondary schools group physical education by homogeneous grade levels—as many as three grade levels are present in each class. The principals complain that they do not have a set of criteria by which to evaluate their programs. The school system contains five large high schools, eight junior high schools, and fifteen elementary schools. Traditionally there has been no coordination between schools of the same level, nor between lower- and upper-level schools.

As the physical education department chairperson of one of the high schools, you have been appointed chairperson of the work group by the school system superintendent. The group is to meet on Saturdays during the spring school term (with extra pay). What will your response be to the following questions:
1. What is the first order of business for the work group?
2. What outcomes should the group try to produce?
3. Who should be brought in as consultants to the work sessions from within the system? From outside the system?
4. What objectives or competencies should be developed and adopted?

School–Community Context

The community is a potent factor in program determination. Wealthy suburban communities can provide handsomely for their schools' physical plants. Inner-city schools with a lower tax base may find it difficult to provide even the bare essentials. Some hard-pressed school districts have been forced to rely on the local PTA group to raise funds to purchase toilet tissue and paper towels. Much improvisation is called for in schools that lack sufficient funding.

The community also affects the type of activities in the program. Northern areas can offer skating, field and ice hockey, and skiing, while southern areas can offer year-round outdoor aquatics. Traditionally and geographically, football and basketball have been popular in the South and Southwest, basketball has also been popular in inner-city areas and the northern areas, and gymnastics has been popular in the Midwest and all the coastal regions. However, many of these activities are becoming popular nationwide. Community expectations and preferences do sometimes suggest certain activities, but professional personnel must work for a quality program without being hampered by geographic or sociocultural stereotypes.

Organizing

Organizing is the second step in setting up the conditions for potentially effective learning. Smooth coordination of teachers, students, and facilities is no accident. Organizing requires much forethought and systematic preliminary action. Some of the organization problems involve teacher assignments, student schedules, facility coordination, purchase of materials, and class organization. Organizational functions are performed by both the principal, as a middle-level administrator, and the teacher, as a classroom administrator. Some typical management objectives for organizing a physical education instruction program are as follows:

to recommend an optimum type of program from analysis of the alternatives
to develop a model faculty schedule
to analyze the school and community context in order to identify all available instructional spaces and materials
to recommend an optimum system of within-class organization for teacher-paced instruction and individualized learning

Personnel Organization

A system of personnel organization functions to divide tasks into manageable units of work. The tasks in education involve both professional and student personnel. Students are not passive in learning; they must actively participate in managing the learning experience. Yet most management tasks are executed by middle-level managers and teachers. Leadership is shared by anyone who contributes to holding the group together or to achieving group goals. Leadership in the physical education program should be structured by a bureaucratic system in direct proportion to the size of the school or school district. Small school systems need little bureaucratic division of labor. In large schools, professional management tasks are typically divided among the supervisor of physical education, the school principal, the department chairperson, and the teacher.

The text and illustrations in Chapter 2 show the organization system traditionally used in school management. The physical and health education supervisor is within the bureaucratic hierarchy to provide systemwide leadership. Individual school principals are the legally responsible agents for their schools, and leadership tasks are frequently delegated to a chairperson in a single school. At the lowest management level, each teacher is accountable for developing and conducting a program for specified classes.

Schedule Construction

The faculty and class schedules of elementary and secondary schools are usually executed by the school principal or counselor. If the status of physical education is to improve in the school, the teachers must seek to advise the schedule makers. For example, in order for a teacher-paced progressional program to work, the students must be classified and assigned to physical education classes by that classification system.

Figure 3.6 A schedule chart coordinating staff and facilities.

Teaching stations

Class periods	West end of gymnasium	East end of gymnasium	Wrestling and tumbling room	Outside field	Health room
1	Hurwitz	Neal	Paul	Hill	Pappas
2	Hurwitz	Pappas		Hill	Russo
3	Pappas	Neal	Paul	Hill	Russo
Lunch { 4	Hurwitz	Pappas	Paul		Russo
5		Neal		Hill	
6	Hurwitz	Neal	Paul	Pappas	Russo
7	Hurwitz	Neal	Paul	Hill	Russo

Scheduling is a major factor in management of a large school. In order to assure efficient use of staff and facilities, a two-way chart should be constructed. In Figure 3.6, the teaching stations are listed horizontally across the top and the time periods vertically in the left column. (Teaching stations are spaces designed for teaching classes with a school facility.) Five teaching stations are shown. After the first instructional unit, the stations can be rotated among the teachers. Total class load for teachers is computed by counting their class periods.

Teaching Stations

The total number of teaching stations and teachers needed for a fall term should be based on a preregistration late in the spring term. The total student demand should be divided by the maximum number of students to be allowed in a class. Many states use twenty-five students as the base class size for payment of state equalization funds. The total class demand is then divided by the number of class periods used in the normal school day in order to determine the number of classes required per time-period. The number of classes demanded at a given period is the number of faculty members and teaching stations needed at that time.

If the maximum teacher load is five classes per day, the total class period demand can be divided by five to determine the number of full-time staff members needed. When the dividend is not equal to a multiple of five, then a part-time teacher is required to share duties in physical education and some other school subject. These computations for class demand and teachers required are based on the assumption of a five-day-per-week program. If the physical education program operates on a system of alternate days or alternate semesters, the class and teacher demand will be reduced proportionally.

Faculty Organization

The total number of periods within a day varies from school to school. Some schools have a six-period schedule, while others may normally have eight periods. Some schools using flexible scheduling may *vary* the time blocks from two to eight periods per day. Regardless of the total number of daily periods, regional accrediting associations recommend allocation of a daily planning period for every teacher. Administrators frequently abuse planning periods by allocating the last period of the day as planning period for the teacher–coaches. If there is an extra payment for coaching duties, the planning period should not be used for coaching. The bulk of the teacher–coach's salary is derived from teaching. Thus the planning period must be used to improve instruction.

Faculty preferences about class and time should also be made available to schedule planners. A teacher may prefer a particular time for the planning period. If there are electives or designated short courses, planners should be mindful of faculty interests and competencies. Special competencies are needed in aquatics and dance, just as in French Club and supervision of the student newspaper.

Faculty organization problems are different for elementary and secondary schools. Most secondary schools are departmentalized, which means teachers instruct in only one subject. Departmentalized classes are sometimes used in upper elementary schools but seldom in lower elementary schools. Elementary schools in grades one through six are generally organized in self-contained classrooms.

If the school uses the self-contained classroom system, two physical education instruction systems are commonly used. In one approach, the regular teacher instructs in language arts, social studies, physical education, and the like. Unfortunately, few self-contained classroom teachers are adequately trained in physical education programming. In a second approach, a physical education specialist takes one or two classes at a time for physical education instruction. Usually the specialist visits each class on alternate days or once a week. Specialists can also be shared between two adjacent schools. Some debate has arisen over the effectiveness of the physical education specialist compared to the classroom teacher. The Workman study (1968) lends some weight to the specialist approach, especially for girls. (The criterion measurements included only five motor and fitness test items.) Apparently, girls respond positively to the motivation offered by the physical education specialist.

Student Scheduling

Student needs and interests theoretically dictate student scheduling. Students should be assigned daily class routines that meet their personal needs. Other factors to be considered are availability of the desired class, the number of students in the alternative classes, and the grade classification of the students in a prospective class. Investigating the effect of three alternative class sizes on learning a tennis skill, Verducci (1969) concluded that the range for effective learning was between 15 and 37 students per class. Student classification and student scheduling are two items about which physical education teachers must educate those who draw up student schedules.

Classification is the process of dividing a population into designated categories. Categorizing students as male or female for physical education instruction is not always valid—and may be illegal according to Title IX. (See Chapter 5 for more discussion of the Title IX guidelines against sex discrimination.) School grade levels are categories arranged in sequential order along a continuum. Both mental and physical performance can be used as bases for classification. Classification methods can be used for assigning students to classes and for dividing students into homogeneous units within a particular class. The basic assumption in student classification is that homogeneous grouping of students facilitates instruction.

The most common method of classifying students for physical education is by grade level. There is considerable variation in maturity within a particular grade level. However, the use of grade-level designation is a quick method, readily available at the time student schedules are drawn up. Students of only one grade level should be assigned to a class, if grade-level classification is used.

Homogeneous student groups can be accurately developed by using physical performance factors. Strength tests (Barrow and McGee 1971) have been successfully used to classify students for instruction and athletic performance. Moore and Falls (1970) also report highly accurate student classification by use of peer-group assessment. Motor ability, physical fitness, and either instructor or peer ratings could all be used for forming homogeneous student groups. Comprehensive testing in the preceding semester is always necessary to determine whether students possess the necessary entry skills for assignment to a specific group. Performance tests are desirable bases for student scheduling because homogeneous skill levels do not restrict highly skilled younger students to participation with unskilled, beginning age-mates.

Alternatives in Program Structure

Several different kinds of programs have implications for schedule construction. Alternatives in program structure suggest various ways in which classes can be organized, for either typical or atypical students. Traditionally, students have been segregated by sex for instruction in a required teacher-paced program. Among the forces precipitating change are the Health, Education, and Welfare Title IX guidelines prohibiting sexism; research in individualization of instruction; and experiments in program flexibility.

Teacher Pacing

B. F. Skinner (1961) and the individualized instruction movement have seriously questioned assumptions favoring complete reliance on teacher-paced methods. Teacher pacing is exemplified when all learners are engaged in the same activities simultaneously, advancing to new tasks only at the direction of the instructor. Lectures and entire class drills are two commonly used teacher-paced methods. Theoretically, more concepts can be addressed this way in the limited time of the school period. Students are assumed to need guidance and motivation toward task achievement. Critics say that complete reliance on teacher pacing is invalid because students learn better at their own (fast or slow) rates.

Student Pacing

A lively book by Gertrude Noar (1972) on individualized instruction is designed to make every child a winner. Since every child learns at an individual pace, at least a third of each teacher-paced class will be hopelessly behind or terribly bored when the rate is set for the average student. Theoretically, every child can achieve the minimal competency standard for an instructional unit if given enough practice time. With individualized instruction, rapid learners can move on to enrichment activities after completing the minimal competency standards. Several variations of student-pacing are described in the paragraphs that follow.

Programmed Text. A programmed text is a series of statements and questions arranged to introduce new material in small steps from the beginning to the end of a learning task. Responses are required periodically, and the steps are small enough to give almost 100 percent positive reinforcement. The learning modules concept is a variation of the verbal input concept. Jarvis (1967) has reported successful adaptation of programmed instruction to learning physical activities. The programmed text can be used in classes of widely heterogeneous composition if the students can read. Programmed texts can also be used as a tool in competency-based programs.

Competency-based Program (**CBP**). CBP is a procedure that can be used in either homogeneously or heterogeneously scheduled classes. Every student behavioral outcome is prespecified. Both the general terminal competencies and specific behavioral competencies are defined by the teaching staff and communicated to the students. As students achieve competencies, they are tested and then allowed to progress to other competency tasks. CBP is also used in contingency contracting. Contingency contracting or *contract grading* is an extension of the competency-based program whereby the student reviews the list of competencies and signs a "contract" agreeing to fulfill certain requirements. The student's grade is contingent upon completion of the contract items. Criterion-referenced grading, discussed on page 108 of this chapter, is readily adapted to CBP.

Homogeneous Subgrouping. When schedule makers refuse to assign students to the physical education class by grade or ability, the teacher can divide the class into homogeneous subgroups. A screening test is given prior to instruction, and the students are then grouped according to their performance on the pretest. For example, in a gymnastics unit a pretest of mat tumbling could be easily given. An elementary-level tumbling pretest could consist of a forward and backward roll and a cartwheel. Homogeneous subgrouping is especially effective when several teachers are assigned physical education classes during the same period. The students can be pooled and reassigned to various teachers after the pretest. Groupings may have to vary as activities change. Excellent young gymnasts grouped with older students for tumbling may not be able to compete with the same older group in a basketball unit.

Coeducational Class Assignment

Initial interpretations of Title IX guidelines against sex discrimination suggest eliminating class divisions based solely on the student's sex and carefully evaluating school policies that discriminate against either boys or girls. Classes can be scheduled separately by sex if the activity so demands. For example, wrestling or men's gymnastics could defensibly be offered to males and women's gymnastics to females. Coeducational classes can be easily scheduled for recreational activities such as archery, badminton, bowling, and tennis. Team sports such as basketball, soccer, and volleyball have also been successfully integrated. Segregation by skill level is allowable, including homogeneous subgrouping within a class. For example, each of two basketball classes could be composed of male and female students of homogeneous skill levels. Where classes are separated by gender, instruction and equipment for both groups must be of equal quality.

Required versus Elective Curricula

Physical education has long enjoyed its status among the required subjects in secondary schools. However, because of competition for school time, requirements are being lowered or dropped. Career education and additional time for specialization, combined with the indifference of physical educators, have contributed to the change.

The shelter of being a curriculum requirement is a mixed blessing. Teachers of required courses are not forced to be sensitive to student needs and interests in enrollment to secure their jobs. Mandatory enrollment assures that virtually the same number of classes will be scheduled year after year. However, several forms of elective programs have been successful. Changing from a required to an elective program does not mean an automatic loss of students and decrease in faculty. Certainly, irrelevant and boring experiences will not be elected, but meaningful experiences are attractive to students. Physical conditioning, team sports, individual sports, and rhythms possess inherent attractiveness to students. Two alternatives to a required-credit program are described in the paragraphs that follow.

Specified Core Curriculum. Authoritarian administrators tend to prefer a prescribed program of physical activities for all students. In the specified core curriculum a regime of calisthenics, gymnastics, team games, and individual sports is experienced by all students. Competency in swimming is frequently a completion requirement. Minimum competency may also be specified in physical education concepts, such as described in Corbin *et al.* (1970). The specified core curriculum can constitute the entire program, or students can elect activities to fulfill general school requirements after the few basic courses are completed.

Elective Curriculum. Assuming that a specified number of credit units are required, the units can either be earned according to an inflexible system where students have no choice of activities or by allowing them to choose activities that interest them. Elective curricula define the activities that are to be offered during a school term. Students then select the courses in which they desire instruction. The system is frequently used in post-secondary schools, though secondary schools could adopt such a plan. Courses may be broadly defined as gymnastics, rhythms, racket sports, or team sports. Specific activities such as golf or basketball could be offered for the duration of a school term. Many schools, particularly large schools, are reluctant to change to an elective program due to the administrative headaches of scheduling. (Use of the school system's computer would minimize the scheduling problem for specific electives.) Near the end of the school term student *time* and *activity* preferences can be computer-sorted. The optimum time and activities can subsequently be used to preregister students by the computer for classes the following year.

The problem of homogeneous scheduling could be partially resolved by writing minimum skill prerequisites for entry into intermediate and advanced courses. For example, a heterogeneous class would probably be enrolled in a beginning tennis class. Those students who achieve the minimum competencies would have the required entry skills for the intermediate-level class. Gender is irrelevant, but students in each class should possess the same skill level.

Elective programs can be initially scheduled by estimating student interest. Prospective class offerings can be determined for subsequent terms by evaluating student elective patterns and asking for preregistration student requests. Curriculum developers should strongly consider free electives for the secondary school whether physical education credits are required or not.

Practice Distribution

If students attend physical education class daily for a school term, the instructor may choose to vary the distribution of activities. The first option is to schedule the unit of instruction in a block plan. The block plan uses massing of instruction time daily for the duration of the unit: a unit of basketball may be conducted five days per week for a four-week unit. A second approach is to alternate two instructional units during a time interval. The partial block plan uses a longer distribution of practice time. For example, a weight training unit could be conducted on Monday, Wednesday, and Friday—with Tuesday and Thursday devoted to an archery unit. A further description of alternatives in distributing practice time appears in Chapter 6. Many elementary programs are partial block plans whereby physical education is alternated during the week with other subjects such as art and music.

Minicourses

The Carnegie unit plan for quantifying the number of credits earned toward graduation is widely used in secondary schools. Some form of reporting is needed, though the Carnegie unit system is limiting. One type of elective program is called the minicourse. Minicourses are short courses of less than one school term in which concentrated effort is devoted to one activity, racket ball or scuba diving for example. The minicourse could be integrated into the school day by allowing students to select two or more minicourses to block out a term, or the course could be taught after school as a continuing-education course. Minicourses differ from other elective schemes in that students are allowed to switch teachers and classmates when going from one minicourse to another within the term. Certification in such activities as life saving and scuba diving has shorter time requirements than the entire duration of a school term. Entry skills may be written as prerequisites for advanced minicourses. The school computer can be used to integrate the scheduling of students for minicourses in the physical education department and other departments.

Off-Campus Courses

Off-campus courses are instructional units conducted off the school campus by the teacher or a designated substitute. For example, a bowling unit could be taught at a local bowling alley. Though the bowling proprietor usually has expertise in instruction, the teacher should retain control of the class by using the proprietor as a resource person. Transportation to off-campus sites during the school day is a problem. Holding off-campus minicourses at night or on weekends could resolve the transportation problem. However, off-campus courses present critical liability issues. Off-campus courses would work best with an elective scheduling plan.

Modular Time Scheduling

The time units of a school day are often firmly fixed before the school term begins. The school day is typically divided into six to eight periods of equal length. Modular scheduling is an innovation based on the assumption that variance among subjects and students necessitates variance in class time. The school may be divided into numerous time intervals of almost infinitely varying size. Seldom is the school day divided into equal time modules. Class length may vary from day to day, depending on the needs of teachers and students. There may be some repetition, such as a schedule repeating itself every five to ten school days. Variation in sizes of time modules is illustrated in Figure 3.7.

Modular scheduling theoretically allows time appropriate for activities and topics at the students' developmental level. Much collective preplanning by the teachers is required for effective use of modular time. Time requests must be made several days prior to the actual need. Obviously all instructors cannot get either all long or all short periods on the same day. If a computer is not available, a "master schedule sheet" must be established in the school so that teachers can avert conflicts in their time allotments. Short modules can be used for lecture or demonstration, long modules for discussion groups. If several teachers are available during a specific module, team teaching is possible. Nixon and Jewett (1964) describe a system in which physical education classes consist of short time modules for instruction, with students dressing in and out in the interim time.

8:00 - 8:30

8:40 - 11:00

11:10 - 12:00

12:05 - 12:25

12:35 - 1:00

1:10 - 2:00

2:10 - 3:15

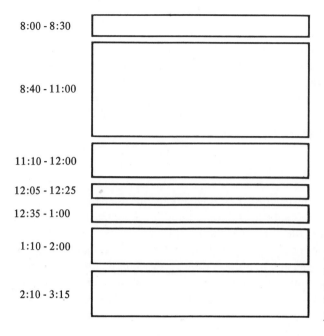

Figure 3.7 An example of dividing one day's schedule into time modules. The relative duration of the modules can vary from day to day.

Organization of the Learning Environment

Few schools possess all the facilities and equipment they need. Physical education facilities are very expensive, and the initial outlay for adequate equipment is also large. Unfortunately, facilities are often planned by architects who know little about their use. Architects have tended to sandwich in rooms that fit their esthetic design rather than defining space utilization and curriculum before proceeding with building design. Chapter 7 deals with long-range planning for facilities and equipment. Here we will discuss utilizing existing space and acquiring or improving equipment.

Using Space

A gymnasium is desirable, but other facilities and areas can be used for physical education instruction. The era of the single-purpose room is over. Taxpayers demand that school facilities be used efficiently by students and the community. A gymnasium built only for use by basketball classes and teams is not economically valid. Multipurpose gymnasiums, rooms, and play areas accommodate programs as variable as the students' needs and interests.

Teaching Stations. A teaching station is the area assigned to a teacher for a class. Figure 3.6 shows a listing of five teaching stations in the top row. Teaching

Southeastern Louisiana University

Figure 3.8 Rhythms, dance, and calisthenics can be conducted in a cleared portion of the classroom.

stations should have some natural space differentiation such as distance or a visual barrier. Visual barriers are desirable, but sound cushioning between teaching stations is even more critical. Designating teaching stations at the opposite ends of a gymnasium can provide enough distance to minimize sound interference.

Analysis of Available Space. Many schools are hard pressed for physical education instruction space. However, a survey of the school site may reveal areas that can be used as found—or easily adapted for class use. Both the teaching station and the activity itself may need adapting. An isolated hall could be used for seated pushball, gym scooters, seated newcomb, calisthenics, and fundamental skills. Classrooms can be used for vigorous activities, such as wrestling or dance, by pushing the chairs aside temporarily. Large trees and the exterior of some buildings could be used for developing repelling skills in an exploring minicourse. Some dressing rooms can be used for calisthenics or weight training. The stage of an auditorium may easily be adapted for gymnastics and wrestling. Outdoor areas also offer possibilities for regular or modified track and field, archery, field sports, and golf instruction with plastic balls.

Organizing Equipment

Equipment is a catalyst for generating student activity. Play is a large part of the child's life, and the presence of play equipment is sufficient to attract students. Playground equipment for free play should be a basic part of every elementary school. Sufficient equipment should be available for class instruction so that at least a third of the students can be actively involved at any time. Where equipment is scarce, groups of students can be rotated as in circuit training. Procedures for purchase and care of equipment are discussed in Chapter 7.

Basic Equipment. Basic equipment for elementary school physical education instruction includes playground balls, team sport balls, perceptual–motor apparatus, multipurpose mats, field markers, rhythm materials, and timing watches. Basic equipment for the secondary level includes mats, gymnastic apparatus, trampoline, team sport balls, records and record player, nets, golf clubs, badminton rackets, tennis rackets, and archery apparatus. Pennington (1966) lists

---

Case Example: ORGANIZING THE PHYSICAL EDUCATION PROGRAM

In Jefferson Junior High there is a chronic problem: too many students in old, cramped facilities. The building formerly housed the high school until a new high school facility was built a decade ago. No renovation was done on the deteriorating building before the junior high moved in. Conditions and morale are so poor that students recently tried to burn the gymnasium by setting a fire under the wooden bleachers. Little major equipment is available because no teacher has stayed long enough to place an order for the next year.

You have been hired by the principal and charged with the specific task of analyzing the situation to make facility, equipment, and program recommendations to the school board. Federal funds have been made available for development of model programs in needy schools. The principal is working up a socioeconomic analysis of the student population, and you are to work up the facilities, equipment, and program details of the federal proposal. Moreover, it is understood that if the project is not funded, some local funds will be available for renovation, and the program is to be started in the fall semester in some form.

In assessing your task, answer the following questions:

1. What type of program will you recommend? Will the recommended program be of the traditional or innovative type? Defend your choice.
2. What type of space arrangements will you recommend? How can multipurpose low-ceiling rooms be used?
3. What major equipment should be purchased to implement the program you recommend? What equipment do you propose to collect or construct locally?
4. If only local funding comes through, what aspects of your program will have priority?

Figure 3.9 Exploration skills such as repelling can be taught by using trees, poles, or the exterior of a building (for advanced classes).

additional items that should be present in every gymnasium as follows: (1) markings for vertical and horizontal jump; (2) peg board; (3) chinning bars; (4) low parallel bars; (5) climbing ropes; (6) balance board and roller; and (7) balance beam. Obviously many worthwhile programs survive on considerably less equipment. But if equipment is not requested, it will seldom be granted.

Improvised Equipment.   Expensive equipment is not always the best dollar value for a physical education program. Many items can be constructed locally by the teacher, PTA, or industrial arts classes. Funds for improvised equipment can be drawn from the school's petty cash or direct parent solicitation. Capon (1974) and Corbin (1972) describe equipment that can be improvised. Balance beams, ladders, jump boxes, geometric crawling shapes, and gym scooters can be constructed with materials from a local building materials store. Old tires from a service station or bike shop can be painted and used for races, markers, or jump mazes. Carpet remnants from a flooring store can be used for padding equipment and as scoot pads on a finished floor. Old bed springs from a furniture store can be covered with thin plywood and canvas to be used as a kiddie bouncer. Eason and Smith (1974) describe an easily constructed multipurpose A-frame cargo net apparatus for perceptual–motor training. A community drive to collect such equipment as old golf clubs, tennis rackets, or miscellaneous sports equipment can be very effective.

Actualizing

Actualizing a physical education program means putting the planning and organizational phases into operation. Actualizing begins when the students come to class and ends when they leave. It involves diverse instructor behavior—from planning class details and teaching methods to adapting activities to student needs.

Initiating the Program

Pupil accounting, orientation of students, and establishment of class routines for checking roll are among numerous details necessary for a smoothly operating program. Of course, these details are only a means to an end and must be kept in perspective.

The First Day

The first class period is an excellent time to orient the student toward worthwhile experiences to come. A positive mental set adopted the first day goes a long way toward encouraging appropriate student behavior during the whole school term.

Pupil Accounting. Students must be accounted for. Students appearing in the wrong class must be directed to the proper class early to avoid their missing important information in the proper class. The central administrative office needs to know early in the class period which students are not in class. The specific method of checking roll is usually up to the teacher.

Teachers are legally responsible for the welfare of students; therefore, systematic accounting must be made of all students. Checking roll is important. Time efficiency is also important, but personalization is more important. Roll check should take only a few minutes to allow most of the class time to be devoted to more productive tasks. The teacher should learn the names of the students quickly. If the teacher can learn to identify each student without laborious name calling during roll check, other means of checking role may be used. Alternatives to roll call by name are: (1) number cards—each student turns his or her number card over when passing the number stand; (2) number spots—each student covers his numbered spot (wall or floor) until roll is completely checked; and (3) squads—the first person in line reports the absences in her or his "squad."

Orientation. The first class period can be profitably spent establishing a positive attitude toward physical education. The skills and abilities the student can look forward to learning should be fully described. Complete discussion of course objectives, basis of grading, and the type of tests to be used help students form a positive mental set. The initial class period is also a logical time for cooperative planning by teacher and students. If contract grading or competency-based programs are used, the initial class period is the time to inform students of these performance expectations. Demonstrations of upcoming activities, tests, and competencies can be effectively used on the first day.

Daily Procedures

Students should be prepared to suit out for activities by the second day. Play is a natural factor in the life of students, and prolonged delay by the instructor dampens spontaneity. Students should be involved in some type of psychomotor activity by the second class period.

Suiting Out. Provision must be made for storage of activity clothing, for suiting out, and for showering. A numbered basket may be assigned to each student. One or two student managers can be assigned to the basket room each period to dispense and receive baskets. Lockers should be large enough to hold the basket and normal school clothing. Quality combination locks are essential for minimizing theft.

Identity is very important in the humanized school. Professional athletes have their name emblazoned on their uniforms. The purpose of the name imprint is to identify the athlete to spectators—but is also bestows personal identity on the player despite the uniformity of the athletic clothing. Similarly, each student's name should be clearly marked in large letters on each piece of activity clothing. Labeling serves two purposes: (1) to identify the student to the teacher and other students; and (2) to discourage theft of activity clothing.

Class Routines. Chaos is not conducive to learning. Neither is strict regimentation. Somewhere between the two extremes of chaos and control lies a lively, viable class context. Early rehearsal in basic class routines can be effective in reducing loss of time. Class routines are for the purpose of protecting the individual student's rights *and* the collective student right to learn. Some routines that should be rehearsed early in the first week are the following:

1. Dressing out.   After baskets are issued, the students should be led through the procedure to be followed for dressing out, showering, dressing in, and basket storage. (The teacher should monitor the dressing area to prevent harassment of younger students.)
2. Roll check.   Walk through the specified procedure for several days or until the students learn the procedure.
3. Formations.   Practice making the line, circle, and stacked line formations from basic squads or the whole class.
4. Attention cues.   Rehearse moving quickly from drill formations and active play to a designated spot for instruction or a different kind of drill. Random bouncing of balls and student conversation hamper the instruction process.

Instructional Strategies

Traditionally one teacher instructs one class for the entire semester. Advantages of the traditional procedure are that it allows (1) time for establishment of rapport between the teacher and each student and (2) subjective performance assessment of each student for individual instruction and evaluation. The theoretical advantages do not always materialize. Alternative instructional models have been suggested to better utilize faculty and other personnel. Refer to Singer and Dick (1974) for systems analysis of the instructional process.

Team Teaching

Team teaching is a method for making best use of instructors by varying the instructors within the staff team. A team is formed by designating various roles to the available personnel within a time period. For example, if there are three teachers assigned to classes in the first school hour, the three would perform three different instructional roles. Figure 3.10 illustrates two forms of team teaching.

Differentiated team teaching maximizes variations in organization of the student group. Students from all classes in a given time period may be amassed in a

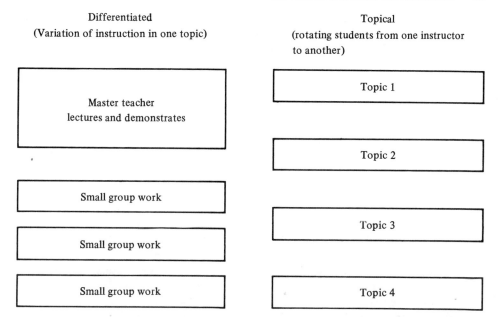

Figure 3.10 Two team-teaching procedures. The size of each rectangle represents the size of the class.

large room for a film, demonstration, or lecture. On succeeding days during the same time period, exploratory groups or discussion groups may be held. Team teaching is more related to personnel organization than to method because after the classes have been structured, any one of several methods can be used. However, the master class is best adapted to teacher-paced methods and use of mass media. In a unit on gymnastics, for example, one mass meeting could be devoted to a lecture and an instructional film. The master teacher could use the second mass meeting to demonstrate basic and advanced skills. Subsequent classes could be devoted to group work in acquiring tumbling skills. Small groups could be rotated from station to station where the other teachers instruct and spot.

Topical team teaching is essentially an extension of departmental organization. Each teacher prepares intensively in a selected field and teaches only one or two specific topics. In topical team teaching, students are shifted from one teacher to another as the topics change. For example, there are four teachers and they anticipate exploring eight physical education activities. Each teacher prepares lessons in two selected areas. As the students move from teacher to teacher they derive the benefit of instructor expertise. There must, however, be a consultation approach to evaluating student progress: The team must get together to decide the course grade to be awarded to each student.

Teacher Aides

Federal programs have brought many paraprofessional aides into the classroom. A *teacher aide* is one who assists the teacher by performing routine tasks. For example, a teacher aide could set up, store, and take inventory of equipment. Whether teacher aides are paid workers or volunteers, the teacher is the professional who is legally responsible for the welfare of students.

Funds for teacher aides are available from some federal programs and often from local sources. Federal programs specify conditions under which their funds can be used, such as with disadvantaged children. Locally funded aides can be used for a wide variety of duties. A routine should be established so that the instructor will not be forced to direct the aide's activity during the class period. A teacher aide's duties can include checking roll and reporting absences, issuing equipment, assisting the teacher in class supervision, reproducing and grading written tests, and recording performance on tests.

Volunteer teacher aides from the local community can be recruited by setting up a continuing program. Little League coaches work as volunteers, so why not a volunteer teacher-aide corps? Departmental needs can be expressed by working through the school PTA or a parent newsletter. Volunteer corps work best when there is some pretraining and when a few hours per week are requested. The aides may be general assistants with an interest in children or former sports competitors interested in working with children in only one sport.

Student Leaders

Leadership development through physical activities is a worthwhile goal. Students can develop leadership skills through practice in being a squad leader. Student leaders can be organized into a formal club program. The leadership role should be rotated among the students. Research has shown that leadership is specific to the situation and can be learned through practice.

A student-leader program is not automatically successful. Much planning, recruiting, and training is necessary. On a noncredit basis, older students can assist in physical education classes in lieu of attending study hall. *In no case should physical education students be student aides in their own class. Advanced students need advanced classes for skill development.* Study halls may be used by developing a school policy that students with a specified grade average (say C+) can go into an aide program. Student volunteers can assist in managing equipment, work with individualized instruction, direct drills, act as spotters, and help in testing. Training for the student aides can be conducted after school or during the activity period set aside for clubs. Student aides can assist, but they cannot be delegated legal responsibility.

Teaching Methods

Teaching methods are divided into three categories for purposes of discussion, but of course the three categories are interrelated in normal instruction flow. They are (1) input methods; (2) practice regimes; and (3) motivation methods. Considerable variation in instructional style is commonly observed, and research suggests that there is no one best set of instructional methods. Categorical statements on methods cannot be made because of such factors as teacher personality, nature of the learners, duration of the task, and structure of the learning task. To find the best way to achieve high levels of student competency, the school manager must consider each of the alternative teaching methods.

Input Methods

Input implies an attempt to communicate information to the learner. The input method may be verbal, visual, or kinesthetic, and it may be applied by one teacher or a group of teachers. Much research has been conducted on input methodology. The status of research has been well summarized by Cratty (1968), Alderman (1974), Robb (1972), and Stallings (1973). Counsilman (1968) and DeCarlo (1963) offer specific recommendations for selected sports skills.

Verbal. Verbal input is communication by the spoken or written word. Words are only symbols that stand for real objects. As representations of reality, words are meaningful only if the reader or listener understands the concept that the words represent. Therefore verbal communication should be used sparingly in the beginning stages of instruction. As learners become more conversant with mechanics and strategy, they can assimilate more detailed verbal input. For example, a football scouting report would be meaningless to a beginner team in junior high school, even though the same verbal concepts in the scouting report form the basis for play tactics in an inexperienced team.

Visual. Visual input is defined as communication by showing the task configuration. Graphic media such as pictures, videotapes, and films show how body segments relate during the activity being learned. Live demonstrations are also effective visual input if the demonstrator is skilled in the task. Since visual input (unlike verbal input) is first-hand observation, beginning learners profit most from seeing how the task is performed. A demonstration has the same meaning regardless of the language spoken by the viewers. More experienced learners can perceive more details than beginners, and highly skilled performers see many subtle details in a demonstrated movement, since they have a vast background of experiences to relate to the demonstration.

Kinesthetic. In kinesthetic input, body segments are manipulated through the desired motions. The learner is relatively passive while the instructor makes the desired movement. The purpose of manipulative input is to enable the learner to *feel* the task motion. Kinesthetic communication is commonly used in demonstrating the flutter kick in swimming. Most learners do not need direct manipulation—in fact, students tend to resent forced movements in the exploratory stage of learning. The method should be reserved for use with the problem learner—and then only after the student demonstrates gross lack of understanding.

Practice Regimes

After task input has been communicated, the student must be involved in a practice regime that will allow rapid and effective learning. All practice does not yield equal results, nor does a great deal of practice guarantee success. Nevertheless, certain practice methods have been shown to produce superior results.

Figure 3.11 Kinesthetic communication may be used effectively only when the student makes gross errors in the learning pattern.

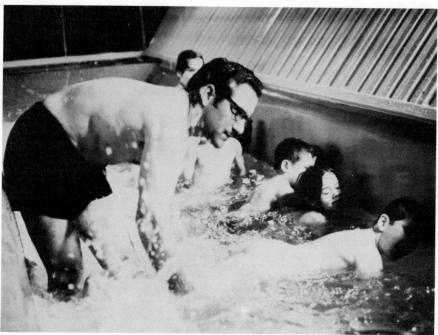

Courtesy Miracle Recreation Equipment Co./Kieffer Associates, Inc.

Size of motor task. The nature of the task is the most important factor in selecting the size motor task unit to be practiced. Some alternatives are the part
method, the progressive-part method, the motor-whole method and the unitary-
task method. The part method involves systematic drills on a segment of a task,
such as the kick in the front crawl swimming stroke. The progressive-part method
employs a sequence of drills, in each of which a new segment of the task is added;
for instance, practicing the front crawl by kicking, then kicking and pulling, and
finally by kicking, pulling, and breathing. The motor-whole method integrates all
the parts of a task simultaneously. The unitary method involves practicing the
skills of a sport by actually playing the game. The motor-whole method has
proved superior to various part methods in swimming. Beginning volleyball
should be taught using the motor-whole method. Golf and tennis should be taught
initially by a combination of motor-whole and unitary-task methods. For a systematic review of the part-versus-whole controversy, see Johnson (1972).

Responsive Practice. Responsive practice is spontaneous student behavior in
response to an unstructured stimulus. Intuitive practice of a golf swing would be
an example of responsive practice. After the learner is told to "hold the club
firmly and hit the ball to the flag," practice trials begin. Another type of responsive practice involves an open-end unstructured task response. For example, the

Figure 3.12 Movement exploration is the process of learning to move in space and time.

Frank Siteman, Stock Boston

students are told to "find a way to get from this side to the other side of the bars." To solve the motor problem, students could respond by crawling through, vaulting over, or pulling up and over. Much movement exploration is responsive practice.

Covert versus Overt Practice. Active involvement in rehearsing a task is essential for progress. However, the learner may either engage in overt practice trials or mentally rehearse fundamentals of the task. Overt behavior can be observed. Covert behavior cannot: It involves only the thought process. Several studies have demonstrated the value of covert practice, but when the covert and overt groups are compared, the overt group is usually significantly superior. Perhaps since both treatments provide significant learning gains, a combination of the treatments would yield results superior to all. Covert practice is seldom attempted in physical education classes, because mental rehearsal is not intrinsically motivating. However, it *is* used by gymnasts before and during competitive routines.

Motivation

Motivation techniques are fundamental to teaching, for without motivation the student will not become involved in learning the task. Fortunately, games and physical activities are inherently attractive to students. Why, then, do many students dislike physical education? Perhaps some programs have been dehumanized, or the natural springs of intrinsic motivation are stopped by ineffective methods. For example, golf units are frequently taught by having students execute repetitive drills from a line. After all the balls have been gathered, the next round of strokes begins. Such methodology is as dull as a basketball unit in which the students dribble, pass, and shoot without ever playing a game.

Motivation and elimination of discipline problems begin with student involvement. Active involvement in interesting activities must begin no later than the second day of class meetings. The three kinds of motivation methods we will discuss are related to the student, the task context, and the instructor.

Student Achievement. The student's drive for achievement is only one student-related factor. Achievement is a complex drive, with the several primary motivators functioning differently in different individuals. Students respond in school to such stimuli as personal inadequacies, social approval for past performance, and parental pressure. Whatever the primary factors, students usually want to achieve.

Natural student motivation to achieve in physical education may be tapped to encourage development of motor skills and physique. Conditioning and body-development units are popular with secondary school boys and girls. The unit may effectively culminate in a power-lifting event or a physical development contest. Research has also shown that secondary students with high sports achievement tend to have correspondingly high social status. Hence the development of motor skills for peer approval may act as a motivator.

Task Context. Direct manipulation of objects can serve to motivate in some activities. Shooting an arrow or hitting a golf ball involves direct manipulation of an implement. The results of a trial—positive reinforcement—are apparent immediately after execution. Competition as a major motivator in athletic performance is discussed in the chapter on tournaments. Legitimate competition can also strongly motivate learning in the physical education class. Some applications of competition in class are (1) balanced-squad competition to culminate a unit; (2) matches or mini-tournaments conducted as a portion of each day's practice; (3) competition against national norms on physical fitness tests; (4) short one-on-one games in team sports; and (5) squad competition in relays such as dribbling and passing. Oxford (1967) describes a successful modified competition for elementary schools. His ideas for a miniature Olympics could be adapted for school use, including many events in addition to track and field.

Physical education classes tend to be proportionally larger than other school classes. By shortening the length of games and making certain other adaptations, the physical education instructor can teach team sports adequately with large classes. Limited equipment and facilities for individual sports present a difficult problem for teaching individual and dual sports to large classes. Specific recommendations for teaching large classes have been made by the Lifetime Sports Foundation and national organizations governing archery, badminton, bowling, golf, swimming, and tennis. General modifications can be made by the teacher, such as shortening the game, increasing the number of players, and decreasing the size of the playing area. Gym bowling is an example of a simulated game in which mechanics, rules, and strategy can be taught. Golf drills and competition can also be conducted in a small indoor or outdoor area by using light-weight wiffle balls (Johnson 1970).

The Instructor. The instructor is the single most important factor in actualizing instructional objectives. Physical education teachers have an inherent advantage over other teachers. The instructor usually possesses activity skills highly valued by students. Therefore, the physical education teacher with some humanitarian interest in the students should easily establish personal rapport with the class. Rapport is enhanced by personal attractiveness, an aura of leadership, and ease in establishing interpersonal bonds. Teacher–student rapport is a potent motivator because it causes students to respond to the teacher's instructions willingly and comfortably. Little extrinsic motivation is required of students when a dynamic leader–follower relationship exists.

Case Example: ACTUALIZING PHYSICAL EDUCATION INSTRUCTION

During supervisory visits to area elementary schools, you notice that the physical education specialists perform the basic instructional tasks reasonably well. Student participation is adequate and the planned instructional program is followed. However, most of the teachers are not providing feedback to the learners during and after their practice trials. Some students take an inordinately long time to reach the minimum competency level. Students are being taught in large units with no individualization. Student errors tend to be repeated during each trial with no comment by the instructor.

As the physical and health education supervisor for the school system, you are concerned about the rate of student progress in the elementary schools. Based on your reading and experience, you feel that the teachers are not performing their feedback functions adequately. In planning an in-service training program for the elementary school physical education specialists, you confront the following questions:
1. What is the best way to present the problems to the teachers?
2. What type and frequency of performance feedback are you recommending that the teachers use?
3. What participation activities can you use in the training session to make the teachers more sensitive to the need of students for feedback?

Controlling

Control of general operations is more critical in physical education than in the traditional classroom context. Movement in vigorous activities produces more injuries, equipment may be lost or stolen, and achievement in the affective and the psychomotor domain is more difficult to quantify than behavior in the cognitive domain. Control procedures in physical education instruction involve both students and teachers. Administrative policies and property control are also important considerations. Some examples of management objectives for administrative controlling are as follows:

to define standardized procedures for measuring student progress in the cognitive, affective, and psychomotor achievement areas
to develop reasonable local norms for physiological and psychomotor achievement tests
to prespecify a strategy for program evaluation
to develop standardized operating procedures for reporting student progress and managing equipment

Student Achievement

Every school activity must ultimately be justified in terms of student achievement. Achievement is defined as behavior modification toward defensible educational goals. Achievement as a product of physical education instruction can and must be quantified for purposes of feedback to the student, the parents, and the school administration.

Terminal Competencies

Once student behavior in classes has been measured, judgment can be made regarding adequacy of student achievement, effectiveness of the instructor, and the value of the physical education program. Important measurement factors in student achievement include: (1) verbal concepts; (2) behavior ratings; and (3) motor components. Performance in the cognitive, psychomotor, and affective domains can be quantified by observation or by objective testing. Student achievement within the four categories of terminal competencies can be assessed by one or more of several measurement strategies.

Physiological Competencies. Factors in the category of physiological development include strength, flexibility, and cardiorespiratory efficiency. An example of a behaviorally stated physiological competency is: "The student will be able to execute twenty sit-ups in sixty seconds."

Physiological efficiency can be assessed through standardized tests. Considerable professional debate surrounds exact specifications for physical fitness and tests for measuring it. Two widely used tests are the revised AAHPER Youth Fitness Test and the Oregon Physical Fitness Test. Many of the test items are fundamental motor skills that the students can practice during or outside class. A tape measure and stop watch are needed to quantify the events that are not repetitive counts. Establishment of permanent markings, such as painting a line on the floor for the standing broad jump, encourages individual practice. Descriptions of several physiological tests are included in Barrow and McGee (1971).

Psychomotor Competencies. Items in the category of psychomotor skill development include proficiency in the fundamental movements, team sports, and individual sports. An example of a behaviorally stated psychomotor competency is: "The student will be able to make ten out of twenty basketball shots taken from the free-throw line."

Standardized tests have been developed for practically every activity in physical education. The basic problem in skill measurement is to structure a condition in which all students can receive the same stimulus. Consequently, many tests use fixed goals or marked walls for the purpose of standardizing testing conditions.

Figure 3.13 Observing social behavior and psychomotor skill is an important method of measuring student achievement.

Tests of badminton, golf, tennis, volleyball, and soccer lend themselves to a marked wall. Using standard conditions for testing increases the reliability of the test. Correlation between scores on wall tests and actual performance in play is usually quite high. A motor test should be administered in each activity to assess the degree of skill acquisition. Valid, reliable, and objective tests of motor skill are described by Johnson and Nelson (1969). Performance ratings are also used in diving and gymnastics.

Activity Concepts Competencies. Activity concepts tap only the cognitive domain. Generally activity concepts include rules and strategy. History of a sport may also be deemed important. An example of an activity concepts behavioral competency is: "The student will be able to describe the serving, receiving, and scoring rules for the game of tennis."

Because of the variability in coverage of subject matter, teachers usually construct their own information tests. Clarity, functioning distractors, and curricular validity are important in constructing information tests. Clarity pertains to the ability of the student to understand the meaning of the test item. *Functioning distractors* in a multiple-choice test are the plausibility and discriminability of two or more of the possible responses. *Curricular validity* is a characteristic of the test-item structure. If history, rules, and playing skills are deemed of equal importance, one-third of the test should be devoted to each of them. More sophisticated construction methods are used for standardized tests. For example, Hooks (1966) has constructed comprehensive knowledge tests for selected activities. Most of the major publishers of activity books also furnish test manuals with their textbooks.

Social Competencies. The affective domain is the most difficult area of human behavior to assess. But the difficulty in measuring values and emotive constructs does not diminish their importance. Knowledge of what constitutes ethical behavior is a quasi-cognitive affective function. An example of a social competency is: "The student will be able to identify 80 percent of the socially desirable behaviors in test items of sportsmanship in basketball."

Although they *can* be faked, attitude scales represent one method of tapping the affective domain. Attitude scales may be used as a basis for determining student grades, but they have greater potential in program evaluation. Students can be painfully frank when they are assured of anonymity. Published psychometric scales for assessing attitudes in physical education include Mista (1968), McPherson and Yuhasz (1968), O'Bryan and O'Bryan (1969), Edington (1968), Kenyon (1968), and Johnson (1969).

Judgment of human performance against the base line of a set model is one of the oldest forms of behavior quantification. The comparison may be relative, all individuals being ranked in comparison to each other. Or the comparison may be against an absolute scale, in which individuals are assigned numerical values representing the degree to which they personify the ideal model. Relative ratings are frequently used in judging such things as beauty contests, and absolute ratings are used in gymnastics and diving. Ratings may be made of ethical behavior, social interactions, and proficiency in sports skill. For additional information refer to Johnson and Nelson (1969).

Marking

Schools traditionally feed progress information back to students and parents. The information may be a number or a letter or a behavior checklist. Grades are one important control agent in the modern school. The grading procedure must be consistent with the school philosophy and program. The evaluation may be based on one of several methods of interpreting measurement data.

Weighting Values. Grade-weighting values are the relative percentages assigned to the various categories of program outcomes. In effect, weighting values quantify the instructor's philosophy of physical education. Each category of outcomes is assigned a percentage value. The categories considered most important are assigned the larger percentages. A somatic realist would probably assign a large percentage to the physiological development category. For example, the percentages may be weighed as follows: physiological efficiency—50%; psychomotor fluency—30%; activity concepts—15%; social efficiency—5%. Assuming that these percentages are used in deriving a student's grade, which objectives are considered most important? If a good teacher concentrates on the most heavily weighted skills, abilities, and understandings, what effect will the percentages given have on the activities selected?

Composite grades can be determined by multiplying the student score by the designated percentage. For example, a student score of 70 on a written test would be multiplied by .30 if the weighting value for activity concepts is set at 30% of the total composite student grade. Grade values for each student in each category would be similarly computed. (Percentage charts should be constructed to facilitate conversion of scores.)

Contract Grading. Contract grading is an extension of the competency-based program concept. After behavioral competencies have been listed, a formal agreement is made between the student and the teacher. A student selects those contract problems in which he or she desires to work. Contracts are valued on the basis of difficulty. The student's grade is based on the number and difficulty of the contracts completed. It is desirable to establish a framework so that at least a minimum number of contracts will be earned in the essential competencies. Fast (1971) has described a successful contingency contract program. The sample contracts appearing here could be used as models for writing contracts in other activities. The student knows of and agrees to the instructional goals. Levels of competency are dependent upon the age and experience of the students. Norms established in previous class performance are defensible bases for specifying competency.

CONTRACTING

All students taking physical education are enrolled in a class. Those who so desire are permitted to pursue units of study of their own choosing; they report to class only for attendance purposes. Copies of contracts for various units are kept in folders in a class area containing materials which will aid the student in the task of fulfilling the contract.

Each student examines the contract work packets for a particular unit and selects the one contract which she wishes to do. Upon completion, a new contract is made. Selections may follow any order so long as the three required work packets are completed.

A worksheet is kept for each student. It records the contract numbers (including the three required contracts and the optional contracts), level, starting date, due date, completion date, point value of the contract, penalty points, bonus points, and the final score. Grades are determined as follows. To earn an A, 100 points must be earned; for a B, 90 points; for a C, 75 points; for a D, 70 points. No contract fails. If the work is not adequately done, it is returned and must be done over.

Sample Contracts—Bowling

Contract 1 (Level 4—20 point value)

Bowl six games at any lane. Keep your score. On a separate sheet state the basic rules for scoring. List the symbols used in scoring and tell their meaning. Your score sheets will be graded for accuracy.

Contract 3 (Level 3—15 point value)

Learn the correct way to pick up and hold a ball. Be able to demonstrate the hand positions, footwork, and release. Further, be able to demonstrate the position of the hand that creates a hook ball, a straight ball, and a backup ball. Evaluation will be based on an oral explanation to the instructor.

B. L. Fast, "Contracting," *JOHPER*, 42 (1971), 31–32.

Achievement Interpretation. After all students have completed a test, such as the Brady wall volley test, the data must be interpreted for use in a standard system of reporting grades. Technicalities of score conversion are described by Barrow and McGee (1971), but the method used reflects the teacher's philosophy of data interpretation. Weber and Paul (1971) describe four approaches to grading in physical education.

Norm-reference grading, or the relative method, is a widely used method of evaluative marking. The underlying assumption is that student achievement will always be described according to the normally distributed curve. Most of the students will make C's; some of the students will earn A's and F's. Norm-reference grading is a group-oriented system that relates individual performance to norm-group performance. Under most school conditions the normal distribution assumption is valid, because most schools are teacher paced. Teachers usually pace the students according to the mean of the class. The rapid learner earns the A and the slow learner earns the F. In reality the norm-reference method maximizes speed of learning. The normal-distribution principle actually assesses rate of learning and not potential to learn. Norm-reference marking is also self-condemning, because most students make C's or lower. If most of the students make

C's or lower, society's commission to the schools to change the behavior of youth is not being adequately fulfilled.

Criterion-based grading, or the absolute method, is a viable alternative to norm-reference grading. The basic assumption is that student achievement standards can be prespecified. Contract grading and student-paced, competency-based programs are examples of criterion-based grading. The student decides how much time to devote to practice. The teacher does not pace the class by moving ahead at whatever is perceived as the mean rate for the group. Small steps are used in setting up the competencies so that any student with normal intelligence can complete the work. Fast learners may finish early and slow learners may require more time, but both can learn the same basic concepts if the time and pacing are flexible. The instructor defines the criterion and the student spends the necessary amount of time to achieve the goal. Weber and Paul (1971) describe four approaches to grading in physical education.

GRADING IN PHYSICAL EDUCATION

There are four currently used methods of assigning grades to pupils in physical education: (1) the relative method; (2) the absolute method; (3) the improvement method; and (4) the impressionistic method.

The relative method, or grading on a curve, measures a pupil's progress as it compares with the performance in the class in which he is enrolled. If a pupil performs at a higher level than the average person, he will receive a below average mark. The grades can be reported as ABCDF, although T scores, Z scores, and percentile scores can be reported. The most important element common to all relative grade systems is that they are based on probability curves.

The absolute method of grading is based on the teacher's predetermined level of achievement. A student must attain a predetermined standard to qualify for a specific grade. Traditionally a score of 70 percent has been considered as passing, with higher percentages for higher letter grades. Scores representing the percent of correct responses are usually converted into letter grades.

The improvement method is a system of evaluation based upon the amount of progress shown during a period of instruction. Progress is frequently determined by a pretest versus posttest scheme. Examples of scores used in the improvement system include percentage gain scores or ratios of posttest scores to pretest scores.

Impressionistic grading is the practice of assigning grades for behaviors that are not related to the specific objectives of the course. Traditionally in physical education such traits as attitude, attendance, sportsmanship, effort, and dress are the kinds of behaviors that have been evaluated.

L. J. Weber and T. L. Paul, "Approaches to Grading in Physical Education," *The Physical Educator,* 28 (1971), 59–62.

Reporting

The primary justification for using student time for measurement is to provide precise feedback to student and parents. Measurement data from the classroom may be used for program analysis or research, but these are secondary to student–parent feedback. Assuming that measurements are regularly taken, the next step is to feed the performance information back to the learner. One important issue in physical education is the type of reporting device. Some argue that physical education should be listed on the regular report card. Other physical educators advocate the use of a special report card to trace progress toward meeting student goals. Either method can be used to report grades derived by norm-reference or criterion-based methods.

Regular Report Card. The assumption here is that if physical education is to have equal status with other school subjects, then course grades should be included on the same card. The principle that "separate is automatically not equal" has been adopted by physical educators who are often as much concerned with their own faculty status as with meaningful reporting to students and parents. Ironically, unless the physical education staff strongly contends for a separate reporting system, school principals will require inclusion in the regular report card.

Special Report Form. To get hung up on academic equivalency to the detriment of the student is to miss the whole purpose of education. Academic subject and faculty status really have little to do with effective behavior modification. The letter grade appearing on a report card is a symbol of achievement, but letter symbols actually convey very little of the student's achievement profile. A more helpful procedure would be to use a special descriptive report form. The special physical education report could be sent in place of a grade on the regular card, or the special form could be included to augment and interpret the symbol reported on the regular form. Factors reported on the special report should reflect the major program components shown in Figure 3.14.

Program Evaluation

Regional accrediting associations require periodic evaluation of all school programs. Review for accreditation purposes forces the school staff to examine the physical education program critically. Actually, the program should be evaluated yearly or bi-yearly in any event. Evaluation of teachers is described in the chapter devoted to personnel management. Evaluation of the instructional program should include management policies, unit content, teaching procedures, and instructional context.

Physical Education Report Form

A - Exceptional
B - Good
C - Average
D - Poor
F - Unsatisfactory

Name _____ Class Period _____ Teacher _____

(six week reports)

Competency Categories	1st	2nd	3rd	4th	5th	6th	Course grade
Physiological development							
Psychomotor skill							
Activity concepts							
Socialization							

Figure 3.14 A special report form for physical education.

Program evaluation must be a cooperative venture involving both managers and instructional staff. Regional accrediting associations also require program review by an outside consultant. Standards for evaluating physical education instruction have been developed by the Texas Education Agency in Austin, Texas; the California State Department of Education in Sacramento, California; and the University of Missouri at Columbia, in cooperation with the Missouri State Department of Education. (A sample evaluation form is included in the Student Guide.) Each local school district may desire to construct its own program standards.

Whether the school is evaluated via a locally constructed or a nationally published instrument, effective use of the data is the important thing. The total average response for the instrument can be reported, but a more meaningful procedure would be to examine the reports of several independent raters item-by-item. A report of the program evaluation and suggested remediation should be given to the school manager and the supervisor of the academic area.

Operations Control

A wide spectrum of general controls are functional in the progressive physical education program. Efficiency of instruction, program accountability, and property control are important administrative functions of the classroom instructor, the department chairperson, and the principal. With operations costs rising, any ineffective or inefficient school program is subject to reduction or elimination. Efficient learning is the only justification for an instructional program. School personnel control procedures are described in the chapter on personnel management. Procedures for control of resources are described in the chapter on fiscal management.

Instruction Control

The assured, self-motivated, professional teacher is the ideal model to which management must be dedicated. However, teachers do not reach professional maturity overnight or without managerial backing. It may be assumed that every teacher needs help and encouragement. Therefore the manager must systematically observe each teacher. Whether the observation is quantified by a supervisory report or an informal notation, the teacher being observed deserves some immediate feedback from the manager. The goal of physical education teacher performance equal to the best instruction in other subjects can be reached by frequent supervision, constructive criticism, and encouragement.

Departmental Policies

A policy is defined as a prespecified course of action developed to attain certain goals. A policy manual should be cooperatively developed by the staff and manager. Policies provide a basis for consistency and impartiality. Yet policies can also become rigid and inhumane. Administrative policies adopted by a departmental faculty may include items pertaining to class records, excuses, class substitutions, advanced-placement examination, uniforms, use of facilities by outside groups, and type of class credit.

Class Substitutions. Various activities are frequently offered as substitutions for physical education. Some of these are school office errand work, ROTC, band, pep squad, and athletics. The decision to allow substitutions may be made by the state education office, the local school board, or the local administration. None of these activities should be allowed to substitute for physical education. When the local department has the choice, it should eliminate virtually all substitution, including credit for athletics. If other groups are to make the decision, the physical education staff should vigorously oppose such substitution.

Advanced Placement. Advanced placement by examination is growing rapidly in post-secondary schools. Students with ability to perform at high levels in mathematics, language, and science achievement tests are exempted from enrolling in lower-level courses. The concept of advanced placement is applicable to physical education, though there are inherent management problems. What test devices will be used? What teaching-load credit should be given to faculty for testing students? What performance criteria should be set for passing the tests? Should students who pass the performance tests be exempted from physical education or placed in advanced classes? Written tests should be used as a preliminary screening device to avoid spending undue time in laborious skill testing. Leighton (1966) presents a detailed discussion of the problem of advanced placement by performance testing.

Case Example: OPERATIONS CONTROL IN PHYSICAL EDUCATION

The physical and health education department at Cooper High School is in an uproar. Several years ago a pilot program of competency-based activities was introduced into the department. With some reservations, older staff members accepted the program on a trial basis. Recently a fervor has arisen over grading. The locus of the problem is the teachers using criterion grading in the competency-based project. Students in a new program have been receiving an abnormally high number of A and B grades. Instructors using the traditional teacher-paced program claim that criterion grading violates the statistical law of normal distribution. Teachers in the competency-based program have been accused by their departmental faculty of being "too easy on grades."

You were serving as departmental chairperson when the competency-based project was approved. During recent faculty meetings, both sides have argued fluently for their position. In trying to resolve the controversy, you ask the following questions in the faculty meeting:

1. What are the basic assumptions of norm grading and criterion grading?
2. What could be causing the apparent difference in student grades?
3. Philosophically, must all teachers on a faculty have the same goals, programs, and grading procedures?

Uniforms. The concept of a uniform physical education costume is a carry-over from historical conditions in which manner of dress reflected social class distinctions. *Uni-* is a prefix meaning "unity" or "oneness." Uniform means one form of dress. With all students dressed alike, class distinctions between rich and poor are theoretically minimized. Now that the original problem of social class distinction has been resolved, what reasons remain for wearing uniforms in physical education? There is some militaristic, disciplinary control associated with uniforms. And they help in making quick distinctions between teammates and opponents in team sports. Contemporary activity clothing might best be described as multiform or polyform. It should be comfortable, washable, and appropriate to the activity.

Class Credit. The type of class credit is one point that is negotiable between the faculty and school administration. Elementary schools commonly use satisfactory (S) and unsatisfactory (U). Secondary schools and colleges have traditionally used the ABCDF system. A recent trend in post-secondary schools is toward recording only credit (CR) or no-credit (NC) on the student's transcript. Revival of the pass-or-fail system is partially based on acknowledged weakness of testing and marking in the ABCDF system. High-drive students are freer to elect courses in which they have interest but no proficiency if they have assurance that their "academic" point average will not be damaged. The two-category credit system is one step toward the elimination of grades advocated by some idealistic educators, but the problem of marking persists. For further study, see Shea (1971).

References

AAHPER. *Knowledge and Understanding in Physical Education.* American Association for Health, Physical Education and Recreation, Washington, D.C., 1970.

ALDERMAN, R. B. *Psychological Behavior in Sport.* W. B. Saunders Company, Philadelphia, 1974.

ALLEY, L. "Athletics in Education, the Double-edged Sword." *Phi Delta Kappan,* 56 (1974), 102–105, 113.

ANDERSON, M. H., M. D. ELLIOT and J. LA BERGE. *Play with a Purpose.* Harper and Row, Publishers, New York, 1966.

BARROW, H. M. and R. McGEE. *A Practical Approach to Measurement in Physical Education.* 2d ed. Lea & Febiger, Philadelphia, 1971.

BERGER, R. A., and D. L. MATHUS. "Movement with Various Resistance Loads as a Function of Pre-tensed and Pre-relaxed Muscular Contractions." *Research Quarterly,* 40 (1969), 456–459.

BETER, T. R. "Effects of Concentrated Physical Education and Auditory Visual Perceptual Reading Programs upon Three Variables of EMR Children." *The Physical Educator*, 30 (1973), 130–131.

BRIGHTBILL, C. K. *Man and Leisure: A Philosophy of Recreation*. Prentice-Hall, Englewood Cliffs, N.J., 1961.

CAPON, J. "Equipment as a Catalyst for Perceptual–Motor Learning." Address to AAHPER Convention, Anaheim, California, 1974.

CORBIN, C. *Inexpensive Equipment for Games, Play and Physical Activity*. Wm. C. Brown Company, Publishers, Dubuque, Iowa, 1972.

CORBIN, C. B., L. J. DOWELL, R. LINDSEY, and H. TOLSON. *Concepts in Physical Education*. Wm. C. Brown Company, Publishers, Dubuque, Iowa, 1970.

COUNSILMAN, J. E. *The Science of Swimming*. Prentice-Hall, Englewood Cliffs, N.J., 1968.

CRATTY, B. J. *Psychology and Physical Activity*. Prentice-Hall, Englewood Cliffs, N.J., 1968.

CURETON, T. K. *Physical Fitness and Dynamic Health*. Dial Press, New York, 1965.

DAVIS, R. "Writing Behavioral Objectives." *JOHPER*, 44 (1973), 47–49.

DeCARLO, T. *Handbook of Progressive Gymnastics*. Prentice-Hall, Englewood Cliffs, N.J., 1963.

DEWEY, J. *Democracy and Education*. The Macmillan Company, New York, 1916.

EASON, B. L., and T. L. SMITH. "The A-frame Cargo Net: A Self-contained Obstacle Course." *LAHPER Journal*, 37 (Spring 1974), 10–11.

EDINGTON, C. W. "Development of an Attitude Scale to Measure Attitudes of High School Freshmen toward Physical Education." *Research Quarterly*, 39 (1968), 505–512.

EISNER, E. W., and E. VALLANCE. *Conflicting Conceptions of Curriculum*. McCutchan Publishing Corporation, Berkeley, Calif., 1974.

FAIT, H. F. *Physical Education for the Elementary School Child*. W. B. Saunders Company, Philadelphia, 1971.

FAST, B. L. "Contracting." *JOHPER*, 42 (1971), 31–32.

GALLAGHER, J. D. "Motor Learning Characteristics of Low Skilled College Men." *Research Quarterly*, 41 (1970), 59–67.

GERHARDT, L. A. *Moving and Knowing*. Prentice-Hall, Englewood Cliffs, N.J., 1973.

GRIEVE, A. "State Legal Requirements for Physical Education." *JOHPER*, 42 (1971), 19–23.

HAVIGHURST, R. J. *Human Development and Education*. Longmans, Green & Co., New York, 1953.

HOOKS, E. W., JR. "Hook's Comprehensive Knowledge Test in Selected Physical Education Activities for College Men." *Research Quarterly*, 37 (1966), 506–514.

JARVIS, L. "Effects of Self-instructive Materials in Learning Selected Motor Skills." *Research Quarterly*, 38 (1967), 623–629.

JOHNSON, B. L., and J. K. NELSON. *Practical Measurements for Evaluation in Physical Education.* Burgess Publishing Company, Minneapolis, 1969.

JOHNSON, M. L. "Social Efficiency: Our Weakest Link." *LAHPER Bulletin,* 31 (Spring 1968), 44–46.

JOHNSON, M. L. "Construction of Sportsmanship Attitude Scales." *Research Quarterly,* 40 (1969), 312–316.

JOHNSON, M. L. "Maintaining Spontaneity in Golf." *LAHPER Journal,* 43 (1970), 29–31.

JOHNSON, M. L. "A Case for Using Large Motor Tasks." *JOHPER,* 43 (1972), 29–31.

JOHNSON, P. C., W. F. UPDYKE, D. C. STOLBERG, and M. SCHAEFER. *Physical Education: A Problem Solving Approach to Health and Fitness.* Holt, Rinehart and Winston, New York, 1966.

KARPOVICH, P. V., and W. C. SINNING. *Physiology of Muscular Activity.* W. B. Saunders Company, Philadelphia, 1971.

KENYON, G. F. "Six Scales for Assessing Attitude toward Physical Activity." *Research Quarterly,* 39 (1968), 96–105.

LEIGHTON, J. F. "Activity Credit by Examination—Pros and Cons." *The Physical Educator,* 23 (1966), 7–8.

LOWEN, A. *Depression and the Body.* Penguin Books, Baltimore, 1972.

LYONS, M. D., and B. LUFKIN. "Evaluation of Tension Control Courses for College Women." *Research Quarterly,* 38 (1970), 663–670.

MAGER, R. F. *Preparing Instructional Objectives.* Fearon Publishers, Belmont, Calif., 1962.

McCORMICK, C. C., J. N. SCHNOBRICK, S. W. FOOTLIK, and B. PEOTKER. "Improvement in Reading Achievement through Perceptual Motor Training." *Research Quarterly,* 29 (1968), 627–633.

McPHERSON, B. D., and M. S. YUHASZ. "An Inventory for Assessing Men's Attitudes toward Exercise and Physical Activity." *Research Quarterly,* 39 (1968), 218–219.

METHENY, E. *Connotations of Movement in Sport and Dance.* Wm. C. Brown Company, Dubuque, Iowa, 1965.

MISTA, N. J. "Attitudes of College Women toward Their High School Physical Education Programs." *Research Quarterly,* 39 (1968), 166–174.

MOORE, G. C., and H. B. FALLS. "Functional Classification for Physical Education in the Upper Elementary Grades by Peer Assessment." *Research Quarterly,* 41 (1970) 519–522.

MOREHOUSE, L. E., and A. T. MILLER. *Physiology of Exercise.* The C. V. Mosby Company, St. Louis, 1971.

MULLER, P. *The Tasks of Childhood.* McGraw-Hill Book Company, New York, 1969.

NAYLOR, J. C., and G. E. BRIGGS. "Effects of Task Complexity and Task Organization on the Relative Efficiency of Part and Whole Training Methods." *Journal of Experimental Psychology,* 65 (1963), 217–224.

NIXON, J. E., and A. E. JEWETT. *Physical Education Curriculum*. Ronald Press Company, New York, 1964.

NOAR, G. *Individualized Instruction: Every Child a Winner*. John Wiley & Sons, New York, 1972.

OBERTEUFFER, D. "Some Contributions of Physical Education to an Educated Life." *JOHPER*, 16 (1945), 3–5, 56–57.

O'BRYAN, M. H., and K. G. O'BRYAN. "Attitudes of Males toward Selected Aspects of Physical Education." *Research Quarterly*, 40 (1969), 343–352.

OXFORD, H. "Elementary Physical Education—The Miniature Olympics." *The Physical Educator*, 24 (1967), 157–158.

PENNINGTON, G. "Equipment Which Should Be Found in Every Gymnasium." *The Physical Educator*, 23 (1966), 171–172.

PUCKETT, J. "Two Promising Innovations in Physical Education Facilities." *JOHPER*, 43 (1972), 40–41.

PURPEL, D., and K. RYAN. "Moral Education: Where Sages Fear to Tread." *Phi Delta Kappan*, 56 (1975), 659–662.

ROBB, M. D. *The Dynamics of Motor Skill Acquisition*. Prentice-Hall, Englewood Cliffs, N.J., 1972.

ROSENTSWIEG, J. "A Ranking of the Objectives of Physical Education." *Research Quarterly*, 40 (1969), 83–87.

SCHURR, E. L. *Movement Experiences for Children*. 2d ed. Appleton-Century-Crofts, Inc., New York, 1975.

SEAMAN, J. A. "Attitudes of Physically Handicapped Children toward Physical Education." *Research Quarterly*, 41 (1970) 439–445.

SHEA, J. B. "The Pass–Fail Option and Physical Education." *JOHPER*, 44 (1973), 44–46.

SINGER, R. N., and W. DICK. *Teaching Physical Education: A Systems Approach*. Houghton Mifflin Company, Boston, 1974.

SKINNER, B. F. "Teaching Machines." *Scientific American*, 205 (1961), 90–102.

STALLINGS, L. M. *Motor Skills Development and Learning*. Wm. C. Brown Company, Publishers, Dubuque, Iowa, 1973.

STRONG, C. H. "Motivation Related to Performance of Physical Fitness Tests." *Research Quarterly*, 34 (1963), 497–507.

ULRICH, C., and J. E. NIXON. *Tones of Theory*. American Association for Health, Physical Education and Recreation, Washington, D.C., 1972.

VERDUCCI, F. "Effects of Class Size Upon the Learning of a Motor Skill." *Research Quarterly*, 40 (1969), 391–395.

VOLTMER, E. F., and A. A. ESSLINGER. *The Organization and Administration of Physical Education*, 5th ed. Appleton-Century-Crofts, New York, 1975.

WEBER, L. J., and T. L. PAUL. "Approaches to Grading in Physical Education." *The Physical Educator*, 28 (1971), 59–62.

WILLIAMS, J. F. "Education through the Physical." *Journal of Higher Education,* 1 (1930), 279–282.

WILSON, C. "Diversities of Meanings of Physical Education." *Research Quarterly,* 39 (1968), 389–394.

WOODEN, J., and J. TOBIN. *They Call Me Coach.* Word Books, Waco, Texas, 1972.

WORKMAN, D. J. "Comparison of Performance of Children Taught by the Physical Education Specialist and by the Classroom Teacher." *Research Quarterly,* 39 (1968), 389–394.

4.

SCHOOL RECREATION

After reading this chapter, each student should be able to:

Describe the educational contribution of a good school recreation program.

Identify the variations of programing.

Develop a comprehensive plan for a year's activities.

Effectively organize staff, students, and facilities.

Describe the methods of instituting successful programs.

Explain controlling processes applicable to school recreation.

119

The tendency for students to play is indomitable. Even in the austere atmosphere of colonial times, students found recreational outlets. The attitude of early schoolmasters toward student recreation varied from tolerance to rejection. In early American education, formal exercise classes were introduced for the health of children. But the medical exercises were not the student's idea of recreation. Stewart (1973) describes how spontaneous play was used as a focal point by students in developing their own school recreation programs. When school officials recognized the educational potential of organized recreation, the spontaneous sports activities were adopted as approved student programs.

Scope of School Recreation

School recreation is an extracurricular program in which student development is fostered without the formal restrictions of class attendance, regulations, and credit. Programs are usually restricted to enrolled students and/or faculty members in a school community. However, some programs include competition between students of more than one school. The physical education instruction program is for skill and concept *learning*, whereas the recreation program is intended for enjoyment and performance. There is also a big difference between

---

THE SCHOOL RECREATION PROGRAM

In a period of worldwide violence, hostilities, and failures of communication, the growth and development of human acquaintance takes a back seat to human selfishness and competitive gains. Such distorted behavior quickly transcends the mere physical relationships. The philosophy underlying our intromural [sic] program, then, seeks to engender a new attitude through play, an attitude we believe can best be described as a "pure play ethic." The attitude implies "play in its purest form, as shared fun which includes acts of participation that are free, honest, trustworthy, and spontaneous." Under the umbrella of the intromural program, the spontaneity will bring errors, but performers are allowed to be free to make errors without punishment because everybody makes errors. The spontaneity will bring honesty, but performers must not take advantage of that honesty because everybody wants to trust somebody. And spontaneity will bring trust; if freedom to make mistakes and respect for honest acts are put before winning, then everyone is someone.

Participation in the intromural program has increased from 15% of the male population in 1971–72 to an astonishing approximation of 70% of the entire university community of 7,000.

What are some of the programs that the intromural department redesigned to accommodate the interest and expressed needs of the university community? The traditional forms of competitive sports were offered, such as: seven-man and nine-woman touch football, two-person volleyball, six-person (coed) volleyball, table tennis, weight lifting, gymnastics, two-person basketball, five-person basketball, track and field, wrestling, arm wrestling, and singles, doubles, and mixed-doubles tennis.

Recreational services included on- and off-campus outings, such as overnight camping and hiking, a day of canoeing, a day of horseback riding and a hay ride, overnight snow trip, dancing with live music.

In response to expressed interest, the intromural department organized chess, bridge, and other card game tournaments, a "Come Sweat Sweet" program which included 100- and 500- mile joggers club, cycling clubs (ten 10-speed bikes were purchased at a nominal fee for the use of the university community), and hours of free play on the athletic fields and gymnasiums with equipment available for checkout for use on or off the campus.

A special clinical area was set aside to offer instruction in certain activities which the participants would like to engage in but were unable to afford the cost or the time during the normal school day. Activities in the clinical area included yoga, archery, master dance workshops, the art of massage, dieting and exercise, and sailing, among others.

The intromural department at the University of San Francisco believes that everybody is somebody, which prompts us to serve as many people as possible. While a large number of people are being served, there are also a great many people serving. They are usually the participants themselves. These participants get their instructions, equipment, and scheduling from the intromural office, but in most cases the competition is run and governed by the performers.

Often we do not use officials to control the games. The participants put into effect the "pure play ethic" and the "honor system." Forty-two intromural five-person basketball teams, 33 ten-person softball teams, and countless chess and card games were among the activities which functioned without officials. Whenever problems of disagreement, misinterpretation of the rules, or infractions were committed, the problem solving and decision making were left to the participants. There were times when the individuals and teams had difficulty agreeing about an incident; in such cases an intromural supervisor was available to aid the participants but not to make the decision about the incident. This procedure has worked successfully.

The next move is to motivate everybody so they feel there is little risk in participating in their choice of play no matter what their ability may be. Incentives are formulated in a manner to make everybody somebody whether they win or lose. The main factor involved in the incentive is the power of scoring points as an individual or a group by mere participation. It should be pointed out that points for winning a place (1st, 2nd, or whatever) can only be one-half of the total points for participation. The significance of this point system can be viewed as an endeavor to underplay winning and to promote participation.

J. L. Taylor, "Intromurals: A Program for Everyone," *JOHPER* 44 (1973), 44–45.

recreation and interschool athletics. School recreation offers low-key sports participation without recruitment for teams. Usually there are no academic requirements for eligibility.

Program Description

The prespecified outcomes of the school recreation program are similar to those of physical education instruction. Obviously, there will be some development of physiological efficiency, psychomotor skills, activity concepts, and social efficiency if the program is conducted according to professional standards. For example, Taylor's "The School Recreation Program" on page 120 implies that the informal recreational context is effective in precipitating positive behavior changes. Note the implied program philosophy and methods. Boys and girls may participate in separate events or together.

Program Variations

The traditional intramural sports concept of school recreation was restricted to competition between students enrolled at one school. However, school recreation implies noncompetitive and competitive activities. The competitive activities could involve students within only one school or students representing several schools. While many activities develop as a spontaneous response to need or interest, some continue on a year-to-year basis. On the following page, Hyatt describes a multischool recreation event that has become a tradition. Though Hyatt is describing an interschool collegiate sports day, the same concept could be applied to lower school levels.

Intramural Activities

The word intramural is a term that literally means "within the walls." Intramural activities involve both sports and recreational pursuits. Traditionally, intramurals have included only competitive sports. But both active events and sedentary activities are being included in within-school recreation. Active events include team and individual sports, jogging, cycling, camping, and frisbee. Sedentary activities include tournaments for chess, cards, debate, and river floating. Continuing-education activities are being offered for nominal supporting fees. Flower arranging, scuba diving, sky diving, and gymnastics are recreational activities which can be arranged.

An all-school play day is usually popular with students and teachers alike. The play day is one day or one afternoon devoted to an athletic event. All classes are informally transferred to the field house or playground for the occasion. Students should be signed up for the various events in advance, and the teachers can act as

THE BIG FOUR SPORTS DAY

When an extramural program involving four different institutions continues to furnish competition between those institutions for a quarter of a century, it must be worthwhile and a description should be of value to many persons.

Big Four Sports Day provides extramural competition between the four large universities in North Carolina in nine activities or events. Students from intramural programs at these schools compete against each other in golf, handball, horseshoes, softball, table tennis, tennis, volleyball, badminton, and bowling. The purpose of Big Four is not only to develop friendships and competition among the students at the different institutions, but to provide the outstanding players in these individual and dual sports with the opportunity to demonstrate their ability in a championship contest.

Each school acts as a host on a rotating basis so that each will host the event every fourth year. About a month prior to the selected date, the Intramural Directors and their student leaders attend a planning conference at the host school which is combined with a dinner meeting to plan the event and discuss any rule changes. . . . The schedule is confirmed and the host school prepares an information booklet and schedule.

Scoring is on the basis of 5 points for first place to 1 point for fourth place for each event. School scores are totaled and a rotating championship trophy is awarded to the winning team.

In 25 years of Big Four Sports Day participation the real winners have been the students, with from 200–250 participating each year. In 25 years, this classic event has served more than 5000 students.

R. Hyatt, "The Big Four Sports Day—A Classic Event," *The Physical Educator*, 28 (1971), 63–64.

officials. Keller (1966) and Oxford (1967) describe programs for play days. Whether it is called a field day, play day, junior Olympics, or miniature Olympics, the program can contribute much to the students and the school.

Extramural Sports

Extramural sports are those athletic contests conducted between intramural teams of two or more schools. The term "extramural" literally means "outside the walls." It is an outgrowth of the intramural program. Extramurals also have the quality of spontaneous informality. Two common methods of team selection are used. The team representing each school can be the team that won the overall school intramural championship. Or the school team can be composed of the "all-stars" selected by vote from various intramural teams. A key difference from participants, with little concern for spectator appeal. Extramural contests are seldom extended further than a few contests after the regular intramural season.

Large school systems have a built-in potential for extramural competition. Each school should conduct its own intramural program, with the winner or top two teams from each school advancing to the systemwide play-off. Upper elementary, junior high schools, and high schools could conduct the extended systemwide athletics.

The type of play-off will be dictated by the sport itself. Junior Olympics events can be conducted on a school day afternoon or Saturday with all interested students eligible—regardless of previous local school contests. Dozens of temporary volleyball courts can be set up on a football field for evening competition in order to allow several teams to represent each school. Basketball can also be successfully adapted to extended intramural play by holding a weekend tournament for the various schools' intramural winners.

Club Sports

Club sports need school sponsorship, and the recreation department is a logical base of operations. Club sports are semiformal interschool athletics. The students bear the responsibility for organizing the group and conducting practice sessions. A particular club, such as a rugby club, should have a faculty sponsor, but there is seldom a paid coach for the team. The intramural director should give assistance in overall planning and scheduling games with other schools. There is a high spirit of amateurism in club sports because the players participate for the pleasure of playing.

Dozens of club sports have developed in colleges and secondary schools. Club sports are more common at the post-secondary level, but they are popular in large high schools where the athletic program serves only a small percentage of the student body. Soccer, karate, flag football, fencing, rugby, judo, and volleyball are among the popular events. Weekend tournaments can be conducted between two or several teams. For further reference to sports clubs see Sliger (1970), Barnes (1971), Johnson (1971) and Denton (1973).

Planning

Although most colleges have had school recreation programs for decades, relatively few secondary and elementary schools have comprehensive programs. Existing secondary school programs are usually dependent upon the sacrificial dedication of a teacher who conducts the program over and above regular classroom duties. Planning is important for existing programs, but it is absolutely essential for initiating new ones. Renner (1972) shares some generalizations developed from trying to initiate a new program. He suggests that every new program needs: (1) adequate administrative support; (2) a dedicated program director; (3) essential facilities and equipment; and (4) a balanced activity plan.

According to the management-by-objectives concept, the administrator is expected to prespecify outcomes. Some typical management objectives for program planning are:

to define the scope and philosophy of the local school recreation program
to identify the program needs and interests of the student body
to develop a comprehensive yearly activity program that is integrated with the interschool athletics calendar and the school calendar
to develop essential departmental policies
to communicate program concepts to students and faculty

Program of Activities

When planning the year's program of activities, the intramural director must resolve several critical problems. Intramural activities must be integrated with the athletic and physical education departments' time schedules. One way of getting maximum use of facilities is to offer a sport before or after its regular interschool athletic season. Activities must be selected in which the students have interest and skill. If students have no skills in a sport, there is little likelihood that interest will warrant offering the activity. Thus it is helpful to coordinate intramural activities with physical education class instruction in a particular sport.

Figure 4.1 Intramural sports such as archery, badminton, and tennis should be scheduled to take place after instruction in these activities has been completed.

Southeastern Louisiana University

The Yearly Calendar of Events

Intramural planners should bear in mind the relative amounts of time necessary to complete tournaments in each of the scheduled sports. Using an enlarged copy of the school calendar, the entry announcement dates, the entry deadline dates, and the closing tournament dates should be marked on the calendar for each sport. Clearance for facility use must be coordinated with other school events, such as interschool athletics.

The complete orientation plan and initial activity can be presented to students during the first days of semester classes. Waiting several days to get started can waste valuable playing time. It is desirable to have a spontaneous special event during the first days of classes. A basketball free-throw contest requires little planning and can introduce students to school recreation. While the special event takes place, groups can be lined up for the initial team sport event.

Activity Alternatives

Selection of the yearly calendar of activities is based on observation and experience. In initiating a new school recreation program, the director must estimate what events will be well received. Continuing with established programs is easier, because the director has participation data on which to base projections.

Experience has shown that successful school recreation programs are flexible in activity programing. Team sports, individual sports, and special events are components of a dynamic sports program. Cultural/creative and sedentary activities can also be included.

Sports. Many students do not want to compete in scheduled tournaments. Informal drop-in centers can provide activity in such events as golf putting and basketball shooting. Team and individual sports are the backbone of competitive school recreation. Team sports are popular at the secondary level. The caliber of play in individual sports largely depends on prior instruction in clinics or physical education classes. Official sports events and modifications are as follows:

Archery (Columbia round and Junior Columbia round)
Badminton (Singles, doubles, and mixed doubles)
Baseball (Co-ed, T-ball, homerun derby, and throw–pitch–hit)
Basketball (Twenty-one, round-the-world, one-on-one, three-person, free throw, pass–dribble–shoot, co-ed, and co-ed two-on-two)
Bicycling (Touring, cross-country race, team cycling, taneur racing, and sprinting)
Boating (Crew, river float, canoeing, sailing)
Boccie ball
Bowling (Gym bowling, individual, team, co-ed, and duck pins)
Boxing (Weight and experience categories)

Broomball
Camping
Cricket
Croquet
Curling
Darts
Diving
Dodgeball
Fencing
Football (Touch, flag, co-ed)
Frisbee
Golf (Medalist, handicap, match, driving, pitch and putt, and low ball)
Gymnastics
Handball (One-wall, three-wall, four-wall)
Hockey (Broom, floor, field, and ice)
Horseback riding
Horseshoes
Ice skating (Figure, racing)
Judo
Karate
Kickball
Motocross
Orienteering
Paddleball
Physical fitness meet
Polo (Broomstick and water)
Pool (Billiards, snooker)
Push ball
Racketball
Roller skating (Individual racing, team racing, and figure)
Rugby
Scuba diving
Shuffleboard
Snow sports (Toboggan, skiing, sledding, snowshoe racing)
Soccer (Five-person, mini-soccer, and co-ed)
Softball (Slow pitch, co-ed, one-strike, home run derby, and throw–pitch–hit)
Speedball (Five-person and co-ed)
Squash rackets
Swimming (Racing, water polo, water basketball, and innertube water polo)
Table tennis (Singles, doubles, and mixed doubles)
Team handball
Tennis (Singles, doubles, mixed doubles, and paddle)
Tetherball
Track and Field (Jogging, decathlon, pentathlon, triathlon)

Figure 4.2 Children have invented many games in response to their needs at various developmental levels.

Terry McKoy, I.O.E.

Trampoline
Tug-of-war
Volleyball (Three-person, doubles, and co-ed)
Weight lifting (Weight categories)
Wrestling (Weight categories and wrist wrestling)

Special Events. Special events conducted in a one- or two-day period add zest to the recreation program. Special events may be of an athletic or cultural nature. Such events help to stimulate interest in the overall recreation program. In setting up the special events, the following principles should be observed: (1) Use a seasonal or general-interest theme. (2) Communicate the idea to the student group. (3) Hold the event in a place where the most spectators will naturally be present. For example, call the fall cross-country run a Turkey Trot and plot the course around several buildings on the school campus. Secure passes for a free Thanksgiving dinner from a local restaurant to be used as awards. Some ideas for special events are:

Circus Night
Pillow fighting
Kite flying
Gym scooter '500' (Individual and team)
Faculty–student rally
Pumpkin-carving contest (Taylor 1974)
Beginner Ski Night (Taylor 1974)

Frisbee Friday (Taylor 1974)
Super Shooter (Taylor 1974)
Tricathlon (Taylor 1974)
Toboggan Thursday (Taylor 1974)
Spring Regatta (Taylor 1974)
"Cyclone 500" (Murdock 1971)
Mountaineer Weekend (Mull 1971)
Spring Spree (Mull 1971)
Winter Weekend (Mull 1971)
Float-A-Thon (England 1973)

Cultural/Creative Events. Instructional clinics, entertainment, and tournaments in table games add new dimensions to the school recreation program. Though intramurals traditionally meant sports events, many types of activities can be scheduled within the school. Events in this category are a change of pace in the athletic program and provide for the interests of more of the student body. The kinds of events are limited only by the inventiveness of the school recreation director. Of course the aid of other faculty members should be enlisted for various events. Some examples of successful cultural/creative events are:

Big-name entertainment (BNE)
Debate contest
Classic films (rental)
Short course (Photography, gardening, dramatics, arts and crafts)
Chess tournament
Checkers tournament
Halloween Hop (dance)

Publicity

Even the best-planned intramural activity programs will lie dormant unless the students and faculty are informed. Initially, new programs in elementary and secondary schools will have to be fully explained to both faculty and students. After some reminding, the faculty will recall their own collegiate intramural experiences, and they will be in a position to explain the program to their students. Some specific procedures for effective intramural sports publicity are discussed in the following paragraphs. See also England (1972), Marciani (1973), and Newman (1973).

The Intramural Handbook

Every competing individual and group should be given a printed or mimeographed school recreation handbook. The handbook serves to inform students of the purpose of the program, lists entry dates for all the year's events, spells out program regulations, and explains the award system. Specific game rules are sometimes included in the handbook, but doing so greatly increases its cost.

The School Newspaper

School newspapers or newsletters are excellent vehicles for telling the intramural sports story. The intramural director should initiate action by contacting the newspaper's faculty sponsor and the sports column writer. Intramural sports are good raw material for a student sports writer. News of coming intramural events, reports of recent contests, and feature articles provide interesting reading for students. See Chapter 11 for details of how to develop a school publicity program.

The Administrative Bulletin

Most large schools have an announcement bulletin mimeographed for circulation to the teachers and students. Schedules of upcoming contests should be included in the bulletin. Specifying teams, time, date, and playing area in the administrative bulletin is a good way to eliminate forfeits due to communications failure.

The Departmental Bulletin Board

Recreation information posted on the departmental bulletin board should include explanation of the program, the yearly activity schedule, rules for current and upcoming sports, a box for entry forms, and pictures of participants. Posted

---

Case Example: PLANNING THE SCHOOL RECREATION PROGRAM

Low student and teacher morale at Lincoln High School strongly signal the need for creative programs. Most of Lincoln's one thousand students live in the surrounding urban neighborhood. The past year witnessed many student fights and much absenteeism, vandalism, and drug abuse.

The principal has secured funding for an after-school recreation director. Assuming that there is also a small budget for operations, what activities could be scheduled for the old school building, auditorium, gymnasium, and playgrounds? What means of publicity would probably be successful in reaching the student body?

---

pictures of sports winners can be made inexpensively with a simple camera. The school photography club may be able to shoot action pictures at significant contests.

Organizing

After preliminary planning and initial program publicity, the next logical step is to organize for action. Organizing should include procedures that guarantee students a strong voice in their program. Organizing includes enlisting the program staff, aligning teams, and coordinating facilities. Since secondary and elementary school programs compete with interschool athletics for facility time, coordinating events is a complex task. Some examples of management objectives for organizing programs are:

> to develop an effective staff organization system
> to select an optimal unit of competition system when the facilities and time period scheduling are specified
> to identify desirable alternatives for funding
> to identify all the facilities in the community available for school recreation

Staff Organization

There is a tendency for programs of all types to drift toward authoritarian management by a few people. The faculty recreation director cannot run an entire program efficiently. And the potential for development of student leadership is neglected if one person makes all the decisions. Student leaders and a student recreation council are needed. School recreation should be a program for and by students wherever possible. Within the staff organization, relationships between positions should be designated on an organizational chart and a job description written for each position. Figure 4.3 shows a sample organization chart for the school recreation program.

The Faculty Director

The role played by the faculty director may range from advisor to managing director. In schools where a program has been operating smoothly, the faculty director can delegate much decision making to trained student leaders. Some faculty directors serve without pay. However, the best method is to pay the director the same additional funds that extra coaching duties offer. One faculty member can direct both the boys' and girls' program, if they are separate.

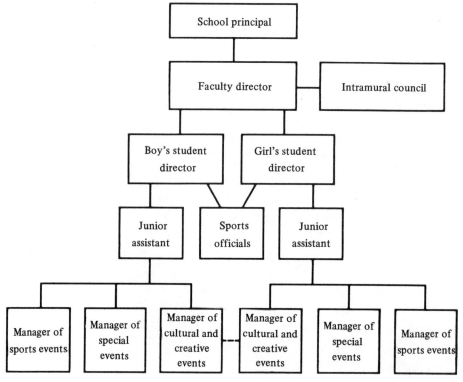

Figure 4.3 A sample organization chart for a school recreation program.

The Recreation Council

The recreation council should be made up of an interested cross section of the student body. Election or appointment by an administrator is possible. Using student government officials and class officers would preclude a separate election. Each representative has one vote, and the group decision is advisory to the intramural director. Membership on the council should be voluntary and members subject to replacement if they miss meetings. Game rules and program regulations are logical topics for council decisions. Protests should be decided by the council with advice from the faculty director. At the end of each school term, the council should meet to evaluate the year's program. Zimmer (1974) feels that student input virtually makes the recreation program.

Student Directors

Much of the actual work of conducting the intramural program should be done by student directors. One student should be appointed to help in the boys' program and another in the girls'. The student director coordinates the work of all other student volunteers. Orientation, event planning, publicity, event supervision, and training of officials are responsibilities that students can perform. Since much time is involved in operating the program, some schools give letter awards to key student leaders. Student directors should be selected from among event managers. Such a program of leadership development will insure good student directors from year to year.

Event Managers

Volunteers interested in a particular event may be designated assistant managers. For example, a basketball manager's assignment would include recruiting officials, checking equipment in and out, and keeping game records.

Officials

Securing competent officials is a perennial problem for intramural team sports at all school levels. Seldom are officials paid for their services at the elementary and secondary level. Some schools are successfully experimenting with honor systems for both team and individual sports (Hopkins 1972).

The common procedure for securing volunteer officials varies with the school. If the regular varsity season has been completed, athletes may be recruited to officiate. Teachers may be recruited to officiate in some games. Some school systems have successfully organized a high school officiating club for both intramural sports and interschool athletics at the upper elementary level. The officiating club could be organized to function as a regular school club. Many of the ideas Stewart (1968) found successful in the post-secondary school context, described in "Intramural officials" below, can be used at other school levels.

Units of Competition

Students who participate in intramural sports must be organized into competitive groups. The units of competition adopted at any school depend largely on the school context. An urban neighborhood school would probably have units of competition different from those of a boarding school or academy. Some common units of competition are described in the following paragraphs. A school also may have several types of organizational units at a particular time—the basic idea is to balance athletic ability between the teams.

Grade Levels

Grade-level units are convenient groupings determined by the grade in which the student is enrolled. However, at the secondary and elementary levels, different

INTRAMURAL OFFICIALS

Competent officiating in athletic contests is important to a smooth-running program whether it is done by staff members, academic teachers, varsity athletes, other students, or by participants themselves on the honor system.

Meetings of team managers are held before competition begins in each sport to discuss eligibility rules, playing rules, and organization and administration of the tournament. These are individuals who are very interested in the program and officials may be recruited from this group.

Occasionally, someone who has been hypercritical of the officiating and thinks he can do a better job does become a good official when offered the opportunity.

Once in a while we have to put a "help wanted" sign on the bulletin board.

With the work manpower situation such as it is, accept officiating candidates from wherever you can get them, and train them for the job.

Education

Meetings for officials are held to discuss administrative details pertaining to them, game rules with special emphasis on variations in national rules which are instituted to adapt the game better to our facilities and the condition of the participants, and mechanics of officiating.

These meetings generally are conducted by the Intramural Director, but on occasion an assistant or someone with special interest or experience in a particular sport may be called upon.

Challenges

We try to impress upon the officials the importance of the work they will be doing, the great responsibility which is theirs, and the authority they possess. Rules are made to provide a fair and equal opportunity and maximum protection and safety for all of the players. Participants in intramurals are there because they are interested and want to have a good time. The quickest way to kill this interest is through embarrassment or injury. It is the responsibility of the officials to help the players to have an enjoyable, worthwhile experience by providing an atmosphere which is conducive to it. In order to do this the officials must know the rules and mechanics of officiating, be impartial and consistent, and "call 'em as they see 'em."

Proper mechanics will enable the official to be in the right place at the right time. Being decisive, blowing a sharp whistle instantly, and use of proper signals will help to convince players, coaches, and fans that the official knows what he is doing and will build confidence in the official himself.

Assignment

An officiating schedule is prepared before the season starts which lists the individuals who are to work each day of the week and is for the entire season. Generally, more officials are listed than will actually be needed (especially on weekends) because inevitably there are conflicts which prevent some of them from appearing. We ask that they inform us at least a day in advance if they will have to miss an assignment.

A schedule is prepared each day which lists the games to be played, the time and location of the games, and the officials for each game. We indicate the officials who are to be referee and field judge in touch football, referee and umpire in basketball, referee in volleyball, and plate umpire in softball, and allow the other officials to decide among themselves which positions they will work.

Most of our officials participate as contestants in the program. This must be taken into account when making assignments. They must be given time off when their team is playing, and they are not assigned to work games in their own division. It is important to avoid placing the officials in positions which may subject them to the possibility of criticism whenever [such] circumstances can be foreseen.

R. E. Stewart, "Recruiting, Training and Assignment of Intramural Officials," *The Physical Educator*, 25 (1968), 32–33.

---

rates of maturation from grade to grade give too much advantage to older students. In large schools grade-level grouping also prevents most of the students from participating, because the size of the player pool is too large.

Homeroom

The student's homeroom or first-period class is a common unit of competition for secondary schools. Units by first-period class have the advantage of early communication of schedules to all the team members. A disadvantage of homeroom or first-period grouping is that some classes have a higher ratio of boys or girls available for a team. First-period industrial arts and home economics are examples of classes that contain a disproportionately large number of potential team members of one gender. When necessary, two classes may be pooled to form a unit of competition.

Physical Education Class

If the physical education teacher voluntarily conducts an intramural program without additional pay, physical education classes may serve as the basic competition unit. Hillman (1972) describes how physical education classes can be used for organizing teams. The teacher can balance the athletic ability in each team in each class. After the class competition is completed, the winners of each class meet in a tournament during an activity period or after school. Care must be taken that the instructional program outcomes are of first priority. Interclass competition would serve as a culminating activity for a unit of instruction.

Clubs

Where students are distributed among existing clubs, these units may be utilized for competition. The friendships already established in a club can help hold the team together during upsets in competition. However, some ambitious students with high athletic ability may recruit other good athletes into the club for intramural rather than legitimate purposes. Recruiting good athletes into various clubs can unbalance competition, causing many forfeits and complaints.

Spontaneous Teams

The use of existing clubs for competitive play is no guarantee of equal competition. In order to prevent the abuse of clubs for recruiting good athletes, a system of spontaneous teams may be substituted. Using only the regulation that "any player can play on only one team during the year if that team enters other sports events," the students are allowed to choose their own teams. Competition may be equalized by having several flights of tournaments for each sport. Any team can choose its level of play, such as A, B, or C flight, based on the players' estimate of their own skill. Players may be allowed to enter as individuals in individual sports if they have not previously been affiliated with a team. Each team selects its own name: "Mildred's Mermaids," "Herman's Hermits," etc.

Finances

How can the school recreation program be financed? Further, considering all of the volunteer leadership what is money needed for in a sports program "of the students and for the students"? School recreation programs are seldom adequately funded at the secondary and elementary levels, even though the program serves more students than interschool athletics. Muller (1971), Van Nostrand (1972), and Ostrander (1973) discuss the funding problem of school recreation.

Sources of Income

Several sources can be tapped to fund recreation programs. The best way to finance the program is with school district taxes. However, there would be very few school recreation programs if tax money were the only source of support. Alternative sources of revenue are limited only by the ingenuity of the program director.

School Budget. Inclusion of intramural sports in the school budget is the most desirable method of funding. Since it can be considered to be essential to the welfare of society, intramural sport easily fits into the category of governmental function. It is a non-proprietary program contributing to optimum student

Figure 4.4 Equalizing competition is a key factor in selecting the best unit of competition.

learning. Being included in the school budget frees the intramural director from menial fund-raising tasks. Even if supplies are not included, the intramural director's salary for extra services should come from school district funds.

Athletic Department. Few if any secondary school athletic departments actually take in enough money to sustain their own programs. Administrative order by the school principal could force the athletic department to share its revenue with intramurals. But forced sharing makes intramural sports an unwanted stepchild of the athletic program. Equipment can be shared when it is not being used for the interschool competition season.

Entry Fee. Entry fees assessed of all participants are one source of revenue. One advantage is that teams are less prone to forfeit if they have put up their own money to play. Nonschool independent weekend tournaments in basketball and softball thrive with entry fees as high as $50 per team. The quality of equipment and officiating could be improved via entry fees. The disadvantage of entry-fee funding is that poor families might not be able to allow their children to partici-pate—and these children's recreational needs may be great. Admission or partici-pation fees for short courses or big-name entertainment (BNE) could provide surplus revenue for other programs. A general activity fee assessed for all students would provide adequate recreation funding.

Special Events. Deriving intramural funds from special events is an undesirable practice but perhaps a necessary one. Candy sales, paper drives, raffles, and car washes require administrative time that is better devoted to the sports program. Admission fees to final play-off contests, all-star games, and games pitting all-stars against faculty are additional sources of revenue for intramurals.

Commercial Involvement. Indirect commercial involvement in public schools has been a fact for decades. Businesses such as Bell Telephone Company and Shell Oil Company have produced and distributed educational films with commercial identification footage. Maas (1974) reports a successful method of getting com-mercial support. He suggests that commercial support of school recreation be (1) innovative with a "soft-sell" and (2) sold to the sponsor on the basis of solid readership interest through intramural participation records. Commercial spon-sorship is ideally suited for advertising events and disseminating results.

Expenses

Legitimate expenses of the intramural program at the secondary and elemen-tary levels include cost of supplies, equipment, awards, and officiating. Supplies for handbook production and general publicity are essential expenses. Equipment may be borrowed from the athletic department and the physical education de-partment, but a separate set of intramural supplies is highly recommended. Awards should be small; it would be a shame to substitute winning a prize for the joy of participating. Picture publicity may mean more to winners than a large, bulky trophy. Officials are necessary in team sports unless a complete conversion is made to the honor system. An officiating club would reduce expenditures for officials.

Time Periods

Almost everything in the intramural program depends on conditions in the school and community. The time periods for play must also be adapted to local conditions. Schools with many commuting students cannot operate after-school or evening programs. Conversely, residence schools and high-population schools in urban communities could use afternoon and evening time periods effectively.

Before School

Students arriving early by commuter bus can take part in many types of sports and recreational game activities. Games of 20-minute duration have been successful in flag football, one-on-one basketball, and floor hockey. Table tennis is also a desirable preschool game because it does not leave players wet with perspiration for the early morning classes. Shooting basketball free throws and wrist wrestling are desirable early morning activities.

Activity Period

Many secondary schools regularly schedule an activity period each week for club meetings and assemblies. Some activity periods can be used to schedule special events such as final intramural matches. Special intramural contests can also be scheduled with an admission fee benefiting the intramural department.

Lunch Period

If the lunch hour is longer than 30 minutes, some time-limit contests can be scheduled. Special arrangements can be made with the manager of the school lunch room to let the players scheduled to play that day go through the lunch line first. Many recreational games and such special contests as one-on-one basketball can be successfully adapted to the lunch hour.

After School

Confrontation between the athletic department and school recreation can be averted by good scheduling and mutual respect. Intramural basketball and volleyball can be scheduled before or after the regular varsity season. Intramural contests can even be scheduled during the season when the facilities are not used by the varsity on the day of a home or away game. Though intramural sports serve more students, the intramural director is invariably forced to schedule around the interschool athletic program. By special arrangement with the school administration, one school day can be shortened to allow for an all-school field day or a similar special event.

Evening

Evening intramural programs have the advantage of almost unlimited use of facilities. This advantage is useless, however, if most students are bus commuters. Evening time periods are excellent for residence schools and neighborhood urban communities. Although evening programs have inherent security and maintenance problems, special events such as basketball or volleyball tournaments in the gymnasium and outdoor volleyball tournaments in the stadium have been highly successful. Milwaukee is known as "the city of the lighted school" because of its extensive evening programs. Evening community education programs can involve students *and* adults.

Weekend

Although weekends are not commonly thought of as intramural sports time periods, many special events can be held on Saturdays. Junior Olympic or systemwide track and field meets can be completed in one Saturday session. Saturday time periods are also desirable for scheduling extramural events and sports club competition.

Facilities and Equipment

There is a trend in colleges to dedicate specific buildings as recreational centers, but the secondary or elementary school recreation program is forced to compete with interschool athletics and cultural events for facilities. Use of a master schedule sheet for all school events helps to eliminate facilities conflicts. Policy statements specifying priorities and scheduling procedures protect the interests of all.

School recreation is not limited to the school grounds. The school campus is usually most convenient for students, and it offers the fewest liability and supervision problems. But resources in the entire community should be tapped. Nonschool facilities can be used by prior agreement with local business people, municipal recreation centers, and churches. Some commercial recreation establishments will even conduct the entire event. Possible facilities beyond the school campus include:

Churches (campus and gymnasiums)
Municipal Recreation Department (golf, swimming, fields)
Bowling lanes
Roller-skating rinks
Ice-skating rinks
Private clubs (tennis, golf)
Movie theaters (big-name entertainment, classic films)
Parks (local, state, national)

Figure 4.5 The most desirable time period depends on the school population, the available facilities, and the nature of the activity.

Terry McKoy, I. O. E.

Southeastern Louisiana University

The ideal of separate equipment for secondary and elementary school recreation is seldom realized. Most school recreation programs share equipment with physical education instruction programs. Well-worn equipment can even be secured from the interschool athletic program. Equipment derived from budgeted funds or from dedicated sales should be listed on the intramural equipment inventory record. Purchase and care of equipment are described in Chapter 7.

Case Example: ORGANIZING SCHOOL RECREATION

Student participation in the Lincoln High School recreation program has been at the fifteen percent level, but the principal believed in the potential of the program enough to secure a "coaching" stipend for the formerly "volunteer" intramural director. The program was sold to the school board as an experimental project. The superintendent of education has expressed interest in such results as (1) increased participation; (2) possible decrease in student unrest; and (3) possible increase in academic achievement.

With a male and female student body of one thousand, what kind of units of competition would you recommend? The school site is urban, and most of the students live within two miles of the school. The interschool athletic program uses the gymnasium and fields when the respective sports are "in season." What time periods should be explored? What additional facilities should be secured for occasional use in the recreation program?

Actualizing

The problem of actualizing is simplified by thorough planning and organizing. Tournament management and student motivation are the two main issues in actualizing. The inherent freedom of recreation gives it a considerable advantage over instructional programs. Its voluntary nature eliminates many actualizing and controlling problems. Some examples of management objectives in actualizing a recreation program are:

  to identify the factors in tournament selection
  to describe game modifications that facilitate recreational competition
  to list motivational alternatives
  to assess the strengths and weaknesses of point systems

Managing Events

Chapter 8 describes the tournament alternatives available for structuring competition. There is a type of tournament adaptable to every intramural situation. Noncompetitive events also require planning and organizing in order to run smoothly. A group of students can be assigned to guide visiting entertainers to the site and to help them set up for the show. See Chapter 5 for guidance in traffic flow and crowd control.

Tournament Methods

The first step in managing tournaments is to define the event, the time limits, and the probable number of entries. A large number of entries reduces the participation of each contestant. A short time interval, such as one week, dictates a short tournament. With varying school conditions, the kind of tournament can be selected that yields the most games in the alloted time.

The second step in tournament management is scheduling the contests. After the tournament draw is made, every game must be numbered and entered on the time, date, and place schedule sheet. Prescheduling contests insures that the total number of games will fit in the limited time available. After the schedule is completed, it should be posted and published by means of announcement sheet or newspaper.

Modification of Activities

"Keep the activity moving!" is the key to successful recreation events. Many nationally regulated sports are paced as much for the spectators as for the participants—especially if television crews are allowed to signal for time-outs. But school recreation is for the participant, not the spectator. School sports can be changed in any manner to fit the situation. Limited facilities, limited endurance, and the large number of participants are factors that dictate game modification. Some examples of game modifications are as follows:

Basketball
1. Twenty-five-minute games with running time—mandatory five-minute half with no time-outs.
2. In co-ed contests the women must play the ball once on each offensive thrust and men cannot shoot from inside the lane.
3. Require a shot within ten seconds in all half-court play, one-on-one, etc.
4. Use interlocking playing periods to provide rest—Teams A–B play their first half, then Teams C–D play their first half on the same court, etc.

Football
1. Everyone is eligible for a pass.
2. No head-on blocking except in the line of scrimmage.
3. Make touch or flag rules.
4. Play for twenty-five minutes running time—use mandatory five-minute half with no time-outs.
5. Use interlocking playing periods.

Tennis
1. Play one six-game set or one nine-game set.
2. Play one six-game set or twenty minutes, whichever comes first.
3. In half-court singles, serve to the court directly ahead and play the alley after a legal serve.

Motivation

Games have their own motivation. However, when rigid programming is executed without student involvement, intramural sports attract much less of the student body to participate. The success story cited by Taylor (1973) reported a big jump in participation when all phases of the program were shared with the students. Additional motivational methods commonly used in intramural programs are discussed in the paragraphs that follow and cited in Sattler and Berres (1974).

Recognition

A well-planned publicity program boosts motivation. Posed pictures of winners and action photos of play may be published in the school newspaper or yearbook or posted on the bulletin board. The names of players and teams can be printed in the school newspaper or circulated in the administrative announcement sheet.

Point Systems

Point systems may be used to unify the intramural program and to encourage wide participation in minor sports events. Points are awarded for entering an event and for placing. Entry points can be deducted for forfeits or added for not forfeiting. Awarding equal points for entering and placing encourages teams to enter all the sports events in order to remain in competition for the overall intramural championship award. More points should be given for team sports than individual sports because more people are required to field a unit. Point systems should be designed to consume no more administrative time than necessary.

Two types of point systems are used in intramural sports. The simplest method is to compute points on the basis of team performance. No account is made of the participation of each individual team member. A second system requires keeping a record of each individual's points for entering and placing. A true overall individual champion can be determined by keeping individual records. The same purpose can be accomplished much more easily, however. If it is desirable to designate an outstanding versatile intramural performer, each team can vote and decide the matter by election. There is little agreement about whether point systems are justified. Curry (1972) offers some anecdotes that question their value.

Southeastern Louisiana University

Figure 4.6 A photo in a newspaper is more satisfying to the winner than being given a large trophy in private.

WHAT'S THE POINT OF POINTS?

What would happen without points? Do our programs really have merit to stand alone without enticing gimmicks to increase participation numbers?

To further elaborate on this point, I would like to share some personal experiences. Three years ago, on our campus in Springfield, one of the intramural swimming teams entered four men in a relay. Of these four men, only three were even deep water swimmers. The fourth individual had to be pulled from the water before the relay was over. When asked why he entered, he stated, "To get the points for my team." In effect, he was making a mockery of the men's program by endangering his life for points.

In 1966, at Raytown High School in the greater Kansas City area, a well meaning young teacher of girl's physical education inititated a point system in her high school intramural program. A highly skilled group of young girls formed a team in the fall and stayed as a unit throughout the academic year. This team built a tradition of winning first in every activity they entered. They had amassed such a large total of points that no one threatened their championship. By the time the softball season rolled around in the spring, this team (which had captured so many intramural championships throughout the year) was the only team to enter girl's intramural softball. The team that played only for points found that all they had was points. No one would play them.

On our Springfield campus, we initiated a point system for Women's Intramural Sports in 1970. The rationale for starting the point system was to encourage more participation in the lifetime sports area. There had been so few entries in the past that at times it had been impossible to hold competition. All of the points were to be amassed toward the all-college championship team to be named at the end of the academic year. As the academic and intramural year progressed, we could see our purpose being fulfilled. Women were entering many of the lifetime sports areas; however, they were doing it purely for the sake of points. At the same time, we began to notice friction developing between old friends and competitive teams. It appeared to us that they were out after the points at any cost. They failed to appreciate the experience of playing equally skilled opponents. Students were seeking championships for points which could go toward the intramural all-college trophy. Informal interviews were arranged with a cross section of the women who were representatives of the various teams participating in the point program. The following results were obtained: many stated that (A) "Winning a basketball championship is unimportant. We are happy about it only because it gets us a few more points closer to the intramural all-college trophy"; (B) "Our team has had several arguments triggered mainly because we failed to earn any points toward the all-college trophy"; (C) "We probably won't enter any more because everyone knows who is going to win the championship"; (D) "It's just not any fun any more. It seems that people are playing for blood or points."

N. L. Curry, "What's the Point of Points?" *Twenty-third Annual Conference Proceedings*, National Intramural Association, Champaign, Ill., 1972, 58–63.

Awards

Trophies are widely used to provide extrinsic motivation for intramural play. Trophies are expensive—and after a few years may become meaningless clutter. If awards are to be given, they should be kept simple, inexpensive, and proportional in value to the contest. Medals and ribbons are as expensive as small trophies, but printed certificates of achievement can be awarded inexpensively. A revolving trophy may also be used to offset the high cost of awards. In the revolving-trophy method, a moderately expensive award is purchased and the winner's name is engraved each year. To insure security of the award it should be displayed in the intramural trophy case.

Case Example: ACTUALIZING THE RECREATION PROGRAM

Most of the students at Lincoln High School have never heard of the school recreation program. Though the director has served on a volunteer basis, a basketball tournament and a jogging club have been formed. With the advent of a "funded" program, expectations for student participation should be higher than the previously posted fifteen percent.

Many special events, intramurals in team sports and individual sports, and club sports are planned. How can the inactive eighty-five percent be motivated to join in? What specific actualizing strategy should be used to encourage participation in the large urban co-ed high school?

Controlling

Many of the fundamental control processes previously described in foregoing chapters are applicable to intramural sports. Specifically, procedure for operations control in intramural sports entails safeguarding property, developing program regulations, and conducting program evaluation. (Although officiating is a control mechanism, the topic has been explored previously under the major heading of staff organization.) Some examples of management objectives for controlling recreation programs are:

to set up standard procedures for equipment control and participant safety
to solicit continuous input from students about program success
to formally assess program effectiveness

Property Control

Standard operating procedure for equipment control in intramural sports requires day-by-day accounting for the flow of equipment in and out of the supply room. Only authorized personnel should have access to supply areas. Sports managers should have access to the equipment needed to conduct their contests. An issue box containing the timer, score book, rules book, and playing equipment should be prepared in advance for check-out to the sports manager. A file card attached to the issue box provides for a quick inventory of the equipment after each day's contests.

Program Regulations

There are two main categories of program regulations: game rules and general regulations. All rules and regulations should be periodically reviewed for relevancy. Although regulations provide a basis for making consistent judgments within the program, it is impossible to formulate a priori rules for every incident that may occur. Rules must also be considered tentative rather than fixed, humane rather than inflexible. The purpose of regulations is to facilitate participation and competition. Regulations foster competition and help to eliminate injuries. Sierra (1972) discusses ways to prevent injury in intramural sports. Many of these concepts are applicable to lower school levels.

PREVENTING INJURIES IN INTRAMURAL SPORTS

Since every type of sports activity offers some risk of injury, with the nature of the sport dictating the type and frequency of injuries which may be expected, accident prevention procedures must be employed in an effort to minimize the occurrence of such injuries. The following is a discussion of several ways in which injuries may be prevented in intramural and recreational sports.

A policy of planning competition for participants with near equal skill and abilities minimizes the dangers of accidents and injuries. Just as interscholastic and intercollegiate athletes commonly have medical examinations prior to participating in competitive sports, so a medical examination should be a requisite for the health protection of the intramural participant as well.

The unskilled person runs a greater risk of incurring injuries, since he does not know how to handle or position himself to exert maximum effort with the least strain. Knowing the rules, techniques, and strategy of a sport is extremely important. Training and conditioning are important factors in injury prevention and control. Opportunities for practice and conditioning should be made available before every scheduled competition.

Where provided, equipment should fit and be free from defects. The use of cleated shoes in football should not be optional, as cleated shoes provide distinct advantages in running, cutting, and blocking. Playing areas should be well-defined and made as safe as possible—for example, the use of padding on walls, restraining lines for players and spectators, and bright colors to define obstacles. Officials and supervisors play an important safety role not only in enforcing rules but also in being alert for signs of injury or illness among the contestants. Up to a point, the more officials assigned to a specific game the fewer injuries will occur. Penalties should be commensurate with the severity of the injury potential of the violation.

L. Sierra, "Preventing Injuries in College Intramural Sports," *JOHPER*, 43 (1972), 66, 68.

Eligibility. Only bona fide students enrolled in the school should be eligible to play in the intramural program. Rules pertaining to scholastic eligibility and probationary status add paperwork and legislate against students who need to participate. Athletes should be allowed to participate in all sports except those in which they have lettered or become professional. The rule for allowing athletes to participate in events other than those in which they lettered is solidly supported by research. Studies on motor skill by Henry (1956) and Bachman (1961) strongly indicate that motor ability is largely specific. Specific ability and conditioning in a sport that has been practiced is not necessarily transferable to dissimilar sports (Hartung 1971).

Forfeit. Forfeits are caused by failure to communicate the game schedule to the team. Teams with winning records seldom forfeit games. Penalties for forfeits can range from loss of entry points or entry fee to elimination from further intramural contests.

Protests. Protests of playing conditions should be filed in writing with the intramural director within twenty-four hours of the contested game. The statute of limitations of twenty-four hours insures that the events will be recent enough to be remembered correctly. Decision calls by an official are not generally protestable. Questions of player eligibility and rule interpretation are legitimate bases of protests. The officials and opponents should be notified that the contest is being played under "probable protest."

Since intramural sports are of the students and for the students, the students themselves should decide the validity of the protest. The intramural council should be convened to review and judge the protest. The options are: Protested game is allowed to stand, the game is given to the protesting team, or the game is replayed if necessary at the end of the season.

Behavior Control. If games are to be the "laboratories of social learning," some mechanism for negative reinforcement of negative student behavior must be available. The following are considered evidence of poor sportsmanship and should result in warning penalty, ejection, or forfeiture of a contest:

profanity
unnecessary delay of game
striking or shoving an opponent or official (ejection from the game and possibility of school disciplinary action)
arguing with officials concerning decisions
derogatory remarks toward an opponent or official
any action the intent of which is to cause injury to an opponent

Program Evaluation

Near the end of each program a systematic evaluation should be conducted. Student reactions to the various activities in the recreation program are barometers of program success. The percentage of student participation can be computed to determine whether all students are being reached. The number of forfeits can indicate a poor selection of activities, wrong play time, or poor choice for units of competition. Other important factors to be evaluated are expenditures, accidents, game rules, and program regulations. In school recreation everything is tentative—change must be made in response to student needs.

Program evaluation must be a cooperative venture involving the director, the student leaders, and the participants. Evaluation forms such as those developed by Wilkerson (1971) and Cable and Grzenda (1972) can be used to get information about the program. A sample school recreation evaluation form is included in Chapter 4 of the Student Guide.

Case Example: CONTROLLING METHODS IN SCHOOL RECREATION

The district school board recently passed a resolution funding a school recreation project for Lincoln High School. You have been appointed program director at your school with an athletic coaching stipend. Few of the students and faculty have ever heard of school intramurals. The school is in a middle-income urban neighborhood. The student body is composed of one thousand students in the ninth, tenth, eleventh, and twelfth grades. Steps have been taken to orient the students and faculty and to get the program started within one month. Write the minimum program regulations necessary to govern the intramural competition, the sports club competition, and the special events. Assuming that considerable equipment will be purchased, how will equipment use be controlled? What safety procedures should be built into the program?

References

BACHMAN, J. C. "Specificity vs. Generality in Learning and Performing Two Large Muscle Motor Tasks." *Research Quarterly*, 32 (1961), 3–11.

CABLE, D., and G. GRZENDA. "Simplified Score Sheets, Officials Evaluation Form, and Program Evaluation Form." *Twenty-third Annual Conference Proceedings*, National Intramural Association, Champaign, Ill., 1972, 59–63.

CURRY, N. L. "What's the Point of Points?" *Twenty-third Annual Conference Proceedings*, National Intramural Association, Champaign, Ill., 1972, 58–63.

DENTON, H. "Promoting a Sports Club Program at the University of Tennessee, Knoxville." *Twenty-fourth Annual Conference Proceedings*, National Intramural Association, Tampa, Fla., 1973, 94–97.

ENGLAND, R. W. "Intramural Newspaper and Hotline." *Twenty-fourth Annual Conference Proceedings*, National Intramural Association, Tampa, Fla., 1973, 142–143.

HARTUNG, G. H. "Specificity of Training as Indicated by Heart Rate Response to Treadmill Exercise." *Abstracts of Research Papers*, AAHPER Convention, AAHPER, 1971.

HENRY, F. M. "Future Basic Research in Motor Learning and Coordination." *Proceedings of the College Physical Education Association*, 1956.

HILLMAN, W. H. "Intramurals Via the Physical Education Class." *JOHPER*, 43 (1972), 63–64.

HOPKINS, P. D. "Intramurals Without Officials." *Twenty-third Annual Conference Proceedings*, National Intramural Association, Champaign, Ill., 1972, 51–54.

HYATT, R. "The Big Four Sports Day: A Classic Event." *The Physical Educator*, 28 (May 1971), 63–64.

JOHNSON, W. P. "The Club Approach to Intercollegiate Athletics in the Community College." *JOHPER*, 42 (1971), 45.

KELLER, R. J. "All School Playday." *The Physical Educator*, 23 (1966), 72–73.

MAAS, G. "Commercial Involvement in Intramurals." *Twenty-fifth Annual Conference Proceedings*, National Intramural Association, Tempe, Ariz., 1974, 68–70.

MARCIANI, L. "Promoting Intramurals: A Publicity Slide Production." *Twenty-fourth Annual Conference Proceedings*, National Intramural Association, Tampa, Fla., 1973, 109–110.

MULL, R. "Innovative Programming." *Twenty-second Annual Conference Proceedings*, National Intramural Association, Blacksburg, Va., 1971, 30–33.

MULLER, P. *Intramurals: Programming and Administration.* 4th ed. The Ronald Press Company, New York, 1971.

MURDOCK, A. "Iowa State 'Cyclone 500.' " *Twenty-second Annual Conference Proceedings*, National Intramural Association, Blacksburg, Va., 1972, 109–110.

NEWMAN, S. "Communications Principles and Tools for Intramurals." *Twenty-fourth Annual Conference Proceedings*, National Intramural Association, Tampa, Fla., 1973, 101–106.

OSTRANDER, H. R. "Innovative Methods of Financing Your Programs." *Twenty-fourth Annual Conference Proceedings*, National Intramural Association, Tampa, Fla., 1973, 109–110.

OXFORD, H. Elementary School Physical Education—The Miniature Olympics. *The Physical Educator*, 25 (1968), 32–33.

RENNER, K. H. "Essential Prerequisites for a New Intramural Program." *Twenty-third Annual Conference Proceedings*, National Intramural Association, Champaign, Ill., 1972, 80–82.

SATTLER, T., and L. BERRES. "Important Issues for Commuter College Programs." *Twenty-fifth Annual Conference Proceedings*, National Intramural Association, Tempe, Ariz., 1974, 129–132.

SIERRA, L. "Preventing Injuries in College Intramural Sports." *JOHPER*, 43 (1972), 66, 68.

SLIGER, I. T. "An Extensive Sports Club Program." *JOHPER*, 41 (1970), 41.

STEWART, R. E. "Recruiting, Training and Assignment of Intramural Officials." *The Physical Educator*, 25 (1968), 32–33.

———. "Brief History of the Intramural Movement." *The Physical Educator* 30 (1973), 26–28.

TAYLOR, D. H. "Special Events—A New Dimension in Intramural Programming." *Twenty-fifth Annual Conference Proceedings*, National Intramural Association, Tempe, Ariz., 1974, 70–73.

TAYLOR, J. L. "Intramurals: A Program for Everyone." *JOHPER*, 44 (1973), 44–45.

VAN NOSTRAND, B. R. "Intramural Budgets." *Twenty-third Annual Conference Proceedings*, National Intramural Association, Champaign, Ill., 1972, 91–98.

WILKERSON, J. "Intramural Recreation Non-participation." *Twenty-second Annual Conference Proceedings*, National Intramural Association, Blacksburg, Va., 1971, 57–59.

ZIMMER, W. R. "Student Input—It Makes the Program." *Twenty-fifth Annual Conference Proceedings*, National Intramural Association, Tempe, Ariz., 1974, 41–43.

5.

INTERSCHOOL ATHLETICS

After reading this chapter, each student should be able to:

Describe the educational contribution of a good interschool athletic program.

Identify and explain special problems inherent in age-level competition.

Describe the management processes specific to a school athletic program.

Successfully complete a short coaching internship.

Evaluate the program and management of athletics in a specific school.

Interschool athletics are solidly entrenched in the American school system. From informal beginnings as student-organized club sports between a few schools, highly organized athletics have spread to virtually all secondary schools. Reasons for the rapid expansion of athletics in the twentieth century are diverse. Social, psychological, and even economic factors have played important roles. School athletics mushroomed because the program filled a void in the participants and in American society. To the participant, athletics represent a new frontier for exploration. To the parent, athletics may represent an opportunity for their child's development and an opportunity to relive vicariously experiences of their own youth. To the spectator, school sports represent entertainment and the chance to identify with something significant—hopefully a winner. Alley (1974) incisively analyzed the educative potential of sports when he wrote:

> I suggest that school athletics, if directed by coaches of resolute integrity dedicated to the optimum development of their charges as individuals, can be an exceedingly potent tool for developing desirable behavior patterns of youngsters who participate. Moreover, the spectators at athletic contests can be favorably influenced as well. A host of factors combine to influence the behavior patterns and personalities of children, and it's well-nigh impossible to establish a cause-and-effect relationship with any factor or group of factors. The point is that athletics are one of the factors operating in the schools, and are probably much more potent in influencing the behavior of youngsters than many of us realize.

Athletic Program Overview

Interschool athletic programs are the highly organized sports activities systematically conducted among several schools. Whereas school recreation activities are programmed flexibly each year, interschool athletic programs are predetermined by school personnel. Prior to the beginning of school the program of activities, the professional personnel, and the schedule for the season are all arranged. Although school athletics are a serious business to principals, coaches, athletic booster clubs, and spectators, everyone should try to remember that sports are only games. The key to maintaining an educational perspective toward the sports program is a proper focus on desirable outcomes. Students—not the perpetuation of school traditions—are most important. Broun (1973), an internationally known sports commentator, offers a unique opinion on the intrinsic value of play. He argues eloquently that sports participation is its own reward and that athletics in the name of school spirit or national patriotism is completely misguided. Losing the regional shot-putting eliminations isn't losing all of the savor of life: there are wider circles than those from which one hurls weights.

School sports usually fall into the category of proprietary school functions. Seldom are all school sports totally funded from tax sources without reliance on gate receipts. Yet, though school sports are proprietary in nature, there is a *major* difference between all school sports and professional athletics. Due to the wide publicity accorded professional athletes, students are prone to mimic the style and attitude of professionals—even the occasional antisocial behavior. As long as athletics are conducted under the jurisdiction of the school, emphasis must be on educational outcomes for the student athlete. Professional sports corporations are little concerned with players beyond their effectiveness in producing winning, money-making teams. Since society funds the school to educate the student, the important factor must be student development—*never* the development of a miniature professional sports corporation operated by the school.

Program Objectives

Regardless of the number of students on the team, education attempts to shape the behavior of students individually in a day-by-day process. Since desirable behavior outcomes are not automatically derived from sports experience, a strategy for education is necessary. The projected outcomes described in Chapter 1 are applicable to physical education instruction, school recreation, and interschool athletics if the programs are conducted on a professional level.

Of course everyone wants to win and no healthy person likes to lose. The issue is not wanting to win, for that goal is universal. Assuming that the purposes of school athletics are educational and not those of a business corporation, the following specific objectives should be program goals:

1. to develop motor skills to the highest level consistent with the student's capacity
2. to perform skills in a context that has high significance to society
3. to develop the ability to interact with team members to accomplish a mutual task, the combined significance of which is valued higher than personal contributions
4. to develop skills in social interaction that will facilitate ethical behavior in everyday affairs
5. to develop knowledge and appreciation of motor behavior through intensive participation
6. to develop a high state of physical and mental health
7. to develop an awareness of the role of competition and cooperation in sports and society

The Scope of a Comprehensive Program

The traditional athletic program has been virtually restricted to two or three team sports for boys. Girls and individual sports have had only a minor part in the action. But progress is being made toward serving more students and wider interests. Legal developments and the growing appeal of individual sports are contributing to program diversification.

The Department of Health, Education and Welfare has prepared a set of nondiscrimination guidelines called Title IX (see Blaufarb 1975). Responding to these guidelines, schools will move toward a balance between boys' and girls' programs. Essentially, the guidelines state that a program is being conducted for boys, a similar program must be available for girls in schools receiving federal financing. Further, co-ed teams are a distinct possibility in sports not involving physical contact, such as golf or tennis. Litigation in the next decade will further define the intent of the law. Additionally, school accountability for sex discrimination has been clarified by rediscovery of the Civil Rights Act of 1871, by which individual board members or administrators may be personally liable for discrimination. As pointed out by Lenaghan and Phay (1973), school board members can no longer use collective immunity as a legal defense against charges of discrimination of any kind.

A comprehensive athletic program includes several sports for boys and girls at all school levels from upper elementary school through senior high school. Metropolitan schools should include team sports at several ability levels, as well as individual sports. A school system should have a separate team for each grade in team sports and a large, multigrade team in the individual sports. The National Federation of State High School Associations (NFSHSA 1972–1973) lists the following sports: badminton, baseball, basketball, bowling, cross country, curling, decathlon, fencing, field hockey, football, golf, gymnastics, ice hockey, lacrosse, riflery, rugby, skiing, soccer, softball, swimming, tennis, track and field, volleyball, water polo and wrestling.

Age-Level Competition

Age-level competition applies to sports participation at grades below the secondary school. In age-level competition the competitive units are generally paired by age or ability level. Preadolescent competition is one of the most controversial topics in athletics. Some schools have age-level or preadolescent competition, though many of the programs are conducted by outside organizations. Well-intended programs conducted by outside agencies include: (1) T baseball (lower elementary ages); (2) Pee-Wee baseball (middle elementary ages); (3) Little League baseball (upper elementary ages); (4) Mini-league football; (5) Pop Warner League football; (6) minor league basketball; (7) minor-league ice hockey; (8) swimming clubs; and (9) gymnastic clubs.

Many scientific and authoritative statements have been made on the pros and cons of elementary school and junior high school athletics. During the scholarly debate, parents and children have acted outside the schools to develop programs of competitive athletics—sometimes to the detriment of the children. Some of the pros and cons of age-level competition are cited here, but the real issue is not

Figure 5.1 Schools that receive federal funding may not discriminate against students by sex.

whether preadolescent competition shall exist—because preadolescent school children *are* participating in athletic programs. These programs could be better under the professional control of teachers (Bula 1971). The schools should be providing sports experience the type and extent of which could then be regulated by professional personnel. Obviously, most of the preadolescent sports drive should be accommodated within the intramural program. Schools must begin to provide educationally defensible alternatives to the sports leagues conducted by volunteers.

The Case Against Age-Level Competition

Many physicians, psychologists, and educators have spoken out against age-level competition below the high school level. Numerous studies of growth and development have reported results seriously questioning both preadolescent competition categorically and specific program management. Dowell (1971) summarizes these factors and provides an extensive bibliography. Of course, competitive sports in the upper elementary grades of four, five, and six are more questionable than in the junior high school grades of seven, eight, and nine.

Physiological. During upper elementary school and junior high school, students are at a precarious stage in physiological development. Rapid growth in height and girth requires most of their available energy, leaving little for concentrated athletic training. If athletic training drains the available growth energy, normal development will be curtailed. Competitive activity at levels below the high school not only involves skeletal growth problems, but also risks damage to developing muscles, bones, and cartilage tissue in joints. Violent and prolonged exercise may overload internal organs, causing both immediate and long-range damage.

Psychological. Competitive sports tend to engender an overload of stress before the student has had an opportunity to develop mechanisms to cope with it. The pressure to win applied by parents and adult leaders easily leads to a frustration syndrome within the developing personality. There is danger that too much competition too soon may cause a reverse effect: the student may abandon noisy sports for calmer pursuits. Every child must have some success in order to develop a normal personality, and competitive sport does little to guarantee reinforcement at critical periods in emotional development.

The Case For Age-Level Competition

Practical educators and sports enthusiasts advocate competitive sports at all school levels. Children are active and adventurous. Organized sports provide a context in which skills can be correctly taught and emotions safely vented.

Dowell (1971) also presents a well-documented case supporting preadolescent competition.

Physiological. Both boys and girls are biologically active in preadolescence, and competition provides encouragement for the movement drive. Girls and boys are nearly equal in physical ability before puberty. Girls' overall athletic perform-ance tends to decrease during adolescence, and it remains to be determined whether this is due to innate physical or psychological differences between girls and boys or to the tendency to assimilate and fulfill societal expectations. Throughout the research studies, properly controlled competition has not been found to be physically injurious to the student. Although high pulse rates have been monitored during preadolescent competition, research evidence indicates that a healthy heart cannot be damaged by exercise. During strenuous competi-tion the preadolescent slows down from fatigue before physiological damage becomes a potential factor. The probable damage to the growth zone of bones postulated by Lowman (1941) has not been validated by field experience and research.

Psychological. Success reinforcement is essential for normal development, but everyone must also learn to live with defeat. Some of society's greatest leaders and athletes have been challenged to excel after various kinds of failure. The preadolescent tends to have periods of serious inward questioning. Sports in-volvement helps to redirect emotional energy outward to worthwhile group goals. Late preadolescents are group-oriented, and sports competition provides a healthy group context for socialization. Athletic ability has been reported to be highly correlated with social status.

Synthesis of the Problem

Obviously, both sides of the issue have some merit. People on the con side tend to be (1) extremely cautious lest damage be perpetrated on developing youth and (2) extremely critical of the way most preadolescent programs are conducted. On the other hand, the people on the pro side of the issue tend to gloss over possible damage in their haste to coach or witness their favorite sport.

The truth of the matter is that most junior high schools and some elementary schools *are* engaged in interschool athletics. Additionally, in metropolitan areas gymnastic clubs, swimming clubs, track and field clubs, and boxing clubs flourish as independent businesses or as a part of legitimate youth organizations. Children will play and eager parents will pay. Private coaching and sports camps also provide competitive experience for youth.

The real problem is how best to provide for age-level competition. Because such mini-leagues as basketball and baseball frequently have coaches untrained in sports skills and ethical coaching, all preadolescent competition should be under

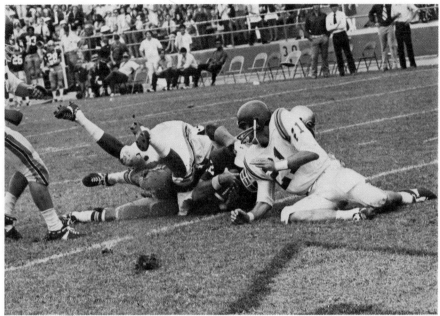

Southeastern Louisiana University

Figure 5.2 It is obvious that there are more desirable sports activities for pre-adolescent students than tackle football.

the control of the local schools with certified teachers as coaches. Competition should be graduated at the upper elementary grades from intramural contests to two-thirds of a secondary schedule at the upper junior high school level. Most of the activity time should be devoted to acquiring skill. Practice sessions must be characterized by *moderate physiological stress* and *low psychological stress.* If preadolescent competition is to be safe and successful, criticisms leveled against the program should be seriously considered and changes made where change is warranted. Bucher (1971) makes some firm recommendations about athletic competition in the various grades.

Planning

Most secondary schools have existing interschool athletic programs. The planning process for existing programs entails taking a critical look at athletics to determine where improvement is needed. Interschool athletic planning in new and existing programs is based on careful projection of student outcomes from the program. Interschool athletics have a broad base of community support, but local and state regulatory organizations are needed to insure that student outcomes are educationally defensible. Some examples of management objectives for administrative planning for interschool athletics are:

> to develop a comprehensive program of diversified activities
> to formulate an overall plan for multilevel school programs
> to identify funding alternatives for a broad base of sports for girls and boys
> to identify the functions of athletic associations

Operational Policies

Each school should develop a statement of philosophy that expresses the spirit of its athletic program. Objectives similar to those we have just listed may be projected from the philosophy statement. Though agencies governing interschool athletics have regulations, the local school needs its own statements of policy. Policies may be outlined in advance, but they usually evolve from trial and error. The Los Angeles City School District, for instance, developed its "Brown Book" of athletic policies (Bakjian 1968). The following categories are critical to management of the athletic program. A descriptive statement can be written for each category by the local school athletic department.

1. representation at athletic association meetings
2. local school athletic council
3. duties of athletic department personnel
4. program of activities
5. scheduling contests
6. length of season and days of prohibited practice
7. purchase and inventory of equipment
8. athletic trips
9. scouting
10. home contests
11. insurance and first aid
12. awards
13. evaluation

Program of Activities

Of course activities such as basketball, football, and baseball may foster desirable student outcomes, but students should have athletic opportunities in individual sports as well. The athletic program must include team and individual sports for girls and boys. The real program will inevitably be a compromise between what the educators want and what the pressure groups want. Factors such as student interest, coaching competencies, and the athletic booster organization often dictate the specific activities in a program. Some desirable activities are:

team sports: baseball, basketball, field hockey, football, ice hockey, lacrosse, soccer, softball, team handball, volleyball
individual activities: archery, badminton, bowling, cross country, fencing, golf, handball, judo, swimming and diving, tennis, track and field, weight lifting, wrestling

Though each school athletic program will not include all of the desirable alternatives, variety is essential. Important criteria in the selection process are as follows:

1. What desirable outcomes are probable?
2. What undesirable outcomes are probable?
3. How many students could be served?
4. How much student and community interest is there?
5. Can existing facilities be reasonably adapted for the sport?
6. How many coaches will be required?
7. Can competition be scheduled with nearby schools?
8. What will be the overall cost?
9. Does the activity fit within Title IX guidelines?
10. Can the activity be integrated into the existing sports program?

Multilevel School Programs

Large urban school systems are frequently criticized for operating a "farm system" of athletics in the feeder schools. If the high school head coach insists that all junior high schools and elementary schools run a carbon copy of the high school offense and defense in team sports, then such an accusation is valid. Every grade level has students with unique developmental problems. Recognition of individual problems means that age-level athletic programs can be tailored to student needs. Sole emphasis on grooming athletes for a subsequent program means that student needs are being ignored.

However, coordination of a multilevel athletic program within a school system is possible. Coordination implies using a common set of terms and definitions within a sport. Coordination may mean that a simplified high school offense and defense may be used at lower grade levels where applicable. (Note: A continuous full-court press defense in basketball would not be appropriate for lower grade levels.) Coordination should include public relations talks and team demonstrations by high school groups for the benefit of the feeder schools.

Funding

Funding is a major problem in conducting interschool athletic programs at all levels. As pointed out by the American School Board Journal (1975), many harried board members ultimately ask the question, "Is athletic programming worth all the cash that is poured in?" In order to determine whether it *is* worthwhile, student outcomes must be quantified and cashflows reviewed objectively. Interschool athletics, intercollegiate athletics, and professional athletics are all feeling the financial pinch (see Lineberry 1973). For decades interschool athletics have received a large portion of direct and indirect school funds. Perhaps the critical economic situation will spur beneficial evaluation of school athletics in terms of educational outcomes.

Income Sources

Tax monies and gate receipts are the two main sources of funds for interschool athletics. All schools rely on tax money to some extent, and most schools generate a portion of their income from paid admissions. In sports that do not produce revenue, the individual participants either furnish their own equipment or hold fund-raising drives to pay for equipment and transportation.

General Taxation Revenue. The degree of reliance on tax sources varies from community to community. Some communities wholly support their athletic programs from tax sources, with gate receipts being returned to the general fund. Full-program funding from tax sources is the ideal situation, because teams and coaches are thereby protected from pressure to win, win, win. Budgeted funding is also more equitable; it is unfair for spectator team sports to be forced to raise funds for the entire athletic program. Even communities that do not contribute tax funds for program operations do make sizable indirect contributions. Indirect tax funding is used to pay the coach's salary and to construct gymnasiums, playing fields, and stadiums. Seldom are facilities or utility costs charged against the gate receipts of the athletic program.

Gate Receipts. While program costs have almost doubled in the last decade, gate receipts have remained stable or have increased only slightly. It is very difficult to transfer the increased costs to the spectator by raising the admission fee while college and professional sports are free when viewed on television.

Gate receipts are funds derived from admissions paid by spectators. Primary funding by gate receipts places tremendous pressure on the program and the coach. Fans come to athletic events to see a winner. And if the home team is not a potential winner, local people do not turn out. There are three ways, or combinations thereof, for schools to have successful gate-receipt funding: season ticket sales, student activity fees, and weekly ticket sales.

The athletic support club should be enlisted to sell season tickets to individuals and businesses. Preseason sales are most successful because losing a few early games seriously dampens ticket sales of all kinds. To facilitate sales, an agreement can be made with the local bank by which the entire cost of the season ticket can be charged to the buyer's Master Charge or BankAmericard account. Or a bank deduction plan can be arranged through participating banks. Printed authorization forms are signed by the ticket purchaser and sent to the bank to authorize deduction of the specified amount from the purchaser's account.

A nominal student activity fee can be charged each student enrolled in the school to pay for cultural, intramural, and athletic events. Payment of the fee entitles the student to be admitted to all school activities.

Recruitment of students and faculty as pregame ticket sellers is a successful method. Prizes can be given to those who sell the most tickets from week to week during the sports season. Of course, ticket sales must not be made during class time. (A strict account must be made of the tickets and the sales money. See also Chapter 7 on fiscal management.)

Expenses

Expenses for interschool athletics are seldom covered by the gate receipts. Expense items include equipment, travel, insurance, officials, training room materials, and uniforms. All expenses increase with inflation. Obviously, new equipment and uniforms cannot be purchased if the money is not available. Certain items are fixed for a particular sport. The state athletic association specifies the exact fee of all officials who work games. Certified officials must be used in all sanctioned games—and all games must be sanctioned. Standard purchasing and cashflow procedures are described in Chapter 7.

Athletic Associations

The feud between regulatory agencies in collegiate athletics has at times become a national issue. Independent agencies governing amateur athletics differ in issues such as jurisdiction and amateur status. Yet intercollegiate and interscholastic athletic associations perform valuable services to the sports community. Some athletic associations are general in nature, covering many sports, while others are restricted to only one activity. (Single-purpose associations, such as for badminton, bowling, and tennis, are cited in the Student Guide.) Athletic associations are necessary to standardize the conditions of interschool athletics. Commonly accepted game rules, eligibility rules, and structured state championships are important association responsibilities.

Terry McKoy, I. O. E.

Southeastern Louisiana University

Figure 5.3 Game officiating is a major source of expense in interschool athletics.

The history of sports has shown that there must be an organization to structure and supervise interschool athletics. Gross abuse of students occurred before athletic associations were formed. For example, there is a problem if school A desires to conduct a low-key but educationally defensible athletic program, while schools B and C subscribe to the "win at all costs" philosophy. Without a regulatory agency superimposed over all competing schools, there is little hope of equal competition. Forsythe and Keller (1972) present an excellent history of athletic associations from faculty sponsors to national agencies. Paterno (1974) recommends the return of local athletic control to a faculty council. But, as Blackburn and Nyikos (1974) point out, faculty councils can easily be annulled by a powerful athletic department, and they can easily be intimidated by administrative action. Strong state and national associations are essential for interschool athletics.

AAU

The Amateur Athletic Union was formed to foster quality athletic competition. The AAU has continually stood for maintaining the amateur spirit in nonprofessional sports. Jurisdiction of events cuts across age levels from secondary school through college and independent athletes. The organization has influence in the area of track and field, gymnastics, and weight lifting. Developing rules for activities, specifying conditions for eligibility, and promoting national competition are important functions of the AAU.

NAGWS

The National Association for Girls and Women in Sport (NAGWS) is an agency within the American Alliance for Health, Physical Education and Recreation (AAHPER). The scope of the NAGWS includes almost all sports in which females regularly compete. The agency has synthesized research, developed rules especially designed for women, and promoted women's athletic participation through national competition in a variety of sports. The organization has been extremely active in improving the status of women's sports. Numerous articles and books about sports have been developed by the NAGWS for publication by the parent organization.

Independent Conference

Independent conferences are often formed when there is no acceptable or available method of structuring interschool competition. Pre-adolescent school competition is largely ignored by general athletic associations. Adjacent junior high schools often form independent conferences to standardize their athletic programs. Private and parochial schools have basic organizational needs that can be met by an independent conference. Private schools may have great difficulty in scheduling games. A conference automatically guarantees a minimum number of scheduled contests and makes possible a conference championship. Of course any independent conference can adopt its own rules and train its own officials.

NFSHSA

The National Federation of State High School Associations (1972–1973) is the most comprehensive organization that regulates high school sports. All the separate state associations form the national federation. Athletics is not mentioned in the title because state competition in nonathletic activities is also a responsibility of the association. Federation bylaws provide guidelines governing player eligibility, conducting contests, and developing playing rules. The federation operates as a nonprofit corporation in which membership is entirely voluntary. Many court cases have evolved to challenge the regulatory authority of the organization. All jurisdictional suits have failed because each state organization is operated by the member schools on a voluntary basis. Much variation exists among the state high school athletic associations. Some associations of the national federation are totally independent organizations, while other associations are agencies of the state. In Texas, for example, the athletic association is part of the state government, while in Louisiana the state association is an independent nonprofit corporation. Principal services of the state associations, in conjunction with the national federation, are as follows:

1. to define the philosophy of interschool athletic programs
2. to develop game rules for the various sports
3. to define the limits of student eligibility
4. to classify schools in order to equalize competition
5. to use the sanction procedure to regulate state, interstate, all-star, national, and international competition
6. to train and assign game officials
7. to provide training films for game officials, coaches, and players
8. to enact disciplinary action against players and schools for major rule violations

---

Case Example: PLANNING AN INTERSCHOOL ATHLETIC PROGRAM

Midwest City High School has fielded only male athletic teams since the school began. In recent years the interschool football program has been highly successful through concentrated recruiting within the school and by requiring all the football players to compete in either track or field events during the spring term. The school also participates in interschool basketball. Midway through the spring term two class-action suits were filed against the principal and the athletic director. The first suit alleged that emphasis only on football, basketball, and track and field discriminates against students whose physical abilities and interests do not fit those sports. The second suit requested the courts to order the school district to provide a program of athletic competition for girls similar to that provided for boys, as mandated by Title IX guidelines. A local judge has issued a restraining order to allow the athletic program to be continued through the current school term. Preliminary hearings for the suits will be held shortly.

You are the athletic director at Midwest City High School. What will be your response in court to the two suits? Will financial capability of the athletic department be a defense factor? Will increased liability for injury be a defense factor?

Organizing

Organizing the interschool athletic program at the schoolwide level includes athletes, staff, facilities, equipment; at the team level, it includes setting up staff and players in the most productive arrangements. Team organization is discussed extensively in coaching texts for various sports (Bowerman 1974, Cousy and Power 1970, Gould 1971, Ralston and White 1971, and Sabock 1973). This sec-

Figure 5.4 A successful coach must be able to organize athletes into an effective team.

Southeastern Louisiana University

tion focuses on the general functions of the athletic director or head coach. Some examples of objectives for administrative organizing are:

to develop a "team attitude" in athletic department personnel
to identify procedures for recruiting and protecting student athletes
to resolve critical issues related to cooperative use of facilities
to describe the principles of game scheduling

The Student Athlete

The principal and the head coach are both responsible for allowing only eligible students to participate in interschool athletics. The general process of organizing student personnel within the athletic program should be a cooperative function of the entire coaching staff, with the head coach of each sport specifically responsible for his or her athletes. Athletic associations' efforts are directed much more toward equalizing competition among schools than protecting the students' welfare. Aggressive coaches often work their athletes hard every day in order to get the winning edge—and other coaches follow suit in order to stay in the same league. Local school districts must protect their students by (1) specifying a moderate length for week-day practice; (2) eliminating weekend and holiday practice; and (3) regulating the number of games in a sport season.

Recruiting

The National Federation of State High School Associations strictly forbids recruitment of out-of-district athletes for high school play. Some independent conferences do allow tuition scholarships for worthy students—some of whom are incidentally talented in sports. However, every successful athletic program must have in-school recruitment. Coaches may recruit students from physical education classes or the intramural program on the basis of their observation of student performance. Frequently, capable students are reluctant to volunteer for the sports program because of fear of failure or lack of self-confidence. A personal invitation by the coach has yielded many students who later excelled in athletics. Of course, preliminary notices of opening workouts should be posted and circulated well before the sport season. Some form of permission sheet must be signed by parents before practice is allowed.

Recruiting conflicts frequently occur within the athletic department. For example, the head football coach may say, "Football is number one, therefore I get the choice athletes." Coaches sometimes "raid" other sports, using flattery and promises to recruit good athletes for their teams. Unwarranted restriction is also an undesirable practice. Some coaches try to force athletes into specializing in only one sport by saying. "If you play football, you cannot play basketball."

Students should be allowed to participate in several sports as dictated by their time, interest, and talent. Forced specialization at the secondary level is a petty manifestation of the "winning is everything" philosophy.

Eligibility

An athlete is generally allowed twelve semesters for high school competition upon entering the seventh grade. Compliance of each team member with age and scholastic requirements of the state athletic association must be verified by both coach and school principal. Error or fraud in stating the official team roster may result in suspension of the school for a year. Players, principals, and coaches under suspension cannot change schools to evade the suspension ruling.

Medical Consideration

Every athlete must have passed a medical evaluation prior to the beginning of practice. Passing a medical examination does not imply perfect health. Students with handicaps often participate; blindness, for example, would not preclude participation in wrestling. Latent medical conditions do sometimes emerge during strenuous activity. If medical examination has not been made prior to practice, the athletic program may be unjustly blamed for causing a condition that existed earlier. Student insurance covering the entire team is a must in modern athletics. The athletic insurance rider may be added at nominal cost to the basic student policy offered to all students in a school. Athletic health insurance may be paid for by the parents, the school, or the local club supporting athletics.

Student insurance with the athletic rider differs in coverage from plan to plan. Standard plans are usually of the type that (1) pays all of the hospital fee and some of the physician's fee—at a considerable premium; or (2) pays the medical expenses after a constant deductible amount is paid by the insured—at less expensive premiums. all student insurance plans should contain a major medical clause by which seventy-five to eighty percent of expenses are paid for extensive medical care. Good business practice mandates shopping for policies and advertising for the "low quality bid" (see Chapter 7).

Athletic Personnel

The various administrative roles in the school system were discussed in Chapter 2. A model organization chart for athletic personnel is shown in Figure 5.5. Staffing the athletic department and arranging for internal communication are significant problems. Much has been written about the pros and cons of coaching certification. Esslinger (1968) and Maetozo (1971) advocate the specific certification of coaches. The logic is that more coaches are needed than are available from the physical education staff. Also, some coaches prefer to teach in other than physical

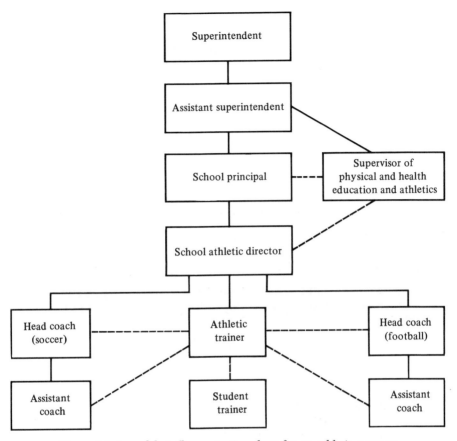

Figure 5.5 A model staff-organization chart for an athletic program.

education assignments. Conversely, many educators feel that broad training in sports philosophy, psychology, and physiology is needed by all coaches. A second major staffing problem is developing nationally in girls' athletics. Girls' sports will continue to increase significantly. Who will coach the girls' teams? There is a shortage of highly trained female coaches, an unfortunate circumstance because girls on the teams can profit greatly from the example of a skilled woman as their coach. Although many men coach girls' teams successfully, not all male coaches are able to do so.

Social psychologists have observed that staff cohesion tends to rise with increased internal communication. Acceptance of individuals in the group tends to be a function of the type and frequency of conversations. And it is obvious that group goals cannot be achieved unless individuals become a cohesive group committed to mutual benefit. Therefore, the athletic administrator should structure conditions for interaction. After-school meetings usually conflict with coaching. But a regular before-school breakfast once a month for the coaching staff and principal can be a vehicle for increased interaction. Pre- and post-season outings for the staff also provide opportunities for communication.

The Principal

The school principal has a *respondeat superior* relationship to the school staff. A principal can delegate authority for program and eligibility lists to staff members. But both the principal and the coach must bear the responsibility for error. Since the principal does have a major responsibility for the athletic program, he or she should meet with the staff regularly for discussion. The principal should also establish a routine of systematic observation to insure that the program is conducted to produce educationally defensible outcomes.

The Athletic Director

The *athletic director* is basically a coordinator. As a middle-level manager, the athletic director must be able to conceptualize what the program should be like and interact with staff members to realize program goals. In small schools the athletic director may double as head coach of a particular sport. In large school systems the athletic director may function at the systemwide supervisory level. The athletic director must have knowledge of sports and maturity in human relations.

The Coaching Staff

Seldom are all coaches able to coach only their specialty sport. It is more common for a head coach in one sport to assist with a second. Or one coach may assist in two or three different team sports. By using the head coach and assistant coach organization, staff personnel can be spread in greater depth throughout the athletic program. Individual sports are generally managed by one coach for each sport. Typical duties of a head coach include: (1) projecting a budget; (2) securing equipment; (3) recruiting students and validating the squad roster; (4) developing a playing schedule; (5) developing an overall strategy; (6) conducting practice and games; (7) accounting for funds and equipment; and (8) coordinating and evaluating staff members. The role of assistant coaches varies with the assignments given by the head coach.

The quality of individuals on the coaching staff is among the most critical factors in the entire school system. The long, close interaction of players and coaches is an ideal teaching situation. Much has been written about the coach in sex-role identification (Werner 1972). Similarly, Porter (1972) maintains that coaching has great potential in enhancing students' character development.

The Athletic Trainer

The trend is toward designating one member of the coaching staff as *trainer* for all sports. In large high schools such designation frees the other coaches for more effort in actual coaching. Legal responsibility for first aid and quasi-medical care can be delegated only to a certified teacher. Where a staff member is available as athletic trainer, a few capable students should be recruited and schooled in the basics of training-room procedures. Development of a senior student trainer and several apprentice student trainers insures continuity from year to year. Athletic supply companies can arrange for local training workshops. Gathering all the coaches and student trainers in a city or district will yield a manageable workshop group. Team physicians and suppliers such as Cramer and Johnson and Johnson can be efficiently used at the district level. The team physician should instruct the student trainers in correct procedures and acquaint them with the limits of their quasi-medical roles. Student trainers cannot assume legal responsibility for executing first aid—though they can perform tasks specified by the physician while under general supervision by the coach. (See also Chapter 10, the Athletic Safety Act (Dellums Bill), and the Forsythe Amendment).

The Student Manager

Student managers are often the forgotten people in sports (Kochera 1971). Managers complement the staff by executing the menial details of cleaning and accounting for equipment. Student managers should be made to feel an integral part of the team. Though managers serve to relieve the coach of equipment duties, they should be rewarded by team travel and team awards. Development of a senior manager with several apprentice managers insures field training of the managers and continuity from year to year.

Cooperative Use of Facilities

Equitable scheduling of facilities is the heart of the conflict between men and women coaches and between the school recreation program and the athletic program. Teams of various grade levels want to use the facilities at the most convenient times. Conflicting demands for the gymnasium and field facilities are made by the various coaches. Some arrogant coaches subscribe to the philosophy that "What is mine is mine, and what is yours is ours!"

In order to resolve the facilities impasse, a set of policies and priorities must be established. These policies should dictate the use of a master calendar for integrated scheduling of facilities. Priorities should be established objectively on the basis of program goals and the number of students involved. Physical education classes must have first priority because of their curriculum relationship. Boys' and girls' athletics should share equally—though the number of students involved may make a difference. Considerate planners will allow younger teams to practice first and older students last. Teams involved in a championship play-off after the regular season should have priority over practice that is just beginning for other sports. School recreation can be integrated into the sharing of facilities by working indoor and outdoor sports slightly out of season. Under no circumstance should athletic teams be grouped together during the last school hour under the guise of a physical education class.

Scheduling Games

A successful athletic season is often defined as winning more than half of the total games. Losing most of the athletic contests is depressing to the team and the supporting community. Professional football has resolved the problem of equalizing competition by reshuffling the divisional teams each year to theoretically produce a balanced won–lost record for each team. Owens (1970) makes a similar recommendation. Twenty-five percent of the contests should be with teams of markedly greater ability. Twenty-five percent of the games should be with teams of lower ability. The remaining fifty percent of a team's schedule should be with schools of ability approximately equal to that of the home team. Thus, every team that makes an above-average effort will have a successful season. Though such factors as district game commitments and school size may prevent the theoretical 50–50 season, scheduling for a successful season is desirable. The development of an ideal schedule is much easier in individual sports than in revenue-producing team sports.

Schedules are frequently worked out one or two years in advance. In order to develop a season schedule, the head coach or athletic director should write preliminary letters to all nearby schools. These letters should state the sport and the alternative playing dates. Tentative schedule agreement may be reached in follow-up telephone calls. A contract or letter of commitment should be exchanged by the schools to finalize the scheduled contests. School districts frequently bring representatives together to develop yearly schedules in order to eliminate protracted communication by letter. Then open dates within district play are filled by contacting other schools. Games with independent teams (alumni, semi-pro, etc.) are usually prohibited by state high school athletic associations.

A contract is a legal document in which two or more parties agree to a specified set of actions. If properly executed by both parties, written contracts are binding. Not only are oral agreements legally invalid, but confusion frequently develops over details. The contract should be signed by official representatives of each school. The standard contract includes school names, date of contest, time of contest, place of contest, ticket guarantee, and other special conditions. Formal contracts may be foregone at the secondary level for some sports. However,

(Please sign and return 2 copies)

MIDWEST CITY HIGH SCHOOL

ATHLETIC CONTRACT AGREEMENT

This AGREEMENT entered into this _____ day of_____,

19____, by and between Midwest City High School and_____

_____ stipulates that:

1. The (basketball, football, etc.) teams of Midwest City High School

   and of_____ mutually agree that

   their respective teams play _____ games and shall meet at

   _____ on _____, 19____

   and at_____ on _____, 19____.

2. The game shall start at _____ at _____

   and at _____ at_____.

3. Midwest City High School agrees to pay the visiting team the sum

   of $_____, and _____ as a guarantee for playing
   said game.

4. The home team reserves the right to cancel said contests without
   penalty for any unforeseen or unavoidable cause.

5. Officials for Midwest City High School home games will be assigned by the State High School Athletic Official Association.

6. _____

   _____

Signed in triplicate
Athletic Council Chairman _____

_____   _____

For Home Team Athletic Director   School

Athletic Council Chairman_____

_____   _____

For Visiting Team Athletic Director   School

Figure 5.6 A model contract for athletic events.

official letters of commitment should be exchanged after schedule plans are finalized. Figure 5.6 shows a model contract which provides both schools with a guarantee of a contest.

Case Example: ORGANIZING A SEASON SCHEDULE

In recent years Midwest City High School has tried to improve its football program by scheduling larger schools in the season's nondistrict dates. The practice of playing more powerful teams has proved disastrous in both injuries and game losses. Midwest High is an AAA school located within convenient driving distance of several other AA, AAA, and AAAA schools. As the incoming athletic director, you find that contracts have been signed for two more years of contests with AAAA schools. Although the fall schedule has been submitted to the state high school athletic association, you have serious doubts about the tentative schedule. What can be done under these conditions to develop a desirable football schedule? Specifically:

1. Is an incoming athletic director bound by the contracts of the former director?
2. Under what conditions can game contracts be voided?
3. What overtures can be made to develop desirable schedules in later years?
4. What criteria should be used in selecting opponents to fill the nondistrict schedule dates?

Actualizing

What does hospitality have to do with staging home athletic events? What do motivation, publicity, and checklists have to do with successful contests? Actualizing begins with team practice and includes transportation, courtesy service, awards, and ticket sales. Actualizing for interschool athletics is the culmination of careful plans and organization. The courtesy and hospitality shown to visiting teams will generally be reciprocated when the home team visits the community whose team it welcomed before. Some typical actualizing objectives are:

to identify the procedures required for athletic team travel
to define the steps in preparing and conducting home contests
to develop guidelines for use of intrinsic and extrinsic motivation in athletics

Preparation for Contests

Individual conditioning sessions should begin well before the first official day of practice. Individual conditioning implies that each athlete accepts personal responsibility for physical fitness and sport skills. Research data (Levitt 1973) indi-

Southeastern Louisiana University   Terry McKoy, I. O. E.

Figure 5.7 Learning to assume personal responsibility for skill and conditioning makes it more likely that they will be carried over into adult life.

cates that there are definite limits to physiological conditioning. Yet few athletes are sufficiently motivated to reach their maximum physiological potential. Preparation for contests includes conditioning, skill development, and strategy.

Practice sessions must be balanced between conditioning and learning skills. Development of strength and endurance are more important in track and field and football. The development of skill is more important in tennis, golf, and basketball. Research has shown that both motor skill and physiological conditioning are specific to the motor task practiced. Therefore, practice sessions must simulate reality in order to produce the greatest overall gains in the limited time an athletic season affords. Gallon (1974) has two excellent chapters on practice sessions in his book *Coaching: Ideas and Ideals.*

Strategy is a major factor in all sports contests—especially in games of skill. Teams well schooled in their offensive and defensive tactics can adjust to varia-

Figure 5.8 *A checklist for travel to athletic contests.*

Check when
completed

☐   1. Confirm game details with host school (by letter or telephone).

☐   2. Secure travel arrangements with common carrier, etc.

☐   3. Plan itinerary for travel, eating, and lodging to and from contest.

☐   4. Draw check from school fund to cover all the expenses and cash the check.

☐   5. Secure and sell the block of tickets provided by the host school.

☐   6. Send itinerary plan to parents of athletes and secure the signed permission slips for all athletes.

☐   7. Prepare official team roster, grade affidavits, and birth certificates.

☐   8. Inform student groups (band, cheerleaders) and adult groups (athletic booster club, parents of players) of itinerary and provide travel map to the contest site.

☐   9. Pack game equipment and assign student manager to guard the baggage. Include first aid supplies.

☐   10. Load equipment, inventory items.

☐   11. Load athletic team personnel, check roster.

☐   12. Check team personnel before leaving each stop.

☐   13. Unload equipment and personnel at contest site.

☐   14. Contact host staff immediately on arrival.

☐   15. Assign student manager to guard clothing and equipment during the contest.

☐   16. Have travel vehicle prepared to leave immediately after the contest.

☐   17. Secure the contract payment from the host school.

☐   18. Account for equipment and personnel before departure.

☐   19. Account for equipment and personnel on arrival.

☐   20. Write courtesy follow-up letter to the host school.

tions of strategy by opponents. In spite of this, coaches commonly use scouting reports as the basis for game preparation. The rationale used to justify the expensive and time-consuming practice of scouting is reactive: "I know that they are scouting us, so we had better scout them." Scouting could be eliminated or minimized by trading game films with schools who play mutual opponents. If scouting is to be used in the athletic program, the following principles should be observed:

1. Scout each opponent only once.
2. Scout only official contests—never scout practice sessions.
3. Scout two future opponents at once when possible.
4. Pay car mileage for scouting trips.
5. Provide passes for visiting scouts (the high school athletic association pass is usually sufficient).

Travel to Contests

Special planning and organizing is necessary for the management of contests played away from home. Management details include coordination of personnel, equipment, and supporters. The checklist shown in Figure 5.8 can be used to insure that all details have been attended to.

Transportation

Since a teacher is individually liable for injury to students while transporting students, it is mandatory that a bonded and insured common carrier be used for out-of-town trips. Charter bus transportation is best for moving the team, the band, and supporting spectators. An alternative method is to employ a certified driver to drive a school-owned or driver-owned bus. In any case, players should not make out-of-town trips in personal automobiles. The state athletic association generally requires that a coach accompany the players on athletic trips. Adult volunteer drivers may have a "guest" or "guest passenger" rider temporarily attached to their basic liability insurance for one or more trips. A guest is a nonpaying rider, whereas a passenger is defined as a paying rider.

Trip Schedule

An itinerary is necessary for parents and for official school information. The time and place of departure, the destination, and the time and place of return will suffice for short trips. More detailed information, including restaurants and lodging sites, is necessary for overnight trips. Mimeographing the itinerary for each parent is good public relations.

Vital Records

The official player roster should be validated before the trip. Eligibility records, parental permission slips, and the game contract should be in the possession of the head coach.

Expense Payment

A withdrawal from the school athletic account should be made to pay expenses for the trip. Expense vouchers must be secured from restaurants and hotels showing the nature and amount of expenses.

Equipment

The student manager should have a checklist of equipment actually needed for travel. Game clothing, towels, playing equipment, and the training kit should be packed and labeled prior to loading. A student manager should be assigned as security agent to stay with the equipment at all times.

Auxiliary Personnel

Tickets for auxiliary personnel should be secured by agreement well in advance of the contest. The band and supporters may travel in a caravan with the players. Details for seating the band and supporters in a group and the time delegated for band performance should be finalized weeks before the trip.

Home Contests

Responsibility for preparing for athletic contests is delegated to the host school. Correctly preparing the site, securing certified officials, handling advance publicity and ticket sales, and procuring a security staff are among the host coordinator's duties. The process of conducting a tournament is described in detail in Chapter 9. Specific items may be delegated as shown in Figure 5.9.

Preparing the Site

The site for the athletic contest must be safe and all components in good working order. The stands must be regularly inspected for safety. The playing surface must be free of obstacles, or existing protrusions must be padded to prevent injury. Public address systems and score boards should be checked prior to the date of the game. Rest rooms should be cleaned and unlocked for use. It is desirable to designate responsibility for preparing the site to a maintenance worker and to provide a detailed checklist.

Courtesy Service

Two weeks prior to the game, both schools should exchange player lists and publicity information. The visiting school should also receive ticket information, ceremonial procedure information, names of the officials, and directions to the playing site. Upon the arrival of the visiting team, a student manager of the host school should be assigned to help the visiting team with incidental needs. The visiting team members are guests, not the enemy!

Ticket Sales

Since most interschool athletic programs depend on gate receipts for funding, ticket sales should be handled in a business-like manner. Tickets for each season's games should be printed in quantity before the season. Tickets of different colors can be used to differentiate reserve sections from general admission. Advance ticket sales may be conducted at a special discount price to eliminate long lines at the ticket booths on the day of the game. Of course, no more tickets should be sold than there is seating capacity in the facility. Reconciliation of the accounts with bank deposit slips should be made soon after each game.

Security

News stories frequently describe player and spectator fights during or after athletic contests. Of course, every seasoned official will have made preparations for a quick departure after the game is over. However, some of the players and spectators must be protected from rampant emotions. Where problems are foreseen, the game may be rescheduled for an afternoon; in extreme cases, the contest may be played without spectators.

Ushers should direct ticket holders to the appropriate seating area. Correctly seated spectators are more easily managed than a milling crowd of fans. Youth clubs and service clubs may provide ushers. Uniformed police officers should be present both inside and outside the playing facility. If the local municipal government will not furnish officers free of charge, the school must secure their services on a paid basis. Ticket-takers are essential personnel in the security system, since they are in a position to screen incoming fans for potential troublemakers.

Publicity

The athletic program must have good publicity to assure community support. Sports information must be accurate. Timing the press releases well in advance of contests gives the news editors an opportunity to plan their own sports coverage. All news media in the community should receive equal treatment, and the same

Tasks	Principal	Athletic director	Head coach	Assistant coach	Student manager	Custodian	Other
				Responsibility Delegated to			
Game contract		X					
Prepare team roster			X				
Verify eligibility of players	X						
Arrange for uniformed security	X						
Confirm details with visiting school		X					
Advertise contest		X					
Sell tickets	X						
Secure admission, gate keeper		X					
Prepare contest area (lines, etc.)				X		X	
Prepare for concession sales	X						X
Clean and open comfort stations						X	
Prepare first aid supplies					X		

| TASKS | RESPONSIBILITY DELEGATED TO | | | | | | |
	Principal	Athletic director	Head coach	Assistant coach	Student manager	Custodian	Other
Courtesy service to visiting team					X		
Turn lights on and off						X	
Open and close playing area						X	
Spectator disruption	X		X				
Accounting for concession and gate receipts	X	X					

Figure 5.9 A checklist for conducting home athletic contests.

information should be supplied to all agencies. Chapter 11 describes the fundamentals of public relations. The overall plan for game publicity should be cleared through the school administration.

Game reporting has long been used for publicity, but it is also a possible source of revenue for athletic programs. Court cases have established the authority of school districts to sell the publicity rights to athletic contests. (See Mohler and Bolmeir 1968). Designation of a radio carrier may be based on bids or on a contract. News media feel slighted if they do not receive game reports following the contest. Prompt reporting of game results increases the probability of news exposure. Out-of-town contests can be reported to local radio stations by telephone soon after the contest.

Case Example: ACTUALIZING INTERSCHOOL ATHLETICS

Midwest City High School has won the right to attend the state girls' basketball championship tournament. The team must travel two hundred miles to the tournament site. If the team is successful in reaching the finals, the staff and players must be lodged and fed for four days. Many of the local fans and school students wish to accompany the team. You are the head basketball coach. How do you answer the following questions:

1. What staff members and players should attend as official school representatives?
2. What factors should be included in the trip schedule—itinerary, cost estimates?
3. What additional permissions or waivers are needed?
4. What method of transportation should be used?
5. How should the trip be financed? Who should carry the money advanced for the trip?

Controlling

Operating control in interschool athletics is among the most critical of all school programs. The large cashflow and the emotions due to psychological identification with the team's fate demand constant monitoring. The athletic associations previously discussed provide a basis for planning and control. Quantitative evaluation usually has less significance for athletics than for the physical and health instruction program. Some typical management objectives for athletic program controls are:

to identify factors critical to cashflow and equipment management

to develop a safety program for interschool athletics

to describe the problem of game officiating and provide a strategy for improving local officiating in sports that do not produce revenue

to identify some of the major problems in management of interschool athletics

Resources Management

Funds derived from gate receipts are public funds, even though they may be earmarked for the athletic program. The financial agent, usually the athletic director, head coach, or principal, must be circumspect in all financial affairs. Any staff member handling significant sums of money should be bonded, the bond being paid by the school district. See Chapter 7 for methods of controlling cashflow.

Financial Audit

An audit is a thorough financial review conducted by a certified accountant. The final audit includes an analysis of income and expenditures and ends with a summary statement of fiscal health. Every athletic program should have a yearly audit. The audit results should be published in newspapers or in the form of a newsletter to all interested parties. A detailed audit dispels suspicions about the use of athletic funds.

Inventory

Athletic equipment is expensive. The philosophy of allowing players to keep athletic equipment places improper emphasis. It is a privilege and honor to represent the school in sports—allowing students to keep equipment implies partial payment for playing. From jerseys to socks, every item of school equipment must be worn only for official practice or contests.

Student managers must be impressed with the necessity of daily property control. Every ball that is used must be accounted for at the end of practice. The final inventory at the end of each sport season should include an analysis of equipment and its condition. Athletes who do not account for equipment should have their grades withheld at the end of the school term until a correct accounting is made. Chapter 7 describes inventory methods and the care of athletic equipment.

Figure 5.10 When deposited in the school athletic account, funds raised by booster clubs become "public" and must be accounted for as if they were tax funds.

"It's from the booster club, men — they say
they're behind us 100 per cent . . . win or tie"

Ol' Coach Publications, © 1966 by Ray Franks Publishing Ranch

Safety

The school may be held liable for the safety of players and spectators. Architectural design and maintenance of facilities must provide for the safety of spectators. Mass sports entertainment produces large gate receipts, but safety problems increase with the number of spectators. While the overall safety of spectators and players is a control operation, much planning, organizing, and actualizing are required. Legal liability is described in Chapter 10, and Chapter 7 gives more details on facilities management.

Crowd Control

The AAHPER (1970) has published an excellent booklet dealing with crowd control at athletic events. Each athletic department should study the facilities in order to develop a standard operating procedure for spectator management. Some renovation of facilities may be required to eliminate problem areas. Basic procedures for crowd control include:

1. adequate lighting of parking lots and areas adjacent to the playing fields
2. uniformed police officers inside and outside the athletic facility
3. separate seating for supporters of the two teams
4. planned spectator flow into and out of the seating area
5. banning alcoholic beverages and mechanical noisemakers
6. having ticket-takers at the gates to watch for "street fighting" weapons
7. use of barriers to separate spectators from playing areas
8. continuous emphasis on sportsmanship during the school term
9. giving free faculty passes to encourage faculty attendance at athletic events
10. playing restful music over the public address system after the contest. Some schools provide a thirty-minute band concert after major sports events.

Medical Care

Competent care of injured spectators and players will eliminate many liability suits. A physician should be present at all contests in contact sports. Many physicians are sports enthusiasts and would serve as the team physician if asked to do so—or the job may be rotated among volunteers. The physician's fee should be based on insurance claims from the student group insurance policy. The team physician can also instruct the student trainers in routine first aid. Approved equipment for transporting fractures should be purchased and carried to the playing area for all contests in contact sports. Since there may be a large number of junior high schools and high schools playing contact sports during a week, having a physician at each game may be impossible. In such cases, standard

Figure 5.11 Facilities must be planned for the rapid exit of spectators and must prevent entry to the playing field.

Ed Keren, I. O. E.

emergency procedures must be rehearsed by the trainer and coaching staff under the initial direction of a physician. A local hospital with a full-time emergency room is the alternative to a physician on the site. Chapter 10 describes preventive safety procedures and includes a standard form for reporting accidents.

Officiating

Securing competent officials is seldom difficult if there are ample funds to pay the fee. State high school athletic associations train and assign officials for such revenue-producing activities as football and basketball. Sports that do not produce large gate receipts may have greater difficulty in securing competent officials. High school track and field meets seldom have paid officials for managing all the events. Track coaches must depend on volunteers and friends. The state athletic association provides forms for evaluating game officials.

Schurr and Phillips (1971) present an analysis of personality factors in sports officials with the intent of identifying those characteristics that are associated with effective officiating. Recommendations are made for the recruitment and training of women officials to call athletic contests. Johnson (1971) states that competent gymnastic judges for high school meets are hard to find. He points out that local groups can be successfully formed for training in officiating specific sports like gymnastics. Wrestling, gymnastics, diving, and track and field are sports in which local training programs may be needed. Training should include knowledge of rules, case interpretation, and considerable field work under various conditions. Several training officials' films are available from the National Federation of State High School Associations.

Evaluation

The sports fan and sports writer continuously evaluate the interschool athletic program. Spectator evaluation is usually based on superficials—winning games and producing star athletes to play in the university conferences. Booster clubs are often highly vocal about team performance. If the principal and coaching staff are not committed to educational goals, they may be caught up in the flood of pressures that would subjugate athletics to community entertainment. Although community input is desirable for program evaluation, professional educators must perform the evaluation process. The projected program outcomes cited in the first part of this chapter should be compared to program realities. Outcomes must be described qualitatively and quantitatively for communitywide publication.

The AAHPER (1973) has produced a tool for evaluation of the interscholastic athletic program. This manual contains an evaluation instrument and recommended standards for the high school sports program. Student outcomes, coaching staff performance, and overall program effectiveness must be considered each year when the program is evaluated. The principal and athletic director share responsibility for program outcomes. A short program evaluation form is included in the Student Guide. Uses of the evaluation data depend upon the research findings. Counseling procedures for low-producing staff members are described in Chapter 8. Open discussion of program evaluation data and plans for improvement should be a function of the athletic department staff.

Problem Areas

Interschool athletics has more than its share of difficult problems. The community wants a winning sports program—without realizing that nobody goes through life as a 100% winner. Emotional identification with the team is illustrated when the sports fan says, "When a player gets tackled, I get tackled. When a player catches a pass, I catch a pass!" Some identification is healthy, but blind identification can lead to spectator fights. Some of the critical problems in athletic programs are cited in the Student Guide.

Program Diversification

The tendency in high school athletics is to focus emphasis on few sports. Typically, emphasis is placed on team sports. Program convergence makes it

Figure 5.12 Officials for swimming and track and field meets are usually semitrained recruits and volunteers.

Terry McKoy, I. O. E.

Southeastern Louisiana University

impossible to serve many students whose talents and interests do not lie in team sports with mass spectator appeal. Ways must be sought to fund sports representing a wide range of student interests. Rugby, soccer, volleyball, archery, badminton, golf, bowling, and tennis are a few of the alternative sports appropriate for the high school level. (See also Chapter 4 for a description of club sports.)

Women's Sports

Interschool athletic competition for women has been as badly neglected as the individual sports program. Because of the recent Title IX guidelines of the United States Department of Health, Education and Welfare, schools receiving federal funds can no longer discriminate against girls in athletic programs. If girls desire to have an interschool athletic program, the school must provide the faculty leadership if a similar program for boys exists. Noncontact sport teams may be sexually integrated. Definite answers to questions about providing separate all-girl and all-boy teams need to be legally clarified via test cases. As shown in the Harres (1968) study, the sample population was generally favorable to women's athletics, and there were no significant differences between the attitudes of men and women toward women's sports. Funding an extensive girls' and boys' program is a problem. Inequities in the number of girls' coaches and the number of boys' coaches will inevitably be litigated. The problem of equitable payment for girls' and boys' coaches can be resolved by using a formula that includes: (1) the length of the sport season; (2) the type of sport; and (3) the number of athletes in the sport.

Drug Abuse

Keelor (1972) writes about the realities of drug abuse in high school athletics. Because of the "winning syndrome" that permeates contemporary society, some coaches have used growth stimulants, pain killers, and behavior stimulants to heighten athletic performance. Individual high school players often hear rumors about outstanding professionals who reportedly use behavior-modifying drugs. Without consultation from physician or coach, players sometimes take dangerous drugs to improve their athletic performance. Not only must the coach refrain from abusing drugs to get better athletic performance, but the coach must also counsel with all players about use of unprescribed drugs. Recognizing that drug abuse is a symptom of personality problems is the first step in remediation. Individual counseling is highly recommended. The tendency immediately to inform the parent must be resisted—it would constitute a betrayal of student trust and could alienate the parent as well. After counseling is under way, the coach can bring the student and parent together to solve their problem.

Ethical Behavior

Although much lip service is paid to the objective of ethical character development in interschool athletics, it is an objective that is not often achieved. With a note of levity, a coach with a losing season frequently retorts, "This year we are working on character development." Obviously, some coaches are better behavior models than others. Significant ethical character development can be achieved through the sports medium. However, several objective studies have shown that the development of ethical character is not consistently accomplished in interschool athletics. Crawford (1957) reported over one thousand incidents of ethically critical sports behavior. Kistler (1957) reported a significant problem in school sports whereby athletes projected the "win at all costs" attitude. Richardson (1962) also reported that athletes in his sample approved the practice of taking unfair advantage of an opponent if they could "get by with it." Ogilvie and Tutko (1971) studied over 15,000 athletes. Their conclusion? "If you want to build character try something else."

The state high school athletic association takes a firm stand on the sportsmanship issue. Schools violating the sportsmanship code are often censured by suspension or probation. However, many insidious acts of illegal behavior that are taught to players go unnoticed in games. If ethical character is to be developed in athletics, the "win at all costs" philosophy must be opposed by school administrators and coaches. Attitude changes can be produced by (1) display of a consistent behavior model; (2) group discussion of critical issues, reaching a consensus for behavior; and (3) reinforcement of behavior changes.

Awards

Athletic awards are extrinsic motivators. State high school athletic associations make specific recommendations about the type and value of athletic awards. Cash awards are barred. Athletes who receive cash other than for legitimate travel expenses violate their amateur status. Jacket or sweater awards should not be presented before the sport season is over. Only one award should be given in any one year. Each school must devise its own criteria for lettering in a sport. The various systems include: (1) recommendation of the coaching staff; (2) playing a minimum number of minutes during conference games—for team sports; and (3) placing in conference meets or tournaments—for individual sports.

Case Example: CONTROLLING THE INTERSCHOOL ATHLETIC PROGRAM

Midwest City High School recently played a football game as home team against Santo Domingo High School. Considerable rivalry, with overtones of racial conflict, has been evident for several years. Much unnecessary roughness was displayed as soon as the game began. The pile-ups took longer and longer to untangle; punching and gouging were seen in the entanglements. A few penalties were assessed by the officials as they tried to cool flaring tempers. During the last quarter, the football game resembled a team wrestling match. Both coaches were marching along the sidelines wildly gesturing to the officials and generally inciting the spectators. The game ended in a tie score.

The principals of both schools filed protests with the state athletic association seeking the opponent's disqualification in the critical district contest. The executive board of the athletic association has scheduled a hearing. As the athletic director, you have tried to analyze the causes of the melee. Assuming that your school is not disqualified from further season play, what preventive measures must be taken to insure that the same thing does not occur in subsequent contests?

References

AAHPER. *Crowd Control for High School Athletics.* American Association for Health, Physical Education and Recreation, Washington, D.C., 1970.

AAHPER. *Drugs and the Coach.* American Association for Health, Physical Education and Recreation, Washington, D.C., 1972.

AAHPER. *Evaluating the High School Athletic Program.* American Association for Health, Physical Education and Recreation, Washington, D.C., 1973.

ALLEY, L. E. "Athletics in Education, the Double-edged Sword." *Phi Delta Kappan,* 56 (1974), 102–105, 113.

AMERICAN SCHOOL BOARDS ASSOCIATION. "What Interscholastic Sports are Really Costing You." *American School Board Journal,* 162 (1975), 19–20.

BAKJIAN, A. "Operating a Massive City Sports Program." *Scholastic Coach,* 37 (1968), 49.

BLACKBURN, R. T., and M. S. NYIKES. "College Football and Mr. Chips." *Phi Delta Kappan,* 56 (1974), 110–113.

BLAUFARB, M. "Retrospect on a Year of Title IX Discussions." *Update,* February 1975.

BOWERMAN, W. *Coaching Track and Field.* Houghton Mifflin Company, Boston, 1974.

BROUN, H. H. "The 1984 Olympics." *Newsweek,* 81 (March 5, 1973), 13.

BUCHER, C. A. "Athletic Competition and the Developmental Growth Pattern." *The Physical Educator,* 28 (1971), 3–4.

BULA, M. R. "Competition for Children: The Real Issue." *JOHPER,* 42 (1971), 40.

COUSY, B., and F. G. POWER, JR. *Basketball: Concepts and Techniques.* Allyn and Bacon, Boston, 1970.

CRAWFORD, M. M. "Critical Incidents in Intercollegiate Athletics and Derived Standards for Professional Ethics." Unpublished Ed.D. dissertation, University of Texas, 1957.

DOWELL, L. J. "Environmental Factors of Childhood Competitive Athletics." *The Physical Educator,* 28 (1971), 17–21.

ESSLINGER, A. A. "Certification for High School Coaches." *JOHPER,* 39 (1968), 42.

FORSYTHE, C. E., and I. A. KELLER. *Administration of High School Athletics,* 5th ed. Prentice-Hall, Englewood Cliffs, N.J., 1972.

GALLON, A. J. *Coaching: Ideas and Ideals.* Houghton Mifflin Company, Boston, 1974.

GOULD, D. *Tennis Anyone?* 2d ed. National Press Books, Palo Alto, Calif., 1971.

HARRES, B. "Attitudes of Students toward Women's Athletic Competition." *Research Quarterly,* 39 (1968), 278–284.

JOHNSON, M. "Providing Qualified Gymnastic Judges." *The Physical Educator,* 28 (1971), 32–33.

KEELOR, R. O. "The Realities of Drug Abuse in High School Athletics." *JOHPER*, 43 (1972), 48–49.

KISTLER, J. W. "Attitudes Expressed about Behavior Demonstrated in Certain Specific Situations Occurring in Sports." *Sixtieth Annual Proceedings of the College Physical Education Association*, 1957.

KOCHERA, R. W. "Your Manager—the Forgotten Man in Sports." *The Physical Educator*, 28 (1971), 93.

LENAGHAN, J. M., and R. E. PHAY. "Individual Liability of School Board Members and School Administrators." *School Law Bulletin*, 4 (1973), 1–6.

LEVITT, S. "The Limitation of Training: Some Implications for Physical Educators." *The Physical Educator*, 30 (1973), 89–90.

LINEBERRY, W. P., ed. *The Business of Sports*. The H. W. Wilson Company, New York, 1973.

LOWMAN, C. L. "A Consideration of Teenage Athletics." *JOHPER*, 12 (1941), 398–399.

MAETOZO, M. G., ed. *Certification of High School Coaches*. American Association for Health, Physical Education and Recreation, Washington, D.C., 1971.

MOHLER, J. D., and E. C. BOLMEIER. *Law of Extracurricular Activities in Secondary Schools*. The W. H. Anderson Company, Cincinnati, 1968.

NFSHSA. *Official Handbook*. National Federation of State High School Associations, Elgin, Ill., 1972–1973.

OGILVIE, B. C., and T. A. TUTKO. "Sport: If You Want to Build Character, Try Something Else." *Psychology Today*, 5 (1971), 61–63.

OWENS, L. E. "Principles of Scheduling." *The Physical Educator*, 27 (1970), 18.

PATERNO, J. "How to Save Intercollegiate Athletics." *Phi Delta Kappan*, 56 (1974), 106–109.

PORTER, C. M. "The Coach as a Character Builder." *The Physical Educator*, 29 (1972), 36–37.

RALSTON, J., and M. WHITE. *Coaching Today's Athlete: A Football Textbook*. National Press Books, Palo Alto, Calif., 1971.

RESICK, M. C., B. L. SEIDEL, and J. G. MASON. *Modern Administrative Practices in Physical Education and Athletics*. Addison-Wesley Publishing Company, Reading, Mass., 1975.

RICHARDSON, D. E. "Ethical Conduct in Sports Situations." *60th Annual Proceedings of National College Physical Education Association*, 1962.

SABOCK, R. J. *The Coach*, W. B. Saunders Company, Philadelphia, 1973.

SCHURR, E. L., and J. A. PHILLIPS. "Women Sports Officials." *JOHPER*, 42 (1971), 71–72.

TAYLOR, J. L. "Intromurals: A Program for Everyone." *JOHPER*, 44 (1973), 44–45.

TUTKO, T. A., and J. W. RICHARDS. *Psychology of Coaching*. Allyn and Bacon, Boston, 1971.

WERNER, P. "The Role of Physical Education in Gender Identification." *The Physical Educator*, 29 (1972), 27–28.

6.

SCHOOL

HEALTH

PROGRAM

After reading this chapter, each student should be able to:

Identify the major health problems in contemporary society.

Plan a school health instruction program.

Relate systems management to health education.

Develop a strategy to involve students in solving community health problems.

195

If health education is viewed as a response to a real problem, the question "Why health instruction?" becomes rhetorical. Even in technologically advanced countries, hazards to health abound, some actually side effects of the progress that has freed us from the epidemic illnesses of past centuries and undeveloped countries today. Politicians, scientists, educators, and laymen rally behind environmental and health causes. Pressure groups demand legislation to improve our quality of life—and to insure that coming generations will have a chance to survive. Health has become not only a national objective, but a national and international imperative as well.

The Scope of School Health

The purpose of the school health program should be to supply health information, encourage good health habits, and foster positive attitudes about health. The three constructs of information, habits, and attitudes are within the domain of the instructional program. The child does not live in a world of ideas, however, but in the real world of family, school, and neighborhood. One community health worker aptly stated the problem of a disadvantaged child when she said

> There is little use in trying to remove intestinal worms from a child in the restroom, or of only teaching him about intestinal parasites in the classroom. The child is infected because his parents do not practice good health habits, such as changing bed linens regularly, washing hands after defecation, etc. Everyone in the whole neighborhood is infected and just worming one is not going to stop the problem.

Obviously, health problems call for a multiphasic approach. Health instruction must be augmented by school health services and a healthful school environment.

School Health Services

Teachers are in closer contact with students, on a long-term basis, than any other professional public worker. The classroom teacher makes daily informal observations of the student. Abnormal health conditions should be obvious to the teacher, because frequent prior observations have provided a base line for comparing day-to-day changes. Therefore, the first line of school health services should be preliminary evaluation by classroom teachers. Subsequent follow-up or systematic screening of all students may be provided by the school or county health team. Adequate records must be kept in a central office to prevent omission and duplication. School health services include both appraisal and preventive programs.

Health Appraisal

Obviously, it would be more desirable to prevent diseases and disorders than to wait until they occur and then apply the cure. It is especially critical that athletes be examined by a physician before participation in sports. Health appraisal means professional medical services supplied by physicians and public health workers. The classroom teacher, the health teacher, and the school nurse are not licensed to diagnose conditions and prescribe medications. After screening, recommendations should be made to the parents about the student's condition and the necessity of seeking medical attention. Some procedures for identifying health problems in a systematic screening program are described in the following paragraphs. See also Willgoose (1974).

Vision Screening. The Snellen test for visual acuity is widely used because of its speed and simplicity. The test can be administered in about one minute, with reasonably valid results. It is helpful for the subject to know the alphabet and the concepts of up, down, right, and left before taking the test.

Auditory Screening. Screening tests for the ability to hear can be administered to an entire class at one time. The conversation voice-level test and the whisper voice-level test can be used to spot problem cases. All students suspected of having hearing problems should be further tested with a puretone audiometer. Hypersensitivity and deafness both occur within the normal school environment.

Health Screening. Overall health screening should be conducted yearly. Some schools require all students to have a medical examination before the beginning of the fall term. If a school does not have such a policy, someone in the system needs to be appointed to screen the students for health problems. The school cumulative health report should be a standardized form (see Figure 6.1) including student's name, age, and address; height and weight; overall body appearance; visual and auditory acuity; record of diseases and immunizations; skin condition; dental condition; and posture.

Preventive Services

The old adage "An ounce of prevention is worth a pound of cure" is certainly true in health. Untold human misery has been caused by failure to take simple, commonly known precautions to avoid serious illness. Immunization and diet are two special preventive health procedures that should be included in school health services. These services are cited here to provide the health teacher with an overall program perspective.

HEALTH APPRAISAL REPORT

(School referral to medical professions)

Student's name _____ Date _____

Address _____

_____ Phone _____

    The following conditions have been observed in the above named student. Apparently, further attention is needed by medical professionals. (Descriptive notes have been made by the school health worker.)

Dental _____

Disease or infestation _____

_____

Emotional _____

_____

Hearing _____

Vision _____

Heart and circulation _____

_____

Nutrition _____

_____

Orthopedic _____

_____

Respiration _____

_____

Skin _____

_____

Other _____

_____

_____

Signed _____

(school health worker)

Address _____

Figure 6.1 A standardized form for health status reporting.

Immunization Program. Only through mass public immunization of every generation can contagious diseases be stopped. Because school attendance is compulsory, the logical place for immunization of each generation is in the school. County medical teams or the school nurse should perform the immunization, and each initial shot and booster shot should be recorded on the student's permanent school health record.

School Lunch Program. School lunch programs were originally instituted to give students a nutritionally balanced meal daily. In recent times the concept has been extended to include breakfast meals for selected students. Meal content has been standardized by federal regulations sent from the Department of Agriculture to the various states. For an example of school lunch regulations, see Nutrition and Technical Services Staff (1974).

Healthful School Environment

Since students spend so much time in school buildings, the school environment should be at least as healthful as the home environment. Most states have structural and health standards that must be met by architects designing public buildings. School facilities should also be attractive and conducive to learning. Some health issues in the school environment are discussed in the following paragraphs. See also Willgoose (1974).

Lighting

The lighting should be of a sufficient intensity to allow comfortable reading at a normal distance. Natural light coming from the side or from behind the student should be augmented by artificial light. Burned-out bulbs should be reported or replaced immediately to minimize eye strain. Halls require fewer footcandles because close reading is seldom done there.

Sanitation

There is no excuse for an unsanitary restroom, classroom, shower room, or drinking fountain. Systematic cleaning and disinfecting procedures must be planned and executed. Chemicals should be sprayed monthly throughout the building to combat insects and rodents. Few things are more upsetting in a learning environment than unsanitary conditions.

Safety Procedures

School safety begins with correct building design and preventive maintenance. Identifying and eliminating attractive but nonessential hazards are also basic safety precautions. Standard operating procedures worked out and practiced *before* any emergency are necessary to guard against local dangers. Fire evacuation routes must be defined and fire drills conducted for students. In areas where tornados are frequent, drill procedures must be practiced until students fully understand the procedure. The local Civil Defense office can be an aid to school safety.

Health Instruction

The question "What information is of most value to the learner?" must be posed continuously by the health educator. With technical information exploding at a geometric rate, concepts presented to students must be weighed for importance and relevance. Furthermore, the learner cannot be viewed as merely the consumer of information. Learners remember, they feel, and they respond with overt behavior. The successful health education program takes every opportunity and creates others to involve students in the learning context. Educators must supply information about health, and they must offer their students opportunities to put good health habits into practice. The more meaningful such practice and the more it makes sense to the students, the more likely they are to carry good health habits into their unsupervised, personal lives.

Value Modification

Clarification and modification of the student's value structure are the most important goals of school health instruction. While no absolutely accurate means of predicting behavior exists, an individual's *value system* generally plays a greater part in determining behavior than what *information* the individual may be able to recall. The relationship between drug information and drug abuse is a good example. As pointed out by Zazzaro (1973), there is convincing evidence that school drug information programs actually interest students in trying drugs by arousing their curiosity. Health education programs that do not accomplish value clarification and value modification are likely to have little behavioral impact on students. Rucker, Arnspiger, and Brodbeck (1969) and Hamin, Kirschenbaum, and Simon (1973) amplify the value concept.

Health Information

All the traditional, statistics-oriented approaches to health education are irrelevant. Certainly accurate information is necessary, but health instruction must be more than an attempt to transmit information from one mind to another. Health education acquaints students with the causes of health problems, their characteristics, and various solutions. Armed with correct information and clear values, students should be more capable of making the choices that will benefit themselves and society. Thus health information complements and provides a rationale for the practice of good health habits.

Misconceptions about health problems are widespread among student and adult populations. Even though more is known about all health problems than ever before, research information is not automatically assimilated by student or adult populations. Health education should function to interpret scientific findings to everyone.

Case Example: SCHOOL HEALTH

After a health screening program, several notes were sent home to parents of children who showed symptoms of intestinal parasite infection. Several irate parents called the school principal to complain that their child had "picked up pinworms at school." Protesting that they had washed, fumigated, and medicated to prevent infection or reinfection within their own households, they demanded that something be done within the school to eliminate the student infection.

The principal confers with you, the health teacher, about the problem. The health screening program has identified a health problem that is now causing a public relations problem for the school. The principal asks you to develop a solution. See also Allensworth (1975).

1. What additional screening and referrals are recommended?
2. Will public health workers be contacted to develop a communitywide strategy?
3. How will the public relations problem be handled?

Planning

The curriculum product is inextricably tied to the process by which it is derived. Classroom-level administrative philosophy predicts not only how the curriculum plan will be developed, but also how the instruction will be actualized. For example, a classical authoritarian health teacher would select all the topics for presentation to the students and present them in factual lectures. Conversely, the teacher committed to participatory management would lean heavily on student needs as the basis for structuring the health curriculum. Local health teachers must be involved in planning the health curriculum for the schools in the school system. Curriculum planners must chart a course that (1) observes state regulations; (2) provides adequate coverage of essential health problems; and (3) satisfies student needs and interests. Some management objectives for administrative planning of health instruction are:

to identify the major health needs and interests of a school population
to devise a systematic program of instruction to meet these student needs
to develop a strategy for bringing administrators, consultants, interested citizens, and health educators into planning the health curriculum

Figure 6.2 The health curriculum is usually balanced between what the students think they need and what the teacher thinks they need.

Program Planning

Curriculum planning must be a continuous process. Schools that meet the needs of the students best are able to do so because they continuously monitor the needs and interests of the student and the local social order. However, curriculum planning is not always successful. State and local curriculum guides may be filed away in a drawer if the teacher does not understand the documents or thinks they are irrelevant.

State-Level Curriculum

Time allotments for academic credit and minimum standards of instructional quality should be established for all the state schools, with supervision and enforcement supplied by the state. In order to set acceptable standards, the state office of education should bring together representative health educators from all over the state at least every five years. This committee should produce and evaluate an instructional guide for use by local personnel in local curriculum planning. Since the local school principal controls the quality of school health instruction, a state health instruction guide is helpful in defining the program to local administrators. On page 203, Cornacchia describes a curriculum conference established on a broad base. Physicians, administrators, and politicians were included in the conference work group, as well as health instructors.

Local Planning

The first step in assuring relevancy of the health curriculum is to bring local teachers into the planning group. There are two major advantages of using local teachers as the primary work group. First, the local health teacher knows the

GUIDELINES FOR SECONDARY SCHOOL HEALTH EDUCATION

Health educators agree it is necessary to reach the school superintendent to improve health education programs. The superintendent or administrative head of a school district is the key to sound instructional programs. Over the years, attempts to reach top school officials have met with limited success. Perhaps the lack of results was because health educators talked to themselves or did little to actually involve administrators. Superintendents have not always been interested, supportive, or well-informed regarding the nature and organization of appropriate or adequate health instruction programs. However, in recent years, administrators have become more concerned with health because they have been confronted in their schools with a variety of health problems of youth such as venereal disease, drug abuse, smoking, teenage pregnancies, and teen-age promiscuity. These problems have often resulted in community pressures for health education programs which have not always been identified as such.

Capitalizing on this favorable atmosphere, a conference of selected educational leaders, including twelve secondary school principals, nine physicians, three school board members, seven health educators, and two professors of education administration was recently convened for two days. School representation came from school districts of varying sizes, geographically distributed. The purpose of the meeting was to develop administrative guidelines for secondary school health education for California schools that would aid in increasing the quality of instructional programs.

As a follow-up to the guidelines that were developed, plans are now under way to (1) obtain formal adoption by the various organizations that sponsored the conference and (2) conduct state regional meetings of school administrators and school board members for implementation.

H. J. Cornacchia, "Guidelines for Secondary School Health Education," *School Health Review*, (1969), 22–24.

situation, the school, the students, the administrators, and the facilities. Second, success of the instructional program depends on the local teacher, and involvement of individual teachers in a group curriculum project tends to foster professional attitudes. Classic studies by Asch (1958) and Sherif (1958) demonstrate the effectiveness of the group decision-making process in attitude formation.

In order to assure that the various health teachers will do more than share their own insights, provision must be made to include outside consultants. As actual group members, consultants can share their experiences and in turn be challenged to respond to the local situation. Consultants may include such persons as physicians, nurses, law-enforcement officers, public health workers, school administrators, curriculum experts, and outstanding health educators.

Teachers in a curriculum work group can accomplish tasks impossible for the individual teacher. Coordination between schools and between grade levels is possible only when health problems are viewed all the way from the elementary school through the high school level. Basic concepts introduced at the lower levels should be reinforced and expanded throughout the formal school program. A comprehensive curriculum guide functions to coordinate instructional effort between schools at the same level and from one grade level to other grade levels. The major topics and subtopics previously identified are arranged in ascending sequential order. Grade placement of subtopics must be coordinated with students' developmental characteristics.

A curriculum guide is a document that defines the objectives, content, teaching methods, and resources pertinent to a field of study. The health curriculum guide should include the following items:

1. nature and purpose of the health instruction program
2. general and behavioral objectives projected for the program
3. developmental characteristics of the learners
4. flow chart of health curriculum topics and subtopics applicable for the various grade levels
5. definition of specific content to be learned
6. suggested methods for teaching various concepts (confrontation techniques, etc.)
7. alternative methods of illustrating or exploring the subject matter (smoking machine, etc.)

Behavioral objectives are useful for prespecifying terminal outcomes. Mager's (1962) method of writing objectives facilitates evaluation of student performance. A partial list of behavioral objectives for a sanitation unit in the various grade

Table 3   *An example of behavioral objectives for health instruction*

Grade Level	Behavioral Objectives for the Sanitation Concept
Senior high	1. To be able to identify local sources of environmental pollution. 2. To be able to utilize liquid and solid waste materials that can be recycled.
Junior high	1. To be able to sanitarily dispose of body waste in an emergency situation. 2. To be able to decontaminate food prior to serving.
Elementary	1. To be able to describe the process of water purification. 2. To be able to describe the ecological cycle of the biosphere.
Primary	1. To be able to cleanse hands and fingers of possible contaminants. 2. To be able to sanitarily defecate and urinate.

levels appears in Table 3. See Willgoose (1974) for a comprehensive list of behaviorally stated health instruction objectives.

Assessing Student Needs

The present and long-term needs of students should define the health curriculum. It is common for teachers to select program content from lists provided in textbooks and/or research reports. Some supervisors continue to tell their teachers to "teach the book" as if its distant author had a mystical insight into local school needs. The truth is that no one knows local health needs as well as the students and their teacher. Though some stimulation is sometimes needed to get them to assess their problems, students readily admit their own and society's needs in an accepting atmosphere. Since society changes, student needs also change. Curriculum planners must be sensitive to nuances of student and societal change.

Student needs can be assessed by administering a needs questionnaire to a reasonable sample of the population affected by the curriculum (see the questionnaire in the Student Guide). Since not all students know their needs, it is also beneficial to administer an omnibus health information test to the student population. Results of the needs questionnaire and the information test can be compared to determine areas of real need. The framework for the health course should be set up in the curriculum guide. Through follow-up discussion with each class, individual health teachers can determine the type and extent of the best health unit for their students. The report by Byler, Lewis, and Totman (1969) entitled *Teach Us What We Want to Know* has broad implications for planning the health curriculum. They found that elementary school children want to find out about babies. Students in grades six, seven, and eight are interested in puberty, sex, and social problems. Social problems are also important in grades nine through twelve. Diseases are of particular interest in fourth, seventh, and tenth grades. Questions about drug abuse tend to be significant in the fifth, sixth, seventh, and tenth grades.

Content Selection

Health education has fallen heir to a variety of interesting and controversial topics. The traditional school curriculum, college preparatory or vocational, has been largely indifferent to the personal problems of students. Approaching health instruction as a method of resolving real problems is highly defensible. To the extent that it confronts significant conflicts in the culture that translate into personal conflicts, health education can rank among the most meaningful of school experiences. Determine whether the state board of education or state legislature has passed compulsory or restrictive legislation on selected health topics. Instruction in drug abuse may be required by state law, and instruction in sex education may be banned by state law. Some of the major topics of health education are cited, with references, in the following paragraphs.

Mental Health

Topics under mental health include the development of personality, response to problems, and behavior during stress. The text by Byrne (1966) is a standard analysis of personality development and structure. Harris (1969) and Newman and Berkowitz (1971) discuss how to cope with stress.

Family Living

Family life and sex education are the most controversial subjects in health education. Some states restrict sex education to anatomy, and other states bar it completely. Topics include anatomical structure, physiology of reproduction, sex role development, values and sexual behavior, marriage and family life, and population control. Schulz and Williams (1969), Burt and Brower (1970), and McCary (1973) offer three perspectives on the topic of family living.

Drug Abuse

Drug abuse is associated with periods of stress. *Uppers, downers,* and *psychedelics* enable the user to escape personal stress temporarily. Accurate drug information without a change in personal values may only produce more stress—and lead to increased use of drugs. Three perspectives on the drug scene are given by Jones, Shainberg, and Byer (1970), Cohen (1969) and Smith, Kline, and French (1968).

Ecology

Ecology is the study of the delicate relationship between the earth, animal life, and plant life. Topics relevant to ecological balance include the plant–animal biosphere, effects of pollution, and alternatives to pollution. Ehrlich (1972) describes the problems of human population growth and Hafen (1972) and Turk, Turk, and Wittes (1972) relate pollution to the biosphere.

Nutrition

Health topics related to good nutrition include the digestive process, nutrients, energy expenditure, and the ideal nutritional state. Cooper (1968) has analyzed the energy cost of various activities. Bogert, Briggs, and Calloway (1966) present an exhaustive treatment of personal nutrition, and Mayer (1968) discusses the problem of obesity.

Care of the Body

Care of the human body includes dental hygiene, conservation of vision and hearing, and good grooming. Schroeder (1971) describes the form and function of the body, and Memmler and Rada (1970) discuss normal and abnormal body conditions.

Disorders and Diseases

Disorders and diseases include the categories of infectious diseases, noninfectious diseases, congenital disorders, and acquired disorders. Discussion should include causes, characteristics, and remedial action for the various maladies. Hein, Farnsworth, and Richardson (1970) and Diehl and Dalrymple (1968) discuss infectious and noninfectious diseases.

Basic Safety

Basic safety education includes home safety, vehicle safety, and first aid. Aaron and Strassen (1966) offer a comprehensive description of vehicle safety. Henderson (1973) presents the rudiments of first aid and home safety.

Medical Services

Selection of the proper medical services is a major health decision. A dentist writing under the pseudonym Revere (1970) speaks frankly about the quality of dental care and the selection of a qualified dentist. Consumer Reports (1971) presents a thorough analysis of the self-medication problem.

Case Example: PLANNING THE LOCAL HEALTH CURRICULUM

The Harris County curriculum supervisor has recently appointed you to chair a health curriculum committee. You are to nominate committee members you would like to have in the work group. The committue will meet initially during the late summer preschool workshop. You are expected to plan the schedule and scope of the workshop.

Harris County schools have been under pressure from the state office of education to improve health education. Typically, health education was assigned to physical education teachers who conducted incidental "rainy day" health instruction. There has been no coordination of curriculum between the elementary and secondary schools. A local plan for health instruction has been approved by the school board, but the outline is grossly incomplete. There is no syllabus or administrative guide for teachers to use in constructing their lesson plans. Health is usually taught in the gymnasium with large classes and limited visual aids. One

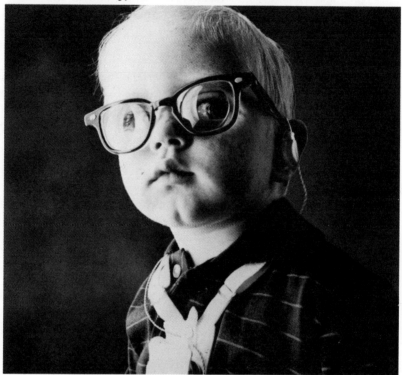

The mother got over her rubella in three days. Unfortunately, her unborn child didn't.

To pregnant mothers, rubella (German measles) means a few days in bed, a sore throat, a runny nose, temperature, and a rash.

But if they're in their first month when they catch it, there's a 40% chance that to their unborn babies it can mean deafness, or a heart condition, or brain damage, or cataracts which cause at least partial blindness.

In 1969, however, an immunization against rubella became available. But when a pregnant mother gets immunized, the prevention may be as harmful to her baby as the disease.

So if unborn babies are going to be protected, it will have to be by inoculating the kids who infect the mothers who in turn infect the fetuses.

And it will have to be done now. You see, rubella epidemics break out every six to nine years. The last outbreak was in 1964. Which means the next one is due any day now.

In the last epidemic, 20,000 babies were deprived of a normal childhood—and 30,000 more deprived of any childhood at all—because no immunization existed.

It would be unforgivable if the same thing happened again because an immunization existed and nobody used it.

 **Metropolitan Life**
We sell life insurance.
But our business is life.

For a free booklet about immunization, write One Madison Avenue, N.Y., N.Y. 10010.

Courtesy Metropolitan Life

Figure 6.3 Students' interest in health problems changes as they mature.

teacher reportedly teaches health units as punishment when the students misbehave in class.

As the health curriculum chairperson, you are responsible for working with the committee to produce a progressional program guide and to recommend personnel, schedule, and equipment for the program to the administration. Specifically:

1. What categories of teachers will you request for the committee?
2. What other personnel will you ask to sit on the committee?
3. Who will you request as committee consultants?
4. What will your work plan be?

Organizing

Program organization is an outgrowth of program planning. Organization involves arranging students and instructional resources to maximize positive effects of the educational program. However, several significant problems must be resolved. Health is taught in many states by physical education instructors who have only superficial training in health education. Often physical educators are neither adequately trained nor very much interested in teaching health. Upper- and middle-level administrators have not characteristically been interested in initiating or enforcing a defensible health program. Managerial objectives for health instruction organization are:

to identify the alternatives in personnel assignment and utilization
to analyze school situations in which the various programming plans could be used
to develop a comprehensive plan to acquire learning resources

Personnel Organization

Health education poses certain problems. First, teaching health as a life process often engenders controversy. Second, health education has not been a priority item in funding and scheduling. Typically, upper-echelon school administrators have not backed the health instruction program equitably. Critical issues of curriculum, scheduling, and staffing have been largely shuffled aside. If math teachers do not understand modern math, they are retrained. If teachers are unprepared to teach sex education or discuss drug abuse, the topics may be dropped.

Student Grouping

Schools are complex establishments, and part of their complexity is an outgrowth of large student populations. School managers try to remain sensitive to the needs of the individual student, but a large measure of this individualized attention gets lost in managing the mass of students. In order to prevent chaos, students must be organized somehow and grouping procedures must be in accordance with Title IX guidelines.

Multigrade Scheduling. Placing students of two or more grade levels into a single class is called multigrade scheduling. Multigrade scheduling is the most undesirable organizational procedure currently practiced in the areas of health and physical education. Physical and health education are two of the few subject areas still afflicted with multigrade scheduling. If second- and third-year concepts are built on first-year concepts, the younger students will be seriously handicapped. However, if the curriculum is entirely flexible to the student interests, "open" learning centers can be structured. Individualized learning has potential value for some health topics.

Grade Scheduling. Organizing students into classes by grades is a desirable practice for health instruction. A fair degree of homogeneity is obtained because grade strata are usually consistent in chronological age. Many more common needs and interests can be served in single-grade scheduling than in the multigrade plan.

A progressional health program is facilitated by single-grade scheduling. Of course it would be most desirable to have students scheduled for health instruction at the development stage in which there was a felt need for the instruction. Students mature at different rates, and therefore everyone in the class may not be ready to study a particular topic. However, scheduling according to interests and needs requires sophisticated computer procedures for devising student schedules. See Chapter 3 for a description and illustration of modular scheduling.

Formulating Student Schedules. Structuring student learning experiences is a complex administrative task. While a large student population minimizes individualization, the *goal* is always a personalized schedule. Most student schedules are formulated by a middle-level administrator, but the health instructor can legitimately request that certain guidelines be followed. Health scheduling guidelines include the following considerations:

1. Use preference sheets administered to students to determine curriculum preferences.
2. Segregate students by gender only for units on family living (if then).
3. Group students by interests, ability level, or grade level.
4. Do not exempt students for such normal physical education exemptions as athletics, ROTC, office work, or physical ailment.

Scheduling Teachers

The educational establishment is justified on the assumption that it gets learners and teachers together. Organization of teachers and students is an interlocking process. Educational managers try to maximize efficiency in the teacher–student relationship by regulating class size and instructional strategy. Both traditional and innovative organizational concepts should be considered in planning health instruction.

Regardless of which organizational plan is used, standard procedure should be followed in formulating the schedule. Ideally, the number of students is divided by the optimum class size to yield the number of necessary teaching stations. State funding is usually based on a class size of approximately twenty-five students. Facilities are also a major factor in determining how many teaching stations are available for health instruction. If block programming is used in conjunction with physical education, health classes should be rotated around one or more health classrooms, with a portion of the semester dedicated to each class. See Chapter 3 for a more comprehensive description of procedures for scheduling faculty.

Multiple Teaching Stations. Contemporary schools are far removed from the early American one-teacher school. Large city and consolidated schools have numerous classrooms for each grade level. The concept of multiple teaching stations for health and physical education is a major organizational breakthrough. Heretofore, some administrators viewed the gymnasium as a large classroom to be completely filled with students each period—under the supervision of a single instructor. Of course, any health program will have a negligible impact upon fifty to one hundred students in an open gymnasium. Convert an adjacent room into a flexible classroom and the potential for health instruction is increased. The health teaching station can be rotated among the classes during the semester. And scheduling via the multiple teaching station plan has good potential for team teaching.

Self-contained Classroom Teaching. Elementary students are usually taught by a single teacher who stays with one class all day, teaching all subjects. Health education within a self-contained unit can be correlated with other subjects, integrated into topical study, or separated as a distinct set of curriculum experiences. Correlated health instruction works well in the lower elementary school grades. Discussion of specific health topics is more frequent in the upper elementary and secondary school grades.

Departmentalized Teachers. Elementary schools may be organized along departmental lines. Most secondary schools use departmental organization. In departmental organization teachers restrict themselves to topical discussion in one subject. Usually upper-level teachers are assigned to teach in their field of major or minor preparation. The health major and minor are popular in college, but in public school departmentalization, health is typically structured with physical education. One of the departmental staff members can be designated to teach all the health block units. Or members of the departmental staff can conduct health block units with their assigned class.

Team Teaching. Team teaching is one of the major instructional concepts developed in recent years. Operating within the department, a *team* is formed by designating various roles to the available personnel. Two alternatives in team teaching are described in Chapter 3. Basically the teaching team is composed of "experts" in restricted content areas. Content areas in health instruction could be blocked into categories such as value clarification, disease and disorders, exercise and health, etc.

Who Should Teach Health?

Nurses, physicians, juvenile officers, and public health workers are the paraprofessionals of health education. All are excellent resource persons; however, none of these people has been trained in planning, organizing, actualizing, and controlling. The individual nurses, physicians, and sheriffs have other demands on their time; they cannot meet with moderate-sized classes on a day-to-day basis. As experts in their respective fields, nurses, physicians, and police officers have information pertinent to health education. The insights of drug addicts and alcoholics can also be valuable. But instead of recruiting the paraprofessionals or the afflicted into schools to *be* the teachers, these resource persons should be used to direct in-service training *for* the teachers. The expert can communicate information to the teachers in a short time, they can subsequently integrate this information into the curriculum.

The Health Educator. If students are to take health education seriously, health teachers must be what they teach. Quality of living is the undeniable interpretation of philosophy. The obese, the alcoholic, the smoker, and the mentally unstable have no business in the school health education field. Personification of the healthful life is the prerequisite to teaching about health.

The health educator must first have an abiding interest in the health area. Secondly, the health educator must have accurate information to communicate to the uninformed. And thirdly, the health educator must have training in the educational process. Health and legal paraprofessionals have the interest and the information, but they are untrained in techniques of goal setting, teaching, and evaluating outcomes. It is the legal duty of the school board to provide competent, trained, professional educators.

Figure 6.4 Teachers are exemplars.

Teacher Aides. The practice of using nonprofessional teaching assistance in the classroom is not a recent development. Early in American education, monitors were used to augment the teaching staff. The use of teacher aides has recently been revived due largely to federal funding. A teacher aide is a trained assistant who performs supervisory and routine classroom functions, including the checking out, accounting, and repair of equipment. Aides can assist in setting up and maintaining demonstrations such as nutrition experiments. However, since aides have limited training and are not certified, they cannot assume the legal responsibility designated to the teacher.

Alternatives in Program Structure

Time for health instruction is a critical factor. If the areas of health and physical education are combined, the time allotment *must* be shared. Time arrangements include the separate course, block time, partial block time, and incidental time. Correlation and integration are sometimes used in elementary schools, but these time-allotment practices are not desirable for secondary schools. An alternative to health instruction within the multiple-grade class organization is the use of a cyclical curriculum. Topics in a cyclical curriculum are repeated every two or three years, thus avoiding repetition with any single student group.

Separate Course

Health taught as a separate course is one of the most desirable practices. When health is separately designated, students develop a positive mental set towards the course. Health is viewed as a distinct entity and not as time taken away from

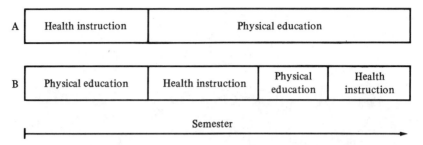

Figure 6.5 Block programming. Two of the many block programming alternatives.

instruction in sports. If state and local boards require that health instruction occupy one fourth of the physical and health education time, then one semester could be designated for health instruction every two years.

Block Time

In *block* programming the unit is continued until complete. Health instruction units can be interspersed throughout the semester of physical and health instruction in varying time slots. The block may vary from one to several weeks in duration. Time blocking is a desirable practice in allotting health time. Time blocking within a semester allows for more flexibility than the separate-semester system, because student needs may not coincide with the semester that the health course is taught. The block plan also allows for a single idea to be pursued daily for one or more weeks until the topic is completed. Mini-units of from one to two weeks can be conducted on selected health topics. A particular health unit can be scheduled at a time during the semester when interest is likely to be highest. Figure 6.6 illustrates some of the alternatives in block programming where health consumes one-third of the physical and health education time. If alternative A is selected, a designated health room can be shared by boys' and girls' classes by rotating use of the room every third of the semester.

Partial Block Time

When two activities are combined into an alternating schedule during the week, the arrangement is called a *partial block* schedule. Health may be taught one, two, or three days per week, alternating with physical education or some other curricular subject. Partial block organization represents widely distributed health instruction time. (Both the separate health course and block programming represent relative massing of instruction time.)

	Monday	Tuesday	Wednesday	Thursday	Friday
A	Band	Health instruction	Band	Health instruction	Band

	Monday	Tuesday	Wednesday	Thursday	Friday
B	Physical education	Health instruction	Physical education	Health instruction	Physical education

One week

Figure 6.6 Partial block programming. Numerous arrangements are possible for alternating health instructions with physical education or electives.

Partial block health instruction is one of the more desirable time arrangements. Health may be conveniently alternated with an elective such as chorus. Partial block scheduling has the advantage of increasing practice time but a disadvantage in failing to maintain continuity. Figure 6.7 illustrates the principle of partial block programming.

Incidental Time

Incidental time allotment implies that little direct attention is given to the topic under consideration. Rainy-day health instruction programs may be well planned in advance and then filed away to await the rain, but relegating health to such inferior status implies that health education is unimportant. Incidental health teaching is one of the least desirable procedures for time allotment. Health may be taught incidentally in physical education, science, home economics, or social studies, but the term "incidental" always implies "by chance" or "as a side issue."

Correlation

Subject correlation is a great idea that is seldom effective in health teaching. A *correlated health curriculum* is structured within traditional subject matter. For example, the biology teacher could include discussion of sex education under the topic of reproduction. Under the correlation plan, health topics are parceled out to home economics, biology, and social studies.

The correlation concept has two major drawbacks. First, specialists in home economics, biology, and social studies feel pressured by health instruction responsibilities, since they are trying to include as much of their specialized subject as possible. Secondly, subject matter specialists are not trained in the content or methodology of health education. The use of correlated health instruction is much more defensible at the elementary than the secondary level.

Integration

Integration is similar to correlation except that the scope is larger. The *integrated health curriculum* is a multidisciplinary approach to a broad topic. The broad topic is of primary importance, and it is viewed from several natural perspectives. For example, if the topic is Africa, its geography, agriculture, wildlife, health, economics, social structure, politics, and culture would be examined. Curriculum integration is a good idea, but there are few teachers prepared to execute it.

Organization of the Learning Environment

Facilities

Provision for one or more designated health rooms is necessary for an effective health instruction program. A specially designated and equipped health room carries a potent message to the student. If the classroom reflects a professional attitude on the part of the instructor, the student senses that important events occur in the room. Health instruction can be no more effectively conducted on gymnasium bleachers than a mathematics class.

The health education room should include enough chairs for the maximum student load. Tables are convenient for laboratory work, but student chairs with a flat writing surface can be jammed together to form improvised tables. Student chairs should not be fixed permanently to the floor. Movable chairs allow work in small groups. A demonstration table, either portable or fixed, containing provision for water and heat should be provided in each health room. A large storage room is also desirable.

Media Coordination

Educational media are tools for supplementing health concepts introduced by the instructor. Media and materials cannot be substituted for the professional teacher any more than a vending machine can be substituted for a competent physician. Wise and timely use of media facilitates student understanding. Media include all learning vehicles and educational tools. Teaching machines, models, charts, film projections, books, and magazines can be used to sustain interest and provide supplementary information. Gillespie (1967) discovered some interesting items when comparing media utilization by culturally privileged and culturally underprivileged first-year college students. The study surveyed health information gained in the secondary school. The culturally disadvantaged tended to seek entertainingly presented information, with little dependence on written sources. The culturally advantaged group tended to use varied sources of information. Both groups demonstrated better recall from magazines than from radio and television.

Case Example: ORGANIZING FOR HEALTH INSTRUCTION

John Tufts High School is located in the interior of a large metropolitan area. The weathered old school building was designed to accommodate considerably fewer than the fifteen hundred male and female students who are occasionally confined in the structure. The surrounding neighborhood consists of stately old houses, now neglected and battered. The unemployment and crime rates are high in the surrounding area.

As Physical and Health Education Department chairperson of the inner-city high school, you have been directed by your principal to upgrade the health instruction program. Usually there are five men and six women teachers assigned to your department. The facilities include two teaching stations for health. Although the block plan for physical and health education has been accepted by the department, very little health instruction has been accomplished.

What will be your organizational procedures? Will you advocate retaining the block organization? Does team teaching seem to offer possibilities for your department? Will you advocate innovations in scheduling? What resource persons will you consider for in-service training?

Actualizing

Planning and organizing processes can facilitate behavior change, but these processes have little direct effect on student behavior. Only when the planned health experiences become part of the students' life do plans and organization become meaningful. The process of confronting the student with relevant concepts is called actualizing. Some examples of administrative management objectives for actualizing in health instruction are:

to identify the alternative methods of health instruction
to get students personally interested in resolving a significant health program

Alternative Methods

The method does make a difference in teaching! Disseminating health statistics and facts by the lecture method is of relatively little value. Any method that does not actively involve the learner has little potential value in changing student behavior. There is no consistently superior teaching method, because appropriate content and method are both dependent upon the task and the developmental characteristics of the learner. Situations vary widely from elementary school through high school. The case against paraprofessionals in health teaching is based on the probability that an instructor untrained in the teaching process will not be able to select the best method for the specific situation. See Sorochan and Bender (1975) for additional method strategies.

Lecture

The *lecture* is a monologue flowing from instructor to learner. The monologue is usually based on a formal outline—either mental or recorded in writing—of the subject matter. Lectures need not be boring—after all, great comedians use the monologue method. A sizable quantity of subject matter can be "covered" in a lecture. However, lecturing does little to insure behavioral change in the student. Lectures are probably the most overused method of trying to change student behavior.

Demonstration

The *demonstration* method is an attempt to involve both visual and auditory communication channels. The lecturer may draw images on the chalk board and show pictures, but the demonstrator presents a model or the real mechanism. For example, a smoking machine with the smoke channeled through a guppy's fish-bowl has a unique impact on the viewers. When the fish turns bottom-up, the effects of smoking become a reality. While it is usually helpful for the instructor to explain some details, verbal communication is secondary to the demonstration itself.

Student or teacher demonstrations can be effectively used in health education. If students are guided to create something they can be proud of, their demonstrations can be more meaningful than a teacher demonstration. Many companies have free or low-cost demonstration kits on health topics; these can be constructed by a student. To avoid embarrassment, the student demonstration should be previewed by the instructor before it is shown to the class.

Critical Incident

The *critical incident* method is a student-centered instruction method structured around a meaningful or pivotal behavior. The incident can be real or hypothetical as long as it illustrates a major point in the general topic under discussion. For example, two high school students are sitting in an automobile and one says to the other, "Come on, smoke one. Marijuana never hurt anybody!"

After the critical incident is selected, the instructor describes the situation to the group. Then, without supplying positive or negative feedback to student statements, the instructor encourages the group to deliberate. During the deliberation process the instructor must ask only nondirective questions. However, the instructor's questions should aid the group in synthesizing their own ideas into a rationally defensible conclusion. In a drug abuse discussion, for instance, the group should weigh possible gains against possible losses.

Confrontation

Confrontation is another debate and decision-making method. Confrontation is attractive in its adaptability to large groups. Once a major issue with implications for social action is communicated to the large group, confrontation can begin.

A set of procedural rules is crucial in the mechanics of confrontation. Usually a simple set of rules (who will speak, when new ideas can be interjected, how an issue can be brought to conclusion, a time limit) and a moderator are sufficient to maintain order.

Next the large group is divided into several small groups. Each small group elects a spokesperson and formulates its own answer to the major question. Each small group's proposal must specify detailed action. After all proposals have been formulated, the spokesperson for each group presents that group's proposal. After all proposals have been presented, any of the proposals can be challenged by the spokesperson of another group. An ineffective spokesperson can be tapped on the shoulder and replaced by another member of the group.

Exploration

Traditional education has emphasized dissemination of information by the teacher. Actually, traditional teacher-oriented methods are better described as "attempted insemination." The learner has too long been forced into a passive role. Intuitive methods that emphasize self-discovery represent an earnest attempt to make learning a meaningful experience. It has been known for decades that firsthand experience is the most meaningful and that it embodies the greatest potential for behavior change. Nevertheless, the exploration method is inherently difficult for mass-production education.

The health teacher's most significant role in self-discovery teaching is in helping the student define the topic. The student must learn to ask incisive questions and to collect data to answer them. Disseminating answers is the easy, less meaningful way to teach. The heart of the intuitive method lies in asking questions that guide learners to discover the answers for themselves.

Programmed Text

The programmed text is the antithesis of self-discovery. With programmed texts the learner can "cover" much subject matter in a short time. Programmed texts emphasize reading and remembering skills.

Programmed texts are based on the principle of immediate reinforcement. Subject matter is divided into very small steps. After each paragraph or series of steps, a test is given to the reader. Learners who answer the self-test questions correctly, are positively reinforced by knowledge of their success. Learners who miss the answers to test questions receive the negative reinforcement of knowledge of their failure. Failure to respond correctly requires the learner to repeat the passage.

Programmed texts require little more than monitoring by the instructor. Learners can proceed at their own rate. Fast learners can proceed to more complex texts on the assigned topic or branch out to other related topics. Commercial programmed texts are available—or teachers may write their own material.

Student Activities

Teacher-oriented instructional methods tend to turn the student into a passive participant in the learning experience. However, there are many activities that can actively involve the learner. These health activities can be used as individual student projects, or they can be used to supplement in-class activities. Some interesting health activities within the capability of many students are suggested in the following paragraphs.

Photographic Journalism

Since words are mediated symbols that represent objects and actions, words are limited in their descriptiveness. Pictures are also symbols that represent tangible objects, but pictures can convey concepts of objects more accurately than words. Photographs can provide the dramatic impact needed to document and promote environmental action projects, for example. The Kodak Company (Kronenberg) has produced an excellent guide to conducting effective environmental projects. The book is written to teach people how to take story-telling photographs and how to use the pictures in a positive and constructive way to improve the community.

Health Movies

Many families own motion picture cameras which they would allow mature children to use for school projects. The child who owns the camera may be required to be the photographer, but the parent can be used as a resource person to teach the child how to operate the mechanism. Short rolls of movie film are inexpensive, and local processors can return exposed film within a week. Other students could make posters for the lead-in title frames and compose the film's

Figure 6.7 Elementary and secondary school students can be taught to apply the basic principles of photography to health problems.

action sequence. Topics for student film production include ecology, safety, disease, and drug abuse. In fact, there are hundreds of possible topics for films in the area of health.

Research Project

Science fairs have given an impetus to student projects of various kinds. Some such projects are only demonstrations, while others outline high-quality, original research. Data-gathering research applicable to health are survey, analysis, correlation, and experimental studies. Topics for original research projects in health include a survey of local attitudes toward pollution and gross analysis of solid wastes produced by a local community.

Diary

A diary is a systematic recording of daily events. It may log all major events, or it may be selective. Students with an obesity problem may find a diary project helpful in weight control, recording the type and amounts of food ingested daily, as well as events and feelings just prior to eating. Subsequent analysis of the diary may reveal patterns of eating and recurring events that seem to precede eating at meal time or between meals. If the student is a compulsive eater, the diary may reveal factors associated with that compulsive behavior.

CHILDREN SPEAK WITH CAMERAS

Nine- and ten-year-old children at Public School 25, District 16, Brooklyn, New York, have been taking pictures of their neighborhood. They send their pictures along with letters to landlords, community leaders, and city agencies, such as the Sanitation and Health Departments. Jean-Paul Kronenberg, the principal of the experimental summer school, explained, "We've built our whole program around the camera because we had to find a way of getting the children interested and involved—a way that didn't require too much money." If you would like more information on the project write to Mr. Kronenberg, Public School 23 Annex, Kosciusko St., Brooklyn, New York, 11221.

J-P. Kronenberg, "Children Speak with Cameras," in Kodak Consumer Markets Division, *Improve Your Environment: Fight Pollution with Pictures*, Eastman Kodak Company, Rochester, N.Y.

Ecology Drive

Most major social reforms have been initiated by idealistic individuals who believe society could be better. Activist students have changed the course of history by methods ranging from toppling government leaders to arousing public sentiment for needed community projects. Successful ecology drives have been conducted by students to clean up selected areas and collect recyclable glass, paper, and metals. Civic action by students not only informs them about local problems but, more important, actively involves them in a behavior-changing experience.

Case Example: STUDENT HEALTH INSTRUCTION ACTIVITIES

Mr. Wright, the school principal, believes in giving students the hard facts of effects and law enforcement regarding drug abuse. Each year he secures the aid of law-enforcement officers who address the student body in an assembly. The law officers usually bring samples of the currently abused drugs, explain their effects, and outline the procedures for apprehending and jailing illicit drug users. Occasionally they bring convicts to talk to the students about their own experiences. One inmate stated, "What will drugs do for you? They'll get you thrown into a lousy jungle, that's what. If you think drugs aren't going to hurt you, just remember it's against the law."

You have been teaching health education for several years, including units on drug abuse. After hearing several of these assemblies, you feel compelled to improve the school drug education program. What would be your analysis of the existing program? See Zazzaro (1973) and Stuart (1971). How might law-enforcement officers be better used in a comprehensive program on drug abuse? What does the research indicate is the most effective method of preventing high-risk behavior?

Controlling

Control procedures supply both the middle-level manager and the classroom teacher with information on student progress from which evaluations can be made. Evaluation quantifies the degree to which educational objectives have been accomplished by the instructional program. Control involves measurement of student behavior, evaluation of student performance data, and administrative action to reinforce or rectify conditions.

Student Achievement

Change in the behavior of students is the objective of the educational system. Changes in attitudes, cognitive processes, and skills related to physical and mental fitness are the major thrust of health education. Behavior change can be quantified by using one or more of the standardized measurement techniques currently available. Both subjective and objective measurement data are valuable in determining individual and class profiles of behavior change. See Chapter 3 for a discussion of grading and reporting procedures?

Information Tests

Both standardized tests and teacher-made tests have their place in the classroom. Standardized health tests are either omnibus tests covering a broad spectrum of topics or restricted tests dealing with only one. Standardized tests are difficult to devise; therefore, they are not particularly sensitive to new developments in the health sciences. Being less elaborately constructed, teacher-made tests are adapted to instruction for local student needs and interests. Some of the published health tests are:

1. Thompson, C. W. "Thompson Smoking and Tobacco Knowledge Tests." *Research Quarterly,* 35 March 1964, 60–68.
2. Kilander, H. F. *Kilander Health Knowledge Tests,* Glenn C. Leach, Publisher, Wagner College, 631 Howard Ave., Staten Island, N.Y. 10301.
3. Adamson, G., and M. W. Sanders. *Emporia Elementary Health Test.* Data Processing and Educational Measurement Center, Kansas State Teachers College, 1200 Commercial St., Emporia, Kansas 66802.
4. Blaylock, R., and M. W. Sanders. *Emporia High School Health Test,* Data Processing and Educational Measurement Center, Kansas State Teachers College, 1200 Commercial St., Emporia, Kansas 66802.
5. McHugh, G., and J. C. Williams. *A Drug Knowledge Inventory, Experimental Edition,* Family Life Publications, Inc., P. O. Box 427, Saluda, N.C. 28773.
6. Health Behavior Inventory (Elementary, Junior High, Senior High and College tests) CTB/McGraw-Hill Co., Del Monte Research Park, Monterey, Calif. 93940.

Attitude and Value Quantification

Attitudes and values are closely related. *Attitude* is defined as inclination toward or in relationship to an object. *Values* involve attitudes, but they also suggest that some objects are of more worth than others. Although it is widely known that attitudes are not entirely adequate predictors of behavior, attitude data does show the disposition of an individual or group toward an object. Most students are quite frank in expressing their beliefs on an attitude scale. See Mayshark (1954) and Sorochan and Bender (1975) for additional measurement devices for the affective domain. Some of the published health attitude scales are:

1. Richardson, C. E. "A Sentence Completion Health Attitudes Test for College Students." *Journal of School Health*, 30 (January 1960), 32–35.
2. Richardson, C. E. "Thurstone Scale for Measuring Attitudes of College Students Toward Physical Fitness and Exercise." *Research Quarterly*, 31 (December 1963), 638–643.
3. *An Inventory of Points of View Related to Health,* California Community Health Education Project, California State Department of Education, Sacramento, Calif. 95814.

Program Evaluation

The direct effects of the health instruction program are measurable by student outcomes. Yet the contributory function of the instructor and the instructional designs should also be assessed. Even school health services and the school environment need periodic evaluation because of indirect effects on student behavioral outcomes.

Health Teacher Performance

Teacher performance can be assessed by observation, student evaluation of the instructor, and evaluation of student progress. Principals and department chairpersons who are providing supervision should look for evidence of effective planning and actualizing. It is highly unlikely that the same lesson plan and teaching methods can be used year after year. There must be evidence that each teacher has attempted to meet student needs. Student projects, animated discussion, and general classroom interest in health are tangible evidence of teacher performance. An instrument for rating general teacher performance is included in the Student Guide for Chapter 8. Teacher attitudes toward healthful living can be assessed using the scale designed by Meise (1970).

Health Instruction Program

All elements in the health instruction program must be represented in the evaluation instrument. Objective review of curriculum, organization procedures, learning activities, and student outcomes should be made by an outside agent. Teachers within the same school system could be grouped into small evaluation teams to rate schools other than their own. Districtwide in-service sessions could be productively used to review the evaluations. A sample evaluation form appears in the Student Guide. Other program evaluation instruments have been published by Anderson (1968) and Mayshark (1954).

School Health Evaluation

Anderson's (1968) *School Health Evaluation Scale* can be used to evaluate the school health environment. The comprehensive scale includes items clustered around (1) safe and sanitary school facilities and (2) healthful school programs.

Case Example: CONTROLLING THE HEALTH PROGRAM

Students at John Tufts High School have never been tested in health instruction classes. Heretofore, health instruction has been "administered" to students mainly as a rainy-day activity. After developing a comprehensive curriculum that specified student outcomes in the cognitive and affective domains, the departmental faculty is asked to devise a defensible plan for assessing the effects of instruction. The plan must be economical because there is little money for supplies.

What types of tests should be used? To what extent should subjective devices be used?

References

AARON, J. E., and M. K. STRASSEN. *Driver and Traffic Safety Education.* The Macmillan Company, New York, 1966.

ALLENSWORTH, D. D. "Common Intestinal Parasitic Infections in the School-age Population." *Journal of School Health,* 45 (1975), 331–338.

ANDERSON, C. L. *School Health Practice.* The C. V. Mosby Company, St. Louis, 1968.

ASCH, S. E. "Effects of Group Pressure Upon the Modification and Distortion of Judgments." In *Readings in Social Psychology,* 3d ed. edited by E. E. Maccoby, T. M. Newcomb, and E. L. Hartley. Henry Holt and Company, New York, 1958.

BOGERT, L. J., G. M. BRIGGS, and D. H. CALLOWAY. *Nutrition and Physical Fitness.* W. B. Saunders Company, Philadelphia, 1966.

BURT, J. J., and L. A. BROWER. *Education for Sexuality.* W. B. Saunders Company, Philadelphia, 1970.

BYLER, R., G. LEWIS, and R. TOTMAN. *Teach Us What We Want to Know.* Mental Health Materials Center, New York, 1969.

BYRNE, D. E. *An Introduction to Personality.* Prentice-Hall, Englewood Cliffs, N.J., 1966.

COHEN, S. *The Drug Dilemma.* McGraw-Hill Book Company, New York, 1969.

CONSUMER REPORTS. *The Medicine Show.* Consumers Union, Mt. Vernon, N.Y., 1971.

COOPER, K. H. *Aerobics.* Bantam Books, New York, 1968.

CORNACCHIA, H. J. "Guidelines for Secondary School Health Education." *School Health Review* (1969), 22–24.

DIEHL, H. S., and W. DALRYMPLE. *Healthful Living.* McGraw-Hill Book Company, New York, 1968.

EHRLICH, P. R. *The Population Bomb.* Ballantine Books, New York, 1972.

GILLESPIE, D. K. "Media Source Use for Health Information." *Research Quarterly,* 38 (1967), 149–151.

HAFEN, B. Q. *Man's Health and Environment.* Burgess Publishing Company, Minneapolis, 1972.

HAMIN, M., H. KIRSCHENBAUM, and S. B. SIMON. *Clarifying Values through Subject Matter.* Winston Press, Minneapolis, 1973.

HARRIS, T. A. *I'm OK—You're OK.* Harper and Row, Publishers, New York, 1969.

HEIN, F. V., D. L. FARNSWORTH, and C. E. RICHARDSON. *Living: Health, Behavior and Environment,* 5th ed. Scott, Foresman and Company, Glenview, Ill., 1970.

HENDERSON, J. *Emergency Medical Guide.* McGraw-Hill Book Company, New York, 1973.

JONES, K. L., L. W. SHAINBERG, and C. O. BYER. *Drugs, Alcohol and Tobacco.* Canfield Press, San Francisco, 1970.

KRONENBERG, J-P. "Children Speak with Cameras." In Kodak Consumer Markets Division, *Improve Your Environment: Fight Pollution with Pictures,* Eastman Kodak Company, Rochester, N.Y.

MAGER, R. F. *Preparing Instructional Objectives.* Fearon Publishers, Belmont, Calif., 1962.

MAYER, J. *Overweight: Causes, Cost and Control.* Prentice-Hall, Englewood Cliffs, N.J., 1968.

MAYSHARK, C. "A Health and Safety Attitude Scale for the Seventh Grade." Doctoral dissertation, Indiana University, 1954.

McCARY, J. L. *Human Sexuality,* 2d ed. Van Nostrand Reinhold Company, New York, 1973.

MEDLEY, D. M., and H. E. MITZEL. "A Technique for Measuring Classroom Behavior." *Journal of Educational Psychology.* 49 (1958), 86–92.

MEISE, W. C. "The Construction and Validation of a Scale for the Measurement of Attitudes toward Healthful Living." Doctoral dissertation, Colorado State University, 1962. (Ann Arbor: University Microfilms, 1970.)

MEMMLER, R. L., and R. B. RADA. *The Human Body in Health and Disease.* J. B. Lippincott Company, Philadelphia, 1970.

NEWMAN, M., and B. BERKOWITZ. *How To Be Your Own Best Friend.* Random House, New York, 1971.

NUTRITION AND TECHNICAL SERVICES STAFF. *A Menu Guide for Type A Lunches.* United States Department of Agriculture, Washington, D.C., 1974.

REVERE, P. *Dentistry and Its Victims.* St. Martin's Press, New York, 1970.

RUCKER, W. R., V. C. ARNSPIGER, and A. J. BRODBECK. *Human Values in Education.* Kendall/Hunt Publishing Company, Dubuque, Iowa, 1969.

SCHROEDER, C. R. *The Human Body.* Wm. C. Brown Company, Dubuque, Iowa, 1971.

SCHULZ, E. D., and S. R. WILLIAMS. *Family Life and Sex Education.* Harcourt, Brace & World, New York, 1969.

SHERIF, M. "Group Influences upon the Formation of Norms and Attitudes," In *Readings in Social Psychology,* 3d ed. edited by E. E. Maccoby, T. M. Newcomb, and E. L. Hartley, Henry Holt and Company, New York, 1958.

SMITH, KLINE and FRENCH. *Drug Abuse: Escape to Nowhere.* Smith, Kline and French Laboratories, Philadelphia, 1968.

SOROCHAN, W. D., and S. J. BENDER. *Teaching Elementary Health Science.* Addison-Wesley Publishing Company, Reading, Mass., 1975.

STUART, R. B. "Teaching Facts about Drugs: Pushing or Preventing." *Today's Education,* 60 (1971), 34–35.

TURK, A., J. TURK, and J. T. WITTES. *Ecology, Pollution and Environment,* W. B. Saunders Company, Philadelphia, 1972.

WILLGOOSE, C. E. *Health Teaching in the Elementary School.* 4th ed. W. B. Saunders Company, Philadelphia, 1974.

WILLGOOSE, C. E. *Health Teaching in Secondary Schools.* W. B. Saunders Company, Philadelphia, 1972.

ZAZZARO, J. "Drug Education: Is Ignorance Bliss?" *Nation's Schools,* 92 (1973), 29–33.

III.
SUPPORTIVE
OPERATIONS

7.

FISCAL

MANAGEMENT

After reading this chapter, each student should be able to:

Perform a cost analysis for an educational program.

Construct a budget for physical and health education, school recreation, or athletics.

Identify important elements in the purchasing process.

Set up a comprehensive accounting procedure for funds and equipment.

Develop innovative methods of storing and conveying sports equipment.

The public's support of its schools is largely based on credibility in financial management. Each school must have standard operating procedures to account for funds and equipment. Accountability does not mean that funds and equipment are rigidly locked away from normal teacher needs. Fiscal accountability does require that all school money and equipment be identified upon entering the system and that ultimate status or expenditure be described. The system used in a school should be accurate yet flexible. Funds and equipment must be continuously monitored *and* accessible to authorized personnel. This chapter will focus on management of finances and of school-owned properties.

Financial Procedures

Two questions may be posed about school finances. "Why is an accounting system needed?" and "What system should be used?" Since large sums of money are handled in the athletic program, what kind of accounting system should be used? All monies that enter the school system—regardless of whether they derive from taxes, gate receipts, donations, or concession profits—must be considered public funds. Money within the public trust must be used only for the public benefit. Public money should not be used for private investment, gifts, or parties. Some examples of management objectives for financial affairs are:

to formulate financial policies for a school budget unit—(recreation depart-ment, etc.)
to relate student outcomes to school costs
to standardize procedures for doing business with educational suppliers (sport-ing goods dealers, etc.)
to promote staff involvement in purchasing and acounting

Financial policies insure efficiency and protect the school manager. For ex-ample, the bond required for school personnel who handle large sums of money is a type of assurance policy that guarantees reimbursement in case of malfeasance. Mainieri and Warnock (1973) present a summary of athletic financial policies. Some questions applicable to financial policies at the elementary and secondary levels are as follows:

1. Who is to be the bonded agent for financial responsibility (department head, principal, athletic director)?
2. What bookkeeping procedures are to be followed?
3. How will the local banks share the time deposits of the school?
4. Who can make cash withdrawals?
5. Under what conditions can withdrawals be made?

Budgeting

A *budget* is a set of financial specifications developed to project expenditures of each of the organizational units. Each major category of items is listed with its designated fund allotment. Items specifically included in the budget are called *line items*. A budget provides the basic organizing procedure for program management. Items within the program budget reflect relative priorities. If basketball, for example, receives twice the amount budgeted for swimming, then management considers basketball more important than swimming. The two common types of school budgets are (1) the tax revenue budget and (2) the zero budget. *Tax revenue budgets* are based on income taxes, property taxes, or sales taxes collected for school operation. Physical and health education instruction and school recreation are organizational units that are usually tax funded. Athletics also receives considerable indirect help from tax funds—coaches' salaries, electricity, and facilities. However, it is common practice to fund much of the athletic program from a zero budget.

Zero budgets are based on gate receipts. The program must produce revenue or solicit contributions to cover expenses. Before an athletic program is initiated, funds amount to zero, though after several years there may be funds carried over from year to year. If cash is needed to start an athletic program from a zero budget, a loan may be secured from a local bank or credit may be requested from a local athletic goods supplier. (The school official who signs for the cash or merchandise may be held liable for payment.)

Cost Analysis

Cost analysis is a procedure whereby all expenditures are related to the total number of students served. Cost analysis for each school program is an essential planning step in financial management. Knowing the cost per student for each program provides a firm basis for budget planning and yearly financial reporting. A comprehensive analysis should include the cost per student for the physical education program, the cost per participant for the intramural program, and the cost per athlete for each interschool sports event. For example, the American School Board Association (1975) has developed a form for computing the real sports costs. That form appears in Figure 7.1.

Figure 7.1 A model form for interschool athletics cost analysis.

Use This Form To Compute Your Real Sports Costs

How much does your school district's interscholastic athletics program *really* cost? [This] form . . . will help you find out, regardless of the specific type of budgeting system used in your district. First, complete as fully as you can all of the subheadings in the six categories listed: salaries, equipment and facilities, game expenses, membership and staff development, insurance, and income from athletics. Compute cost subtotals for each category, then add subtotals to obtain a total cost figure. Subtract revenue from total cost to determine total net athletics cost. Divide the total net athletics cost by the total number of students in high schools covered by the interscholastic athletic program to determine the net per-student cost. Divide the total net athletic cost by the total number of students participating in interscholastic athletics programs to determine the "net per-participant cost."

EXPENDITURES

Salaries. (List the portion of an employe's salary directly related to interscholastic sports. Often that portion is listed separately in an employe's contract or it can be computed on the basis of the amount of "employment time" an employe spends on interscholastic sports.)

Athletic director	$_____
Head coach	_____
Assistant coaches	_____
Trainer	_____
Buisiness manager	_____
Supervisors for cheerleaders	_____
Supervisors for marching band	_____
Special maintenance crews (those whose work is directly related to interscholastic athletics—not regular groundskeepers	_____
Others	_____

Subtotal for salaries $ _____

Equipment and facilities. (List material—new, replacement or repairs—used exclusively, or nearly so, for interscholastic sports.)

Uniforms for athletic team members and for marching band members and cheerleaders	$_____
Athletic equipment (balls, bats, nets, protective gear)	_____
Laundry and cleaning costs	_____
First aid supplies and medical equipment	_____
Utilities (those directly related to interscholastic sports, such as lights for night games, etc.)	_____

Others _____

Subtotal for equipment and facilities $_____

Game expenses. (List those attributable to interscholastic sporting events.)

Transportation $_____

Meals and lodging   _____

Travel insurance   _____

Salaries for officials   _____

Personnel (ticket sellers, ushers,
   security persons)   _____

Maintenance (list costs for field
   and stadium preparation
   or rental)   _____

Entertainment costs (for halftime
   shows, if any)   _____

Special additional costs (tournaments, playoffs, special
   meets)   _____

Other   _____

Subtotal for game expenses $_____

Membership and staff development.

Cost for membership in professional organizations
   (coaches' organizations, athletic
   groups, accreditation agencies) $_____

Clinics, seminars, workshops and
   publications for athletic team
   members and athletic department
   staff   _____

Mileage and per diem payments
   for athletic staff attending
   special meetings   _____

Other   _____

Subtotal for development $_____

Insurance

Medical $_____

Liability   _____

Other   _____

Subtotal for insurance $_____

Total Costs: $_____

INCOME FROM ATHLETICS

Gate receipts $_____

Concessions   _____

(Be sure to subtract from these first two whatever share of revenue goes to band, clubs, cheerleaders or other special groups.)	________	
Donations	________	
Radio and/or television coverage	________	
Income-producing publications	________	
Other	________	
	Total Revenue:	$________
Subtract revenue from costs to show net athletic costs:		$________
Total number of students in high schools covered by interscholastic athletic programs analyzed here:		________
Total number of students participating in interscholastic athletic programs analyzed here:		________

(Reprinted, with permission, from The American School Board Journal, *June 1975. Copyright, 1975, the National School Boards Association. All rights reserved.)*

The *cost factor* is derived by totaling all program expenditures and dividing the sum by the number of participants. Cost analysis may also be made for individual items such as equipment, transportation, and salaries. An additional cost analysis for daily operation can easily be computed by dividing the total number of program days into the cost per student that was computed previously. Figure 7.2 shows a sample cost analysis for interschool sports. See Abdelsamad and Hunt (1973) for further guidance in analysis of capital expenditures.

Figure 7.2 A sample cost analysis for interschool sports.

What Five Districts Spend for Interscholastic Sports

How much do [*other* school districts] spend on interscholastic sports? To find out, *The American School Board Journal* asked superintendents of a sampling of school districts to complete [Figure 7.1]. Below are listed the actual cost figures for interscholastic athletics programs in the five surveyed school districts. The five were selected as representative of different enrollments and settings. Districts A and B serve industrial cities of approximately 100,000 population. District C is a wealthy suburban district where per-student expenditures exceed $2,000. District D serves a nonmetropolitan community of 33,000 population. Tiny District E serves a rural population.

CHARACTERISTIC	DISTRICT A *Medium-sized industrial city*	DISTRICT B *Medium-sized industrial city*	DISTRICT C *Wealthy suburban area*	DISTRICT D *Small city*	DISTRICT E *Rural area*
Enrollment	14,410	14,500	4,500	1,523	250
% of students who participate	25%	9.5%	31%	35%	46%
Total cost	$321,898	$162,835	$138,954	$77,441	$25,140
Income from athletics	$76,159	$50,000	$11,923	$22,600	$3,314
Net cost	$245,739	$112,835	$127,031	$54,841	$21,826
Estimated % of total high school budget	4.4%	3.5%	0.6%	5%	4%
Income as a % of total costs	23%	31%	8.6%	29%	13%
Net cost per student in school system	$17.05	$7.78	$28.23	$36.00	$87.30
Net cost per participant in sports program	$68.26	$82.36	$91.32	$102.89	$187.79
Salaries as % of total costs	54%	40%	47%	45%	34%
Equipment and facilities as % of total costs	25%	27%	24%	23%	28%
Game expenses as % of total costs	18%	26%	25%	26%	30%

Budgetary analysis should also be related to behavioral outcomes. Since traditional types of budgets tend to communicate more in "accountant language" than in "educator language," an alternative budgeting method was developed. PPBS (Planning Programming Budgeting Systems) is an attempt to relate outcomes to expenditures. Avedisian (1973) presents a summary of the traditional and PPBS approaches to financial management.

PLANNING PROGRAMMING BUDGETING SYSTEMS

Physical education programs, as you and I know them in the professional sense,—the class, adapted, and athletic programs—are facing a major crisis in public education simply because the educational dollar is so hard to obtain. We simply cannot, and should not, sweep under the rug of complacency such manifest problems as drug abuse, property tax increases, racism, discipline, and cutbacks in program and personnel. We must tell it like it is and avoid a tendency of school personnel to freeze under these pressures and cast our hopes, ideas, and research in concrete. The time for adaptability and action is now. Thus, the traditional method of preparing physical education budgets—the incremental and function-object oriented way—will not work. What then is the approach to the problems of our day?

One effective answer is PPBS—Planning Programming Budgeting Systems—a revolutionary and practical idea which has been sweeping through educational circles. The focus of attention is on output (accomplishments) rather than upon input (things we buy). Balls, bats, and gloves do not become the issue, but . . . instead, the spotlight shines on programs and performance.

Planning Programming Budgeting Systems means the following: Planning in terms of establishing objectives; programming which concerns itself with a group of activities designed to achieve specific objectives; budgeting via priority allocation of resources; and evaluation as a systems approach "when the parts are connected for the purpose of analysis."

The Darien Public School Budget is presented in three different ways. The first is the traditional school budget which we call the line-item budget. This can be seen in summary and then in line-item detail. The format of this budget tells us easily what is spent on salaries, and on textbooks and on teaching supplies, and on equipment, etc. It is strictly input oriented. It tells us what dollars are being spent and what materials or services we are buying. But, what cannot be readily ascertained is what the citizens and students are getting for their money in terms of the learning that goes on in classrooms.

The second budget format is called a unit budget. This is the format that has been used for the past four years and is called a Responsibility Center Budget. This format is a modification of the traditional line-item budget in that it . . . is distributed in such a manner that additional questions can be answered; e.g., this format permits us to compare expenditures in one elementary school with another elementary school. It permits us to answer the question, is there a balance of effort in expenditure between the elementary schools and the secondary schools? But still this format is strongly input oriented and does not answer the questions that concern taxpayers about the increased financial support required annually to operate schools.

The third format is called PPBS. A planning programming budgeting system, PPBS attempts to get at the real questions and to answer them as fully and as carefully as possible and to demonstrate value received for dollars supplied as far as is humanly possible. It attempts to get at the relationships between programs and the resources which are required to accomplish the goals of the Darien Public Schools. In short, it attempts to connect output and input.

Note: The Darien Public Schools plan to discard the Line Budget and Unit Budget at the beginning of the fifth year, or 1974. It is wise to include the three different budgets until such time as the staff and the public have time to learn the principles of PPBS.

C. T. Avedisian, "PPBS—Its Implications for Physical Education," in *Administrative Theory and Practice in Athletics and Physical Education*, edited by P. Hunsicker, The Athletic Institute, Chicago, 1973.

Budget Items

Assuming that the total revenue from all sources is known or can be projected from experience of recent years, the budget can be constructed according to major headings. Each instructional, recreation, and athletic program should be classified separately according to the following item headings.

Capital Outlay. Construction of facilities or payment on bonded indebtedness are the major factors in capital outlay. Major purchase of equipment to be fixed to a facility site can also be capital outlay. Basketball backboards and stadium bleachers, for example, are part of capital outlay.

Contractual Services. Contracts are often let by schools to individuals or companies for special services. Contractual services may include laundry, security officers for games, transportation for athletic teams, automobile maintenance for driver education, office machine repair, and stadium rental. All items must be advertised well in advance of the bid opening. Contractual services apply only to businesses and not to regular school employees—even though yearly employment contracts may be signed.

Contingency. The best laid plans are often disrupted by unforeseen events. A contingency item is an estimated amount budgeted to pay for miscellaneous items and unforeseen emergencies. Contingency funds are flexible and can be used for petty cash, capital outlay or contractual service overruns, repair of damage caused by weather disasters, and general cost overruns caused by inflation. (During inflationary periods, an amount equal to twenty percent of the repair and contractual service budget might well be designated for contingency.)

Equipment. Initial investment in equipment for instruction and athletics is a significant part of the school budget. Diversified long-range planning for purchase of equipment will ultimately provide the school with all the desired apparatus, though the total program could not be outfitted in a single year. Equipment replacement must also be considered in the yearly budget.

Insurance. Student health insurance may be carried by the school or the individual participants. Broad, comprehensive damage and liability insurance for the school is usually funded by the local school board. If the school itself contributes to an insurance program, the policy should be selected through competitive bids.

Personnel Services. Personnel services include the base salary and coaching stipend of teachers. Most salary budgets are managed through the central school board office. But if a lump sum is designated to each school for coaching stipends, the principal and athletic director must divide that amount on the basis of priorities among sports events.

Supplies and Materials. Training-room supplies and instructional materials are important factors in program success. The amount of public funds school systems designate for instructional supplies varies from a low of twenty cents per student to as much as three dollars or more per student. Supplies and materials include athletic tape, gymnastic chalk, and ditto paper.

Steps in Budget Construction

Line items to be included in a budget should be evaluated and ranked cooperatively by the staff. Line items identifying major expenditures, such as for gymnastic apparatus, may be shuffled out of or into the budget to arrive at a composite total. Most organizational units within the school, such as the physical education department, will have jurisdiction only over equipment and operational items. The central administrative office budgets capital outlay, teachers' salaries, and maintenance costs. Though variations exist, the following method is standard procedure for budget development.

Program Review. Compare the cost analysis and inventory with the projected program. Cost analysis per pupil for each program must be made. A comprehensive inventory report reduces the chance of wasteful duplication. Budget decentralization should call for each head coach, head trainer, and the head of the

Figure 7.3 Line items of the budget should be evaluated and ranked cooperatively by the staff.

physical education department to submit requests for the next year based upon review of the previous year and projections for program changes. For example, if archery is going to be added, a heavy allowance will be needed in the capital budget to prepare for this sport. Certainly the football coach will need to project the attractiveness or unattractiveness of the next season's opponents played at home, the strength of the home team, and any other factor which might affect possible income.

Previous Budget.   Compare each line item in the previous year's budget with the projected budget. Differences between the new budget and the old should be explained in marginal notes or on additional sheets. Increases in requested funds for line items should be explained and justified in an attached sheet called an *addendum.* Inflationary cost increases can be projected by telephoning local distributors for informal estimates.

Line Item Values.   Label every major category of items, such as capital outlay, contractual services, etc. Subheadings under each line item may specify the amounts requested for instruction, intramurals, and the various sports events. For administrator convenience, the amount budgeted for the previous year and the requested amount should be posted in separated columns on the righthand side of the budget sheet. In all cases the proposed expenditures should balance with the proposed income.

Submitting the Budget. The new budget should reflect the best thinking of the staff as they evaluate past programs. After the line items are completed, the tentative budget should be submitted through the proper administrative channels. The physical and health education department chairman and the athletic director should submit their proposed budgets to the school principal. Any items deleted by the school principal or central office must be renegotiated or dropped. Renegotiation is possible if money can be cut from other categories in a compromise effort. A budget is tentative until approved by upper-level school administrators.

Purchasing

Purchasing is the actualizing process in school business management. School systems spend millions of dollars annually for physical and health education and athletic materials. Classroom supplies, health education models, and sports equipment are a few major categories of purchases. Both materials and services are purchased by school systems, and every school manager must know the alternative methods and procedures commonly used in making purchases.

The timing of purchases and the quantity of materials needed for the year can be estimated by looking at the previous year's class log and adjusting for any

Figure 7.4 When to order and receive athletic equipment. (From Athletic Handbook, *2nd Ed., 1974, with permission from Rawlings Sporting Goods Company.)*

Athletic Equipment Buyers Agenda

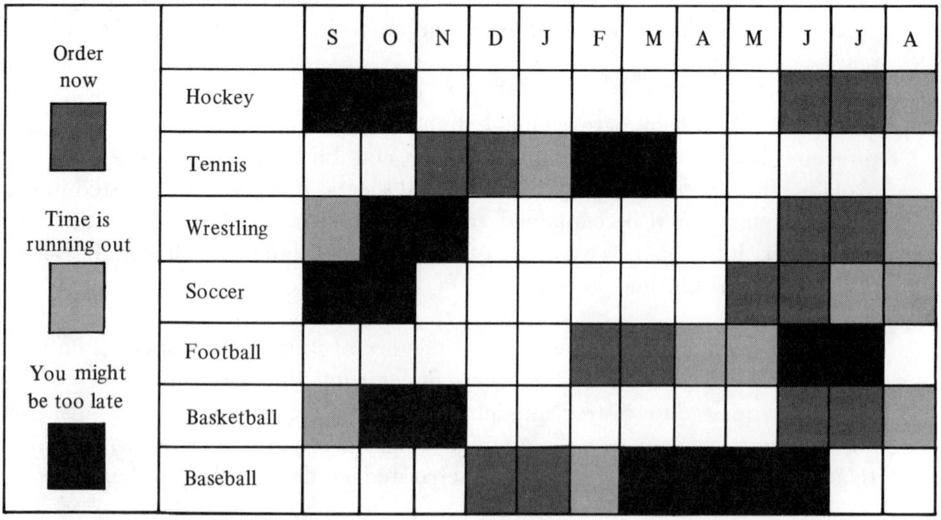

Legend:
- Order now
- Time is running out
- You might be too late

Sport	S	O	N	D	J	F	M	A	M	J	J	A
Hockey												
Tennis												
Wrestling												
Soccer												
Football												
Basketball												
Baseball												

Courtesy the *American School Board Journal*

Figure 7.5 School administrators and educational suppliers do not want to call it graft to accept favors from vendors, but what else would you call it?

known changes—more students enrolled, shorter season, increased price of admission, etc. Of course, new programs must be equipped wholly on the basis of estimates. Materials for a new program can be estimated by considering the number of students, the number of times the materials are to be used, and the breakage potential. If possible, all materials should be ordered and received several months prior to expected use. Figure 7.4 shows an ordering schedule for purchase of athletic equipment.

Representatives of educational supply companies frequently give gifts to school officials on whom they call. The salesperson does not directly state, "This is a bribe that I am offering to get your business." Many of the gifts are quite innocently given and received. Even so, every department head and athletic director must refuse offers of free dinners, personal athletic equipment, and the like. Accepting gifts from vendors places the school official in a compromising position that is very difficult to explain.

Methods of Purchasing

Two methods of purchasing are commonly used in schools. Both direct buying and bid buying have a place in school business management. Some items are purchased best when bids are let on specified items. Other materials and services may be acquired only through direct purchase.

Bid Buying. Bid buying is the procedure by which specifications are drawn up exactly defining the item to be purchased. A list of product or service specifications is sent to a large number of potential suppliers, inviting them to submit bids. At the designated time the bids are opened and the "quality low bid" accepted. Bids that do not meet the specifications should be rejected. If all bids are the same, schools usually prefer to buy from a local dealer. After the low bidder is selected, an order for the actual materials must be placed through the school business office. Bidders usually specify the length of time that their bid is valid. With common price fluctuations, few bidders will hold a bid price valid for more than ninety days. Bid procedures must be begun at least six months prior to the date the supplies or services are needed in order to allow for correspondence and shipping. It is most helpful to the athletic director if those vendors bidding on a particular item are asked to submit a sample for review. This will give the athletic director an opportunity to evaluate differences in quality. A bid specification sheet is illustrated in Figure 7.6.

Figure 7.6 *A bid specification sheet. The specification may be advertised in a newspaper or sent to regional suppliers.*

Att: Mr. J. Smith

MIDWEST CITY SCHOOL DISTRICT
MIDWEST CITY, IOWA
Note to Bidder

CONDITIONS:
    Bids for the following equipment are herewith solicited. Sealed bids will be opened at one o'clock P.M. on March 30, 1977. The quality low bid will be accepted. Substituted items may be accepted. It is assumed that the prices quoted will be valid for a period of ninety days from the bid opening. Suppliers can bid on all items or one item, etc.

EQUIPMENT:
    20 Carlton 4.7 metal rackets strung with multi-ply nylon.
    10 dozen Carlton "International" nylon shuttlecocks.
    10 dozen Penn "Centre Court" tennis balls, white.
    10 5' × 10' bonded foam lightweight folding mats with velcro fasteners on ends and sides.
    2 6' diameter push balls with canvas duck cover and rubber bladder.
    1 12' × 12' Cargo Climbing net. Must be 3/4" diameter rope with 12" squares, polypropylene rope preferred.

Direct Purchase. Much time is required to submit bid specifications and evaluate the actual bids. If the price is known to be relatively constant for all suppliers or if the equipment is needed right away, the direct purchase method is superior. In direct purchase, the list of item specifications is sent to a reputable supplier in the form of a purchase order. The supplier can ship the items immediately without bidding and waiting to see who was the low bidder. Some goods and services are available from only one company. Local purchase is best if prices are equal. If several local suppliers handle the desired merchandise, purchases can be divided equally among them. Purchase all baseball equipment from store A and all basketball equipment from store B, for instance. Local dealers are usually more liberal with credit to schools than are out-of-town low bidders.

Purchasing Procedure

After determining what items are in the inventory and what items are approved in the budget for purchase, the educational manager is ready to buy. Preliminary decisions about bid buying or direct purchase must be made early. The first actual step toward purchase is to draw up the item specifications. The model number and description must be included for each item. If substitution is to be allowed, the acceptable substitutes should be specified in exact detail. The phrase "quality low bid" on the bid form protects the school from being forced into acceptance of inferior goods and services. The Rawlings (1974) *Athletic Handbook* contains many suggestions for preparing purchase orders.

The second step is to get cost estimates. Manufacturers' catalogues usually list prices, but the actual dealer price is considerably less than the list price. Since the usual markup in sporting goods is forty percent or more, the opportunity for a dealer to sell a large quantity of items at one time usually reduces the actual cost to the school. Some state governments regularly bid standard items, such as janitorial supplies, on a statewide basis. This statewide bid price is called a *state contract item.* Local schools can generally use the low state contract price to their advantage.

The final step in purchasing is to forward a purchase requisition to the central business office. A requisition vouches to the company that the goods will be received and paid for. A separate requisition should be made for each company that is to supply goods or services. Each requisition must include specifications as well as the catalog number and amount of each item ordered. A model purchase requisition is shown in Figure 7.7. Items costing less than $25.00 can be purchased directly with funds from petty cash. Some standard purchasing practices are as follows:

1. Prepare the budget and equipment orders early (prior to the end of the preceding school year).
2. Specify the desired size, color, and model numbers of each item.
3. Request bids from several local and area merchants.

PURCHASE REQUEST

Requested by_____

For (school) _____

Address_____

Approved (principal)_____ Date _____

Budget number _____

Vendor _____

Address_____

Catalogue number	Item description	Unit cost	Number of units	Total

Figure 7.7 A model of a purchase requisition. A separate request should be completed for each vendor company.

4. Use bid buying whenever possible.
5. Do not accept items substituted by the vendor if they do not meet specifications.
6. Prefer quality merchandise that can be used for several years over cheap equipment that must be purchased yearly.

Accounting

Though it entails some planning, organizing, and actualizing, accounting is mainly a control process. Control of finances is an important factor in school athletics because of the amount of money handled. Converting public funds for private use is embezzlement. Embezzlement of school funds is a criminal act. And mishandling of funds quickly reverses any positive public relations efforts. Booster clubs and PTA groups will work for the school to no greater extent than school officials are dedicated and honest.

Principles of Accounting

Sound money management is essential in a long-range educational program. Someone in the school must be designated the financial agent. Debts incurred for physical education instructional materials are usually backed by school district assets. Districts must raise their own athletic funds if they use the zero budget. If the school's athletic fund is independently financed, someone within the organization must become the financial agent and personally sign for the purchase of goods and services. If the athletic program does not raise enough income to pay its incurred debts, the athletic director or department head may be held personally liable. A periodic balancing of the departmental account is essential. The process of balancing assets and liabilities is called *accounting*. Separate accounting may be made for cash and credit received and for unremitted accounts receivable. Publication of the financial summary is a fundamental duty of public organizations.

Records. Every individual and organization needs to keep accurate records. Each transaction should be recorded in the ledger and the voucher or bill of lading placed in the appropriate file. Records of income and expenditures protect the school manager and the school patron. Tax-deductible gifts should be recorded in the school ledger to protect the patron. Many local citizens make a substantial contribution to programs such as athletics and music. Cash transactions should always be validated by a cash receipt signed and dated by the recipient. It is good business practice to deposit *intact* all amounts received.

Accounting Definitions. Any monetary event that occurs in an organization is called a *transaction*. Recording all transactions is called *bookkeeping*. Though there is no clear difference between bookkeeping and accounting, bookkeeping tends to describe the act of making records, whereas accounting is the process of reviewing and summarizing financial status. Accounting elements include assets, liabilities, and summary statement. Assets include property, equipment, bank accounts, interest on money, gate receipts, accounts receivable, and patron gifts. School liabilities are financial obligations to creditors; they may include bank notes, credit extended by sporting goods companies, bonded indebtedness on facilities, and various unpaid bills.

Accounting Procedure

Small schools and untrained personnel often use the simpler single-entry accounting procedure. Standard columnar ledger pads of from twelve to twenty columns will suffice. One page should be marked "Cash Receipts" and a second

Cash Receipts

	Source	Date	1 Received	2 Deposit	3 Reserve Seat	4 Ticket Sales Advance Sale
1	Booster Club Gift	Aug. 25	1000 00	1000 00		
2	Football Tickets	Sept. 1	2100 00		2000 00	100 00
3	Football Game	Sept. 8	5710 00	5710 00		
4	Football Game	Sept. 12	3505 00	3505 00		200 00
5	Football Game	Sept. 26	3800 00	3800 00		250 00
6		Cash Balance	14015 00	14015 00	2000 00	550 00
7						
8						
9						
10						

Cash Disbursements

	To	Date	1 Amount	2 Athletic Equipment	3 Game Officials	4 Office Supplies
1	Wilson Sporting Goods	Aug. 26	900 00	900 00		
2	Officials Assn.	Sept. 2	300 00		300 00	
3	Misc. Game Expense	Sept. 3	500 00			
4	Stamps (Cash)	Sept. 4	50 00			
5	Midstate Supplies	Sept. 4	150 00			50 00
6	Misc. Game Expense	Sept. 8	800 00		300 00	
7	Misc. Game Expense	Sept. 14	800 00		300 00	
8	Misc. Game Expense	Sept. 26	800 00		300 00	
9	Universal Gym	Sept. 28	3000 00	3000 00		
10		Total Expense	8200 00	3900 00	1200 00	50 00
11						

Figure 7.8 A model for recording receipts and disbursements.

Cash Receipts

6 Gate Receipt	7 Candy	8 Concessions Drinks	9 Programs	10 Athletic Boosters	11 Other Collections	12
				1000 00		
5000 00	110 00	200 00	400 00			
3100 00	100 00	105 00	300 00			
3000 00	200 00	150 00	200 00			
11100 00	410 00	455 00	900 00	1000 00		

Cash Disbursements

6 Training Room Supplies	7 Candy	8 Concessions Drinks	9 Programs	10 Game Security	11 Gate Manager	12 Other Expenses
	50 00	100 00	200 00	50 00	100 00	
						50 00
100 00						
	50 00	100 00	200 00	50 00	100 00	
	50 00	100 00	200 00	50 00	100 00	
	50 00	100 00	200 00	50 00	100 00	
100 00	200 00	400 00	800 00	200 00	400 00	50 00

Balance brought forward from last month $255.50

RECEIPTS

Season ticket sales	$310.00	
Ticket sales	805.00	
Booster club contribution	500.00	
PTA donation	55.00	
Concession sales commission	340.00	
Game program sales profit	200.00	
Total revenue	$2,210.00	
Total cash resources		$2,465.50

EXPENDITURES

Equipment purchase	$850.00	
Facility rental	400.00	
Transportation	200.00	
Officials' fee	600.00	
Total expenses	$2,050.00	
Balance of cash on hand		$415.00

Figure 7.9 A model financial report.

page "Cash Disbursements." Every transaction should be recorded on the correct page. Figure 7.8 shows how to set up the respective pages with column headings.

Debits and credits correctly recorded are an accurate method of proof. Periodic comparison of credit total and debit total is called taking a *trial balance.* For further information see King and Lightner (1973).

An annual financial report should be published for the athletic program. Since the physical education and intramural departments are commonly funded with tax money, those finances are reconciled through the regular school budget. A *financial statement* reconciles the receipts and disbursements through a specified date. A sample financial statement summarizing all transactions for an athletic program is shown in Figure 7.9.

Property Management

Physical and health education and athletic facilities are rapidly being constructed or expanded (Suran 1974 and Hoy 1974). New types of equipment and equipment organizers are becoming commercially available. The educational manager has responsibility for the acquisition, use, and control of equipment. An important precept is that administrative convenience should never preclude use by faculty and students. Some examples of property-management objectives for school administrators are:

> to produce staff-devised plans for facilities remodeling or construction
> to enlist the staff in developing and enforcing property-management procedures
> to organize equipment for easy access and inventory

Equipment Planning

The advantage of long-range planning for acquisition of equipment has been discussed. Property acquisition without a long-range plan is likely not to yield an adequate inventory of equipment. Buying one major piece of athletic apparatus, one piece of gymnastic equipment, and one multipurpose mat can strain the annual budget. But such purchases made yearly, according to a long-range acquisitions plan, should yield a well-equipped program within five years.

Systematic replacement of major equipment must be built into the long-range plan. Depreciation of equipment can be prorated over the expected number of years of service. The *prorated annual cost* represents the actual cost per year. If a piece of major equipment costs a thousand dollars and lasts ten years, the cost to the school is only one hundred dollars per year. Budget items for major equipment are better defended on their yearly depreciation cost than as a large initial expense.

Central storage and disbursement of major equipment can be effectively used in a citywide or countywide school system. Since small rural schools do not have enough money to buy elaborate equipment, a check-out system could be developed. For example, gymnastic equipment could be stored at a central location during the off-season and moved from school to school for instructional units. Of course, the cost of moving the equipment must be considered in the plan.

Planning Facilities

School facilities must be humanized to promote the development of desired student outcomes. Schools and other public buildings may be monuments to an architect's cleverness, but once buildings are completed, students and faculty must live with any structural mistakes. Because of the long-term commitment that construction represents, physical and health educators have a professional obligation to offer input into building programs. Weinstock (1973) cites some

Courtesy Nissen Gymnastic Co.

Terry McKoy, I. O. E.

Figure 7.10 The prorated yearly cost of an expensive piece of apparatus may make its great initial cost more palatable to upper-level administrators.

requirements for acceptable school buildings. In order to make school a good place to learn, the following conditions should be met.

1. Human scale. Physical settings must be related to projected users and their need to identify with surroundings (small for elementary students).
2. Personal territory. Students and teachers need a place they can feel is their own (locker or tote tray).
3. Spatial variation. Rooms in the building should vary in size (for team teaching, individual conferences, etc.).
4. Spatial order. The space should permit people to arrange themselves in relationships dictated by the work and should offer privacy (noise abatement and visual screens).
5. Manipulability. Portions of the building should be able to be used independently of other subspaces (classrooms should be shut off during athletic contests).
6. Access to information and tools. Serviceability and convenience to learning resources are the main considerations in designing space (storage rooms open directly into learning centers).
7. Optional seating and work surfaces. Variations in seating and working surfaces must be built into the facility.
8. Work esthetic. A place that is interesting, useful, and relevant should also be attractive to its users (use color, texture, and murals).

New construction is only one way to provide facilities. With the projected decrease in school population, fewer new buildings will be constructed. Old buildings can be renovated at a small portion of the cost of new construction. The Educational Facilities Laboratory (1961) study showed that heated physical education areas composed twenty-two percent of the high school facilities, and seventy percent of all school property was used for physical education. Yet physical educators have not characteristically been active in facilities planning. It is imperative that they be more active! On page 254, Coates defines the guilding principles of facilities planning.

An excellent resource guide for physical education and athletic facilities construction has been developed by a coalition of the Athletic Institute and the American Association for Health, Physical Education, and Recreation (1974). The AAHPER has also published facilities manuals for dance (1972) and dressing rooms (1972). Bucher (1971) describes the fundamentals of constructing physical and health education facilities and also illustrates innovations in building design. The Educational Facilities Laboratory Report (1961), also a classic in the field, shows building and site design specifically applied to physical education.

THE PHYSICAL EDUCATOR AND FACILITY PLANNING

Guiding principles for construction generally accepted by school personnel are as follows:

1. The facility should be developed and coordinated as a part of the total school–community master plan.
2. Facility design must take into consideration the future long-range needs for the building and be planned as a functional segment of the total building.
3. Physical education personnel should be involved in the early planning between building committee and architect.
4. Educational consultants should be invited to participate in the planning and to evaluate the work of the planning group.
5. Traffic patterns for spectators and students should provide for movement through corridors and spaces with a minimum of congestion.
6. The facilities should be designed for flexibility in order to provide for a full program of activities.
7. Facilities should be located in areas that are easily available to students but provide isolation from other instruction.
8. Safety and healthful environment should be given prime consideration in facility design.
9. Planning must be realistic and consider the financial situation of the community.

E. Coates, "The Role of the Physical Educator in Facility Planning," *The Physical Educator*, 28 (1971), 88–91.

Managing Use

Equipment is purchased for use, and use causes damage. Unfortunately, other factors also cause damage, such as vandalism, weathering, and lack of preventive maintenance. *Equipment* is defined as movable materials designed for repeated use, whereas *supplies* are consumable materials designed for a single use. Principles in managing use are directed to (1) facilitating the use of equipment and (2) maintenance procedures.

Facilitating the Use of Equipment

Equipment piled high in a storage room represents an expensive daily cost in instructors' time spent securing instructional materials. The storage room should have clearly marked shelves for each group of items. The type and number of

Figure 7.11 A well-organized equipment storage room saves teachers valuable instruction time.

items should be posted on the shelves for daily inventory. Equipment can be grouped by sports families or in alphabetical order.

Several commercial suppliers have developed equipment organizers that can be transported directly to the teaching station. A two-wheeled, heavy-duty-wire cart is useful for storing and conveying heavy baseball and golf equipment. Discarded grocery carts will serve for storage and transport of lighter equipment. Nylon mesh bags are a necessity for carrying balls to and from the teaching stations. Weight training programs were formerly hazardous because of loose weights and the risk of falling with a full set of weights. The development of consolidated multistation units for weight training should reduce accidents and increase usage. A list of equipment suppliers is included in the Student Guide.

Caring for Equipment

Quality athletic equipment is made to withstand rough abuse for several seasons. Upon request, each manufacturer will supply specifications for cleaning and maintenance. Athletic garments should be purchased with due consideration for maintenance. Most knit polyester fabrics can be laundered, reducing the cost of cleaning game clothing. Dry cleaning may preserve fabric color, but washing in water is usually needed for perspiration stains. Leather basketballs and footballs can be cleaned with water and a commercial cleaner. Daily maintenance can easily double the useful life of athletic equipment. The cost of a washer and dryer for the department is shortly repaid in convenience and increased equipment life. Consult the Rawlings (1974) handbook for specific details on equipment care.

Equipment control begins and ends with a comprehensive inventory. The type and quantity of each item of equipment must be recorded at the beginning and end of the year. Procedures for periodic equipment accounting should be made and a standard operating procedure for checking out should be instituted. A formal system such as is shown in Figure 7.12 may be called for in large school systems. The instructor who signs out a designated number of items is responsible for the return of that equipment. Large items should carry engraved identification, and small items should be marked with paint or ink.

Arrangement of the storage room can facilitate usage and control. It should be centrally located near the teaching stations. Dutch doors are desirable if an attendant is available. Student workers and teacher aides may assume attendant duties in the equipment room.

Close equipment control must become second nature to all instructors. Though equipment is of only instrumental importance in the teaching process, loss of equipment may preclude continuation of worthwhile activities. Every teacher should be given a complete copy of the equipment inventory. Staff should cooperate to plan effective methods of control. For example, issuing a football to a designated squad leader is better than simply giving the ball to the squad in general. The squad leader is identified and held accountable for the piece of equipment. An example of an inventory form appears in Figure 7.13.

Figure 7.12 A formal check-out sheet for equipment control.

Equipment control

Teacher	Date out	Date in	Description of equipment items	Number of items
Eisenberg	1/5/77		Basketballs	12
Pender	1/5/77		Golf Clubs – – – – – – – – –	– –24
			Golf Balls – – – – – – –	– 56

SCHOOL RECREATION
INVENTORY FORM

Name _____

Date _____ Room or location _____

Type of equipment	# New	# Used	Condition of equipment	# Discarded

Figure 7.13 A model equipment inventory form.

Case Example: MANAGEMENT OF FISCAL AFFAIRS

Both the athletic director and the principal of Boone High School agree that each sport must independently manage its own fiscal affairs from a zero budget. The head coaches of all sports must raise their own funds, keep their own books, and inventory their own equipment. The school provides team transportation, coaches' salary and facility rental costs. The head coaches must raise funds for equipment, uniforms, and supplies.

You are the head baseball coach in the first year of the school's baseball program. A local sporting goods dealer has agreed to furnish uniforms and equipment to the team at a discount price if you will sign as the responsible financial agent. You realize that if the gate receipts do not cover this expense, you will have purchased twenty baseball uniforms of various sizes for yourself.

Develop a plan for financing purchase of the necessary baseball equipment. Describe how the money will be raised, how you will set up your bookkeeping system to account for the transactions, and how you will control losses and damage to the equipment.

References

AAHPER. *Dance Facilities.* American Association for Health, Physical Education and Recreation, Washington, D.C., 1972.

AAHPER. *Dressing Rooms and Related Service Facilities for Physical Education, Athletics and Recreation.* American Association for Health, Physical Education and Recreation, Washington, D.C., 1972.

ABDELSAMAD, M. H., and E. H. HUNT. "Capital Expenditure Analysis: Key to Financial Management." *Administrative Management,* 34 (1973), 63–65.

AMERICAN SCHOOL BOARDS ASSOCIATION. "How to Figure Your True Sports Costs." *American School Board Journal,* 162 (1975), 21–24.

ATHLETIC INSTITUTE AND AAHPER. *Planning Facilities for Athletics, Physical Education and Recreation.* The Athletic Institute and American Association for Health, Physical Education and Recreation, Chicago, 1974.

AVEDISIAN, C. T. "PPBS—Its Implications for Physical Education." In *Administrative Theory and Practice in Athletics and Physical Education,* edited by P. Hunsicker. The Athletic Institute, Chicago, 1973.

BUCHER, C. A. *Administration of Health and Physical Education Programs Including Athletics,* 5th ed. The C. V. Mosley Company, St. Louis, 1971.

COATES, E. "The Role of the Physical Educator in Facility Planning." *The Physical Educator,* 28 (1971), 88–91.

EDUCATIONAL FACILITIES LABORATORY. "Shelter for Physical Education." Architectural Research Group, The A & M College of Texas, College Station, Texas, 1961.

HOY, J. T. "What's New at W. M. U." *Athletic Administration,* 8 (1974), 22, 24.

KING. J. W., and A. S. LIGHTNER. "A Good Start in Accounting." *Business Education Forum,* 28 (1973), 27.

MAINIERI, D. J., and R. H. WARNOCK. "A Summary of Financial Policies in Selected Community Colleges in the United States." *Athletic Administration*, 8 (1973), 26–27, 29.

RAWLINGS. *Athletic Handbook*, 2nd ed. Rawlings Sporting Goods Company, St. Louis, 1974.

SURAN, C. "A Dream Come True." *Athletic Administration*, 8 (1974), 12–13.

WEINSTOCK, R. "How To Make Sure Great Schools Get Designed for Your District." *American School Board Journal*, 160 (1973), 25–27.

8.

PERSONNEL ADMINISTRATION

After reading this chapter, each student should be able to:

Identify the procedures of staffing an organization.

Take part in an employment interview as employer and applicant.

Evaluate the performance of staff and administrator.

Identify the critical factors in staff–staff and administrator–staff relations.

Develop a strategy for minimizing turnover.

Develop a strategy for improving manager and staff production.

The idea of having schools to perform society's educative function is valid, but the intended function of the school is seldom fully realized. There is too much truth in the mismanagement depicted in the films *To Sir With Love* and *Conrack* and the book *Up the Down Staircase.* The following quotation from Bower (1973) describes the behavior of two school principals, but all school administrators must be sensitive to the damage incompetent management can do.

> I think the perfect cartoon of a principal is a very frightened man out on a cold day with few clothes on, about to dip his toe in cold water. They're frightened of getting wet or jumping into anything. Perhaps communities make them that way—playing safe is safest. But it sure doesn't encourage me to try anything new or even think about it anymore. I feel sympathy for him, but I'm frustrated, too. He's supposed to evaluate me but he's never observed me teaching, never once. A vice-principal or visiting principal would come in but my principal would sign the evaluation. They write up all these stupid things that have nothing whatsoever to do with you as a teacher. It's all so much nonsense.

Modern science has left few physical problems unsolved, but the basic "people problems" remain and multiply. The most critical issue in contemporary society is how to handle problems of human interaction. People complicate matters with their own character complexities, their own prejudices, and their own unresolved needs.

Similar personnel management problems crop up in classrooms, on athletic teams, in the school staff, and in business organizations. The concept of organizational management is as old as social institutions themselves, and scientific management was begun more than half a century ago by Taylor (1947), who first presented his ideas on scientific management in 1909. Obviously, much research on management efficiency and social psychology has been done since. Yet the task of applying the principles of organizational management and social psychology to school administration remains extremely challenging.

Specific problems of staffing, motivation, evaluation, and work-group harmony are examples of management functions in personal administration. The familiar concepts of planning, organizing, actualizing, and controlling also appear in subdued form in this chapter. The major thrust of this section is to cast scientific, philosophical, and practical concepts into functional form in physical and health education.

Selection of Staff

Staff selection is the planning and organizing facet of personnel management. Staff members needed are teachers, coaches, and teacher aides. Planning is needed in staffing because staff competencies must fit into the overall organizational aim. Organizing is intrinsic to staffing because organizing is the process of fitting tasks and people together. Staff members are the critical catalyst between projected educational ideas and modification of student behavior. Some examples of management objectives for staff selection are:

to analyze an organization and determine the work competencies needed to achieve full productivity

to write behavioral job descriptions that identify the job activities

to select staff members

to identify the elements of orienting staff to the school

Job Analysis and Description

Assuming that there is a long-range management plan for the school, competency patterns should be periodically analyzed for each staff position. Each worker plays a designated role in achieving stated organizational aims. Good management demands job analysis and a job description for every position in the school, including both existing and prospective staff positions.

Job Analysis

Job analysis is the process of reviewing the organization's goals, the success of recent production efforts, and the competency patterns demonstrated by the staff. Stewart (1967) studied the work diaries of one hundred and sixty managers to determine the tasks in which they engaged. Research in job analysis is also called the *critical-incident technique*. Obviously, different competencies are required to play the various positions on a team. Similarly, different personality profiles and competency patterns are needed in operating a school. For example, personality profiles of successful teachers tend to include (1) empathy for other people; (2) moderate to high drive level; (3) conscientiousness; and (4) a moderate level of sensitivity. However, the personality requisites of various school management and teaching assignments may vary from school to school. Mandell (1974) used extensive interview and observation techniques to identify performance factors in athletic team positions. His description of the personality profiles characteristic of a football team—another complex organization—is included to depict procedures for job analysis and illustrate the idea of differential staffing.

A PSYCHIATRIST LOOKS AT PRO FOOTBALL

At the coach's invitation I began to observe and interview the players of the San Diego Chargers. My function was to provide the coaches with a clear understanding of these men and their positions, and to make personal comments and recommendations.

It took more than a year of quiet observation and conversation to break down the barriers between the players and me. In all I conducted over 200 interviews—on the practice field, on the plane to games, etc.

My first observation to the coach was, "I can tell whether the player is on the offensive or defensive unit just by looking at his locker. The offensive players are clean and orderly while the lockers of defensive men are a mess."

I began to differentiate the personality profiles of these men without prior knowledge of requirements for their specific positions. It became clear that in addition to athletic ability, motivation, and commitment, a suitable personality for his particular position is the most significant factor for a player's survival in the NFL.

Offensive linemen, for example, tend to be conservative, ambitious, tenacious, and precise. A sacrificial attitude toward the welfare of the team is integral to the offensive lineman.

The center, who often has to call the signals, is usually the brightest. The offensive guard may be more aggressive. Loyalty and commitment are characteristics of the tackle.

The wide receiver is a very special human being. He is narcissistic and vain, and basically a loner. Essentially brilliant and not too friendly, he's rarely a popular member of the team, and often lives by himself.

Quarterbacks are the most difficult of the offensive players to categorize. Given outstanding intelligence and skill, the major determinant of their success appears to be self-confidence—a self-confidence that is akin to super-arrogance.

The defensive-team members are the renegades. Compared to the offensive line they are basically angry, restless, intolerant of detail, and barely under control.

The linebacker is a combination of control, brutality, and internal conflict. He wants to look good to himself and becomes extremely depressed when he fails.

Given roughly the same amount of athletic ability, why do some men fail and others succeed in pro football? In other fields as well, appropriateness of personality to one's role may be the most significant single determinant of success and happiness.

A. J. Mandell, "A Psychiatrist Looks at Pro Football," *Saturday Review/World*, 2 (1974), 12–16.

Periodic evaluation should be conducted to redefine the cluster of job competencies needed for each staff position. The overall organization of a school staff is not a static picture on a line-and-staff chart; school structure must change with changes in the expectations of society. Job analysis must be carried out periodically to insure that all needed competencies are represented on the staff. For example, emphasis on lifetime sports at the high school level is a nationwide trend. A physical education department that is only competent in team sports needs to be retrained in lifetime sports. And new faculty and replacements should be hired with emphasis on competencies in individual sports.

Job Description

A *job description* is a summary of the major tasks executed by a certain employee. Every staff position in an organization should have a job description. Complete disclosure of the job description helps both employer and employee. A prospective employee needs to know what will be expected. The practice of keeping a distasteful assignment in the background until after the school year begins results in strained administration–staff relations and low productivity. Writing job descriptions in behavioral terms insures a clear understanding during employment and a reference point for employees as they begin their jobs. A sample job description follows.

Title: Supervisor of Physical and Health Education

Duties: The supervisor of physical and health education for the Dakota City School System will report to the assistant superintendent for instruction and will have the status of executive consultant to the school principals and teachers. The specific management functions to be accomplished are:

1. To instigate long-range curriculum and facilities planning
2. To develop a systemwide yearly budget for physical and health instruction, school recreation, and athletics
3. To develop evaluation guides for student testing and program assessment
4. To identify and publicize significant programs and needs within the various schools
5. To conduct in-service training for elementary and secondary teachers

Salary: Open and dependent upon academic degree and number of years of experience.

Requirements: Master's degree in physical and health education including course work in school management. A valid teaching certificate and three years of successful classroom teaching are required.

The Dakota City School system is an equal opportunity employer.

Securing Candidates

Filling vacant public school positions can no longer be done in secret. Executive guidelines and review by the United States Department of Health, Education and Welfare require advertisement of all job openings. The federal courts continue to review schools for possible discrimination. Placement and promotions should reflect proportionality of race and sex. It is critical that employers maintain a register of all applicants. If the number of applicants from minority groups is low, it will be necessary to show just cause. It is suggested that recruiting efforts be made at those institutions with predominant black or female enrollment.

Prospective candidates for an open position can be secured from several sources. Colleges and universities with programs in teacher preparation usually have a placement service. Independent companies offer placement service for a fee to the prospective teacher. Professional associations sponsor placement service during area conventions.

Placement Services

Colleges and universities with programs in teacher education are eager to place their graduates. The institution's teacher-placement service is a mediating agent to bring candidates and employers together. Graduates register with the placement service, specifying areas of interest. Prospective employers are provided names, credentials, and recommendations of available candidates. Many placement centers have facilities available for on-the-spot interviews with the narrowed field of candidates. Direct communication with regional university departments of physical and health education can also produce quick results.

Professional Associations

National and district AAHPER conventions sponsor placement services to members. Because so many potential employers and applicants attend such meetings, contact between employer and candidate is convenient and informal. All candidates complete a registration form defining their job interests. Prospective employers review the files to select the candidates they want to interview. Professional conventions provide an excellent context for interviewing a large number of potential candidates in a short period and at a low cost to the interviewing school.

Within the System

If a middle-echelon or other highly desirable position is to be filled, personnel within the system should have as much chance as outside recruits. The pros and cons of filling line positions with inside personnel are lengthy. If inside persons are not allowed to compete for more responsible positions, low morale will result. Staff members may feel tied to a low position. Their only alternative is to leave the institution for another position in which there is real opportunity for advancement. Thus valuable staff members may be lost unnecessarily.

If outside persons are not considered for appointment, faculty in-breeding can be a problem. Outside persons bring new dimensions to the local situation. The free exchange of ideas representing divergent ways of thinking should provide a more dynamic situation. If correctly channeled, the new ideas brought in by outside recruits can increase production.

The problem of filling a vacancy from inside or outside the system is not really as difficult as it may seem. It can be resolved by following a twofold plan of action: (1) publish the job notification widely and (2) evaluate all candidates on the basis of merit. Though there is usually some local pressure to quickly accept someone within the system, the community as a whole will be shortchanged if other qualified people are not considered.

Assessing Applicants

Industrial psychologists test and interview, using statistical tools to project the probability of success for each applicant. Principles and procedures developed by business and psychology have wide application. If staff production is to be increased in schools, objective methods of selecting staff must be employed.

Assuming that people will behave in the immediate future in a manner consistent with their immediate past, educational records and employer evaluations should predict the probability of an applicant's success. Both objective and evaluative data should be collected for each applicant. Some relevant categories of information are described in the paragraphs that follow.

Background Information

The personnel administrator should secure direct, independent statements from those who know the candidate. Former associates, ministers, professors, and administrators can supply information regarding reputation. An omnibus rating sheet, such as the one shown in Figure 8.1, can be developed to gather information from several sources on several facets of the applicant's qualifications. A category dealing with ethical character is nearly always included. Ratings and letters of recommendation must be received directly from the evaluator. (Letters of recommendation carried by the applicant should be given very little weight, since forgery is possible.)

Educational Experiences

Academic achievement and teaching success are not synonymous. The correlation between school achievement and teaching work success is typically no greater than .50. Academic achievement is measured by the courses completed and the point average attained. Each applicant should furnish an official transcript of all college credits.

Physical and health education teachers need both planned curricular experiences and extracurricular experiences. Preparatory theory class and classes in motor-skill acquisition are essential. While in the teacher education program, the physical and health education major should also have participated in interschool athletics and intramural sports. The kind and extent of extracurricular activity should be noted. Some administrators weigh grades and extracurricular experiences equally. Field experience has shown that people with involvement in extracurricular activity have a good basis for coping with the high stress of teaching.

MIDWEST CITY SCHOOL DISTRICT
MIDWEST CITY, IOWA

Date _____

To _____   Re _____
     (reference)   (applicant)

Address _____   For _____
                                       (position)

_____

The above named applicant has given your name as a reference for a position in our school system. Your evaluation will be kept confidential. Rate each category (1) below average, (3) average, or (5) above average. Use numbers only.

1 2 3 4 5 Unobserved

1. Model for gender identification by students

2. Overall health and appearance

3. Scholarship in major teaching areas

4. Scholarship in minor teaching areas

5. Competency in team sports

6. Competency in individual sports skills

7. Rapport with students

8. Ability to effectively organize

9. Ability to effectively communicate

10. Ability to motivate students

11. Ability to control students

12. Competency in coaching

13. Acceptance of responsibility

14. Overall projection of professionalism

How long have you known the applicant? _____

In what relation have you known the applicant? _____

_____ Would you hire the applicant for this position? _____ Additional comments _____

_____

_____

_____

Date _____ Signed/Official title _____

Figure 8.1 A model evaluation form.

Work Experiences

The beginning teacher who has only student teaching experience to report is untested. Work experience teaches dependability, worker interaction, and perseverance. After studying one category of beginning workers, Renee (1974) reported that the most common weaknesses of new employees were undependability and inefficiency. Camp leadership, recreation leadership, and work experience outside education should be reported. Whether candidates earned a sizable portion of their educational expenses is also an important consideration.

Capabilities

Numerous tests are available that purport to measure almost all the traits thought to relate to production. Information tests, attitude scales, personality inventories, and motor-performance tests can aid in selection of personnel.

Education deals largely with transmitting information. Physical and health education as a subject area has amassed much information of value to the student. However, teachers must be conversant with this information before they can transmit it. State departments of education specify minimum certification programs for teacher education, but there is considerable variation in course quality among institutions. Until the teaching field becomes a self-regulating profession that rigorously and objectively examines college graduates prior to professional fellowship, individual administrators must protect themselves by making their own evaluation.

Standardized Tests. Standardized tests have been published purporting to measure general capability to teach and specific preparation in the subject area. The *National Teacher Examination* is a widely used device for quantifying the degree of professional preparation. The Educational Testing Service of Princeton, New Jersey, uses active professional teachers as consultants in developing their tests. Intrinsic validity and test norms are based on responses from teachers and college seniors. The tests tend to discriminate between groups in the various stages of professional preparation.

The *National Teacher Examination* contains two distinct parts—a common examination and area examinations. The common examination covers professional information; English expression; the fields of social studies, fine arts, literature, science, and mathematics; and nonverbal reasoning. The area examinations individually cover the subjects usually taught in schools. Each test contains one hundred or more questions pertaining to a specific area. The tests are timed, with less time allowed than is usually necessary for completion. Because of the shortened time allotment, the tests reward reading speed and minimize conceptual skill. The *National Teacher Examination* is an achievement test, not a test of teaching potential or competency. It measures verbal interpretation of hypothetical teaching situations.

Date _____

Interviewer_____

Applicant _____ For_____
　　　　　　　(name)　　　　　　　　　　　　(position)

_____
　　　　　　(address)

_____

After the applicant has left the room, complete the rating form. The rating categories are (1) below average, (3) average, and (5) above average.

　　　　　　　　　　　　　　　　　　　　1　2　3　4　5　Unobserved

1. Overall health and appearance

2. Ability to communicate

3. Knowledge of subject area

4. Knowledge of student charac-
　　teristics

5. Interest in the position

6. Direct eye contact

7. Friendliness

8. Degree of appropriateness for
　　the job

9. Positive professional outlook

10. Attitude toward students

11. Philosophy of teaching/coaching

Strengths: _____　Weaknesses: _____

_____　　　　　_____

_____　　　　　_____

_____　　　　　_____

_____　　　　　_____

Figure 8.2 A checklist for summarizing an interview.

Interview. The interview is a gathering device for subjective data. A trained interviewer can derive information that could not otherwise be obtained. Some businesses commonly interview each prospective employee twice. The first interview is used as a rough screening device, and the second interview provides information to be used as a basis for final selection of the proper candidate. Figure 8.2 is a checklist for use in summarizing the interview.

The trained interviewer looks for characteristics that conform to the job description. Contrary to what might seem obvious, a well conducted interview is a highly structured affair. The adroit interviewer leads the prospective employee from topic to topic without using notes. Occasionally the interviewer will pause to pursue a lead into greater depth. After the candidate leaves, the interviewer fills out a checklist and makes additional notes. The key to interviewing is to ask a question and then *listen*. The following list is made up of questions often asked in an employment interview.

1. Why do you want this job?
2. What qualifications do you have for the job?
3. What is your philosophy of education?
4. How do you deal with discipline problems?
5. Do you feel that your family will adapt well to the community?
6. Are you interested in research and innovation? What research and experimentation have you done?
7. How would you handle the tasks specified in the job description?

Both interviewer and candidate profit from an interview. The candidate needs to know specifically what tasks are expected, what the school and community are like, and what the possibilities of advancement are. Certainly salary is important, but salary should never be the first question raised by the candidate. To discuss salary *first* reveals a shallow, mercenary attitude. The first considerations are the job itself and the administrative philosophy prevailing in the school. The candidate should be persistent in interviewing the interviewer to gain a clear understanding of these topics.

Since the interview is a subjective data-gathering device, the interviewer should be aware of its inherent weaknesses. Many people can put on a good show for an interview. The glib, witty, congenial candidate is not necessarily the best candidate. These are desirable traits, but they are no guarantee of adequate background information or real motivation. Interviewing is notoriously unreliable as a single tool for selecting candidates. Asking candidates to conduct a "sample class" with regular students would give them an opportunity to demonstrate field competency. Reliability is increased when the candidate is interviewed by several members of the staff successively. It is becoming common practice for members of a department to interview desirable candidates in teams of two or three faculty members. After all of the faculty and administration have interviewed the candidates, a faculty meeting is held to make the selection. Three sample interviews appear in Chapter 8 of the Student Guide.

Orientation

Near the end of the final interview, both parties should arrive at some form of tentative agreement. A letter of commitment can be signed during the interview. Or one or both parties may reserve the right to seek interviews with other parties. The candidate may want to consider several jobs before making a commitment. The personnel manager may want to examine the field of candidates thoroughly before making firm offers. However, the interview should not end before both parties become aware of their relative desirability to the other. The candidate should know if he or she has a chance to secure the job. The personnel manager should find out whether the candidate is interested in accepting the position. It is unethical for a candidate to accept a position only to break the contract and shortly thereafter accept a more desirable position. If the school district is expected to live up to its contract, the individual teacher should also be expected to honor the formal agreement.

Contracts for Employment

A contract is an agreement by which two or more parties bind themselves to perform specified functions. In the frontier days, one's word was supposedly one's bond. Presently it is common practice to draw up and sign contracts. A properly signed contract is legally binding. Though school districts seldom exercise the option, a teacher may be forced to remain at a school because a formal contract exists.

For the protection of both parties, an employment contract should specifically delineate the tasks, related duties, and minimum compensation. Some systems prefer to hire personnel for an unspecified school somewhere in the district, rather than specifying in the contract the school and assignment to subject area. Most school employment contracts contain a clause by which the school board can require the performance of secondary teaching duties, such as hall supervision, attendance at occasional evening activities, bus duty, etc. A departmental staff handbook should be given to each person with whom a contract is signed. The staff handbook acquaints the staff with community relations, job descriptions, departmental organization, policies, advancement procedures, and grievance redress.

Tenure

The concept of teacher tenure was developed to protect teachers from being fired for such reasons as (1) participation in local political campaigns; (2) to make room for employing a friend or relative of administrators; (3) disagreement with administrative philosophies. Though the specifics vary from state to state, tenure laws do insure equitable treatment of veteran teachers. Beginning teachers are typically on probationary status. Tenure is generally received after two to five years of employment by a school district. Coaches may receive tenure as teachers, but the additional coaching assignment is not subject to tenure.

Staff Production

What goes on in the classroom is the essence of education. Teachers *should* teach as pure professionals to the highest level of their ability. But the fact is that some teachers do little more than mediocre work. Why? Teachers are human beings, and human beings can become motivated or discouraged. The circumstances that motivate one teacher may alienate another. Since a sizable portion of physical and health educators perform only at a minimally acceptable level, a study of staff production is needed to remedy the situation.

Some productivity factors and manifestations of disaffection are extremely subtle. Ponder (1971) found that teachers who taught in schools with a closed administrative climate took significantly more days of sick leave than teachers in schools with an open climate. He also found that student health attitudes were positively related to class emphasis, and student absenteeism was positively related to hindrance (teacher factor). Teacher sick leave was positively related to disengagement and hindrance and negatively related to "esprit," intimacy, trust, and consideration.

Staff production in schools is an actualization problem. It includes both the amount of progress made by students toward stated educational goals and the level of teacher performance in facultywide projects. Teacher production need not imply the school-as-factory idea by which teacher–machines spew out packages of duplicate students. Staff productivity should be equated to quality and quantity of teacher performance—a reasonable standard of accountability for student outcomes. Some management objectives for improving staff production are:

to identify the factors that enhance and discourage teacher productivity
to develop a strategy for raising teaching and coaching to full productivity
to define procedures that administrators can follow to raise morale, reduce turnover, and increase productivity in terms of student outcomes

Factors in Staff Production

What causes a health educator to work nights and weekends to prepare for classes? Why do athletic coaches devote hours beyond the required time to developing a team? Conversely, why do many physical education teachers "roll the ball" out to their classes and seldom attend a professional meeting? The answer to these questions may be that human beings are extremely complex, and that factors necessary for motivation are not present. Some teachers feel that physical education is not important in the eyes of fellow teachers, administrators, and parents, and that their main job is coaching. This attitude negatively influences the quality of physical education instruction.

School Environment

The work context can be a potent factor in production level. Industrial psychologists have explored environmental factors associated with high production. Though environmental conditions alone do not dictate production level, factors such as lighting, noise, room temperature, and materials do have an effect.

Classes. Each state education office makes a recommendation for the maximum size of elementary and secondary classes. The practice of "dumping" two or more academic classes into a physical education class seriously impedes teacher production. If physical education teachers do not take a stand against this kind of administrative action, they deserve to have an untenable number of students. Unfortunately, it is the students who suffer. One teacher can only give a fraction of the actual instruction time to each student: fifty students means one-fiftieth of the class time for each individual.

Instructional Materials. Adequate instructional materials do not cause good teaching, but effective teaching is hampered without them. Such basic equipment as balls, mats, and space for movement are essential to all physical education programs. Though much of the basic material for both health and physical education can be developed by the innovative and enthusiastic teacher, many unmotivated teachers use lack of materials as an excuse for poor teaching.

Assignment. Some teachers thrive on teaching handicapped children. To such teachers, small gains over a long period make the process worthwhile. Coaches tend to want to work only with the child gifted in motor ability. Each teacher has a preference for grade level and type of student. Where teachers are assigned to classes on this basis, competency and production level *should* be high.

Instructor Personality

Many dedicated teachers work at a high production level largely because of the psychological gratification. On a personality test, such teachers would score high on the factor of nurturance. They feel a need to help others. Elementary school physical education teachers and special education teachers would tend to have a high nurturance drive. Other personality factors such as achievement drive, dominance, and self-confidence function to affect teacher performance and stu-

Profile 4   Professional Team and New Coach   Coach _ _ _ _ _   Team _____

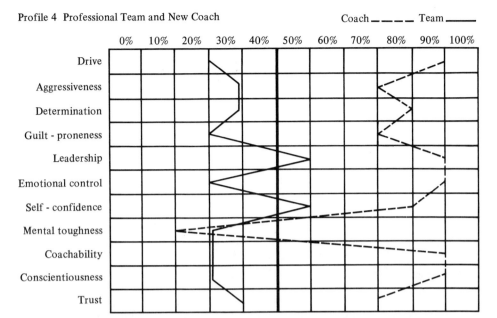

Figure 8.3 Profile of a professional team and a new coach. (Reprinted from Modern Medicine, © *1972 by the New York Times Media Company, Inc.)*

dent interaction. Ogilvie (1974) cites a case where a wide difference in personality factors existed between the team and the coach. Apparently, little basis initially existed between the coach and the team for sharing goals and procedures. (See Figure 8.3.)

Administrator–Staff Interaction

Outstanding athletic coaches inspire their teams to high achievement. The work group—whether a team or a staff—needs leadership to perform well. The manager must be able to communicate, to set goals, and to instill self-confidence in the work group. Administrator–staff interaction is based on the leader's credibility, support of the staff, and steps toward achievement of goals. A key element in administrator–staff interaction is two-way communication. Again the leader is responsible for initiating and maintaining effective communication.

Motivation

There are many theories of work motivation. Workers have been viewed as "disorganized rabble" (Mayo 1960). Psychologists who attempt to define work as "basic need fulfillment" have difficulty explaining why people continue to work

Figure 8.4 Because threats and compensation fail to instill long-term high-level motivation, other methods must be examined.

after enough money is earned to provide for all foreseeable needs. Salary increases and similar material incentives do always increase productivity.

Modern theory on work motivation takes into account the worker, the task to be accomplished, and the context. Teaching is considered a profession, but because of the bureaucratic nature of large school systems, the managerial group must function to motivate teachers. Considering the professional nature of the staff, the complexities of the teaching process, and the coordination problems of a multiteacher school, no simple authoritarian theory of threats and rewards is appropriate. Atella (1974) gives a summary of work motivators. Interestingly, his list of motivators for building worker confidence and organizational goal achievement does not include a single material incentive!

People respond to various motivations. Two teachers may teach effectively for different reasons. McGregor (1969) offers some basic concepts of actualizing that apply to both management of teacher behavior by administrators and management of student behavior by the classroom teacher:

1. The expenditure of physical and mental effort in work is as natural as play or rest. . . . Depending upon controllable conditions, work may be a source of satisfaction . . . or a source of punishment. . . .
2. Man will exercise self-direction and self-control in the service of objectives to which he is committed.
3. Commitment to objectives is a function of the rewards associated with their achievement. The most significant of such rewards, e.g., the satisfaction of ego and self-actualization needs, can be the direct products of effort directed toward organizational objectives.

4. The average human being learns, under proper conditions, not only to accept but to seek responsibility. . . .
5. The capacity to exercise a relatively high degree of imagination, ingenuity, and creativity in the solution of organizational problems is widely, not narrowly, distributed in the population.
6. Under the conditions of modern industrial life, the intellectual potentialities of the average human being are only partially utilized.

The behavioral consequences of productivity and growth cannot be isolated one from another. Managers who are totally production-oriented have their heads in the sand. Managers can encourage individual growth and achievement of personal goals within the organizational framework in order to increase productivity. Though many immature teachers may initially require managerial prodding, wise management seeks to create the kind of environment that will foster personal motivation within each employee.

Achievement

Recognition of the dignity of work is a fundamental base for production. To strive toward and achieve significant goals is a pervasive need in Western civilization. Achievement in initial tasks generally raises hopes for achievement in more difficult tasks. For example, a health teacher who is praised for trying innovative methods with one class will be inspired to continue looking for better ways of teaching.

The administrator should use the achievement factor in motivating teachers by counseling with each teacher to set goals for self-realization. The concept of becoming the best teacher possible is a powerful motivator that can improve the individual and increase instructional quality. Each department head must also show the significance of teaching by rewarding excellence. The concept that every teacher must try to become an administrator in order to be an outstanding person must be repudiated once and for all. Coaches have a sense of significant achievement because local sports fans place high value on athletics. But the main thrust of education is in student outcomes, not on winning. The administrator's responsibility is to continuously dignify the career of teaching. Naming outstanding physical education teachers and giving merit raises for real accomplishments are two methods of motivating for achievement.

Participation

Participatory management is the process by which staff members are involved in making decisions relevant to their jobs. Participation in production management is synonymous with egalitarian administrative philosophy. In early classic studies of group participation, Lewin (1958) and White and Lippitt (1947) showed that the egalitarian principle works in production situations. Though Mayo (1960) was not the prime investigator, his study of work dynamics in the Hawthorne plant indicates that participation in relevant decisions was a factor in increased production. Likert (1961) also concludes from his studies on business operations that participatory management can function to increase productivity.

The school administrator can use the motivational force in participatory management by (1) listening to the ideas of teachers; (2) putting their ideas into practice and giving credit to the originator; (3) using group decision making in faculty meetings and committee work; and (4) performing routine management details and using faculty only for solving significant problems. Formation of the departmental policy manual, curriculum development, and construction planning are significant functions that demand the participation of faculty members.

Job Enrichment

Job enrichment is the process by which staff members are given more autonomy for executing their work. The concept is related to Gestalt psychology, because it assumes that people work best when they can relate details to a large, meaningful task. Though the idea of differentiated staffing and team teaching holds some promise of effectiveness, team teaching can become an "assembly line" task for teachers on the lower levels. Teachers in self-contained classrooms offer each unit of instruction only once. Departmentalized physical and health education classes cause teachers to repeat, giving similar treatment to subsequent classes. Job enrichment includes allowing teachers to work with each student long enough to develop teacher–student rapport and increasing the amount of authority each teacher has to make decisions.

Compensation

Taylor (1947) believed that pay rates were the most important factor in production once the person was fitted to a job. He believed that the right work task and the right compensation would create a "mental revolution." Compensation is the pay that a worker receives for the tasks performed. Compensation is an incentive to work, but it does not always cause a mental revolution. Compensation can take the form of base pay at a flat rate or merit pay for quality work. Merit pay for instructors is a thorny problem because of the difficulty in assessing teacher production. However, as managers have found out, teachers and other workers do not perform at a moderate or high level just because they are to be paid for their efforts. It is not uncommon for teachers and industrial workers to perform at only one-half or one-third of their true production potential.

The use of merit raises shows some promise for improvement in teaching. If assessment of instruction were made by objective procedures like those cited in the later section of this chapter on staff evaluation, then merit raises would be

Figure 8.5 Job enrichment implies delegation of meaningful authority and a basic trust that the worker will perform well.

meaningful. Assessment must be accurate. Giving a merit raise to a low producer on the physical education staff would pose a major morale problem. The chief criticism of merit raises is that the largest increases tend to go to compliant staff members who build up the ego of the department chairperson, the athletic director, or the supervisor.

The Administrator and Unit Production

What effect does manager behavior have on teacher productivity? Manager effectiveness depends partly on the manager's capability, partly on how long the teachers have worked together, and partly on staff leadership within the work group. As Taylor (1947) found, an entrenched work group may successfully resist managerial leadership. On the other hand, May (1960) reported extremely good results when managers interacted with the work group in carrying out the leadership process.

Molding the Work Group

The department head, athletic director, or head coach has the responsibility of molding the staff into an effective unit. The morale level and production "tone" of the staff are determined by the middle-level administrator directly responsible for their performance. If this manager is cynical and complacent, little teaching will be done. If the manager is a sensitive and striving professional, the probability of effective teaching will be high. In a sense, all effective managers must be pragmatic dreamers. The dream is the ideal of what schools could be, and pragmatism must translate that dream into concrete steps toward improvement. Every outstanding physical and health education program and athletic program is the product of a leader who set high goals and worked toward them in small, positive steps.

Production Norms

The generally accepted rate of a staff's teaching effectiveness is called the *production norm*. Production norms can be seen and measured. Comparative measurements of two independent schools of like grade levels would indicate their relative production levels. Each teacher tends to develop a production norm which deviates little from the teaching rate of other staff members. Research on norm development by Sherif (1958) and Asch (1958) clearly shows that the other individuals in the group exert subtle influence to determine the group norm. This research implies that if a new professional teacher joins a staff where physical education is "taught" by rolling out the balls for play, the new teacher will tend to become cynical and disaffected like the other teachers. In order to foster high production and avoid such discouraging situations, the manager should be familiar with the following concepts.

Dynamism. In order to move the staff toward professional production, the manager must show willingness to be professional. Effort must be systematically applied to overcome staff inertia. Dynamism implies movement. Developing new teaching ideas, getting staff members to believe in themselves, and causing the group to formulate staff goals are dynamic skills of an egalitarian manager.

Power Consolidation. Realistically, every staff is not capable of instantaneously moving into high-level teaching productivity. Many physical and health educators have grown accustomed to doing little, and they will resist change. During rapid organizational change, power must be taken from the resistant teachers and temporarily consolidated in the manager. The principle of power consolidation has been used by every political government that has ever been formed. In order to get results from dynamic management techniques, the executive needs effective leverage. Managers in schools and industry use salary, threat of removal, job reassignment, and loss of privileges as levers in power consolidation.

Norm Modification. Research has shown that problem-solving group interaction is the most effective method of improving established norms (Lewin 1958, Coch and French 1958, and Morse and Reimer 1956). Individual conferences may alert teachers to the difference between their own teaching level and the desired teaching level. But the effect of group pressure is so strong that participation by the group in resetting group norms is essential for sustained change. Consolidation of power aids in setting the stage for norm modification. Faculty meetings should be the primary mechanism for modifying the production norm. Problems should be presented and discussed and a consensus reached by the group. Interaction and discussion are important, but the quality of the group consensus in accepting the new production norm is at least equally critical.

Figure 8.6 Conflicts between management and staff are resolvable when both accept their common humanity as a basis for understanding their individual needs.

Staff and Manager Relations

Both teachers and managers view their own job as the most significant in the school operation. When executives consult with the staff, they tend to do so with condescension, feeling that lower echelon personnel are not capable of making important decisions. On the other side, staff members often point out examples of administrator incompetence. Administrators and instructors (management and labor) seem to have at least a mild feeling of contempt for each other. Though such mutual contempt is widespread, no specific school has to follow the general tendency. The quality of administrator and staff relations is a manageable factor, and it is a responsibility of the manager. Collins (1974) also points out a significant problem in staff–manager relations. She incisively states that every manager must avoid the paranoia that leads him or her to believe that somebody is conspiring to undercut the leader's status.

Manager Competencies

Managers must perform the critical functions of planning, organizing, actualizing, and controlling. Though some tasks are executed directly by the manager, most will be performed by staff members to whom the specific job is delegated. In his witty book *The Peter Principle*, Lawrence Peter (1969) explained why things go wrong in organizations. His slightly cynical contention is that most executives are working at their level of *incompetence*—otherwise they would be promoted to more responsible jobs. In a sequel, *The Peter Prescription*, (1972) Dr. Peter resolves the dilemma of incompetence with a strategy for the developing of creativity, confidence, and competence. Significant elements of manager competence are cited in the following paragraphs.

Decisions. Administrators make decisions of greater magnitude than teachers. For example, the staff must be evaluated. Those who are performing well should be rewarded, and staff members who are not performing adequately must be retrained or released. New staff members must be selected. Someone in the organization must make the "hard-nosed" decisions and enforce them. Seldom is there sufficient time to gather all the facts pertinent to a decision. Political repercussions must also be considered. Decision making is usually a pragmatic trade-off between what is best and what is expedient.

Decisions may be made by the manager or shared with the staff. Theory Y (McGregor 1960) was formulated to explain why authoritarian industrial managers failed to increase productivity. The essence of theory Y is that the average human being is self-directed and that people will normally accept and even seek responsibility for decision making. Theory Y is in opposition to theory X, which holds that working staff cannot by nature make decisions and must be coerced to work by constant supervision. For example, the authoritarian theory X assumes that physical education teachers need much supervision. Theory Y assumes that physical and health education teachers can be trained to high productivity through trust, delegation of responsibilities, and reinforcement. Penzer (1973) explains the concept of theory Y and its inherent problems, and Scott (1972) presents some long-range problems in delegating authority.

Every school manager must develop a systematic method of getting and giving information. Reports by instructors on class performance, observation of instructors, individual discussion with instructors, and staff meetings are a few productive methods of getting and giving information. Memos and periodic newsletters are also used frequently to give information to the staff.

Feedback to Staff. There is no single managerial factor more important than feedback of information to the staff. *Feedback* is defined as information gained by a person about something she or he did or attempted. A cheering crowd is feedback to a runner who stretches toward the finish line. A friendly handshake and commendation by the manager is an example of feedback to a teacher. Feedback usually has positive (acceptance) or negative (rejection) overtones.

Negative feedback ranges from coldly ignoring teachers to forthright rejection of their efforts. Not all teaching attempts are successful—and some teachers make little attempt at all at success. After observation, review of student performance, and review of teacher performance ratings, the department chairperson must confer with each instructor about the relative success of the instructor's efforts. The objective data and observation reports should describe the teacher's performance profile. If the profile is low in several major categories, retraining or dismissal is necessary. Retraining is the more humane approach—perhaps in cooperation with a mature teacher model. A permanent file must be kept on each

Figure 8.7 Acceptance of staff members as worthy human beings is communicated by body language as well as by words.

staff member by the athletic director or physical and health education department head. The individual instructor must know what is in the file. If the supervisory reports are continuously negative, the file may be used to validate a decision to dismiss the staff member. Even if the data show low production, the mature manager will be able to convey rejection of the teacher's *performance,* not rejection of the teacher as a human being.

Positive feedback conveys the idea of acceptance and reward. Positive reinforcement is the most powerful tool known for the shaping of human behavior. The whole concept of behavior modification is based on judicious use of positive reinforcement. Positive feedback is generally synonymous with positive reinforcement—though feedback is much more specific and may not carry an extrinsic reward.

Theory Y postulates that people basically want to do an acceptable job. Though Atella (1974) recommends instilling slight apprehension in employees as a motivator, the major emphasis of his article is on providing guidance, support, and reward. The manager's supportive feedback to individual teachers will do more for overall staff relations and for teacher productivity than large measures of negative feedback and constant supervision.

Personnel Problems

Typically, some members of each school staff have problems working with each other, and staff members have problems with the administrator. Many apparent problems can be attributed to misunderstanding and the failure to communicate. Other problems relate to job descriptions that prescribe responsibility for performing certain duties. Some deep-seated personality conflicts, usually arising from unmet needs, can only be resolved by reassignment.

The manager must act as a referee over the staff and between staff and self. Most staff problems can be resolved by conferences wherein a mutual plan is developed to avoid future confrontations.

Personnel Evaluation

Staff effectiveness should be assessed each year by objective and subjective devices. To complete the school's assessment of effectiveness, the staff should anonymously evaluate the management each year. Anonymous evaluation by the staff would provide some unique information not directly obtainable by the manager. Some examples of management objectives for personnel evaluation are:

to develop a strategy for yearly management and staff assessment
to develop standard procedures for processing personnel evaluation data
to develop a procedure for "spot checking" teacher productivity during the year
to develop counseling procedures for evaluation feedback to manager and to staff members

The concept of accountability dictates that student achievement and teacher performance be evaluated regularly. The formal accountability procedure adopted by the Kalamazoo schools assumes that both teaching effects and effectiveness can be measured. It is described on the next page.

Measurement of Instructor Performance

The purpose of evaluation is to improve instruction. As recipients of instruction, students are in a unique position to report their own observations. That students see what is going on in the classroom each day increases the reliability of their judgment. A middle-level supervisor who observes a particular teacher infrequently may or may not get a representative view of the teacher's performance. Secondary school students should be mature enough to provide performance feedback. Of course, student evaluations should be accepted as only one piece of evidence about a teacher's performance. Student evaluations may be used by the teacher who seeks to improve instruction. Student evaluations should also be used by the middle-level administrator as an aid in counseling teachers. If the school district owns or leases a computer, the students can make their responses on a scan sheet.

Radebaugh and Johnson (1971) analyzed teacher behavior to determine the factors that are identified with excellent teachers. By using the framework identified by Radebaugh and Johnson or the factor analysis research by Medley and

HOW 'MAZOO RATES TEACHERS ON PERFORMANCE

In Kalamazoo, Michigan, teachers are held accountable for how much and how well their students learn. Each teacher is the subject of a detailed evaluation, the result of which is his or her *Teacher Performance Profile*. Various components are weighted differently. Students rate the teacher on a *Student Opinion Questionnaire*. For example, eleventh graders are asked questions such as: "Does this teacher show an enthusiasm for the subject?" The teacher is evaluated by the Principal on a *Teacher Evaluation Form*. Five to fifteen of the teacher's peers evaluate the teacher on *Peer Image Questionnaires* that ask questions such as "Does he/she contribute his share of time and energy to faculty activities and concerns?" The teacher also evaluates himself on three questionnaires—the same ones his peers, students, and principal used.

The teacher is evaluated in terms of his or her students' achievement gains. Students in grades one through nine take the *Metropolitan Achievement Test* in September and again in May each school year. Academic achievement of secondary school students is determined on criterion referenced tests.

American School Boards Association, "Here's How 'Mazoo Rates Teachers on Performance," *American School Board Journal*, 161 (1974), 43.

Mitzel (1958), you can construct a local evaluation tool. Figure 8.8 is a teacher evaluation form created by writing descriptive items for several factors considered crucial to effective teaching. The "open records" federal legislation should be viewed as a positive step toward productivity feedback. Teachers need to be apprised of supervisory evaluations in order to make needed improvements.

Production Counseling

Evaluation involves measurement and the comparison of measurement data against established performance criteria. A department head knows what a good teaching effort should be. Measurement data of teacher performance must be compared to a standard of "reasonable production." The minimum data for staff evaluation should be a rating by the students, the instructor's self-rating, and a rating by the department head. Evaluation conferences with the manager and each individual teacher should be the most productive sessions of the school year. Past performance can be examined and goals for the future can be set.

After the measurement data is condensed into a performance profile, each teacher should be called in for a conference with the department chairperson. Such conferences have traditionally been one-way feedback sessions from

INSTRUCTIONAL EVALUATION FORM

DIRECTIONS: *Do Not Write on This Form.* The purpose of this activity is to gather information which may be used to improve instruction. If your answers express your frank and honest reactions to the questions, the results will give your instructor information which can be used to accomplish this purpose. As you read through and respond to the items below, you may feel that one or more particular items do not apply to this particular course. If you feel that an item does not apply, you should not respond to that item; otherwise, mark your rating of each item with one of the following on the standard answer sheet that has been supplied: 1 (superior), 2 (good), 3 (average), 4 (below average), 5 (poor). We realize that you are not an expert, but we do want you to be as frank and honest as possible.

1. Speaks distinctly and in an engaging voice.
2. Appears poised and self-confident in the classroom.
3. Is able to hold my attention in the classroom.
4. Appears to know the subject matter being taught.
5. Subject matter is explained as clearly as possible considering subject.
6. Uses effective examples, illustrations, and/or visual aids.
7. Lectures meaningfully related to textbook materials assigned.
8. Examinations appear representative of the materials assigned.
9. Homework and assignments add to my understanding of the course.
10. Classroom activities, excluding lectures, add to my understanding of the course.
11. Grading of the course is objective.
12. Is able to gain my participation readily.
13. Plans and organizes lectures and/or activities effectively.
14. Meets class regularly and punctually.
15. Grades and returns tests promptly.
16. Gives adequate information concerning test results.
17. Classroom time is used effectively.
18. Makes me feel at ease in class.
19. Appears to be impartial in dealing with students.
20. Is willing to provide outside help and guidance.
21. Makes it possible for students to feel that they may ask questions.
22. Makes it possible for students to feel that they may express their opinions.
23. Courteous and tactful toward students.
24. Free from distracting mannerisms.
25. Appears enthusiastic about the subject matter.
26. Stimulates my interest in further study of the subject.
27. Overall teaching ability.

Figure 8.8 A sample teacher evaluation form. (Courtesy Southeastern Louisiana University.)

manager to teacher. Application of theory Y would substitute a free, two-way exchange of ideas and problems.

The main fallacy of traditional personnel management has been its complete lack of understanding of the individual teacher's personality. Coaches are recognizing the need for understanding the personality of each athlete. If an athlete scores low on the self-confidence factor, the coach must handle that athlete differently than an ebullient, highly self-confident athlete. Counseling with teachers to promote productivity is similar to counseling with athletes. To get each individual to perform near capacity, the counseling must fit the individual. A physician would not write the same prescription for all patients. Neither should a department chairperson interact the same way with all teachers. Essentially, the manager must assess the personality of each teacher by test or observation. Such factors as drive, determination, creativity, self-confidence, sensitivity, and emotional control should be included in assessing a teacher's personality. Only by knowing teachers and their performance can the manager be really effective in work counseling.

Case Example: STAFF PRODUCTION

When Mr. Humbuck accepted the position of city supervisor of physical and health education, he had decided to get acquainted with the situation before structuring an action plan. Six months after assuming duties, he began trying to put his plans into effect. He sent detailed memos to each of the eighty teachers under his supervision describing the curriculum plan and specifically detailing the changes expected.

Upon visiting each school later in the year, Mr. Humbuck found that the inexperienced teachers had put some of his directives into practice, but none of the older teachers even remembered receiving them. At the end of the school term, Mr. Humbuck evaluated his year's effort and concluded that he had not accomplished anything. The teachers continued to use the methods they had previously used. There was no systematic testing and reporting on a systemwide basis. There was no progression of activities from lower to higher grades. His efforts to change the staff operation had been virtually ignored. (The previous supervisor had espoused the laissez-faire philosophy, functioning mainly to coordinate equipment purchases and to schedule interschool athletic contests.) The superintendent of schools has demanded positive changes—especially in physical and health instruction programs.

To complicate the situation, there are conflicts between men and women physical and health education teachers over facility use. The school has a fifty–fifty black-white teacher ratio. There is little communication between the black and white teachers and some open hostility on the coaching staff.

Based on this description of the school district, what are the major problems? What strategy should be followed to get production started?

References

AMERICAN SCHOOL BOARDS ASSOCIATION. "Here's How 'Mazoo Rates Teachers on Performance." *American School Board Journal,* 161 (1974), 43.

ASCH, S. E. "Effects of Group Pressure Upon the Modification and Distortion of Judgments." In *Readings in Social Psychology,* 3d ed. edited by E. E. Maccoby, T. M. Newcomb, and E. L. Hartley. Henry Holt and Company, New York, 1958.

ATELLA, J. T. "Instilling Apprehension Delicately." *Administrative Management,* 35 (1974), 56–57.

BOWER, E. M. *Teachers Talk about Their Feelings.* National Institute of Mental Health, Rockville, Md., 1973.

COCH, L., and J. R. P. FRENCH, JR. "Overcoming Resistance to Change." In *Readings in Social Psychology,* 3d ed., edited by E. E. Maccoby, T. M. Newcomb, and E. L. Hartley. Henry Holt and Company, New York, 1958.

COLLINS, L. "Do You Have What It Takes To Be Board President?" *American School Board Journal,* 151 (1974), 17–19.

LEWIN, K. "Group Decision and Social Change." In *Readings in Social Psychology,* 3d ed., edited by E. E. Maccoby, T. M. Newcomb, and E. L. Hartley. Henry Holt and Company, New York, 1958.

LIKERT, R. *New Patterns of Management.* McGraw-Hill Book Company, New York, 1961.

MANDELL, A. J. "A Psychiatrist Looks at Pro Football." *Saturday Review/World,* 2 (1974), 12–16.

MAYO, E. *The Human Problems of an Industrial Civilization.* The Viking Press, New York, 1960.

McGREGOR, D. *The Human Side of Enterprise.* McGraw-Hill Book Company, New York, 1960.

MEDLEY, D. M., and H. E. MITZEL. "A Technique for Measuring Classroom Behavior." *Journal of Educational Psychology,* 49 (1958), 86–92.

MORSE, N., and E. REIMER. "The Experimental Change of a Major Organizational Variable." *Journal of Abnormal and Social Psychology,* 52 (1956), 120–129.

OGILVIE, B. C. "Personality Traits of Competitors and Coaches." In *Issues in Physical Education and Sports,* edited by G. H. McGlynn. National Press Books, Palo Alto, Calif., 1974.

PENZER, W. N. "After Everyone's Had His Job Enriched, Then What?" *Administrative Management,* 34 (1973), 20–22, 76, 80.

PETER, L. J. *The Peter Principle.* Bantam Books, New York, 1969.

———— *The Peter Prescription.* Bantam Books, New York, 1972.

PONDER, L. D. "The Relationship Between Organizational Climate and Five Health Related Factors in Selected East Tennessee Elementary Schools." Doctoral dissertation, University of Tennessee, Knoxville, 1971.

RADEBAUGH, B. F., and J. A. JOHNSON. "Excellent Teachers—What Makes Them Outstanding." *Clearinghouse,* 45 (March 1971), 416–417.

RENEE, M. A. "What Business Wants from Beginners." *Administrative Management,* 35 (May 1974), 55–57.

SCOTT, R. H. "You Owe It to Yourself to Delegate." *Administrative Management,* 33 (December 1972), 77.

SHERIF, M. "Group Influences Upon the Formation of Norms and Attitudes." In *Readings in Social Psychology,* 3d ed., edited by E. E. Maccoby, T. M. Newcomb, and E. L. Hartley. Henry Holt and Company, New York, 1958.

STEWART, R. *Managers and Their Jobs.* Macmillan & Co., London, 1967.

TAYLOR, F. W. *Scientific Management.* Harper & Row, Publishers, New York, 1947.

WHITE, R., and R. LIPPITT. *Autocracy and Democracy: An Experimental Inquiry.* Harper & Row, Publishers, New York, 1947.

9.

TOURNAMENTS

After reading this chapter, each student should be able to:

Describe each type of tournament.

Describe the various applications of tournament competition in physical education classes, school recreation, and interschool athletics.

Correctly structure the competition in each type of tournament.

Conduct a successful tournament in a practical situation.

A good tournament produces balanced competition climaxed by the final victory of the best athlete. Interest should build from the first round of play to the final decisive contest. There are always many who claim to be the superior player. It is competition that separates the best competitor from the challengers. Hence one disadvantage of competition in education: it produces too many losers. Technically, in a sixteen-competitor tournament, fifteen players lose (see Alexander 1970 and Bessier 1967).

Managing Competition

A *tournament* is an orderly series of contests in which skill is tested. The word tournament is derived from the Old French word *torner* which means "to turn." Thus, a tournament is an advent in which participants compete in systematic order. In medieval times the tournament was a knightly sport in which men in armor engaged in matched contests to exhibit skill and courage. In modern terms a tournament is a contest or series of contests held to systematically determine the winner from a large field of challengers. For example, professional golf tournaments usually consist of several rounds played on successive days. The lesser skilled players are eliminated from a field of more than one hundred golfers, leaving the top players to compete in the final rounds.

Competition

The true goal of school competition is to contribute to the development of the individual student. Professional and other nonscholastic competition may legitimately have goals such as prizes or money. Schools, by contrast, function only to

Figure 9.1 The joust was an early form of structured competition. Each knight would compete in the war game when his turn came.

change student behavior in positive directions. Competition in the school contest must be viewed as a means to an educationally justifiable end, rather than an end in itself.

Marshall (1962) presents the classic concept of competition. As an idealist, he contends that the value of competition is within the process itself. His case is easiest to understand in terms of, say, track and swimming events, where time and distance are the performance criteria. From the long-range perspective of human life, the idealized competitive process becomes clearer. Physical education fails if exercise stops with the end of the academic program. At age thirty and onward, the ability to regularly *complete* a mile run becomes more important than high velocity. Marshall's premise of competition against forces becomes valid when viewing sports competition against the background of legitimate personal and social values.

COMPETITION: FOR BETTER OR WORSE?

There are several major areas in which competition performs a contributory function. Though game competition has several different meanings, it is difficult to imagine sports without the element of competition. To fully understand the fundamental problem, the question should be posed as to what the competitor is competing against.

The real competition in sports is against nature, not against another person or team. The batter faces the theoretically impossible task of hitting a sphere thrown with tremendous velocity and spin. The objective of the runner is the 9.4-second hundred or the 46-second quarter mile. The golfer takes along an "opponent," but the real objective is in hitting the ball where he wants it to go.

We can view competition as either a struggle against opponents or as the applying of skill to overcome obstacles. In a sense the skill is "matched" against that of an opponent, but to so define competition is to avoid what should be obvious. For example, try mountain climbing. There are other companions in a climbing party, and each person reaches the goal; participation and individual achievement is the physical accomplishment.

Playing the game is the thing, and here is the crux of the matter. Victory over *persons* instead of over a difficult obstacle is only a social distortion of the true story. With a team or a wrestler, the obstacle to be overcome is literally the other players, but personal enmity is not the major factor. The desire to excel is potent, but this does not imply that defeat of other persons is a prime motive. Not every competitor can finish first in an event of competition, but everyone that overcomes physical forces to complete a task is a winner in a very real sense. Many of the great competitors in history have been technical losers.

M. S. Marshall, "Competition: For Better or Worse?" *School and Society*, 76 (1962), 321–324.

Structuring Competition

There are four major categories of tournaments. Each of the four types have inherent advantages and disadvantages. The tournament director must select a tournament that will produce a winner within an allotted time. A quick tournament is not necessarily the best tournament. Within the time allotted, the tournament must yield maximum participation. As shown in Figure 9.2, there is an inverse relationship between speed of deciding a winner and amount of participation in the tournament.

Competition is a tool used by professional educators in encouraging student achievement. The choice of type and amount of competition is a professional decision that must be made on the basis of the task and the individual students. Inappropriate use of competition can produce disastrous results, as pointed out by Noar (1972). Management decisions must be made about the type and extent of competition to be used in classes, recreation, and athletics. Some typical management objectives for administering school competition are:

to identify the sources of competition in schools
to correctly match type and extent of competition with student and context

Figure 9.2 Commonly used tournaments classified according to the amount of participation and speed of deriving a winner.

MATCH	*Fastest decision* ↑	*Least participation*
Meets		
Stratified matches		
ELIMINATION		
Single		
Single-consolation		
Double		
ROUND ROBIN		
Split		
Single		
Multiple		
CHALLENGE		
Ladder		
Pyramid	*Slowest decision* ↓	*Most participation*

to eliminate undesirable competition—that which produces negative effects

to develop an alternative strategy to motivate individuals for whom competition is not indicated

to correctly execute tournaments in classes, recreation, and athletics

Directing a Tournament

Tournament directors may not be seen by spectators or players, but organized competition cannot exist without them. The term *tournament director* identifies the person who performs the administrative tasks of managing competitive events. A tournament director can be an instructor who conducts competition in a physical education class, an intramural director, an athletic director, a track coach hosting a meet, an independent tournament promoter in professional boxing, or a state high school athletic association director managing a statewide play-off. The tournament director functions to initiate the call for entries, to structure the tournament brackets, and to actualize competition. During the tournament, the director must enforce regulations, secure and pay officials, and make all physical arrangements. The specific problems of planning, organizing, actualizing, and controlling are discussed herein for several kinds of tournaments.

Selecting a Tournament

There is an ideal tournament for almost every situation. The ideal tournament for continuous YMCA handball competition would not be ideal for a state basketball play-off. Differences between the YMCA and the state play-off tournament lie in the type of game and the type of players. A handball ladder tournament must be scheduled for the convenience of the individuals, within the players' own time schedule. Conversely, the state basketball tournament precludes school work for several days while the event is completed. In choosing a specific kind of tournament, the director should consider all pertinent factors. How many teams or players will be invited or allowed? How many days can the tournament run? What facilities are available? What is the nature of the activity? What day should the tournament end in order to attract the most spectators?

As shown in Figure 9.2, the director can select from a wide variety of tournaments, considering such factors as the type of sport, the number of participants, and the availability of facilities. The following principles should be used as guidelines for the instructor, recreation director, or coach who is selecting a type of tournament.

1. *Select a tournament that is consistent with the nature of the activity and its traditions.* For example, football contests with all the time-outs, pomp, and ceremony usually last for two hours. And the activity itself is fatiguing.

Ed Keren, I. O. E.

Figure 9.3 Spectator interest is a major factor in team sport competition between schools.

Southeastern Louisiana University

Therefore, only one game is scheduled per week during the season. Since it is desirable for all the teams in the conference or district to play one another, a round robin tournament is used to structure football competition.

2. *Select a tournament that will produce a winner in the available amount of time.* Estimate the number of possible games by multiplying the courts by the number of playing times available. In a tennis tournament where there are six courts, allowing two hours per match during an eight-hour period, at least twenty-four matches should be possible. Of course, the type of sport will largely dictate the length of the rest period between matches.

3. *Select a tournament that will allow the participants as much play as possible.* Elimination tournaments are never used in district or conference team sports, because a long season is needed to recoup the expenses of equipment, etc. Use a challenge or round robin tournament whenever the activity and time permit.

4. *Select a tournament that is consistent with the characteristics of the participants.* Young players will be exhausted and lose interest if the tournament is too long. In a recreational setting such as a YMCA, mature adults respond well to an individual sport challenge tournament. Handball and squash are largely played by mature youths and adults; therefore, competition can effectively be structured with challenge tournaments.

Planning a Successful Tournament

Attention to detail is the key to directing a successful tournament. Large tournaments need a tournament committee to help with the management. The *tournament committee* should be composed of the director and several knowledgeable adults. Committee members can assist in planning, organizing, actualizing, and controlling. Committees can also serve an important function in making judgments in protest cases.

Players and coaches are most interested in the type of tournament and the playing schedule. As soon as the tournament structure is set, a complete playing schedule should be developed. If time permits, send an advance copy of the playing schedule to each participant to allow all to arrive at a convenient time.

Provision for playing areas and player accommodations is an important factor in the caliber of tournament play and in developing a positive attitude toward future tournaments. Physical arrangements for play include having sufficient ceiling height for badminton, having a firm floor surface for basketball, and having well-marked lanes for track events. Housing arrangements must also be made in advance. Visit local hotel managers and get bids for housing the visitors. Housing all the participants at one place can reduce prices while increasing general camaraderie among players. Sometimes, members of the home team house visiting players, and the visitors later reciprocate.

Early in the year prior to the tournament, draw up a checklist of tasks including the following items:

1. Clear the use of facilities with the central school office.
2. Secure bids or commitment for housing the visitors.
3. Apply for tournament sanction with the national governing board for the sport.
4. Publish an announcement describing the tournament, the time, the place.
5. Purchase the necessary equipment and supplies.
6. Purchase the awards and have them inscribed (an enterprising director can get local merchants or civic clubs to donate trophies in exchange for advertisement in programs and the like).
7. Secure entries from the participants; the entry blank can be sent out with the announcement.
8. Schedule the contests throughout the tournament.
9. Secure game officials and arrange their rotation schedule.
10. While the tournament is in progress, check with the players and coaches for problems that may have arisen.
11. Have a tournament committee available to mediate any disputes that may arise.

Effective Scheduling

Scheduling is the process of assigning a date, time, and place for every contest in a tournament. All indoor events can be scheduled precisely—outdoor events must be tentatively scheduled. Scheduling should be considered a tool to facilitate competition. A schedule must be flexible in order to serve the best interests of all concerned. In informal tournaments, such as tennis, golf, and badminton, the schedule should be very flexible. Informal tournaments are conducted for the benefit of the players, not the spectators. However, spectator sports and all major tournaments must begin and end within the allotted time.

When setting up the schedule of play, consider such factors as the length of a normal game and the recovery ability of the players. Allow ample time for warm-up and introduction of players in team sports. Always try to alternate teams to prevent one person or team from competing twice in succession. A back-to-back game schedule for any team would seriously impair their play—and their chances. Track and swimming meets must be scheduled to balance the competition and rest periods of the entrants.

Southeastern Louisiana University

Figure 9.4 Cross-country meets do not require laned tracks or a formal course.

Terry McKoy, I. O. E.

Match Tournaments

Match tournaments are the simplest of structured competition. A *match tournament* is defined as structured competition wherein all competitors compete simultaneously or in successive order. The match tournament is commonly used in track and field, because many schools can compete at once. Match tournaments could not be held in such sports as football, because games involve a response to an opponent. Match tournaments can be as simple as a dual swimming meet or as complex as the massive Olympic track and field meets.

There are two types of match tournaments: meets and stratified matches. *Meets* are restricted to simultaneous competition of all participants in a heat or event. *Stratified matches* are those contests in which participants are paired systemati-

Figure 9.5 Golf competition can be structured for various forms of meets, stratified matches, and elimination tournaments.

Southeastern Louisiana University

Figure 9.6 In gymnastics and trampoline, contestants are rated one at a time on the basis of form.

Southeastern Louisiana University

cally according to some factor such as size or ability. All team match tournaments are set up on a cumulative point system. Individuals score points for placing in each event, based on a predetermined value system. The *team score* is computed by adding all the points won by all the individuals on a team. Meets may also consist of a number of different motor tasks. For example, track and field events are included such as relays, distance runs, shot-put, and the long jump. Each sport in which the match tournament is used has evolved its own variations. For example, several trials are allowed in field events, but only one trial is allowed in each running event where there are sufficient lanes for all the runners.

Meets

In small meets all contestants can participate at the same time. In large meets preliminaries must be scheduled prior to the final events. Those athletes who score best in the preliminaries are eligible for participation in the finals. An alternative method in track events is to schedule two or more heats for a particular event and rank the runners by their times after all heats have been run. Some major meets climax a series of regional meets which are actually preliminaries to the national meet. Meet competition is used in a medalist golf play, handicap golf tournaments, gymnastics and trampoline, track and field, and aquatics.

Stratified Matches

Stratified matches pit individuals of equal rank against each other. It is always assumed that a fair estimate of ability or size has been made. Each participant competes against only one opponent during the entire match. Stratified matches are highly desirable for some types of dual school competition because competition is equalized by pairing. Stratified golf matches between two teams are called *Nassau scoring*.

Stratified matches are commonly used for dual competition between schools in such events as tennis and badminton. Prior to competition the players on each team must be ranked by the coach from highest to lowest according to ability. The number-one player on team A must play the number-one player on team B. Similar pairings are made with successively lower-ranked players. After the singles competition is completed, ranked pairings for doubles should be made. Team scoring for stratified tennis matches is one point for each victory. The team score is computed by adding all the points from matches won, both singles and doubles. In dual competition for boxing and wrestling, the participants are stratified according to weight rather than ability.

Figure 9.7 In order to protect each team from ranking manipulations, starting rosters should be exchanged simultaneously.

Elimination Tournaments

Elimination tournaments are widely used in classes, recreation, and interschool athletics. Several variations of the basic elimination tournament are also common. Three variations are (1) single elimination; (2) single elimination plus consolation; and (3) double elimination. Elimination tournaments are used in all national tennis competition and in state high school football, basketball, and baseball play-offs. The Muller (1971) continuous playback tournament is a variation that insures ranking of all the competing teams.

All elimination tournaments are constructed like a family genealogical tree. This is because both are based on perfect powers of two: two, four, eight, sixteen, thirty-two, sixty-four, etc. (Counting backwards from yourself there are two parents, four grandparents, eight great-grandparents, etc. Thus any direct-lineage family tree may serve as a model for the structure of any basic elimination tournament.)

Single Elimination

In the *single elimination tournament* everyone except the winner is defeated once. Losing contestants are eliminated from the tournament, leaving the winners to play each other. The total number of matches in any single elimination tournament can be computed using the formula $M = N - 1$. The symbol M represents the total number of matches to be scheduled. N represents the number of participants or teams. Therefore, if $N = 16$, the total number of matches will be $16 - 1$, or 15.

Single elimination tournaments are used when it is necessary to derive a winner in a short time. A state basketball championship play-off, for example, is usually conducted in one week. District champions from AAAA, AAA, AA, and A divisions constitute a large number of teams. The large number of teams, limited playing courts, and short time available dictate the use of a single elimination tournament.

Planning

In order to construct a single elimination tournament, determine how many people will be participating in the tournament. When conducting an invitational tournament, invite only the number of players needed to fill the tournament. The first round blanks are called *slots*. The tournament bracket is easily constructed if the number of contestants is a perfect power of two. If the number of players is not a perfect power of two, choose the next highest number that is. For example, if there are seventeen participants, a thirty-two–slot tournament *must* be executed. The thirty-two–slot tournament *must* be used because single elimination tournaments are drawn with the idea that all byes will be eliminated by the second round. (A *bye* occurs when a participant does not have an opponent for that particular round.) If there are seventeen participants and thirty-two slots in the first round bracket, there will be fifteen byes, or unfilled slots, in the first round. In the second and succeeding rounds, there will be no byes—every participant will have a schedulable match.

After the tournament director has determined the size of the bracket, the first round slots are drawn in a column. Vertical lines are added on the right to connect each pair of slots, as shown in Figure 9.8. Traditionally, the winners are advanced to the right side of the bracket until only one participant remains undefeated. (Unlike the family tree, tournament eliminations grow sideways.)

Organizing

Once the bracket structure has been determined, the director fills the slots with the names of the participants. Filling the slots of a single elimination tournament usually involves the following sequential steps:

1. *Seeding.* Seeding is the arbitrary placement of certain participants in such a way that the better players will not meet each other before the last rounds of play.
2. *Byes.* Byes are used to fill vacant slots in the brackets when the number of participants is not a perfect power of two.
3. *Draw.* Drawing is the designation of players to the slots remaining after the seeds and byes have been fixed.

The tournament director must be objective and fair in all decisions. Though seeding is arbitrary, it is always based on a record of outstanding performance prior to the tournament. It would hardly be fair to have the two best participants play each other in an early round of the tournament. Usually no more than one fourth of the participants are seeded. Seeding is usually begun by placing the best player in the upper slot in the top bracket. The fourth-ranked player is placed in the lower part of the top bracket. The third-ranked player is placed in the uppermost section of the lower bracket, and the second-seeded player is placed in the lowest slot of the bottom bracket. The intention is to prevent the best players from playing each other before the quarter finals. If they live up to their records, all four of the seeded participants will be playing in the semifinals. Seeding should be omitted if no information on the prior performance of the participants is available. Seeded contestants should be listed beside the tournament bracket, as shown in Figure 9.9.

If the number of participants is not a perfect power of two, byes are written into the tournament bracket to fill the slots that will not be used. Seeded teams

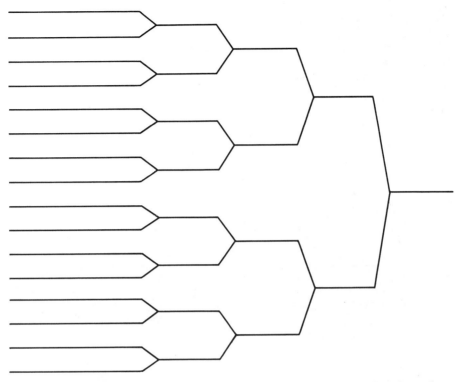

Figure 9.8 A sixteen-slot single-elimination tournament. Competition takes place where the diagonal lines connecting the slots meet.

should receive the first available byes, and the remainder should be distributed as evenly as possible throughout the bracket. A bye should not be placed immediately below another bye. All byes should be fixed in place before the names of any nonseeded players are drawn for the remaining slots.

There are two different ways of making a tournament draw. Players may be *randomly* selected to fill the several remaining slots, or the tournament director can *systematically* place participants in the various slots. In random selection the slots remaining after seeding are numbered, and those contestants who have not been seeded are placed in the slots by chance. Each participant draws a number, and his or her name is written in the corresponding numbered slot. Chance drawing for position is especially important in regional play-offs and other major tournaments.

Informal tournaments can easily be organized by placing participants in the slots remaining after the byes have been set. Figure 9.9 shows how a tournament draw can be made by arbitrary placement. Notice that the placements prevent two players from the same school from playing each other in the initial rounds.

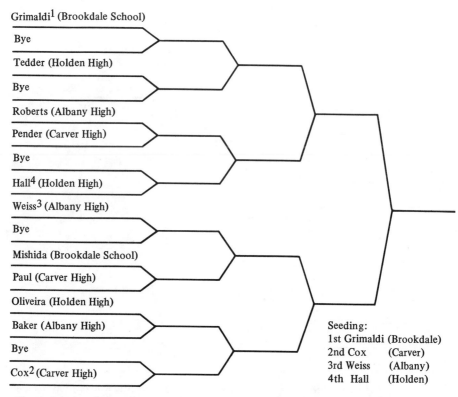

Figure 9.9 An eleven-player single-elimination tournament organized by the systematic placement method. Four players have been seeded.

Regardless of which method is used to organize the draw, the tournament director must never use placements to aid his or her own school. After the tournament draw is announced, no changes should be made except to correct gross errors.

Actualizing and Controlling

The name of the winner of the first round of play is written on the line that extends to the right of the vertical line connecting the slots. The game score is written underneath the line that bears the winner's name. The winners meet in the next and succeeding rounds until only one undefeated player remains. A player who loses one match is dropped; hence single elimination means, "As soon as you lose once, you are out of the tournament."

So that participants may know the specific time that they will play a match, the director should schedule the matches in sequential order all the way to the finals.

Single elimination tournaments are easily scheduled. Following the principle of *proceeding down* the column in each successive *round* of matches, sequential numbers are placed at the points that denote matches. As shown in Figure 9.10, each match has a number that can be associated with a schedule for time and place. Note that where a bye is entered in a slot, a match designation is omitted in the number sequence. Each column should be completely numbered all the way to the bottom (byes excepted) before moving to the top of the next round of play. If the tournament bracket is constructed on a large sheet of poster board, the time and place can be written adjacent to the sequential match number.

Single Elimination-Consolation

In order to provide additional competition for those players who lose their first match, a loser's bracket can be added to a single elimination tournament. Addition of a consolation bracket insures that each participant will play at least two matches in the tournament. The term consolation is derived from the verb "to console," which means *to sympathize constructively*. Even when losing their first match, the losers are consoled because they will then enter another tournament. If seeding has been used in organizing the tournament, there is a good chance that after the first round of play competition will be relatively equal in the consolation tournament, as well as in the single elimination still going on to determine the overall winner.

Figure 9.10 A seven-player single-elimination tournament showing a sequential schedule. Note that the numbers in the sequence are placed where the diagonal lines meet.

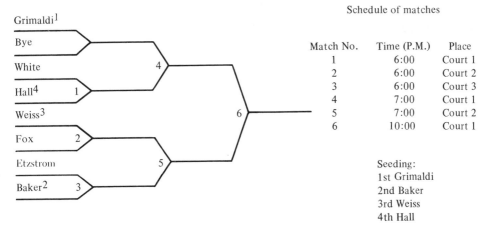

Schedule of matches

Match No.	Time (P.M.)	Place
1	6:00	Court 1
2	6:00	Court 2
3	6:00	Court 3
4	7:00	Court 1
5	7:00	Court 2
6	10:00	Court 1

Seeding:
1st Grimaldi
2nd Baker
3rd Weiss
4th Hall

Planning

The *single elimination–consolation tournament* is really two tournaments in one. The main bracket to the right is a single elimination tournament. After the first round of matches is played, a loser's or consolation bracket is formed to the left. The consolation side is formed in the same manner as the single elimination bracket.

Organizing

A single elimination–consolation tournament is organized at first just like a single elimination tournament. The consolation tournament begins after the first-round matches of the single elimination tournament have been played.

The winner on the consolation side is not the second place winner; that title is "consolation winner." There is no comparative relationship between the status of the consolation winner and that of the winner or runner-up of the single elimination tournament. Due to ignorance of tournaments, some sports writers may report the consolation winner as the third-place finisher. A reasonable estimate of third place could only be determined by scheduling a match between the two losing semifinalists, as shown in Figure 9.11.

Organizing players, byes, and seeds is not necessary in consolation tournaments because these processes should already have been used in developing the single elimination structure. The losers of the first round of matches are recorded in the slots to the left of the first-round structure. If a player had a bye during the first round of the tournament and lost the first match (in the second column), that player should be brought back across to the left side and entered into the consolation tournament (see the lower bracket in Figure 9.11).

Actualizing and Controlling

Actualizing the consolation tournament is similar to actualizing the single elimination tournament. Both sides of the tournament should be played to conclusion. The winner of the consolation side is *not* to be matched against the winner of the single elimination side. To do so would violate all the underlying assumptions of both types of tournaments.

The combination single elimination–consolation tournament is scheduled similarly to a single elimination tournament. The director should attempt to balance play on both sides of the bracket to prevent any player from having to play two games in succession. (In small tournaments it is sometimes impossible for the director to prevent successive games.) The game schedule should be arranged to complete the consolation side before the single elimination side. Scheduling by this principle prevents an anticlimatic finish and insures that the best match of the

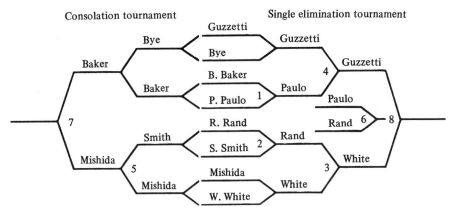

Figure 9.11 A seven-player single-elimination–consolation tournament including a playoff for third place. Note the game schedule arrangement.

tournament is the concluding game. A well-scheduled tournament moves at a deliberate pace, slowly building player and spectator interest through the final contest.

Single elimination–consolation tournaments are effectively used in small tennis tournaments for which ample courts are available. Nearly all regional badminton tournaments have consolation events concurrent with the single elimination bracket. Consolation tournaments are also commonly used in invitational basketball and football tournaments.

Double Elimination

Double elimination tournaments are similar to other elimination tournaments, but all contestants remain in championship contention until they have lost *two* games. More participation is possible because every entrant is allowed two losses. In single elimination–consolation tournaments, only the losers of the first round of matches (the consolation players) are allowed two losses before being dropped from competition. The total number of matches in any double elimination tournament can be computed using the formula $M = 2N - 1$ or 2. M is the number of matches to be played. N is the number of participating units. The formula $2N - 1$ represents the maximum number of games, and $2N - 2$ represents the minimum number of games for any given number of participants. For eight participants in a single elimination tournament, seven games would be scheduled; in a single elimination–consolation tournament, ten games could be scheduled; and in a double elimination tournament, either fourteen or fifteen games would be scheduled. The double elimination factor doubles the amount of participation.

Planning

Since each player must lose twice before being eliminated, a double elimination bracket is drawn in a slightly different way from a single elimination bracket. After the number of participants is determined, the number of slots and byes is calculated in the same way as for a single elimination tournament. The left-hand brackets are drawn so that losers of the first round are returned to the left side. The first round on the left side is similar to the beginning of a consolation tournament. Succeeding pick-up brackets must be drawn on the left side so that losers of the second and succeeding right-side rounds are returned to the left. Return of right-side losers to the left side in a double elimination gives each losing player the opportunity to win the tournament even after losing one match. Losers of second and succeeding rounds are always crossed to a higher or lower bracket on the left side. Cross-bracketing losers prevents two teams from playing each

Figure 9.12 A fourteen-player double-elimination tournament. Note that the sequence of matches is balanced between both sides.

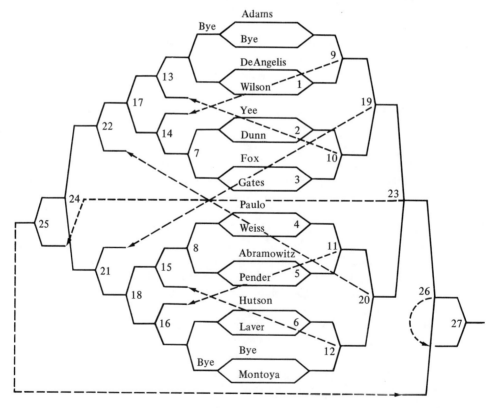

other twice before the semifinals. L-shaped boxes are drawn on the winner's line for every even numbered left-side round, as shown in Figure 9.12. Broken lines drawn from point of loss trace routes followed by right-side losers. The route lines for right-side losers must be drawn in before any game is played in the tournament in order to avoid controversy.

Organizing

A double elimination tournament is structurally different from a single elimination tournament. Double elimination tournaments have the advantage of eliminating seeding and random drawing. Even if the best two teams meet early, they can still play again in the finals of the tournament. Cross-bracketing losers from the right side makes seeding and random drawing superfluous. Crossing means that a person who starts off in an upper bracket and loses is brought to the left-hand side and down one whole position. Losers are systematically "seeking their own level" and playing someone in the lower or higher section.

After all tournament pairings have been completed, the winner from the left-hand side is brought back around, and a match is scheduled against the winner from the right. However, an additional game may be necessary. If the winner of the left-hand side, who has lost once, defeats the winner of the right-hand side, the winner of the right-hand side has only lost once. To declare a winner at that point would not fulfill the requirements of the double elimination tournament. If the winner of the left-hand side defeats the winner of the right-hand side, another game between them must be scheduled. Then the loser of the rematch will have lost two times, and the winner of the rematch will be the winner of the double elimination tournament.

Actualizing and Controlling

The principle to follow in scheduling double elimination tournaments is that rounds are to be played systematically from left to right on the main bracket and from right to left on the once-eliminated side. A balance between left and right sides is thereby achieved in scheduling the games. Play that alternates from right side to left side allows rest periods for the participants. It is common practice to begin the scheduling of games at the top of the bracket. Games will be scheduled only where two opponents actually meet; if a player has a bye, the game will not be scheduled. Beginning from the top and going downward, games should be numbered consecutively and matches scheduled throughout the tournament. Numbers should be inscribed where the two opponents' names appear. Games should be numbered beginning on the right-hand side and then alternating with the left-hand side of the tournament bracket.

Double elimination tournaments have more games to be scheduled on the left-hand side than on the right-hand side. Obviously, the left includes those people who have played a match to completion on the left, *plus* those who were recently eliminated from the right. Since more matches will be scheduled on the left than on the right, it will be necessary to play two rounds of matches on the left before going back and playing one on the right. In a fourteen-player double elimination bracket, the first round would be played on the left, the third round on the right, and the second, fourth, fifth, seventh, eighth, and tenth rounds on the left. The sixth and ninth rounds are played on the right. The left-hand winner is brought back around to the right side for round eleven. If the winner of the right side loses the eleventh round (see Figure 9.11), an additional match is played.

Round Robin Tournaments

The basic idea in *round robin tournaments* is to cause every participant to play every other participant in the division. If there are eight participants, each player will play seven matches. Although challenge tournaments frequently last longer, only a round robin tournament insures that every person will play every other person. Round robin tournaments provide many games for each participant, but they cannot be used in all situations. Considering the number of games, scheduling becomes increasingly difficult as the number of players or teams exceeds eight. Available time and facilities will not always allow a round robin tournament. The total number of matches to be played in a round robin tournament can be computed by using the formula $M = \dfrac{N \times (N-1)}{2}$. If $N = 6$, then $M = \dfrac{6 \times 5}{2} = \dfrac{30}{2} = 15$ matches. Round robin tournaments are widely used for structuring season play in interschool and professional activities. A single

Figure 9.13 A single round robin tournament is commonly used for district baseball competition and for small recreation league play.

Ed Keren, I. O. E.

round robin is used for conference and district football competition. A double or triple round robin tournament is often used for basketball, baseball, and tennis in regular season play.

Single Round Robin

Single round robin tournaments may be used when it is desirable for every player to compete against every other player. A true winner can be determined in round robin tournaments, because the person with the best overall record should be the superior player. Unlike elimination tournaments, round robin tournaments afford each participant an opportunity to defeat the player who eventually becomes the champion.

Planning and Organizing

The basic process in structuring all round robin tournaments is to rotate the players systematically until all possible pairings have taken place. Horizontal, vertical, or chart rotation can be used. The vertical column rotation method described here is one of the least complex.

As shown in Figure 9.14, identifying numbers are given to all participants. Each participant keeps this original identifying number throughout the tourna-

Figure 9.14 A sixteen-player split round robin tournament. Note that the lower half of the original list is the lower flight.

ORIGINAL GROUP

Number	Name	FIRST ROUND OF UPPER FLIGHT
1	Anderson	1 – 2
2	Baker	
3	Fernandez	8 – 3
4	Hartung	7 – 4
5	Hebert	
6	Marlar	6 – 5
7	Morrissey	
8	Paul	FIRST ROUND OF LOWER FLIGHT
9	Pender	9 – 10
10	Ponder	
11	Russell	16 – 11
12	Setti	15 – 12
13	Sweatt	
14	Theriot	14 – 13
15	Tryniecki	
16	Waller	

An eight-team round robin (even number of participants)

1 – 2	1 – 8	1 – 7	1 – 6	1 – 5	1 – 4	1 – 3
8 – 3	7 – 2	6 – 8	5 – 7	4 – 6	3 – 5	2 – 4
7 – 4	6 – 3	5 – 2	4 – 8	3 – 7	2 – 6	8 – 5
6 – 5	5 – 4	4 – 3	3 – 2	2 – 8	8 – 7	7 – 6

A five-team round robin (odd number of participants)

x – 1	x – 5	x – 4	x – 3	x – 2
5 – 2	4 – 1	3 – 5	2 – 4	1 – 3
4 – 3	3 – 2	2 – 1	1 – 5	5 – 4

Figure 9.15 *Two single round robin tournaments. Note that the upper left position remains fixed while the other numbers rotate in a clockwise direction.*

ment. Using the vertical column rotation system, the numbers are rematched for each round of the tournament. Except for the upper left-hand number, all numbers are rotated one position clockwise for each successive round of play, as shown in Figure 9.15.

The upper left position in the vertical pairings is called "robin." All players are systematically rotated around the robin position. If the number of participants is even, the robin position is a player. When there is an odd number of players, an *X* is inserted for robin in the upper left position. The first row match $(X - 1)$ should not be scheduled for an odd number of players because the upper left player has drawn a bye. A round robin schedule is shown in Figure 9.16.

Figure 9.16 *Schedule for a four-player round robin tournament.*

Game	Round one
A	1 – 2
B	4 – 3

SCHEDULE OF GAMES

Game	Time	Date
A	1:00	4/21/77
B	2:00	4/21/77
C	1:00	4/22/77
D	2:00	4/22/77
E	1:00	4/23/77
F	2:00	4/23/77

Game	Round two
C	1 – 4
D	3 – 2

Game	Round three
E	1 – 3
F	2 – 4

Number	Player	# Won	# Lost	# Tied	Percent
1	Pender	_____	_____	_____	_____
2	Schwartz	_____	_____	_____	_____
3	Tryniecki	_____	_____	_____	_____
4	Paul	_____	_____	_____	_____
5	Christopoulos	_____	_____	_____	_____
6	Russell	_____	_____	_____	_____
7	Anderson	_____	_____	_____	_____
8	DiNatale	_____	_____	_____	_____

Figure 9.17 A reporting form for round robin tournaments.

Actualizing and Controlling

Several methods may be used to record results of round robin tournament play. For informal tournaments the winner of each match can be circled as results are reported. A tally can be made for the performance of each team by counting the number of times each team's number has been circled. Figure 9.17 illustrates a convenient method of tallying results of round robin tournaments. The individual percentage can be determined by allowing one point for a win, one-half point for a tie, and no points for a lost game. In the event of a tie in percentages, the team that won when the tying teams played each other would be declared the winner.

Split Round Robin

Split round robin tournaments can be used for round robin play in a large field of participants (professional baseball, basketball, and football for example). Professional football is divided into two competing leagues. An elimination play-off may be used to determine an overall champion between the split groups. The split round robin idea can be used successfully in school recreation to reduce the total number of games if the league is large.

Planning and Organizing

There are two major approaches to planning and organizing split round robin tournaments. One method is to equalize ability level between the split groups. Heterogeneously grouping several ability levels will give each of the split groups an approximately equal number of high- and low-ability teams. A second approach to organizing split round robin tournaments is to separate players by ability grouping into two or more tournament flights.

The process of constructing the rounds for each group in the split round robin tournament is similar to setting up a single round robin tournament. Figure 9.14 shows how the original group of participants can be split into two or more subgroups. The dividing line may be quite arbitrary, as in separating the upper and lower divisions of the roll in an activity class.

Actualizing and Controlling

When an original group is split into more than one subgroup, the number of games to be scheduled is reduced roughly in proportion to the number of new subdivisions. A sixteen-player round robin tournament will consist of one hundred and twenty games. By dividing the group into two flights, it is necessary to schedule only fifty-six games. The specific processes of structuring the competition are similar to the procedures described in single round robin tournaments.

Multiple Round Robin

In a *multiple round robin tournament*, every player plays every other player two or more times. Double and triple round robin tournaments are commonly used in scheduling interschool basketball and baseball. Professional baseball teams play each team in their league as many as six times per season. Leaders may be indentified at the completion of first and subsequent rounds of play to add interest to a long playing season. A multiple round robin tournament is drawn similar to a single round robin tournament. After the first series of pairings, a second round is drawn. To reduce confusion, the same identifying numbers should be used for each set of rounds.

The number of games to be scheduled in multiple round robin tournaments increases in proportion to the increased number of complete rounds. Usually the second and subsequent series of rounds are scheduled in the same order followed in the first round. If a systematic schedule is not followed for second and subsequent rounds, care should be taken to prevent two teams from playing each other in back-to-back games. Professional baseball uses a multiple round of play within each league.

The record format shown in Figure 9.17 can be applied to multiple round robin tournaments. Each team's total number of games played is divided into its total number of games won. If a team played ten games and won eight games, the percentage of games won is $8.00 \div 10 = .80$, or 80%. In professional baseball, the percentage calculations are carried out three decimal places.

Challenge Tournaments

Funnel, ladder, pyramid, crown, and spider web tournaments are all *challenge tournaments*. All challenge tournaments operate on the same basic principle: a lower-ranked player challenges a higher-ranked player in hopes of exchanging ranks. Persons in lower ranks try to move up through the ranks to the highest position. Geometric models are always used in setting up challenge tournaments.

Challenge tournaments can last as long as the tournament director desires. A balance between maximum amount of play and maintenance of interest in the tournament itself is the major factor in determining how long a tournament should last. Challenge tournaments are often used in individual sports to determine team ranks for interschool stratified match play. Athletic clubs and YMCA's often have challenge tournaments running continuously without a designated end date. Challenge tournaments are rarely used in team sports because of the difficulty of getting two teams together at one time and place on short notice. Challenge tournaments could provide motivation for internal competition within school clubs backing an individual sport such as tennis or golf.

Ladder Tournaments

Competition in a *ladder tournament* is structured like a step ladder. A player is placed on each rung of the ladder, and the players on the lower rungs try to replace higher-ranked persons by challenging up. Obviously, players do not want to move down the ladder. Therefore, a contest ensues when a challenge is properly issued by a player of lower rank. Ladder tournaments work best when there are ten or fewer participants.

Planning and Organizing

In order to initiate a ladder tournament, the director should rank the players from lowest to highest ability. The highest skilled players should initially be placed on the lowest rungs of the ladder and the lowest skilled on the highest rungs. The tournament will quickly become stagnant if the best players are placed on top at the beginning. Starting the best players on the lower rungs will also insure that most of the participants will play the other participants.

Players should be listed vertically in the form of a standing step ladder. A peg board with golf tees inserted makes a good backing. Small hooks screwed into a wood backing, with name tags attached, are very convenient to use (see Figure 9.18). The tournament structure should be stored in a showcase or otherwise protected from mischievous shuffling of names. A tournament for each skill level should be constructed if ladder tournaments are used for a large number of

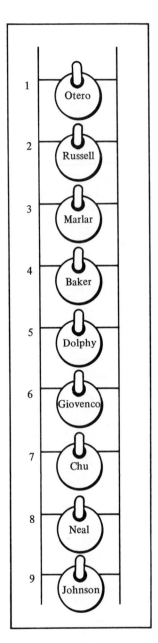

Figure 9.18 A nine-player ladder tournament constructed by using screw hooks, wood backing, and cardboard name discs. Participants can change the standings themselves as challenge matches are played.

participants. If several flights of ladder tournaments are set up, players at the top of their ladder may challenge the lowest-ranked player in the next higher ladder.

Actualizing and Controlling

In order to activate a ladder tournament, organization and regulations should be posted. Because players operate the tournament themselves, everyone should understand the special regulations governing challenges and general match play. Special regulations vary from tournament to tournament. The following items are typically used in challenge tournaments.

1. Players can challenge only one or two positions higher than themselves.
2. A challenge is considered valid if the player above has been properly notified.
3. Higher-ranked players who do not respond to a challenge within two days forfeit their position to the challenger.
4. A player who is challenged must play that match before challenging up.
5. Once a challenge is played, the challenged player may have one week to challenge up before being challenged again.
6. All positions are frozen at midnight on the final day of play. Challenges pending at that time are not considered valid.

Pyramid Tournaments

A *pyramid tournament* is a sophisticated type of challenge tournament in which participants move in horizontal *and* vertical lines. The top of the pyramid is the highest ranking position. All the players try to move to the top position by challenging up. Like other challenge tournaments, the pyramid is most useful in school recreation.

Planning and Organizing

In Figure 9.19, a pyramid tournament is drawn in such a way as to decrease the number of positions by one with each successive row. Challenging is more flexible than in ladder tournaments, because challenges can be issued to ranks at the side position or to positions above the rank held. A larger number of participants can be included in one bracket when a pyramid structure is used.

Actualizing and Controlling

In order to begin a pyramid tournament, the players' names should be inserted in the various slots. As in the case of ladder tournaments, a dynamic situation is created when the best players are initially placed in the lower positions. Although

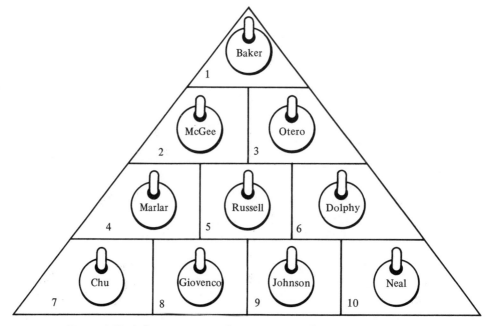

Figure 9.19 A four-row pyramid tournament with ten participant slots.

several variations are possible, the basic idea in pyramid tournaments is to challenge and defeat a player on your row before challenging up. After you have defeated a player on your row, you may challenge a player on the next. All individual slots should be numbered, which will allow for ranking within rows as well as the usual ranking of rows from lower to higher. A set of regulations similar to those prescribed for ladder tournaments should be developed. The type of activity and the type of player should be considered in developing these rules. Rules governing the pyramid tournament should be distributed to all participants. Since the participants arrange their own matches, the tournament director's primary tasks are to establish the structure and to adjust the ranks of players as match results are reported.

Informal Tournaments

The fact that certain tournaments have habitually been used in particular events does not mean that tradition must always be followed. A regulation single elimination tennis tournament is not practical for classwork. The two-out-of-three, six-game sets could not be played in one class period. But in physical education classes and intramurals, modifications can be made in order to complete a tournament within a short time. In physical education classes a tournament should be concluded within one to five days in order to keep interest high.

The physical education instructor and intramural director can modify the game and tournament to fit available time and player skills. A round robin basketball tournament can be held in a few physical education class periods if the games are shortened to fifteen minutes of straight clock time. A round robin tennis tournament can be held to culminate a unit if the matches are reduced to fifteen minutes of playing time on a lengthwise half court. (The serve should be made to the service court directly across the net. After the serve, the alley can be used for play.)

Modifying Length and Characteristics of the Game

A badminton instructor with six courts can complete a modified singles tournament in one class period. A game shortened to seven points can be played on a lengthwise half court. The first person who reaches seven points calls "game," and the first round of play is completed. A moderate-sized class can complete a round robin tournament, and a large class can complete an elimination tournament in one period. Having everyone rotate when a winner is called eliminates the waiting period common in tournament play when games are completed. Half-court tennis and most team sport tournaments can be similarly modified to fit within a class period.

IDEAS FOR BADMINTON INSTRUCTION

Competitive Drills and Modified Games

The introduction of competition into a practice or drill session does much to stimulate the interest of students. Many of the developmental drills included in this report are adaptable to competition.

Double Doubles

This is an original game developed by a teacher for use in large badminton classes. It should be played according to the official rules for doubles *except* that there are four people on each side of the net instead of two. Two people on each side are allowed to serve, after the first service, as in an official game. When the side is out, the two people on the back half of the court on the side which is just coming in to serve step forward to become the servers. Then they serve until the side is out. Then the back court players on the other side step forward to exchange places with the forecourt players, thus becoming servers, etc. It is important that the player in the back court, behind the receiver of service, steps back far enough to allow the receiver space to make an adequate return. The two playing the forecourt should be warned not to back up too far to make a return. The players in the back court are able to watch the front players to avoid colliding with them.

Half-court Singles

By using only half the court from center line to outside boundary line for doubles, beginners may attempt playing singles early. The center line may be extended to the net temporarily with tape. This game enables four people on a court to play a regulation singles game (or less if desired).

Game for Dropping Off the Player Who Makes An Error

This modified game is played as a regular doubles game where there are extra people to go on a court. After a rally is completed, the player who makes an error is replaced by someone waiting to play. After each rally is completed, a replacement comes into the game. The one who leaves the game waits his turn to start back on his side. Replacements can be assigned to each side of the net.

Whistle Tournament

This game may be adapted for singles or doubles play. Courts are numbered, and players fill courts and play. Play is continued for a pre-established length of time. At the end of this time, the director or instructor blows a whistle. The winners on each court move up and the losers move down. First court winner stays on court 1, while loser on the last court also stays where he is. The ultimate winner of the tournament will be winner of court 1 at the end of the period or session of play.

Lifetime Sports Education Project, *Ideas for Badminton Instruction*, 2d ed., American Association for Health, Physical Education and Recreation, Washington, D.C., 1966.

Modifying Tournament Procedures

Single elimination–consolation tournaments can easily be modified for class use in some individual sports. The observant instructor can determine who the better players are. Setting up the first round with a highly skilled player paired with a less skilled player speeds up the first round of play and prepares a tournament for each ability level. The less skilled compete with each other on the consolation side, while the more skilled players move to the single elimination side. If there is enough time, longer matches can be played in the final round.

For individual sports such as badminton or tennis, a round robin tournament can be quickly set up on the courts without drawing up the rounds. With one line of tennis nets, the player in the farthest left-hand court is designated as robin.

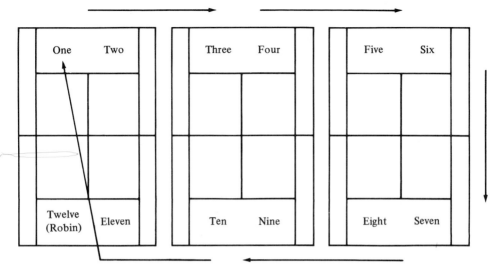

Figure 9.20 The first round of a twelve-player round robin half-court singles tennis tournament. In order to find second-round pairings, the players move clockwise bypassing the lower left-hand court.

Robin stays in her or his court, and with the completion of each set of matches the players rotate around robin to make new pairings, as shown in Figure 9.20. If there are two or more strings of nets, a split round robin with elimination finals can be scheduled.

References

ALEXANDER, I. E. "Nature of Means–End Relationships in Sports." *Proceedings of SDAAHPER*, Columbia, S.C., 1970.

BESSIER, A. R. *The Madness in Sport*. Appleton-Century-Crofts, New York, 1967.

LIFETIME SPORTS EDUCATION PROJECT. *Ideas for Badminton Instruction*, 2d ed. American Association for Health, Physical Education and Recreation, Washington, D.C., 1966.

MARSHALL, M. S. "Competition: For Better or Worse?" *School and Society*, 76 (1962), 321–324.

MARTENS, R. *Social Psychology and Physical Activity*. Harper & Row, Publishers, New York, 1975.

MULLER, P. *Intramurals: Programming and Administration*, 4th ed. The Ronald Press Company, New York, 1971.

NOAR, G. *Individualized Instruction*. John Wiley & Sons, New York, 1972.

10.

MAINTAINING LEGALITY IN OPERATIONS

After reading this chapter, each student should be able to:

Define and give an example of the basic legal concepts that apply to physical and health education.

Identify the various legal agencies dealing directly with education and describe their respective functions.

Describe the critical legal areas of school operations that are manageable by school personnel.

Describe the legal action that could follow a school injury.

Analyze a teaching situation for possible hazards to student health.

There is an air of finality about the courtroom that causes one's anxiety level to rise—especially if the case is personal. Good community relations for all school programs begin with legal/ethical operations. Full financial disclosure and adherence to professional ethics is expected of teachers and administrators. The most progressive physical and health education program is marred if a legal suit evolves from an unforeseen incident. Even if the teacher is successfully defended in court, there will be much anxiety, and possible reversal by an appeals court keeps stress high for months or years.

Prevention is the first line of defense against a court suit. All possible sources of student injury or inequitable treatment must be anticipated and eliminated. This chapter presents some of the issues involved in maintaining legality in the operation of physical and health education programs.

Basis of School Law

In order to understand state and national legislation and judicial interpretation, it is essential to know the rudiments of legal terminology and legal theory. Most present laws and interpretations have deep historical roots. In other cases, the letter and spirit of the law have changed with the times. For example, the "separate but equal" doctrine has historical precedent, but recent desegregation decisions and Title IX antidiscrimination concepts regarding sex are more consistent with the contemporary sociopolitical climate.

Legal Terms

Both the prospective teacher and the prospective administrator need to know the elements of civil law. Physical and health education programs are inherently susceptible to civil action as redress for grievances. Some essential legal terms are as follows:

> *Attractive nuisance* An attractive condition that may be hazardous. Children are impulsively attracted to such play objects as swimming pools, playground equipment, obstacle courses, etc. The age of the child is a factor in evaluating the attractiveness of an object or situation.
>
> *Civil suit* Litigation brought about to seek redress for a wrong or injury to an individual or a specific group. Most school cases are civil suits instigated to gain repayment for damages or to seek specific action by school officials.
>
> *Defendant* The one charged with wrongful action. In civil suits the case is brought against the one who committed the allegedly wrongful action.
>
> *Foreseeability* The predictability of dangers inherent in a situation allows possible hazards to be anticipated. This concept is derived from the concept of the "reasonable man" in English common law.

Figure 10.1 *Physical education teachers are legally responsible for the instruction and safety of their students.*

Southeastern Louisiana University

Ed Keren, I. O. E.

Liability A state of legal responsibility. The teacher's assumption of responsibility for children is a defined liability condition.

Negligence The failure to correctly discharge the responsibilities of one's position. A teacher may be held negligent for not executing any action—and also for executing the wrong kind of action.

Precedent A decision made by a high court on a particular case which then serves as a guide for later cases. The concept is derived from the Anglo-Saxon *stare decisis*, meaning "to stand by the cases."

Plaintiff The one who brings civil suit. In civil suits the case is brought by the offended. The term is derived from the concept of the cry of an injured party—a plaintive cry.

Respondeat superior The administrator is responsible for the acts of subordinates, as in a master/servant relationship. Administrators and teachers fall within the concept; school boards, however, tend to be exempt from such responsibility.

Tort A legal wrong resulting in injury or damage. Teachers' malpractice usually comes under tort or tort liability suits.

Ultra vires Beyond the bona fide limits of legality. The teacher who administers corporal punishment to a student off the school grounds and outside of school-sponsored activities is acting without legal support.

Vis Major A chance occurrence or a natural happening. Tornadoes are natural phenomena. (Those who view the Supreme Deity as austere and oppressive have called the same occurrence an "act of God.")

Genesis of Legal Concepts

Two schools of legal thought have evolved through the ages. The oldest legal philosophy is called *common law*. Common law defines the normative behavior that people consider acceptable to their society. Murder, rape, stealing, and perjury were usually defined as unacceptable within the social group—though such behaviors were often approved when the victim was someone outside the social group. Common law persists in modern times in the practice of "common law marriage." The Hebrew people considered that all other societies lived under the common law philosophy.

Most of the states in the United States have their roots in English common law because of the English colonial influence. The English people formulated a series of concepts based on traditions handed down to them from other cultures. Legal enactments may be made in English common law countries, but interpretation of cases is based largely on precedents. A precedent may continue indefinitely, only to be changed when sociopolitical philosophy changes. For example, in English common law each person is responsible for himself or herself and his or her property. A teacher transporting students in a defective automobile which he or she owns may be successsfully sued for injuries suffered by students.

The second school of legal thought is manifest in codified law. *Codified law* is defined as a set of standards or procedures written down and issued by proclamation or edict. The written official laws may be issued by rulers or a committee commissioned to write the laws. The earliest codified law is the ancient Babylonian Code of Hammurabi. Prescriptive moral standards of Christians, Mohammedans, and Hebrews are codified law. The legal structure of European countries and the state of Louisiana is based on codified law, as in the Napoleonic code. Under codified law a judge decides the merits of the case by comparison to the written law. The judge is not bound by verdicts previously rendered in similar cases. However, both written laws and common law interpretations may be used. Concepts such as child abuse have been clearly legislated, but other conditions, including teacher–student relationships, are not fully defined.

Fundamentals of School Law

Liability suits against schools and teachers have become a common occurrence. In New York, New Jersey, and California, teachers and school districts frequently lose negligence suits brought against them. In other states it is virtually impossible to win a negligence suit against a school district. The variation in vulnerability to suit is a function of the state legal structure. Physical and health educators should be able to answer the following questions about the state in which they are employed:

1. What is the relationship of state government to the people that are governed?
2. Are citizens permitted to sue the state government to collect for damages to their individual rights?
3. What special behavior is expected of teachers that is not expected of people engaged in other jobs?

Sovereign Immunity

Sovereign immunity is the special position enjoyed by some states in which the government cannot be sued without its consent. Under the doctrine of governmental immunity, the parents of a student killed in football practice are powerless to press a case for damages—the suit would be dismissed from court without a trial. The coach, as an officer of the school, is also free of liability.

Sovereign immunity has its roots in the kingships of antiquity. As kingdoms were carved out and stabilized by strong leaders, power was concentrated in the hands of a few dominant individuals. If the king intentionally or accidentally committed an offense, who had the power to bring him to justice? The king and his ministers were accountable to no one. Kings of antiquity and some modern governments are apparently beyond accountability for injury to private citizens.

The basic premise of sovereign immunity is alive and well in the United States. If "the government can do no wrong," then government officials are protected from negligence suits.

Not all the states uphold the concept of governmental immunity, however. Several variations of accountability have emerged in various states. In New York, Arizona, and California, governmental immunity has been declared invalid. Conversely, Colorado and Kansas courts have upheld the sovereign immunity concept. Many variations exist in other states. In Pennsylvania, school systems cannot be sued for negligence when performing a governmental function, but the district can be sued when engaged in proprietary functions. Another variation occurs in Minnesota, where the school district can be sued for negligence if it has purchased liability insurance (Garber 1967). There follows a summary of a court suit resulting from defective recreation equipment.

SPANEL v. MOUNDS VIEW SCHOOL DISTRICT N 621 118 N.W. 2nd 795., *Supreme Court of Minnesota, December 14, 1962.*

A five-year-old boy was injured on a defective kindergarten slide. A suit was brought against the school district, the principal, and the teacher in charge. The case was dismissed in the lower court under the doctrine of governmental immunity from tort liability.

The Minnesota Supreme Court upheld the dismissal of this action, but prospectively overruled the doctrine of governmental immunity as a defense to tort claims against school districts, municipal corporations, and other governmental units, except the state itself, arising with respect to torts committed after the 1963 legislature adjourned, subject to any statutes presently or hereafter limiting or regulating the prosecution of such claims.

Counsel informed the court that legislation was planned for the 1963 session to give affected government entities a chance to meet their new obligations, and until then the court felt that they had a right to rely on the immunity, with advance notice that they should take out liability insurance to protect themselves against financial losses in the future when the defense of governmental immunity would no longer be available to them.

Note: The 1963 legislature restored the governmental immunity rule as a defense in actions against school districts, but provided that when a school district procures liability insurance, then during the period the insurance is in effect and to the extent of the coverage, it becomes subject to the statutory provisions relative to liability for torts committed by the school district or its officers or employees, acting within the scope of their employment or duties, whether arising out of a governmental or proprietary function.

NEA Research Division, *The Pupil's Day in Court: Review of 1963*, National Education Association, Washington, D.C., 1964.

Although many states protect public funds by denying the possibility of negligence suits, teachers are usually responsible for both malfeasance and nonfeasance, as shown in the Vermont case of *Eastman* v. *Williams*, 207 A 2d 146 (1962). The major protection of teachers is the fact that few teachers are wealthy enough to make lawsuit attractive to the plaintiff. Professional liability insurance is available at modest cost—usually through the state teachers' association or the AAHPER. One of the major tenets of English common law is that every person is responsible for her or his own. Under the responsibility concept, and considering further civil rights statutes, every school employee and board member may be held responsible for wrongful acts. Another possible liability protection for teachers is provided in some states by statutory "save-harmless laws" in which the school district must indemnify teachers against legal judgments. Save-harmless statutes essentially cause the school district to become indirectly liable.

Legal Functions

Being an agent of the state, the school may perform several distinct types of community services. The extent of services is determined basically by what the community wants. If it is the "will of the people," taxes may be levied for recreation and community college services. Both the extent of services and the type of services are regulated locally. School services are legally classified as governmental functions or proprietary functions.

Figure 10.2 Athletics are usually classified as school proprietary functions because of the gate receipts derived from them.

Ed Keren, I. O. E.

Governmental Functions. If the school is engaged in performing a service considered essential for the welfare of society, it is performing a governmental function. The physical and health education instruction program is an example of governmental function. Physical and health education instruction is required in most states and is optional for credit in others. It is evident that the general public supports these programs as governmental functions. The collection of funds from students for a uniform does not alter the governmental function. Intramural programs usually fall into this category.

Proprietary Functions. Supporters of athletics frequently defend their programs on the basis of "making money for the school." Proprietary function pertains to the collection of revenue and the operation of a program that brings revenue into the school. Gate receipts cause school athletics to be placed in the category of proprietary functions. The athletic program does not need to show a profit to be classed as a proprietary function. The difference between the two types of school functions is clearly illustrated in Pennsylvania. If a student is injured in a gymnasium during a physical education class, the school district cannot be sued. However, if the same injury occurs during interschool basketball, the school district is vulnerable to liability suit.

Duty Relationship. Parents do not send their children to school to have them return home maimed because of negligence on the part of school personnel, as shown in the case of *Feuerstein* v. *Board of City of New York,* 202 NYS 2d 524 (1956). School personnel are considered public servants who voluntarily perform their professional tasks for the welfare of the state. Being agents of the state, teachers are remunerated for their services.

Teachers are legally considered to function in a quasi-parental relationship to the students. The teacher–student duty relationship was originally based on the principle of *loco parentis.* The teacher is responsible to act as a prudent professional with some of the parent's authority. The action of teachers must be reasonable, as dictated by their professional training and assumed responsibilities. American society does not allow teachers to severely neglect or mistreat students, and similarly society does not allow parents to severely neglect or mistreat their own children.

The degree of responsibility varies with such factors as age and ability of the child. Elementary school children require constant supervision by either parents or teachers. The degree of teacher responsibility diminishes as the student matures, and since all eighteen-year-olds have full citizenship, the stand-in parental responsibility has little validity for university professors. The original *in loco parentis* concept cast the teacher as a parent surrogate with full parental authority to regulate student behavior. Recent judicial philosophy is redefining the teacher–student relationship. Instead of being in place of the parent, the teacher will be held as partaking of a professional relationship akin to that between physician and patient. Of course custodial care will continue to be expected of teachers, but absolute teacher authority over the child is not assumed. Students do not give up their rights when they enter schools.

Statutory Processes

Laws are formal statements by which a society is governed. In an egalitarian society, laws are passed by consent of the governed. Responding to the voice of the people, laws can be made, amended, or abolished. Perceiving that a society cannot long stand without a mechanism for educating its youth, the American democracy has seen fit to establish laws providing for the orderly socialization of the young.

School management is primarily a function of state and local governments. Consequently, school law varies from place to place. For example, some states may prohibit the use of public school tax funds for support of athletic programs, while in other states athletics is viewed as an integral part of the curriculum. Some states have compulsory physical and health education programs, while others have elective programs.

Legal Enactments

School laws are enacted almost entirely by state and local governments. General school laws within the state are formulated by state legislatures or state agencies. Problems of a local nature are handled by the local board or its administrative officers. The federal government influences state and local programs by specifying conditions under which appropriated funds can be secured.

Federal Law

Although millions of dollars are spent annually on local school operations, there is no reference to education in the United States Constitution. The Tenth Amendment to the Constitution states, "The powers not delegated to the United States by the Constitution, nor prohibited by it to the States, are reserved to the States respectively, or to the people." Responsibility to educate is a "power not delegated," and the states have the right and duty to establish public education.

Federal programs influence schools at the elementary, secondary, and university levels. Federal funds may be used to purchase physical education equipment and teaching materials. Some federal funds are specifically for use in disadvantaged areas. Other funds, such as those for drug abuse education, may be spent for the general student group.

State Law

Regulation of education at the state level is accomplished by (1) constitutional law; (2) state legislative enactments and appropriation; and (3) state board of education rules. Constitutional law is concerned primarily with structure. The state legislature can enact practically any type of law, but educators are most concerned with appropriation of tax monies. The state board of education is an organization created by state law to administer programs in education. State legislatures can act to specify curriculum: witness bans on sex education and the requirement of Americanism versus Communism.

State School System

The states have followed a common pattern in assuming their responsibility to educate. Legal enactments at the state level provide for state-level executive control and financing by the state school board and the state school superintendent. Control and financing are shared with the local school government unit

Figure 10.3 The functional relationships among state and local school organizational bodies.

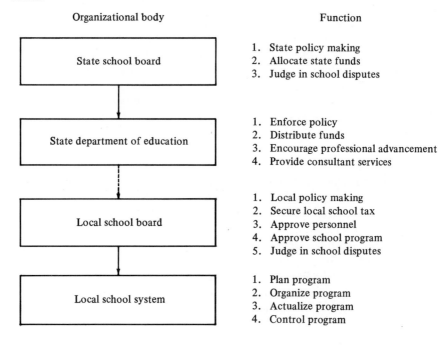

Organizational body	Function
State school board	1. State policy making 2. Allocate state funds 3. Judge in school disputes
State department of education	1. Enforce policy 2. Distribute funds 3. Encourage professional advancement 4. Provide consultant services
Local school board	1. Local policy making 2. Secure local school tax 3. Approve personnel 4. Approve school program 5. Judge in school disputes
Local school system	1. Plan program 2. Organize program 3. Actualize program 4. Control program

(city, county, or independent school district), but the state maintains final executive control. Figure 10.3 shows the respective functions of the various agencies.

State governments implement educational systems through a body called the *state board of education*. Usually state boards establish policies, adopt standards, and regulate state-level financing of the local school operation. In order to accomplish the complex task of regulating all local schools, executive structures called state offices of education are established. The state board may regulate athletic programs, approve or disapprove the requirement of physical and health education, and establish minimum requirements for teacher certification.

The *state office of education* executes the policies of the state school board. The *chief state school officer*, or state superintendent, acts as chief executive over the state education office. Within the state office there are usually supervisors for each major area. The state supervisor of physical and health education acts as liaison between the state office and the local school. In some states the state supervisor acts as a coordinator or consultant-by-invitation, and in other states the supervisor takes the role of inspector/controller. If a law or ruling is made concerning education by the state legislature, state courts, or the state board, it is the final responsibility of the state office of education to execute the act.

Local School System

The local school board functions similarly to the state-level school board. Basically, the local board is concerned with raising funds, approving programs, establishing policies, and rendering judgment in local disputes. The board consists of lay persons, not educators, who are elected or appointed. Like the state board, the local board members are advisory. While acting in good faith as a governmental body they are usually not personally liable for their own actions nor for the actions of their school employees. This principle is illustrated in *Vendrell* v. *School District No. 260*, 360 P 2d 282 (1961).

As executive officer for the school board, the local school superintendent may be elected or appointed. The superintendent and the superintendent's staff cause the local school system to operate. Since most school systems are sizable and complex operations, the superintendent employs several middle- and lower-level executives. Principals, supervisors, and athletic directors perform the middle-level management functions.

The local school system is most influential in determining the caliber of physical and health education programs. The local board should employ a supervisor who is a specialist in physical and health education to provide systemwide leadership. The local board should approve a syllabus for systemwide use. Local programs seldom rise any higher than the level of funding and leadership provided on the level of the local school system.

Case Example: FUNCTION OF THE LOCAL SCHOOL BOARD

Several retired military men in the school district have been actively trying to establish a Junior ROTC program in the high schools. Their method has been to contact local board members individually and later to schedule representatives from the Army, Air Force, and Navy to sell the board on the program. Each of the military representatives strongly emphasizes the ROTC program of physical training through calisthenics and marching drill. After all the presentations have been heard, the board votes to approve the program as a substitute for the physical and health education requirement.

1. What similarities are there between the outcomes of a military physical training program and those of a physical and health education program? What differences exist?
2. What can physical educators in the school district do collectively to combat this proposal?

Critical Areas of School Operations

The first line of protection against litigation is a professionally defensible school program. During court litigation, the reasonable man concept from common law is repeatedly used as a reference point. When acting reasonably and in good faith, school personnel stand a good chance of avoiding negligence judgments. Specifically, school personnel can protect themselves from liability suit by professional behavior. In the following paragraphs, the idea of "professional action" is applied to several physical and health education functions.

Planning

Planning includes making decisions about the type and extent of the curriculum to be offered by the school. Planning entails prespecifying terminal competencies and implies a strategy for outcomes achievement.

Activity Program

The type of activities offered in physical education programs lend themselves to one major form of school torts. Local boards have the implied responsibility and authority to approve the school curriculum. The professional teacher should know the developmental characteristics of the student and be able to match appropriate activities to student needs. If an official syllabus is available, a teacher who follows the syllabus approved by the board has a good measure of protection from related lawsuits. The court may disapprove of the activity, as in the case of *Bellman* v. *School District,* 11 Calif. 2d 576; 81 P 2d 894 (1938). However, if the school board has approved of the activity, the individual teacher should not be held liable. In the Bellman case, the court maintained that the girl was required to perform a tumbling stunt inherently dangerous for her age and ability, but the school board had approved the activity in its syllabus. If the appropriateness of an activity is questioned, the teacher should refer to three reference categories: (1) the official school board syllabus; (2) the activities usually included in the syllabi of other, similar schools; and (3) textbooks or authority figures. (The Red Cross organization is considered the authority for swimming.) Let us look at a case where the teacher did not follow the district-approved curriculum plan.

KEESE v. BOARD OF EDUCATION OF CITY OF NEW YORK 235 N. Y. S. 2d
300, *Supreme Court of New York, Trial Term, Kings County, Part 3, December 3, 1962*

A 13-year-old junior high school girl was injured when kicked by another player in a game of line soccer. The Board of Education syllabus listed line soccer as a game for boys and stated that after sufficient skill has been acquired two or more forwards may be selected from each team. The syllabus called for 10 to 20 players on each team and required a space of 30 to 40 feet.

The physical education teacher divided some 40 or 45 girls into two teams to play in a space 50 feet wide and 60 feet long. The girls were not experienced players.

An expert witness testified that avoidance of the danger of accidents requires a restriction to no more than two people on the ball at one time. The witness criticized the board syllabus permitting the use of more than two forwards. She testified that before junior high school pupils should be allowed to play line soccer, they should be given experience in kicking, dribbling, and passing.

There was evidence that the teacher in charge allowed six to eight inexperienced girls to be on the ball at a time, but no evidence was presented that adequate instruction was given.

The court held that an injury from the melee was, if not inevitable, at least reasonably foreseeable. The teacher had showed a complete disregard for the safety of her pupils, and since the pupil was injured as a direct consequence of the teacher's negligence in a game in which she was an involuntary participant, she was entitled to be awarded damages.

NEA Research Division, *The Pupil's Day in Court: Review of 1963,* National Education Association, Washington, D.C., 1964.

Figure 10.4 Activities must be geared to the abilities of the students. Testing for prerequisite "entry skills" before allowing students to attempt advanced stunts helps to protect the teacher from negligence suits.

Controversial Activities

Controversiality depends on the local community. Sex education is banned in some states. Instruction in social dance may be an issue in other communities. As described in the following paragraph (Bower 1973), activities applicable to instruction in relaxation or value clarification can precipitate an uproar.

Case Example: SCHOOL ACTIVITIES AND PARENTAL CONTROVERSY

The most agonizing thing that ever happened to me in teaching was with parents. Last summer I learned something about group processes and I thought it would help my class. I know that group process stuff can be dangerous but I only did harmless stuff. We did simple things such as lying on the floor, mentally exploring our bodies. Then we got up and walked around with our eyes closed. Parents started calling up asking that their kids be withdrawn from the class so they wouldn't be exposed to me. And a contingent of parents announced they were going to "take care" of me as soon as they got "their ammunition ready." And a month later a woman called up and said her daughter had had her blouse ripped off and all that guk. All lies, phoney. I had permission from my principal. I asked the parents to come and face me with their accusations and they refused. They said I was to go to one of their homes at 7 o'clock in the evening. I refused. I felt it was risky and would put me at a great disadvantage, with all those people ready to tear into me. I felt they could come and see me in my own environment where it concerned them, and on my terms. Nothing happened, and nobody ever said anything to me; they just took their kids out of my class. I was terribly upset. (Bower 1973)

Organizing

The physical education instruction program, school recreation, and interschool athletics account for most school accidents. Professional foresight regarding school facilities, equipment, student–parent information, and staffing is essential to preventive action.

School Facilities

School boards are in a position to create a safe school environment. As trustees of public funds, school boards cause buildings to be planned and erected. It is expected that public funds are used to give proper maintenance and repair to equipment and facilities. The cases of *Bard* v. *Board of Education*, 140 NYS 2d 850 (1955) and *Domino* v. *Mercurio*, 234 NYS 2d 1011 (1962) serve to illustrate the responsibility of local school districts to provide a safe environment. The *Domino* v. *Mercurio* case illustrates the persistent jeopardy in which people unwittingly place themselves. Teachers are liable for failure to regulate the use of facilities.

DOMINO v. MERCURIO 234 N. Y. S. 2d 1011, *Supreme Court of New York, Appellate Division, Fourth Department, December 6, 1962.*

The school board and two teachers assigned as playground supervisors were sued for damages for injuries received when a softball player fell over a bench on the school playground. Benches supplied for use of the players were appropriated by the spectators who overflowed onto the ground in front of them. Ropes and standards were available to restrain the crowd, but the teacher supervising the crowd did not consider their use necessary. On two occasions he stopped the game and ordered the spectators back, but they again gradually drifted forward and were not ordered back.

The jury found that the playground supervisors had been negligent. The question on appeal concerned the liability of the board of education.

The appellate court held that the doctrine of *respondeat superior* was applicable and that under this doctrine the board was liable for the negligence of its employees. Therefore, there was no need for the jury to be charged or find that the board had been negligent in selecting or employing the supervisors before the board could be held liable.

Two judges dissented on the ground that there was no evidence the playground supervisors had been negligent. They said there was no evidence of how, when, or by whom the bench had been moved and its position obscured from view of the supervisor. The dissenters reasoned that if the location of the bench constituted a hazard to the players, defendants could not be held liable for permitting it to be there unless and until they had notice thereof.

NEA Research Division, *The Pupil's Day in Court: Review of 1963*, National Education Association, Washington, D.C., 1964.

Students enrolled in physical education classes present a different problem from either recreation or athletics. Activities in physical education classes required or elective are assigned activities—and in a sense compulsory. Even if an activity or stunt is specified as optional, the instructor may not be able to enter assumption of risk as a legal defense. Both instructors and coaches are liable for assuming their share of the "safe environment" responsibility.

Though not usually the prime cause of unsafe facilities, the classroom teacher is the local regulator of facility use. Inherently dangerous areas are legally termed *nuisances* and are to be avoided. Allowing two softball games to be played on the

Figure 10.5 Unsafe use of outdoor facilities. Two softball games should not be played in such a small area.

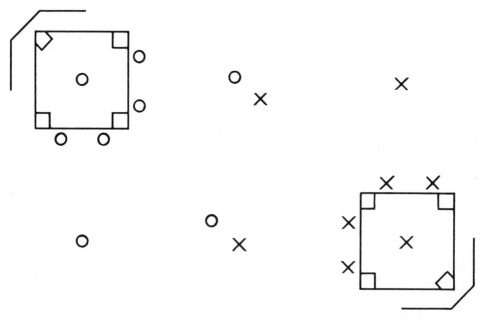

Figure 10.6 Foreseeing inherent dangers in the use of equipment is a competency expected of professional teachers.

same small field is an example of unsafe use of facilities, as shown in Figure 10.5. Laying out two basketball courts side by side with a common sideline is also an unsafe practice. School districts may be liable if they own an "attractive nuisance," such as a deep unfenced ditch near the school playground. However, *teachers* become vulnerable if they assign their classes to play near a dangerous place.

Equipment

A classroom teacher is not financially responsible for repairing school property but *is* responsible for reporting the matter to the school administration. Acting as both instructor and supervisor, the teacher must prevent students from using defective equipment. For example, the court found the instructor negligent in *King* v. *Haley*, 334 Michigan 146 (1931) for requiring students to climb a frayed rope. The plaintiff was injured when the frayed rope broke. Sudden breakage of equipment recently checked presents an entirely different legal problem from deliberate use of worn or damaged equipment. Dangerous equipment such as bows, arrows, trampoline, and hanging ropes must be stored safely or made inoperative immediately after use.

Student–Parent Information

When students are to participate in any extracurricular event, or when field trips are planned, parents must be informed. A consent-to-attend form, signed by the parents, should be filed with the school before the trip. Many schools require a waiver to be signed by student and parents prior to any participation in athletics.

Contrary to popular belief, waiver forms are totally invalid for minors. The parents may believe that they have signed away all rights to suit, but no one can waive the rights of a minor—not student, parents, grandparents or legal guardian.

Staffing

School boards must employ competent personnel to instruct and supervise students while they are at school. In the case of *Britton* v. *State*, 103 NYS 2d 485 (1951) it was shown that student assistants were not sufficiently instructed to assume the *in loco parentis* teacher responsibility. Instruction and supervision by student teachers must be generally supervised by a professional instructor. The case of *Garber* v. *Central School District*, 251 App. Div. 214; 295 NY Supp. 850 (1937) illustrates the necessity of employing professional instructors to fulfill the *in loco parentis* responsibility. In the Garber case, the court maintained that a custodian was not sufficiently trained to assume supervisory duties. However, the case of *Ragonese* v. *Hilferty*, 191 A. 2d 426; Md Ct. of Appeals (1963) indicates that certain roles within the school can be assumed by properly trained and designated nonteaching personnel. The court held that a school bus driver and a safety patrol student are sufficiently responsible for the specific task of monitoring school bus riders. Apparently volunteers and paraprofessionals can assume limited responsibilities with students.

Figure 10.7 Pole vaulting is a hazardous activity for which step-by-step instruction must be given prior to the first full trial.

Southeastern Louisiana University

Actualizing

After planning and organizing have been completed, the program is ready to begin. The first order in program actualizing is instruction. Transportation and first aid are also important parts of the total physical education program.

Instruction

All teachers who fail to act as prudent professionals are vulnerable to liability suit. Failure to provide instruction would be negligence by nonfeasance, and providing incorrect instruction would be negligence by malfeasance. Combatives, gymnastics, swimming, some field events, and contact sports are activities in which instruction is necessary prior to participation. In the case of *Mastragelo* v. *West Side Union School District*, 42 P 2d 634 (1935), for example, the teacher was declared negligent for allowing two students to box without prior instruction. One of the boys received a blow to the head which resulted in a fatal cerebral hemorrhage.

Transportation

The best precaution against transportation accidents and school liability is to have all students transported by common carrier. A common carrier is insured and bonded, and the drivers are trained to handle large vehicles. Many school buses are owned by private drivers whose route is appointed by the school board. Privately owned school buses are desirable common carriers, because initial liability rests with the driver–contractor rather than the school district or the teacher. A teacher who drives a school-owned bus to transport students to various activities renders both self and school district potentially liable. School teachers transporting students in private automobiles assume personal liability. Courts have held teachers personally liable for accidental injury to a pupil even when the teacher was benevolently taking the student to get medical aid.

First Aid

First aid places teachers in a precarious position. Teachers must render first aid, and the first aid rendered must be correct. In one case of an early-season football illness, a player collapsed with extremely high temperature, reddened skin, and high pulse rate. The coach did nothing to reduce the temperature of what he should have recognized as heat stroke. The courts sustained a personal liability decision against the coach for negligence in the death of the student.

Figure 10.8 Prompt, correct first aid helps the injured student and reduces the possibility that the injury will lead to legal action.

Southeastern Louisiana University

Controlling

Though the administrative process may be broken down into four component parts, in teaching and coaching many of the parts are almost simultaneous. Supervision of teachers and students are important elements of control. Insurance and contracts are also essential legal controls.

Supervision

There is a distinct difference between teacher and school board supervisory liability. Teachers are expected to fulfill their assignments, but the school board is responsible for foreseeing areas in which supervisory assignments are necessary. For example, the cases of *Satariano* v. *Sleight*, 54 Cal. App. 2d 278; 129 P 2d 35 (1942) and *Forgnone* v. *Salvador Union School District*, 41 Cal. App. 2d 423; 106 P 2d 932 (1940) serve to document school district responsibility for providing adequate supervision.

It is the duty of the school district to provide adult supervision while students are on the school premises. Teachers are sometimes assigned general supervision duties, but they are *always* responsible for the classes specifically assigned to them. Teachers are expected to be at the site where their classes are held. In a seemingly unfair decision, a teacher was held to have been negligent when he left his class unsupervised in order to administer first aid to one of the class members. In the case of *Miller et al.* v. *Board of Education. Borough of Chatham. N.J.*, Sup. Ct. L. Div. No. L — 7241–62 (1964), the students had been warned to stay off the apparatus while the teacher attended to an injury of one of the other students.

The act of teacher supervision implies preventive action if an event is foreseeable and remedial action if accidental injury occurs. In the case of *Ogando* v. *Carquinez School District*, 24 Cal. App. 2d 567; 75 P 2d 641 (1938), the courts maintained that adequate supervision would probably have speeded first aid to the hemorrhage and would have saved the child's life. Class or area supervision

Figure 10.9 Close supervision is essential in activities such as trampoline.

Southeastern Louisiana University

does not imply minute regulation of every pupil (the Ogando child ran through a glass door). General observance of students in the activity area is sufficient in most cases.

Control procedures are occasionally needed while students are engaged in drills. During practice sessions, care must be taken to prevent weaker students from being overwhelmed. Pairing of students of different sizes can be a dangerous practice. Though soccer is basically a minimal-contact game, a modified soccer contest precipitated a successful negligence suit. In the case of *Brooks* v. *Bd. of Ed. of N.Y.*, 205 NYS 2d 777 (1960), the teacher was found negligent for injuries sustained in a mismatched contest in kicking a soccer ball. Similar injuries could occur in the contact sports and in combative activities such as wrestling and boxing.

Insurance

There are several types of insurance available to schools to cover perils in physical and health instruction, school recreation, and interschool athletics. School insurance is used to protect the insured against perils such as liability and medical health situations. Every teacher and school district should review its insurance needs with an insurance counselor. Insurance of particular legal interest to teachers and coaches is reviewed in the paragraphs that follow. It should be noted that insurance coverage is always limited to the amounts designated in the policy. The procedure for letting bids was described in Chapter 7.

Liability. Liability insurance protects the insured against negligence by both omission and commission. *Omission negligence* pertains to behavior that the teacher did not perform as he or she should have, such as failure to render first aid. *Commission negligence* pertains to malfeasance: performing the wrong acts, such as improperly transporting victims with spinal fractures. Teachers are universally liable personally, though school board members have not been held personally liable. Recent rediscovery of the Civil Rights Act of 1871 (Lenaghan and Phay 1973) has precipitated cases in which the pointed conclusion is that *every person who deprives someone else of constitutional rights is thereby vulnerable for liability action in federal courts.* Essentially, the federal statute circumvents any state governmental immunity in several categories of suits.

Typically, liability insurance policies cover the teacher or school employee up to $100,000 per incident. If more than one liability incident occurs, the company guarantees the maximum amount for each occurrence. Inasmuch as insurance companies do not want to lose liability cases, the teacher involved also has the advantage of being defended by a skilled attorney. Liability insurance for educators seldom costs more than twenty dollars per year. Group plans like those purchased through athletic organizations usually cost much less. The AAHPER has worked cooperatively with an insurance company to develop a low-cost liability plan for members.

Health. Health care insurance is legally significant for interschool athletics. When a student is injured, immediate medical care can prevent aggravation of the injury. If a teacher has an uninsured student transported by ambulance to a hospital for medical treatment, the teacher is responsible for paying both the ambulance and medical bills. A group plan for student health insurance is offered by many companies at a nominal price. Coverage for interschool sports is an add-on item to the basic student health insurance plan. The school district or athletic booster club may pay a portion or all of the athletic add-on health coverage. Health care insurance should be mandatory for athletics, because any expenses will be readily paid by the company and the parents will be less disposed to sue for damages.

Contracts

Written, signed contracts are essential documents for managerial control. Contracts are used for teacher personnel, athletic contests, and building programs. A contract gives each party the assurance that specified conditions will be fulfilled. Many school districts require that teachers sign contracts on a year-to-year basis. Teachers can be required to fulfill the contract if the school district desires, even though a more interesting job is available. Tenure is a type of contract in which the school district assures the teacher of continuancy. Tenure does not assure a particular assignment in the school district, and coaches can get tenure only as teachers. Coaches may be relieved of their coaching duties even after they become tenured as teachers.

Some schools sign contracts for interschool athletic contests. The contract assures the complete schedule of a season's contests. Contracts for athletic events specify the time, date, and place of the contest. Contracts for athletic events may also stipulate the type and source of officials. An assurance bond may be provided by each school to insure that the contest will be played as scheduled. Of course, contracts may be voided by mutual agreement of both parties. (See Chapter 5 for a sample athletic contract.)

Negligence Litigation

Tort liability is in the category of civil law. Some school and teacher suits do not involve injury. If civil rights have been violated by improper testing or improper grade computation, the student may win the equity suit. When an injury occurs, the injured party may seek to win redress in litigation. Yet many legitimate suits are never filed by the plaintiff, and some are settled out of court, especially when the defendant's insurance company sees that the defendant has a weak defense. The following summary should serve to acquaint the potential teacher, coach, and administrator with standard legal procedures.

The Injurious Incident

In order to have a legitimate case, the plaintiff must be able to show that some kind of injury has occurred. Evidence is needed. If there is an alleged physical injury, that injury should be verifiable by medical examination and testimony. Every teacher should view every significant injury as a potential lawsuit. All student grades should also be defensible and accurate. It is to the teacher's benefit to record and remember pertinent details.

Duty for medical care is limited to the administration of first aid. After temporary and immediate care is rendered, the parents should be notified. Teachers are not bound to call ambulances or to take students to medical centers. The teacher who orders an ambulance or requests medical aid may be forced to pay the medical and ambulance bills.

Since each significant injury is a potential lawsuit, reporting must become standard operating procedure. The report should be completed soon after an incident occurs. Pertinent details should include the name of the injured and the date, time, and place of injury. Details of events preceding and following the incident, narrated by identified witnesses, are valuable in courtroom examination. A standard form from the National Safety Council (see Figure 10.10) can be used, or each district can develop its own accident report form. The report should include the date of the incident, who was involved, who were the witnesses, a description of the incident, specification of the care that was given, and the teacher's name. A copy of the report for each significant accident should be retained by the teacher, and one copy should be filed with the supervisor.

Initiation of the Lawsuit

When a tort or civil wrong has occurred, the plaintiff may go through court procedure to collect for damages. The first step is usually to retain a legal advisor who will plead the case before the court. If the teacher pleads innocence of the allegation, the trial is heard in a court of equity. If the defendent admits error, "no contest" is entered on the court record. The court must then decide how much money is to be awarded to the plaintiff.

Elements of a Valid Negligence Case

The lawyer for the plaintiff is the first person to evaluate the prospective case. If the evidence indicates a strong case of negligence, the plaintiff's lawyer may file the case in the local clerk of court's office. If the evidence is not sufficient to warrant civil action, the lawyer recommends that the plaintiff has no case. Due to the time and expense of a trial, most weak cases are never filed. When a civil wrong is alleged to have been committed by a teacher or school district, the

(check one) ☐ School Jurisdictional ☐ Non-School Jurisdictional	**RECOMMENDED** **STANDARD STUDENT ACCIDENT REPORT** (See instructions on reverse side)	(check one) Recordable ☐ Reportable Only ☐

School District:
City, State:

General

1. Name			2. Address		
3. School		4. Sex Male ☐ Female ☐	5. Age	6. Grade/Special Program	
7. Time Accident Occurred Date:		Day of Week:		Exact Time:	AM ☐ PM ☐

Injury

8. Nature of Injury

9. Part of Body Injured

10. Degree of Injury (check one)
    Death ☐   Permanent ☐   Temporary (lost time) ☐   Non-Disabling (no lost time) ☐

11. Days Lost
    From School: From Activities Other Than School: Total:

12. Cause of Injury

Accident

13. Accident Jurisdiction (check one)
    School: Grounds ☐   Building ☐   To and From ☐   Other Activities Not on School Property ☐
    Non-School: Home ☐   Other ☐

14. Location of Accident (be specific)	15. Activity of Person (be specific)

16. Status of Activity	17. Supervision (if yes, give title & name of supervisor)
	    Yes ☐
	    No ☐

18. Agency Involved	19. Unsafe Act
20. Unsafe Mechanical/Physical Condition	21. Unsafe Personal Factor

22. Corrective Action Taken or Recommended

23. Property Damage
    School $ Non-School $ Total $

24. Description (Give a word picture of the accident, explaining who, what, when, why and how)

Signature

25. Date of Report	26. Report Prepared by (signature & title)
27. Principal's Signature	

This form is recommended for securing data for accident prevention and safety education. School districts may reproduce this form adding space for optional data. Reference: *Student Accident Reporting Guidebook*, National Safety Council, 425 N. Michigan Avenue, Chicago, Illinois 60611. 1966. 34 pages.

Courtesy National Safety Council

Figure 10.10 A standard accident report form.

plaintiff must demonstrate that certain conditions were present. Peterson, Ross-miller, and Volz (1969) summarize these conditions as follows:

1. The defendant had a duty to protect the complainant against unreasonable risk of injury.
2. The defendant breached the duty—that is, failed to protect the complainant from injury.
3. The breach of duty by the defendant was the proximate cause of the complainant's injury—that is, a direct and unbroken chain of events existed between the breach of duty complained of and the complainant's injury.

Filing the Suit

The concept of bringing suit is derived from the term "pursuit." The offended pursues the defendant with due process of law in order to gain redress for injury. A brief proposition is filed with the clerk of court of original jurisdiction. In describing the beginnings of a legal suit, Black (1957) states that "an action is 'commenced' . . . as soon as the summons is signed and sealed in good faith, for the purpose of immediate service, and that purpose is not afterwards abandoned."

Typical Case Procedure

In the American court system, civil cases are tried in the presence of the opposing sides. The principal participants are the defendant, the attorneys, the judge, the jury, and the witnesses.

Court of Record

The court of original jurisdiction conducts the preliminary round of litigation. Through due process conducted by the judge, the attorneys attempt to present the facts of the case to the jury. The plaintiff (if the injured party is living) may relate his or her side of the story to the court. The defendant can testify in his or her own behalf. The defendant does not have to make self-incriminating statements, however. Witnesses of various kinds may augment details of the incident. Expert opinion may be furnished by a physician or a physical education curriculum expert. The jury, after proper instruction from the judge, must decide the legitimacy of the plaintiff's claims. Gauerke (1959) summarizes the basic court procedure as follows:

1. A lawsuit usually results from a disagreement as to legal rights.
2. The first step in a court procedure is the issuance and delivery of a summons.

3. The statement of the case by the plaintiff (the party who initiates the court action) and the answer by the defendant are known as court pleadings.
4. In a defendant's demurrer he temporarily admits the declaration of the plaintiff but alleges that no law makes him liable. The issue is determined by the trial judge.
5. The trial is a legal process by which the evidence in the case is brought before the twelve persons for their verdict.
6. Prospective jurors may be rejected by the attorneys if their knowledge or occupation would tend to make them partial to either party.
7. Witnesses, after having testified, are usually subjected to cross-examination to attempt to expose weaknesses in their statements.
8. The verdict entered in the court records by the judge becomes a judgment.
9. The carrying out of the verdict according to court instructions is called the execution.
10. If errors have been committed in the original trial, the defense may appeal to a court of higher jurisdiction. Then it is the plaintiff who becomes the defendant if and when the case on appeal is accepted by a higher court.

Appeals Court

The losing side in the original hearing *may* appeal its case to the next higher court. After examining the report from the inferior court of record, the appeals court may sustain or reverse the lower court's decision. An appeals court can also declare a mistrial, or it can agree with a lower court's decision but change the amount of damages to be paid to the plaintiff. For example, in the case cited previously of *Domino* v. *Mercurio*, 234 NYS 2d 1011 (1962), the playground supervisors were found to be negligent. The question was posed as to who should pay the damages assessed by the court of record. The question on appeal concerned the liability of the school board. If the appeals court decided that the doctrine of *respondeat superior* was valid, who should pay the damages—the teachers or the school district?

Case Example: ADMINISTRATIVE PRECAUTIONS AGAINST NEGLIGENCE

You are the director of physical and health education for the city school system. The following incident occurred in a neighboring city's athletic program:

Early in September the football coach was conducting a scrimmage. The afternoon was hot and the high school boys were sweating profusely under their full protective gear. After forty-five minutes of continuous action, one of the boys lay down and complained of feverishness and headache.

The football coach observed that the boy's forehead was hot and dry and that his heart was beating very rapidly. With the aid of a manager, the coach assisted the injured player to the shower room where he was wrapped in a soft blanket. The coach directed a warm shower on the blanketed boy and called the boy's parents.

Four hours later the boy died of massive brain damage, heart failure, and kidney collapse. The dead boy's parents sued the city school district for $1,500,000 in damages for the wrongful death of their son. The case is now lodged in an appeals court.

In trying to prevent a similar occurrence in your school district, you set up a negligence prevention program. You have certain administrative prerogatives that can be used to develop the program. Specifically, what will your program consist of? How will you present the program to the teachers under your jurisdiction?

The Teacher as Defendant

When teachers execute their responsibilities in a reasonably prudent manner, they are fairly safe from damage judgments. Teacher self-protection should begin with a professional quality physical and health education program. Students who have experienced lead-up and readiness activities in lower grades should be prepared for more strenuous and complex activities. A progressive program should include screening of students, defensible activities, elimination of hazards, and constant supervision. Specifically, the following items should be observed in a program involving vigorous gross body activity.

> Students should be screened for inherent health hazards—preferably by a physician.
> The program of activities should be approved by the school board.
> Activities in the program should be selected on the basis of student ability level.
> Safety procedures should be incorporated into the instructional phase (see skill progressions).
> Equipment and facilities must be regularly inspected for dangerous conditions.
> Teachers must attend their supervisory posts at all times when they have responsibility for students.
> Accidents must be reported on a standard form and sent to upper-echelon school executives.

Scope of Negligence

Teachers may be held liable for both nonfeasance and malfeasance. That is, teachers may be held negligent if they perform no action and also if they perform the wrong action. In order to protect students in their trust, teachers must act and they must do the right thing. A real dilemma arises when a teacher must leave the class in order to administer first aid to an injured student. But generally the "reasonable man" concept of professional behavior is the legal standard. The case

Figure 10.11 Every injury has potentially disastrous personal and legal consequences.

of *Welch* v. *Dunsmuir School District*, 326 P 2d 633 (1958) serves to illustrate the necessity for professional teacher behavior. During the early phase of fall football practice, the Welch boy ran through a contact football play. Though apparently injured, the boy clasped the coach's hand while lying on the field. The coach had assistants carry the boy off the field on a stretcher. After being carried off the field, the boy could no longer use his hands or feet. The official medical diagnosis was a fractured neck and complete hand and foot paralysis. In the ensuing case, the courts awarded a large sum of money to the plaintiff for personal damage attributed to the coach's negligence.

Possible Legal Defenses

"The best-laid schemes of mice and men go oft astray." Accidents can occur in physical and health education in even the best programs. However, the prudent teacher is not without powerful defenses. It should be noted that all the defenses listed herein are not applicable to all cases. If a negligence suit occurs, the teacher, school district, and defense attorney review the case and plan the best defense strategy. Some of the possible defenses are shown in Figure 10.12.

Immunity

Some states deny that governmental agents can be sued for negligence. "Save harmless" statutes protect the teacher from some liability action. Sovereign immunity can protect school boards as agents of the state, but the identity of government agent is not applicable to the individual teacher. In several states both teacher and school district can be brought to court. However, teachers are

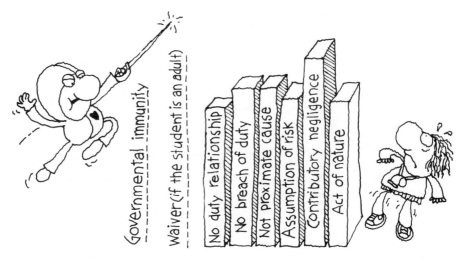

Figure 10.12 The possible legal defenses against a negligence suit. Not all of these alternatives apply to every situation.

not usually paid well enough to establish large estates. Unless the plaintiff is particularly vindictive, suing the individual teacher produces little reward for plaintiff and plaintiff's attorney. If insured, the teacher and the school board will usually be sued for the maximum allowable within the policy. In some cases where governmental immunity is upheld, the school district has paid the court judgment even though the teacher was found negligent.

No Duty Relationship

A teacher stands in the place of the parent while the student is under the teacher's jurisdiction. However, once the student has temporarily severed the relationship, as in going to another class or going home, the teacher is not in a modified *loco parentis* condition. The case of *Hill* v. *Board of Education of Central School District New York*, 237 NYS 2d 404 (1963) serves to illustrate the point. An elementary school pupil had left the school grounds and was on his way home when he was injured. The courts held that the school district had no duty to the departing student.

In order for no duty relationship to be a valid legal defense, it must be established that the student–teacher relationship had not commenced or that the relationship had been dissolved. Obviously, the complete student–teacher relationship cannot be delegated to student monitors even though student leaders can give some assistance. One teacher can assume temporary responsibility for another teacher's classes. Allowing a few students to go out to a play area early without supervision is a risky practice. Absence from the class is not a valid case of no duty relationship.

There are some interesting ramifications of the duty relationship concept. Generally, if there is no legal duty and if one party did not *cause* the injury to another party, then no legal responsibility forces a person to act. For example, Leibee (1965) defines duty to provide first aid as follows:

> At common law no individual has to give assistance to a "stranger" unless he is at fault in exposing the "stranger" to an unreasonable risk of harm. There are, however, relationships which require the rendering of assistance—relationships such as that of a father or mother to their child, husband or wife to a spouse, and doctor to a patient (under certain circumstances). Should assistance be given to a "stranger"? The individual rendering such assistance may be required to answer in a court for his actions–inactions. If the defendant has begun part performance, or has attempted to render aid, it is clear that he has voluntarily started to act; he is thereafter liable for his negligence.
>
> However, even though a person may himself be under no obligation to render aid to one in peril, he is at all times required to use reasonable care to see to it that he does not prevent others from giving assistance to the person in danger, and this applies to both negligent and intentional interferences with aid being given to another.

No Breach of Duty

Black (1957) defines breach of duty as "the neglect or failure to fulfill in just and proper manner the duty of an office. . . ." To claim no breach of duty is to maintain that the "reasonable man" concept has been satisfied. Breach of duty might include both failure to act and failure to act properly, arising from ignorance, willful intent, or forgetfulness. Once a substantial duty relationship has been established, the next step is to establish that the duty was handled in a competent manner.

In the case of young children, the field may be reversed by the judge. Instead of defending himself against testimony by the injured student, the teacher may be forced to supply evidence to show "why he should not be held negligent in his duty." Very young children may not be able to remember the details of an accident. Therefore, the burden of proof may be placed on the defendant.

Successful defense by school personnel using the concept of no breach of duty has been made in court. In the case of *Nestor* v. *City of New York*, 211 N. W. S. 2d 975 (1961), the courts decided in favor of the school district. A boy was struck by a bat on a school playground while the teacher was rendering general supervision to the area. The court supported both the school board and teacher in concluding that they had fulfilled their duty to the student.

Not Proximate Cause

A successful negligence suit must establish that there was a close relationship between the teacher's action or inaction and subsequent effects on the student. Black (1957) defines proximate cause as "that which, in a natural and continuous sequence, unbroken by an efficient intervening cause, produces the injury, and without which the result would not have occurred." Thus, the school board or teacher pleads that injury to the student was caused by a potent third person or force. The actual proximate cause may be attributed to the teacher, the student, another student, or an act of nature. In *Welch* v. *Dunsmuir School District*, 326 P 2d 633 (1958), cited previously, the football coach was clearly the proximate cause of aggravating the injury.

Conversely, in the case of *Read* v. *School District No. 211*, 7 2d 502, 110 P 2d 179, the Read boy sustained a back injury from playing touch football in a gymnasium, but the teacher was found innocent of the charges. The court held that the teacher had adequately supervised the game and was not the proximate cause of the accident. Certain questions recur in this sort of defense. How much time is necessary to "break" the chain of events of proximate cause? Are other factors more important than simply the passage of time?

Assumption of Risk

Under certain conditions a school district may be able to successfully plead that the plaintiff assumed responsibility for the risk taken. Assumption of risk is possibly a valid defense in athletics and intramurals—but not in the physical education program when the student is performing compulsory activities. Black (1957) defines assumption of risk as "a term or condition in a contract ... either expressed or implied from the circumstances ... by which the [contractee] agrees that dangers of injury ordinarily or obviously incident ... shall be at his own risk." Voluntary attendance at a school or professional basketball game is an example of assumption of risk. An assumed risk is founded upon the ability of the risker to recognize the possible dangers inherent in an activity. A child old enough to propel herself on a swing may know of the dangers of falling out of the swing. However, assumption of risk never precludes responsibility for safe environment and supervision.

School districts have the same responsibility in voluntary recreation and athletics as in compulsory physical education. They are responsible to furnish a safe environment, proper instruction, and adequate supervision. In *Welch* v. *Dunsmuir School District* the plaintiff was voluntarily engaged in interscholastic football practice. Assumption of risk was not a legitimate defense, because it was apparent that the supervising coach did not act as a reasonably professional teacher.

In the case of *Ingerson* v. *Shattuck School,* 185 Minn. 16, 239 N. W. 667 (1931) a spectator suffered a leg fracture when two football players rolled over the sideline and struck her. Players had run out of bounds several times before the incident occurred. The courts ruled that the plaintiff had sufficient knowledge of the dangers inherent in standing so near the boundary line. In what situations would asumption of risk be a potentially valid defense? In what situations would the judge probably not allow that defense?

Contributory Negligence

When the injured party is of sufficient maturity to foresee the possible results of action, contributory negligence may be claimed by the defense. Black (1957) defines contributory negligence as "any want of ordinary care on the part of the person injured ... which combined and concurred with the defendant's negligence, and contributed to the injury as a proximate cause thereof, and as an element without which the injury would not have occurred." If contributory negligence can be sustained, the defendant is usually cleared. Courts in the United States do not follow the Oriental practice of attempting to ascertain the percentage of negligence attributable to each party.

Anyone familiar with teaching knows that students frequently act in an unreasonable way. Young children are considered less capable of reason and forethought than adults. Mature students are held more accountable for their actions. Leibee (1956) describes court perspectives on pupil accountability in this way:

> As to children, one group of courts follows the criminal standard and looks at the age of the child. These courts have generally divided children into the following groups by age:
> 1. Between 1 and 7 years of age there is no capacity for negligence.
> 2. Between 7 and 14 years of age there can be a *prima facie* case of incapacity, but it can be rebutted.
> 3. Between 14 and 21 the child is presumed to be capable of being negligent, but this presumption could be rebutted.
>
> Another group of courts uses a method which requires looking into the child's *experience, background, capacity (intelligence),* and *age.* The standard is whether a child of this age, background, capacity, etc. could be negligent. In determining whether a particular child was in fact negligent, the objective standard is abandoned for the standard is whether a reasonably prudent child of the same age, capacity, etc. would have acted in this way. Courts will let a jury consider the deficiencies of experience of a child but not of an adult.

Contributory negligence was an attempted defense in the litigation *Satariano* v. *Sleight,* 129 P 2d 35 (1942). The seventeen-year-old plaintiff sustained a brain concussion when crossing the street from the gymnasium to the athletic field. The courts decided in favor of the plaintiff, disallowing the degree of maturity common to a normal seventeen-year-old boy. Kidd (1971) gives an account of an accident in physical education class. Assuming that the gymnast was a secondary school student, would contributory negligence be a factor?

AFTERWARD IS TOO LATE

The following narrative is presented in the hope that it will motivate physical educators and coaches to reassess the steps they now take toward preventing injuries and to remind them again of the imperative need for safety precautions.

"Coach, will you watch my new move on the flying rings?"

"Okay, okay," I shouted back, "but be careful; you're very high on your swing."

"Don't worry, Coach, I'll be all right," replied Bruce as he pulled to a piked position at the front of the swing. "Just watch the next move."

"Aha," I thought, "he is going to do a snap-down back uprise, but he is starting a little soon ... he'll never make it up!" Then, as he was at the bottom of his snap-down and starting upward, his hands came loose.

"He's going to show me a cut-off dismount!"

I froze. My legs felt like boards on a sawhorse—stiff and straight, yet weak. If the boy was not trying a dismount and was actually falling, I was in no position to break that fall. Bruce's body continued to rise higher and backward from the rings. I could only assure myself that he would make it to his feet—his body would rotate just that far. But as he neared the mat, his feet had rotated too far. Then it happened! Bruce's head and body hit the canvas with a brutal impact. I stood petrified with disbelief. This could not happen to me. I could not possibly be seeing one of my boys breaking his back or neck. I just could not. Other coaches, yes, but not me.

Still stunned, as if charmed by a snake, I felt repelled from the spot where Bruce lay. Noticing the jerking motions of his body amid the rising puff of dust which surrounded him, I managed to move forward in a staccato manner. I fell on my knees beside him grabbing his shoulder, holding him pinioned to the floor in an attempt to stop his convulsions. I had never seen the rolled whites of eyes before, but Bruce's eyes were solid white. His breath came in gurgles, groans, and slopping gasps. Blood flowed freely from his nose and dribbled from one ear; his body was still jerking and twitching like a beheaded chicken.

Suddenly, Bruce stopped moving, and just as my body began to relax in relief, stark reality battered into my consciousness. Was Bruce dead? I felt the blood drain from my face, and nausea tormented my stomach. A sick silence filled the gymnasium.

I looked up and there were the ambulance attendants. They laid Bruce on the stretcher and quickly walked away. An agonizing thought tormented my mind. Bruce might never again be a daring young man on the flying rings, and I realized that I, too, had experienced the menace of coaches and physical educators—a tragic accident.

Epilogue

The following safety precautions are recommended to guard against the occurrence of tragic accidents like the one just presented.
1. Make students acutely aware of the hazards involved in gymnastics prior to any performance.
2. Always know what the performer is going to do.
3. Insist upon proper lead-up stunts.
4. Insist on the use of safety belts when there is the slightest doubt as to the performer's ability, or the stunt is considered hazardous.
5. Know where to spot the performed stunts.
6. Teach the gymnasts to insist on proper spotting by competent individuals.
7. Have definite accident procedures to follow in case of injuries.

Thomas R. Kidd, "Afterward Is Too Late." *The Physical Educator*, 28 (1971), 120–121.

Similar safety precautions could and should be developed for every sport in which the possibility of serious injury exists, whether in a physical education classroom or on an athletic field.

Act of Nature

When an accident occurs in a safe environment with correct instruction and well-supervised conditions, the defendant may plead that the event occurred by pure chance. Black (1957) defines an act of nature as one that "results immediately from a natural cause without the intervention of man, and could not have been prevented by the exercise of prudence, diligence, and care." For example, when a boy charges into the line of scrimmage and sustains injury, that injury may be attributable to chance. However, that the injury occurred by chance does not preclude subsequent mishandling by the teacher.

Act of nature is not applicable as a defense in all cases, even when weather turbulence is a factor. If a student is injured by lightning while in a classroom, act of nature should be a legitimate claim. Conversely, if a teacher did not foresee the possibility of lightning danger in turbulent weather and grouped the class under a tall tree in the playground, act of nature would be a questionable defense. It is common practice to clear outdoor play areas and swimming pools if weather turbulence is imminent.

In the case of *Kaufman* v. *City of New York*, 214 N.Y.S. 2d 767 Sup. Ct. 23 New York (1961), the plaintiff's parents sued when their son was terminally injured in a

Figure 10.13 Courts have ruled that some categories of accidents in vigorous activities cannot be foreseen or prevented even by close supervision.

basketball game. Two boys bumped heads while scrambling for a rebound, and the Kaufman boy was severely injured. The courts held that the incident could not have been prevented by the closest of supervision. Attempts to gain possession of a free ball are a natural part of playing basketball. The collision was simply a chance occurrence.

Case Example: NEGLIGENCE SUIT AGAINST THE INSTRUCTOR

A seventeen-year-old high school boy died as a result of a cerebral hemorrhage sustained during an intramural basketball game. The fatal injury occurred as two students collided while running headlong in opposite directions. Two basketball courts had been laid out in the gymnasium in such a way that both courts used the centerline of the main court as a sideline. At the time of the incident a player from the other court had charged "out of bounds" to recover a ball, and upon crossing the mutual sideline collided with the son of the plaintiff.

The game was being officiated by a member of the varsity basketball team. The intramural director did not see the fatal accident. Immediately after it was apparent that a serious incident had occurred, the intramural director covered the boy with a blanket and called his family.

The parents of the dead boy are suing you, the teacher, for $100,000 to recover for the wrongful death of their son. The legal brief names you as negligent in discharging your duty as a teacher.

What will your specific legal defense be? Review the details of the case again and prepare your defense strategy. Who will be your witnesses? What points will you allow the plaintiff's attorney to establish without contesting them?

References

BLACK, C. *Black's Law Dictionary,* 4th ed. West Publishing Company, St. Paul, Minn., 1957.

BOWER, E. M. *Teachers Talk about Their Feelings.* National Institute of Mental Health, Rockville, Md., 1973.

GAUERKE, W. E. *Legal and Ethical Responsibilities of School Personnel.* Prentice-Hall, Englewood Cliffs, N.J., 1959.

KIDD, T. R. "Afterward Is Too Late." *The Physical Educator,* 28 (1971), 120–121.

LEIBEE, C. *Tort Liability for Injuries to Pupils.* Campus Publishers, Ann Arbor, Mich., 1965.

LENAGHAN, J. M., and R. E. PHAY. "Individual Liability of School Board Members and School Administrators." *School Law Bulletin,* 4 (1973), 1–6.

NEA RESEARCH DIVISION. *The Pupil's Day in Court: Review of 1963.* National Education Association, Washington, D.C., 1964.

PETERSON, L. J., R. A. ROSSMILLER, and M. M. VOLZ. *The Law and Public School Operation.* Harper & Row, Publishers, New York, 1968.

RESICK, M. C., B. L. SEIDEL, and J. G. MASON. *Modern Administrative Practices in Physical Education and Athletics,* 2d ed. Addison-Wesley Publishing Company, Reading, Mass., 1975.

11.

COMMUNITY RELATIONS PROGRAM

After reading this chapter, each student should be able to:

Describe the major factors in a school's continuing public relations program.

Analyze the public relations needs of a specific community.

Identify the principles of public relations.

Describe the media used in public relations programs.

Write news releases.

Identify state, district, and national movements that can be correlated with the local public relations program.

Analyze the effectiveness of a community relations program.

Public relations (PR) programs are used every day in business, government, and education. *Public relations* is broadly defined as management of information to achieve organizational goals. Public relations programs range from the slick multimedia campaigns of businesses, the military establishment, and political candidates to the soft-sell information programs of nonprofit institutions and schools. Some public relations people have earned bad reputations because they insincerely tried to misrepresent poor products in glossy, attractive packages. But all public relations must not be rejected because of unscrupulous PR men—schools need good community relations in order to exist. Good community relations does not happen by chance; it is the product of a professional school curriculum and planned public relations activities.

The Need to Tell—The Right To Know

The Gallup Polls of Attitudes Toward Education (1973) indicate that education is one of the main concerns of the United States citizen. Every citizen should be concerned about public education because tax dollars fund the schools. Public concern can be roughly equated to public support. Voters fund programs of which they are informed and of which they approve. Programs discontinued by voting citizens are either poorly publicized or out of step with community needs. In addition, the new "right to know" laws have put public schools into glass houses (Knowles 1973).

Program Reports

The school needs to tell about school life, and the supporting public has a legal right to know what is happening to its tax funds. Schools are involved with two of the most highly valued concerns of local citizens—their children and their tax dollars. Therefore, public relations programs must be twofold. First, programs dealing with student outcomes are of vital interest to parents. Second, every taxpayer wants to know that tax dollars are being honestly and wisely spent. The school must practice full disclosure with both curriculum outcomes and finances.

Public relations programs must be continuous. Monthly, quarterly, or annual reports in news media show the public that educators are active. Periodic feedback to the supporting community tells the voter that school people appreciate continued support. Intensive public relations campaigns used only to "sell" bond issue programs will ultimately fail. The voters eventually realize that they are being "used" to supply funds for programs they never hear of again. The news article by Sheehan (1973) illustrates the positive kind of media support that physical and health education needs. Most citizens do not know of the potential benefits of a comprehensive program. News articles can inform the public about the deficiencies of local physical and health education programs and describe the benefits a model program offers. Several of the agencies that provide free materials and illustrations are cited in a later section of this chapter.

Community Support

The financial support of local voters can never be taken for granted! Many special sales taxes, maintenance taxes, and bond issues are currently being rejected by voters throughout the United States. Parents are basically concerned about education, but inflation, civil rights issues, and ignorance contribute to the failure of communities to fund new or existing programs.

Until the present decade, each neighborhood had its own school. The neighborhood school virtually insured parental awareness and support. Recent civil rights action has mandated changes in this situation. Close parent observation has decreased with increased school consolidation and student busing. Parents are often unfamiliar with metropolitan school programs. Therefore, it is necessary to use a multimedia approach to school public relations.

In Chapter 1 the reciprocal relationship between the public and the school is thoroughly discussed. The public sends children to the school with the implicit request that child behavior be changed in several defined areas—reading, writing, arithmetic, etc. Every school exists on a commission from the public to educate youth, and report cards are not sufficient to describe what the school is actually doing. Parents and other citizens must be informed of new and existing programs to insure their continued support in approving bond issues and general tax funding. The use of the special physical and health education report card described in Chapter 3 conveys specific feedback to parents. For example, student performance on the AAHPER Youth Fitness Test can be meaningfully compared with national norms for feedback to parents.

Planning

Effective public relations programs are deceptively simple—the program is unobtrusively structured in a manner that attracts attention only to the school activity in focus. Wise planning eliminates the "show business" approach. People can be positively influenced toward schools without ever being aware of a public relations program as such. But effective, unobtrusive school public relations programs do not occur without planning and forethought.

Which Public?

Most public relations campaigns are not directed to the general public. Certain segments are singled out for sales and political campaigns. Similarly, information on school activities may be directed to a segment of the population. Information on bond issues is directed to voters, but athletic publicity is written for the sports fan. Just as a publisher of children's books tries to get the attention of young readers, physical and health educators must earmark their public relations program for the desired "audience."

A community population can be subdivided into several categories. Students and parents are a major group. Athletic boosters are a second major group. The school administration, school board, and teachers are an oft-neglected group. Political leaders and social action organizations are potential allies that can be rallied for support. For example, the national-level Parent Teachers Association recently urged all local chapters to investigate their school's health services and health instruction programs. Whether the target group is the general public or a specific segment, every public relations program must be designed to inform and motivate a target population.

What Information?

School public relations is not a whitewash! Financial reports, successful programs, and unsuccessful programs should be fully disclosed. Obviously, successful programs should receive the larger share of publicity. The disappointing results of unsuccessful programs will eventually become public knowledge, and school personnel who disclose them are in the best position to minimize their negative effects, ending with a positive plan for future programs.

Certain incidents of a sensitive personal nature should obviously not be publicized. Generally, the news media will publicize information on newsworthy events and plans, but remember that news reporters are also interested in sensational school incidents. The incidents cited as court cases in Chapter 10 are examples of situations requiring extreme discretion on the part of school personnel. Indiscreet release of preliminary details by school personnel can prejudice an ensuing liability case. Admission that an injury occurred, the time and date of the injury, and the general type of activity during which the incident occurred *can* be given to news media upon request.

A balanced public information program should be planned for the entire school year. The school, department, and athletic budgets should be published early in the year. Information on the weekly athletic program is essential for funding of athletics that depend on gate receipts. Special feature stories can be developed around new programs, outstanding teachers, or unique student achievement. A

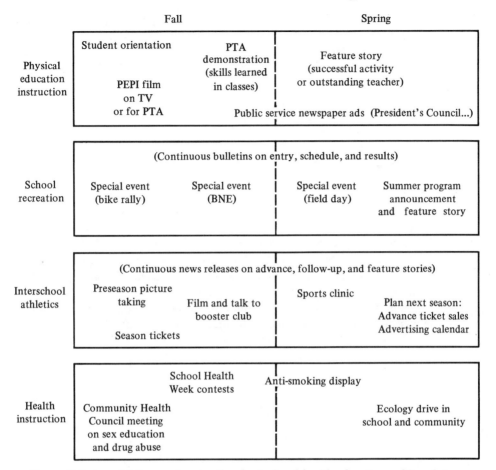

Figure 11.1 A model for preplanning the physical and health education public relations program (for junior high school).

definite time schedule for regular information reports and special-interest feature stories must be prescheduled in accordance with the school calendar. Figure 11.1 shows a model for preplanning the yearly public relations program.

Physical education instruction, health education, school recreation, and athletics provide natural raw material for public relations. Communicating information is not restricted to news articles. Each athletic event is a demonstration of student achievement. Special events such as gymnastic demonstrations for the PTA and other groups can be effective. The really effective school public relations programs are those that regularly bring the public into the schools *and* take the students out into the public. Nothing conveys the physical and health education achievement message as effectively as live demonstrations of student skills and learning experiences.

Principles of Public Relations

Lists of public relations principles have been formulated by numerous authors (Voltmer and Esslinger 1967; Resick, Seidel and Mason 1970). Such summary statements are concepts distilled into key points. The following list of public relations principles is amplified in preceding or subsequent parts of this chapter.

1. Develop a school program that is worthy of reporting. Whitewash wears off quickly, and the inadequate school program is glowingly reported only to be embarrassingly revealed.
2. Determine immediate and long-range public relations needs. Physical educators, health educators, and athletic coaches must develop a positive public image. Planning consecutive information articles and special events during the school year functions to shape public opinion.
3. Define the target population. Information relative to grading in physical education is of interest mainly to students and parents. Other population segments, such as athletic supporters, are interested in only one facet of the school program of activities. The information publicized should be of interest to the desired target population.
4. Produce good news stories. News stories must include all the relevant facts. Articles must be interestingly written, and press releases should be relatively free from bias or value statements.
5. Make the public relations program continuous. If an advance story is publicized by the news media, the same news media deserve a follow-up story. Press releases should be generally preplanned to capitalize on reader interest in upcoming and recently concluded events.
6. Monitor the effects of the public relations program. Is the target population getting the message? Public attitudes can be determined by observation and simple polling.

Organizing

Organizing is the process of arranging the program components that were prespecified in the planning phase. Organizing in public relations involves designation or training of staff personnel and selection of the appropriate media. Though few staff members in the school have experience in public relations, with some training in media selection and resource development, a staff member can function effectively as an information agent.

School Personnel

Who is responsible for good school public relations? Obviously, one person cannot carry the entire program. Development of a physical education departmental image is a responsibility shared by management and staff. In reality the public relations image is the publicized "way of life" that professional educators live from day to day. Physical and health educators are paid not only for what they do, but also for what they are. The image is very important.

The Importance of All School Personnel

Every school employee, from the principal to the custodian, is an ambassador of good will to the public. A surly janitor or a cold department chairperson alienates student and public. Faculty meetings should include discussion of ways to improve public relations. Certainly the minimum expected of a physical education or athletic department is to be courteous to students, parents, and visitors. If a staff is operating a professional program, it is only natural that they share their ideas with others.

Students are also direct representatives of the school. Athletic teams are official school ambassadors. Athletes are privileged to represent their school, and a high level of ethical behavior should be expected. Physical and health education students are always unofficial public relations representatives. Students usually speak frankly and freely. If the school program is challenging and progressive, the net result will be an unsolicited positive report to parents and friends.

The Public Relations Staff Member

"That which is everybody's business is nobody's business," is an old adage with direct application to school public relations. All teachers find plenty to do during the day with their classes, planning, and supervision duty. Good teachers also find time to do special things like public relations. Each physical and health education department and athletic staff should designate the public relations responsibility to one staff member. Time released from the duty roster of building supervision could compensate for the extra load. The designated staff member may not do all the actual work, functioning instead as an organizer and program pusher. Ideas in this chapter, concepts explained in the reading list in the Student Guide, and help from a local news editor will serve to train the public relations coordinator.

Student Assistants

It is desirable to train several students to help in the public relations program. Athletic coaches frequently work with a local reporter or newspaper editor to train interested students in the art of sports writing. Students can easily learn how to keep game statistics and write a running account of the action. The professional reporter will know what statistics and stories can be used. After the program to train student sports information managers has begun, the senior leaders can recruit and train younger students. Of course, the student information manager's work must be reviewed for accuracy by the professional teacher.

Resource People

Numerous kinds of resource people are available in every community for use in the school public relations program. Knowledgeable physicians and nurses can be asked to speak or write for program support. Newspapers print public service advertisements, and both radio and television stations are required to broadcast public service announcements. Newspapers cannot afford to pay enough reporters to cover all high school games in a large city. A local freelance writer can be hired to report an individual school's games and the stories sold to a local newspaper.

A community advisory committee can also aid in school public relations. The committee members should be selected from citizens active in civic affairs. The advisory committee should function as a citizen liaison between the public and the school administration. Advisory committee groups have been effective in planning bond issues, developing programs for controversial subjects, and raising funds for special projects.

Public Relations Media

Public relations media are the vehicles by which the school program's message is conveyed to the target population. Actually, "media" is the plural form of the word "medium." The medium should not attract attention to itself, but rather it should be the unobtrusive means by which the message is dynamicly conveyed. Many of the media used by business (such as radio, television, and newspapers) can be used successfully by schools.

The School Conference

Parents and other target populations can be brought into school affairs. Small group-discussion sessions may be scheduled during the day, or a parents' day can be devoted to class observation. PTA meetings also offer opportunities for telling the physical and health education story. School groups supporting athletics usually initiate dialogue with the coaching staff. Athletic booster clubs commonly hold regular monthly meetings during athletic seasons.

The School Bulletin

Important concepts can be effectively transmitted to parents by use of a mimeographed bulletin. If the bulletin is sent out to correspond with the issuance of report cards, the probability of parental perusal will be increased. The bulletin may include an introduction to new or old programs, research reports, or an explanation of grading. Obviously, only the parental population will be reached by bulletins transmitted by students.

Demonstrations

Parents want to see their children perform. Securing the participation of a large number of students in a demonstration virtually assures the presence of a large number of parents. Scheduling the demonstration during a natural gathering of people also insures public exposure for the program. Half-time at football and basketball games is a good opportunity for exhibition of physical education instruction and the school recreation program. The demonstration should be informative rather than just entertaining. Gymnastic events, a badminton exhibi-

Figure 11.2 Special physical education exhibitions involving a large number of students virtually assures that a large number of parents will come—to see their children perform.

Terry McKoy, I. O. E.

tion, a table tennis match, or a wrestling match could be used for a half-time show. A high skill level is required for half-time demonstrations, but if the entire event is to be focused on physical education, well-rehearsed class activities can be presented by students of moderate skill.

Radio and Television

Local broadcasting stations are interested in maintaining their own community relations by publicizing area news. Schools can capitalize on local broadcasting needs by supplying information about upcoming events and the results of completed events. Regular news stories and feature stories may be broadcast, but station managers are busy people. The school public relations coordinator must initiate communication with local stations about significant school events. Broadcasters will not use all their story leads, but alerting them will increase the probability of occasional coverage for special stories. Athletic events are reported regularly; sell radio time to local merchants known as "broadcast boosters."

Newspapers

Professional physical and health educators are often guilty of writing for the wrong population. Professional journals contain many informative articles that should be shared with the general public. Exercise physiologists tend to write sophisticated articles for other exercise physiologists. The real need, however, is to inform and convince the general public about the values of exercise! Therefore, researchers and program managers must begin communicating with the sociopolitical world of public life.

Newspapers are widely used by athletic departments to publicize their programs. It is the task of the physical and health educator to become friends with the media people and to share the message of physical and health education with them. The sports editor and the general editor are power allies for good school public relations. At times of high business advertising or political campaigning, it may be impossible to get news stories printed. During the fall and winter seasons, most newspapers are filled with football news. Late winter, spring, and summer are off-seasons for business advertising and for many spectator sports. Newspaper editors will fill every page with an ad or a story. So have a physical and health education story on deposit with the editor for that open spot on the page!

Actualizing

Preparation of publicity information is a skill that can be learned through experience. Printed matter is called *copy*, and photographs or line drawings are called *illustrations*. Information developed by a school staff member is called a *news release,* while an article developed by a reporter is called a *news story.* News releases should be sent to all local newspapers and radio and television stations. If news items are to be publicized on a certain day, the date of the news release should be specified. All public media need to have the final copy at least two days before the intended date of release.

Preparing News Releases

News copy is commonly divided into three categories: the advance story, the follow-up news story, and the feature article. All news copy is written with a common set of principles. Clarity is important. Short sequential sentences adapt well to the short lines of news print. News columns are usually composed of three to six words per line. Therefore, most paragraphs in a news story contain only one or two sentences. All news copy must be double spaced.

Advance Story

An *advance story* is a public notice of an upcoming event. The advance-notice news release ranges from one hundred to five hundred words—usually only one double-spaced page of copy will be printed in a newspaper. Little journalistic flair is needed to tell the basics of who, what, when, where, and how. The basic items should briefly arouse public interest in the event and tell prospective spectators the time and place of the event. Advance-story news releases should be in the hands of the media news managers five days before the event. Publication should be requested to begin two days before the scheduled event. *The Daily Star* gives us a good example of an advance news story.

TORS EYE SCOTTIE

HAMMOND—The Purple Tors are looking for their first win over Scotlandville here tomorrow night as 7-AA cage action warms up in the second round.

The Tors are fresh from a 48–42 win over Belaire Friday night.

Both Hammond and the Scots are tied for first in 7-AAAAA with a 3–0 slate.

The Scots have scotched Hammond twice during the first round, 79–58 and 49–34. Both games were played on the road by the Tors.

The basketball game begins at 7:00 P.M. at the Hammond High School gymnasium.

"Tors Eye Scottie," *The Daily Star,* Hammond, La., Feb. 3, 1975.

Rick Smolan, Stock Boston

Southeastern Louisiana University

Figure 11.3 Clear action pictures add interest to all kinds of news stories.

Follow-Up News Story

The *follow-up news story* is a summary report of an event. Follow-up reports are usually longer than advance stories—from two hundred to a thousand words. Only the highlights of a sports event or an exhibition should be reported. Statistics are important in a follow-up sports story. Follow-up stories should be written objectively, though more actual space can be devoted to local individuals or teams. *The Lion's Roar* offers a good example of a follow-up article about a post-secondary event. The format would be the same for an event at other school levels. The reason that universities get more publicity than other schools is that the universities have a professional staff writer to produce news copy.

JINX BROKEN WITH 23–8 WIN

For the past six years a damper has been put on SLU's week-long homecoming activities when Southeastern dropped the homecoming football game before returning alums.

Southeastern's 1974 football Lions broke what had almost become an annual homecoming tradition.

Defense was the name of the game Saturday afternoon as SLU snapped the "jinx" with a 23–8 win over Northeast Louisiana, increasing its season record to 5–1.

Tommy Saia accounted for the Lions first three points of the game, booting a 27-yard field goal with 11:26 showing on the second-period clock.

Pass interceptions by John Klumpp and Freddie Bedford along with a blocked punt by Hamp Steward set the stage for a 17-point second quarter, and the Lions' offense moved the second-half kickoff 83 yards for a score to put the game out of reach.

The Green and Gold amassed 348 yards in total offense and held Northeast's attack at bay until the Indians finally scored in the last 5 minutes of the game.

"Jinx Broken with 23–8 Win," *The Lion's Roar*, Hammond, La., October 31, 1974.

Feature Story

A *feature story* is an in-depth report on a significant event or a noteworthy person. Little-known Olympic events have been recently publicized in the *JOHPER*. Successful athletes frequently grant interviews that are written up as feature stories. Successful programs in exercise physiology have been published in national news media. Film documentaries, most nonfiction magazine articles, and some newspaper articles are classified as feature stories. The focal points of a feature story are the background details that go unpublished in regular news articles. Though Brad Davis is a university player, the article about him is a good example of a feature on school athletics.

BRAD, HAMMOND HAMMER

BATON ROUGE—Brad Davis, the "Hammer" of the LSU offensive weapon, was born to play football.

Oft compared to Billy Cannon, Davis is explosive in his own right, and when the Hammond youth picked up eight yards early in the fourth quarter against Kentucky, an LSU career-rushing leader was born—with a career record of 1,884 yards.

The story began in Hammond, forty miles east of Baton Rouge. Davis was a prep All-American and was named outstanding back in the state. After leading the Hammond Tors to the Triple-A state title, a vigorous recruiting battle was triggered, but the "Hammond Hammer" was destined to matriculate at Tigertown.

He was chosen on the All-SEC sophomore team and was the Tigers' second best rusher with 560 yards in 1972. Davis only scored once that year, but that touchdown was a pass from Bert Jones that gave the Bengals a 17–16 win over Ole Miss after the horn sounded the end of the game.

As a junior, Davis had a banner year, rushing for 904 yards to erase the single-season rushing mark at LSU that had been held by Art Cantrelle. After a slow start, he became one of the nation's premier backs and proved his all-around ability against Auburn by running, catching a touchdown pass, and throwing a 24-yard aerial to set up another score.

But Davis saved his best effort for the battle with the Alabama Crimson and White, ripping through the vaunted Tide defense for 143 yards on 17 tries including a 40-yard run that saw him break a half-dozen tackles and then outrun the secondary to the end zone.

Brad closed the season in a personal duel with John Cappeletti of Penn State, outgaining the Heisman Trophy winner 70 to 51 yards in the Orange Bowl.

"Brad, Hammond Hammer," *The Daily Star*, Hammond, La., October 29, 1974.

Photographs

Good photographs enhance reader interest in news articles. Photography is an art that must be studied—*and* learned through trial and error. Good photography equipment is helpful in making a quality product. Studying angles and picture composition is essential. Developing and printing can be self-taught. The public relations coordinator must generally rely on a student photography club or a professional freelance photographer.

Black and white glossy prints are required for use in newspaper printing. The minimum camera equipment is a 35-mm reflex (through-the-lens) instrument. A

1/500-second shutter speed is necessary for action pictures, while a 1/1000-second shutter speed is required to "stop" the action in some sports. The negatives should be reviewed before printing to find the best frames. The frame that is selected should be "cropped" for the printer in order to isolate the desired action. A telephoto lens also helps to isolate the action and give clear pictures for field events like football and soccer. For further reference on photography, see Sussman (1973).

Films

Athletic contests are commonly recorded in 16-mm motion pictures, shot at the standard twenty-four frames per second. Game films for analysis can be shot at lower speeds, but television stations prefer films shot at thirty-two frames per

Figure 11.4 Clear, centrally focused pictures are usually most desirable for augmenting news copy.

Terry McKoy, I. O. E.

Southeastern Louisiana University

Figure 11.5 Blurring some details by focal adjustment or the use of a slow shutter speed can produce the illusion of fast action.

second. The rate of filming depends upon the purpose and the available light. Weekend developing service can be obtained for black and white film, but color film usually takes longer. Filming should be introduced and concluded with action shots. If an athletic event is being recorded, shooting the clock and scoreboard occasionally will help to identify playing sequences. A home movie camera can be used for some events, but a large-reel telephoto movie camera is needed for field sports.

Motion pictures are commonly used for player analysis by the coaching staff. However, athletic booster clubs enjoy seeing the game film, as narrated by the coach. Film clips can also be sent to television stations for publicity. A composite film may be made showing what a physical or health education program should be like—or what the local program is like. Several excellent films have been produced for public relations purposes by national organizations.

Coordinating Local, State, and National Programs

The local school public relations coordinator for physical and health education has available several professional resources. State and national health physical education, and recreation organizations are coordinating their efforts to get nationwide publicity. If the national professional image of physical and health

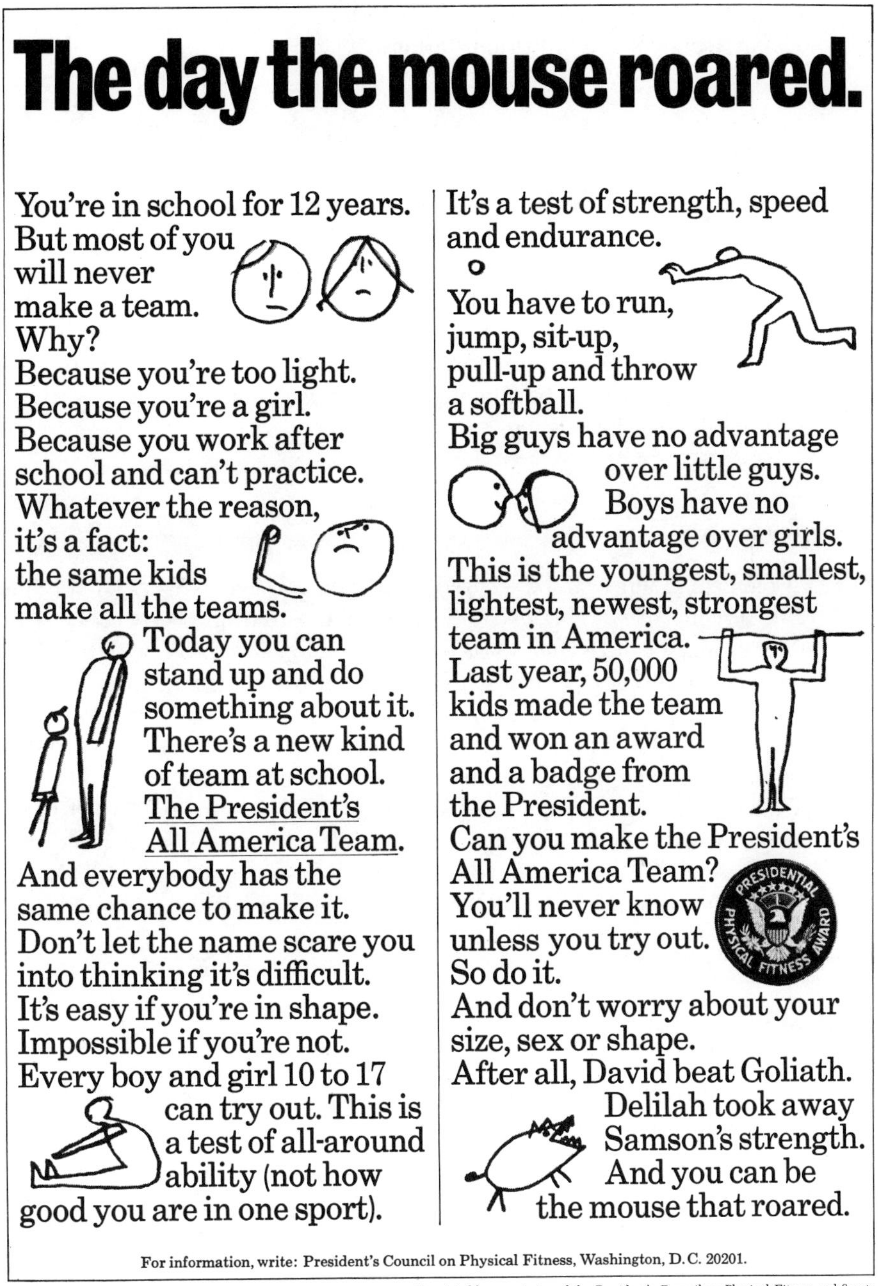
The day the mouse roared.
You're in school for 12 years.
But most of you will never make a team.
Why?
Because you're too light.
Because you're a girl.
Because you work after school and can't practice.
Whatever the reason, it's a fact: the same kids make all the teams.
Today you can stand up and do something about it.
There's a new kind of team at school.
The President's All America Team.
And everybody has the same chance to make it.
Don't let the name scare you into thinking it's difficult.
It's easy if you're in shape.
Impossible if you're not.
Every boy and girl 10 to 17 can try out. This is a test of all-around ability (not how good you are in one sport).
It's a test of strength, speed and endurance.
You have to run, jump, sit-up, pull-up and throw a softball.
Big guys have no advantage over little guys.
Boys have no advantage over girls.
This is the youngest, smallest, lightest, newest, strongest team in America.
Last year, 50,000 kids made the team and won an award and a badge from the President.
Can you make the President's All America Team?
You'll never know unless you try out.
So do it.
And don't worry about your size, sex or shape.
After all, David beat Goliath.
Delilah took away Samson's strength.
And you can be the mouse that roared.
PRESIDENTIAL PHYSICAL FITNESS AWARD
For information, write: President's Council on Physical Fitness, Washington, D.C. 20201.

Figure 11.6 The President's Council on Physical Fitness and Sports will furnish high quality ads that can be run in the local newspaper as a public service.

education is to be improved, quality information must be disseminated through local newspapers and television stations.

Mat Service

A *mat service* is the providing of professional quality photographs or other illustrations for use in local publications. The President's Council on Physical Fitness and Sports, Washington, D.C., provides excellent materials that can be published in local newspapers. Public relations is also one of the major concerns of the American Alliance for Health, Physical Education and Recreation, 1201 Sixteenth Street NW, Washington, D.C. Many articles published in textbooks or professional journals can be obtained free for local publicity by writing the author and publisher for permission.

Film Sources

Free loan of films can be secured from agencies such as West Glen Films, 565 Fifth Avenue, New York, N.Y. Several of the free films are concerned with athletics and health. The AAHPER has developed a project called PEPI—an acronym for Physical Education Public Information. Two important films for interpreting physical education to the public have been developed by the AAHPER and PEPI project. The first film is *All the Self There Is* and the second film is entitled *Every Child a Winner*. Both films demonstrate the value of physical education to the development of an integrated personality. The PEPI materials are available from the state coordinator; contact the state association for health, physical education, and recreation. Other sources of publicity films are the Athletic Institute, Chicago, Ill., and respective state departments of education.

Controlling

The principles of good public relations do not change. To effectively inform and to motivate toward beneficial action are the purposes of public information programs. In order to insure effectiveness, you must determine whether the desired impact was achieved. Businesses commonly obtain feedback by printing cut-out coupons in advertisements. The number of coupons collected on sale items indicates the net sales effect of the advertisement. School public relations programs must also be attuned to reality by (1) defining the target population; (2) publicizing the needed information; and (3) observing the effects of the program.

Monitoring the Program Output

There are two main areas of public relations monitoring. First, the school staff must be aware of what is being said. Publishers sometimes make errors in reproducing copy supplied to them. Reporter interpretation of school events may not be entirely complimentary. Systematic review of publicity is usually sufficient to determine what is being said by the media people. Remember that a hostile reaction to adverse publicity is the worst possible way to handle public relations. Second, observation must be made to see if the target population got the message. If the target population was the parent group, a telephone survey to a few "friends" and "enemies" should produce a reasonable approximation of the program's impact.

Handling Complaints

Every organization that is active will eventually get some negative feedback. Criticism implies that someone disagrees with what is being done—to them or to others. Theunissen (1967) advocates taking a positive approach whereby complaints are turned into compliments. Behind every complaint is a condition that motivated the critical action. Misunderstanding of policy, ignorance of purposes and grading, and teacher negligence cause many complaints. A complaint left unresolved may result in a lawsuit.

When handling complaints, the school staff must listen, and then retrench to areas where the teacher and the person who complains have a mutual agreement. For example, one frustrated girl who had been double promoted to a higher grade found she could not learn to shoot a basketball successfully. Finally, she exclaimed defiantly, "I don't see why everyone has to take this dumb P.E.!" After a cooling-off period in which the pressure to achieve has been removed, the teacher should counsel the student. Starting with the student's obvious interest in academic achievement, the instructor could relate the value of physical activity to her immediate and long-range goals. Obviously, not all public relations problems are easily solved, but listening to complaints and working together to solve the problem is a positive step toward a desirable image.

Case Example: PUBLIC RELATIONS PROCEDURES

Fredricksburg High School has had internal problems with management, curriculum, and student unrest in past years. Teachers "race the students to the doors" in the afternoon after the dismissal bell. The physical and health education curriculum was evaluated "poor" by a recent accrediting team. Students have protested various conditions such as the dress code (including the physical education uniform) and the gross lack of instructional quality at the school. To make matters worse, the former football coach was indicted for assault on the opposing coach in a fight that followed the last football contest.

In trying to remedy the situation, the school board has hired a completely new management team for the school. The new principal has initiated "Operation Turnaround" in which professional concepts of school management are to be used. You have been hired as chairperson of the physical and health education department, athletic director, and head basketball coach. Assuming that you will immediately upgrade the instructional and athletic programs to a professional level, what will be your procedure for improving school public relations? Who will do the actual public relations work? What will be your overall public relations strategy?

References

"BRAD, HAMMOND HAMMER." *The Daily Star*. Hammond, La., October 29, 1974.

THE GALLUP POLLS OF ATTITUDES TOWARD EDUCATION, 1969–1973. Phi Delta Kappa, Bloomington, Ill., 1973.

"JINX BROKEN WITH 23–8 WIN." *The Lion's Roar*. Hammond, La., October 31, 1974.

KNOWLES, L. W. "New Right to Know Laws Put Schools in Glass Houses." *Nations Schools*, 91 (1973), 94.

RESICK, M. C., B. L. SEIDEL, and J. G. MASON. *Modern Administrative Practices in Physical Education and Athletics*. Addison-Wesley Publishing Company, Reading, Mass., 1970.

SHEEHAN, G. "The New Phys Ed Is a Winner." *Register*. Red Bank, New Jersey, February 21, 1973.

SUSSMAN, A. *The Amateur Photographer's Handbook*, Thomas Y. Crowell Company, New York, 1973.

THEUNISSEN, W. "Turning Complaints into Compliments." *The Physical Educator*, 24 (1967), 35.

"TORS EYE SCOTTIE." *The Daily Star*. Hammond, La., February 3, 1975.

VOLTMER, E. E., and A. A. ESSLINGER. *The Organization and Administration of Physical Education*, 5th ed. Appleton-Century-Crofts, New York, 1975.

INDEX

383